Negotiating
Caribbean Freedom

Caribbean Studies

Negotiating Caribbean Freedom

Peasants and the State in Development

MICHAELINE A. CRICHLOW

LEXINGTON BOOKS
Lanham • Boulder • New York • Toronto • Oxford

LEXINGTON BOOKS

Published in the United States of America
by Lexington Books
An imprint of The Rowman & Littlefield Publishing Group, Inc.
4501 Forbes Boulevard, Suite 200, Lanham, Maryland 20706

PO Box 317
Oxford
OX2 9RU, UK

Copyright © 2005 by Lexington Books

British Library Cataloguing in Publication Information Available

Library of Congress Cataloging-in-Publication Data

Crichlow, Michaeline A.
  Negotiating Caribbean freedom : peasants and the state in development /
Michaeline A. Crichlow.
      p. cm. — (Caribbean studies)
  Includes bibliographical references and index.
  ISBN 0-7391-0914-6 (cloth : alk. paper) — ISBN 0-7391-1037-3
(pbk. : alk. paper)
  1. Peasantry—Jamaica. 2. Farms, Small—Jamaica. 3. Agriculture—-Economic
aspects—Jamaica. 4. Agriculture and state—Jamaica. 5. Political participation—Jamaica. I.
Title. II. Series: Caribbean studies (Lanham, Md.)
HD1531.J3C74 2004
306.3'64'097292--dc22   2004018653

Printed in the United States of America

⊗™ The paper used in this publication meets the minimum requirements of American
National Standard for Information Sciences—Permanence of Paper for Printed Library
Materials, ANSI/NISO Z39.48-1992.

To the memories of my grandmother, Ursula Sue-Crichlow, who taught me that living a life of dignity was also part of political struggle; and my mother, Bertha Louisy-Crichlow, whom I knew far too briefly. Those memories, I draw closely.

Mud-caked feet of a Haitian cane-cutter in the Dominican Republic.
Photo by Victor Camilo (circa 1980s)

Contents

Series Editor's Introduction

In *Negotiating Caribbean Freedom* Michaeline A. Crichlow puts her finger on all the relevant buttons concerning the role of the peasantry and the state in the development process. And while she does not press all the buttons with the same force, she nevertheless calls the reader's attention to the most salient issues. Crichlow takes an intellectual and recent historical tour of the world of the small agricultural producer in Jamaica and the perspective she adopts is located somewhere between the dependency theorist and the postmodern critic. Her primary aim is to analyze the complex relationship between the state and nonstate sectors, and how the formulation of development policies in agriculture reflected the economic interests of those elites who controlled the postcolonial state apparatus.

One of the special features of Jamaica's contemporary political economy is the way in which class struggle has come to be cast by leading commentators as a tribal contest. Unlike other countries such as Trinidad, Guyana, and even Suriname, where ethnic divisions are writ large on the political stage, and where some like Lloyd Best have spoken of ethnic tribalism, the Jamaican reality is markedly different. For given the specific pattern of colonial settlement and slave labor recruitment in Jamaica, the overwhelming mass of the population today rightly claims some form or degree of African descent. This has made for a most complex and fascinating mix of social identities based on color and shade tinged with a pronounced embrace of Afrocentrism that complements well the populist appeals of Rastafarian culture and its roots in Africa. In a society where most are "racially African," then, it is to the nuance of color and shade as in "black," "brown," "high brown," "yellow," "light skinned" and "white" that one must turn for a popular appreciation of the picture of social stratification in Jamaica. For the concept of "class," as conceived by Marxist analysts, is roundly downplayed for political and ideological reasons.

However, while ethnic tribalism does not exist in Jamaica, commentators on the political scene prefer to speak of "tribalism" in their assessments of political attitudes and affiliations. For in a situation where the traditional divisions based on class have been muted by the politics of Afrocentrism, and where most claim Africa as the mother country, ordinary working people, whether rural or urban, have come to distinguish themselves more in terms of their political affiliations. Thus, the tribes of which they speak are those linked to the two main political parties: the liberal, social democratic Peoples National Party (PNP) and the conservative, populist Jamaica Labour Party (JLP). Supporters of these two parties comprise the "tribes" in question, and the violence they visit on one another is filled with the venom and blind loyalty commonly associated with tribal violence in other parts of the world.

Given the thoroughness of British colonial rule and the hegemony of racial thinking it secured, it was not surprising that the postcolonial order inherited by the (white and high brown) leading local elites would similarly be marked by racial and elitist concerns according to which the subordinate (and darker complexioned) populations were denied social and economic opportunities, and made to feel inferior and ineffective. Development for the new leaders, the junior partners of international capital, meant the use of the state as a means for entrenching further dependent capitalist development under the rubric of national sovereignty. And in order to realize the types of plans and policies that such development required, it was necessary to enlist the allegiance of the ordinary working people, the so-called sufferers, who were the vehicles to be used in implementing their development plans and vision.

This is where the politics of cultural nationalism and the economics of dependent capitalism come together in the cementing of underdevelopment. For the political appeal of the postcolonial elite was one of nationalism or nation building. It embraced the rejection of (white) Europe and played on populist sentiments of ethnic and national purity. But though unique, the Jamaican case is nevertheless most instructive of other countries within the Caribbean region, where the institutions of dependent development (including the postcolonial state) and the patterns of exploitation that characterize the region today, are easily traceable to the class interests of the local political and economic elites and their collaboration with the imperialist classes. For the latter the Caribbean represents three principal and related phenomena: a) cheap and abundant resources, b) a conveniently located market outlet for commodities produced and manufactured in the metropolitan countries, and c) a ready supply of cheap labor. From the perspective of the local elites, on the other hand, the survival of political regimes in the various countries is tied to the specific development policies they pursue and the degree to which they are able to accommodate the demands of outside imperialist interests. In all of this, the direct small producers are squarely on the front line.

Anton Allahar
October 2004

Acknowledgments

I thank all the taxpayers of the Americas whose contributions provided the University and Foundation grants I received to enable this research: The Ford Foundation, Arts and Humanities Initiative grants; International Travel grants from International Programs; Old Gold Fellowships, from the College of Liberal Arts and Sciences, the University of Iowa; and faculty development support from St. Lawrence University.

Thanks also to the staff of the Documentation Center at the University of the West Indies, Mona, Beverly Lothian, Norma Davis and Audrey Chambers, who were very helpful in finding obscure and difficult to locate documents. The staff of the Statistical Institute of Jamaica, and the Ministry of Agriculture, in particular Dr. Marie Straughan, and those of RADA too aided me considerably.

I would like also to acknowlege my friends who hosted me throughout my sojourn, providing tremendous encouragement and concrete support, namely, Erna Brodber, Omar Davies, Claire Forrester, Carmen Tipling, Jean Anderson, Olive Senior, Faye Wright, Patricia Northover, Marcia Sepaul, Ralph Premdas, Annie Paul, the late Dickie Coke, and many others. To the numerous smallholders whom I observed and questioned on my numerous trips to the "islands": The Windward and Leeward Islands, Jamaica, and Trinidad. To my special friends in Choiseul, St. Lucia, Theresa, Joy, Mary and her children, and Ma Eliza who made my stay there enjoyable and worthwhile. I acknowledge also my father and stepmother who accommodated my liberal freeloading.

To those upon whom I imposed to read sections of earlier drafts: Patricia Northover, who also suggested the book's final title, Charles Carnegie, Louis Moyston, Dale Tomich, the late Terry Hopkins (who reminded me that peasant was a relational concept. "Where were the landlords?" he asked provocatively); also my long standing friends Terry Thomas, Omar Davies, Faruk Tabak, Margaret Bass, and Carolle Charles. Jane Collins provided much needed intellectual support and encouragement. Brian Waniewski offered tough editorial suggestions. My youngest friend, two-year-old Sarah Naima, provided hours of delightful childish diversions during the manuscript's final moments of revision.

As an undergraduate at UWI Mona, my favorite classes were Sociology of Development, taught by a no-nonsense lecturer, Elsie Franc, and Sociological Theory, taught by a constructive cynic, named Herman Mckenzie. Those classes stimulated my interest in "peasants," and the disciplinary conceptualizations that attended them. I really wanted to know how people like my late grandmother who was a very modern subject, a piano-playing, Bajan cane-farmer, came to be so narrowly construed by well-meaning academics.

Thanks to Dehring, Bunting and Golding for permission to use the advertisement in chapter 7, the Epilogue, and to Louis Moyston for allowing me to quote so generously from one of his lively newspaper columns. This is my work, these are my errors.

CHAPTER 1

Development's Agrarian Culture

> The fact is that the Caribbean was the first overseas outpost
> of European Imperialism and Capitalism, was "western-
> ized" and "modernized" and "developed" before most of the
> colonial world had even become colonial, and that the peo-
> ples of the Caribbean are the peculiarly disenfranchised
> beneficiaries of centuries of Western capitalist solicitude.[1]

I am interested in exploring how certain notions of agricultural development
were visited upon a segment of Jamaican society, viz. rural working peoples, in
exchange for their support of nationalist and postnationalist state agendas, and
the ways in which those connections became unraveled, creating a different kind
of rural space. I focus on land-based working peoples, whom for the sake of lin-
guistic brevity, I call smallholders, as they were central to the procedures of development. The relationship between smallholders and elements of the postcolonial state is difficult to characterize within the rubric of subordinate and
dominant, for the relationship is complicated not by variations within an essentially oppositional context, a popular argument in much literature, but by a co-
incidence of various agendas, oppositional in some respects, which serves to produce more governable subjects via submission, consent, and participation, as
noted by poststructuralists. Capitalist development became institutionalized in
an agricultural sector linking formal and informal economic activities nationally
and internationally in complementary alliances. Resultant social configurations
came to define the hierarchy of agricultural production on the island. This book
will aid those who are concerned with illuminating the past not for its own sake,
or as a container for "correct interpretation," but as a means of understanding
the present so as to get beyond it. The present in Jamaica may seem like a long,
dark night of many knives, but darkness relies for its relief on light, and certainly

1

there have been brighter moments in Jamaican history. Visiting Jamaica, where I came of age in the late 1970s, I am struck by the daily toil that the majority of hard-working people there endure. Also, I am embarrassed by the ease with which many middle-class Jamaicans disparage the working poor. With the unraveling of the liberal democratic postcolonial project, as Scott would put it, it is urgent to consider alternatives to both the authoritarian democratic state practices Jamaica has known and the tribal politics that its peoples have been drawn into without recourse to grievance or change.[2] An enormous amount of unthinking needs to be done, as Immanuel Wallerstein might say.[3]

Unthinking development linked to political paradigms necessitates an understanding of the past, in this case, foremost, the discursive and institutional modalities of economic development linked to state re-formation and citizen-making. A preoccupation with solving economic quandaries touted as foundations for brighter tomorrows carries with it a cultural understanding of what a liberated, free Jamaica might look like. Despite many institutional reforms, I believe that no governing regime has deliberately effected any major structural transformation of Jamaica's postcolonial landscape, try though they might. Nevertheless, one cannot deny the ideological visions of new sovereignty implicit in paeans to the "new Caribbean man," a vision popularized during the William Demas era, though long extant.[4]

I hope neither to map a programmatic development nor to propose a political agenda for the future, but rather to elucidate how the past was constructed, how certain visions affected it. How did development policies come to serve as the principal vehicle and the message in the formation and reformation of ruling elites and the institutions of the state, significantly influencing the relations between state and nonstate arenas?

The increased popularity of poststructuralist analysis makes indisputable the process whereby populations are discursively represented and institutionally targeted by elements of the development "industry," not least among them, the state through agricultural development policies. Many of these studies focus on what gets produced under the rubric of development rather than on the failures of the projects' objectives, as had been the common technique. These perspectives have created substantive knowledge about the nature of the relationship between subject populations and the agencies which conceive the plans that shape the lives of participating and nonparticipating populations in specific locations.[5] Arturo Escobar and others "locate development as a discursive field, a system of power relations which produces what Foucault calls domains of objects and rituals of truth."[6] For these poststructuralists, development is a kind of apparatus "that links forms of knowledge about the Third World with the deployment of forms of power and intervention, resulting in the mapping and production of Third World societies and segments of populations within."[7] Using a Foucauldian framework, James Ferguson examines the development apparatus for its "instrumental effects" in Lesotho. His method allows us to focus not on the failure of various aspects of development planning, which is a pervasive focus of those examining Caribbean development, but on what is produced and made normative. He argues that the unintended consequences of development policy led ultimately to the bureaucratization of peasant existence in Lesotho, evidenced by more and more peasants standing in line for state institutions' rubber stamp. Though neither production, productivity nor the livelihoods of subject persons is enhanced by the development industry, power is increasingly filtered through government or state agencies.

These useful insights move us beyond the intentions of planners, the failures of policy, the faulty operation of projects, and a taxonomy of the relationships among administrators and participants, all of which have served as a means of evaluating a project's worth for, focus though poststructuralist discourse analysis might on the textual production of development, there is a need to study more concretely how development's target populations reconcile their needs with their involvement in development projects. In short, what makes development attractive to those who engage its promises?[8] Although violence has often been used in the implementation of development projects not all development depends on discursive or material coercion.[9] However malignant and disastrous development's effects, sometimes those marginalized, or those about to become so, staunchly support its aims or its actions. They support policies that seemingly undercut their independence, or erase their agency, or so we think. How do we account for this empirically and theoretically? Do we see an anomaly backgrounded by the frequency with which its opposite occurs, or a "false consciousness," or an outgrowth of what Michael Hanchard in the Brazilian context calls the hegemonic principle?[10] How can we move beyond case studies to a perspective that incorporates different locations, geographic and historical, comparing for example the case of Lesotho, where there is manifest opposition between the state's and citizenry's needs, to those small states of the Caribbean where development was (and still to some extent is) tied to a notion of citizenship that presupposes working peoples' collusion with development's agenda. How do we configure these differences theoretically, making sense of them in light of alternatives to development, or an alternative sort of development? How do we account for moments when resistance and opposition are suspended in state/nonstate relationships, when "hidden transcripts" either do not exist or cannot be unearthed with the limited tools of the researcher, when alliances seem to outweigh oppositional relationships?

Acknowledging that aspects of underdeveloped economies and cultural dispositions are products of development but ignoring how men, women, and children have become development's targets limits what can be said about development's effects and, more importantly, how alternative kinds of development or alternatives to at least a certain kind of development might come to exist.[11] Early conceptualizations of development and its latter-day critiques, whether from a political-economic or a poststructuralist standpoint, overlook relationships that arise between clients and agencies of development during periods of fluctuating hegemonies, when for some reason their agendas converge. Consider the early period of decolonization, the immediate postcolonial period, which seemed to engender a great deal of consensus, arguably the case in the Caribbean. Intermittent consensus between state and nonstate arenas led to development, that in turn, as Lloyd Best states, created Caribbean societies. I refer to world development, as in the early formation of the capitalist economy, which historically underpins world-systems theory.[12] Because development of that sort created these places, the oppositional relationship typically seen in postcolonial societies was not entirely operative. I seek to implicate ordinary Jamaicans in the reproduction of development projects and, therefore, in the agricultural sectors' resultant social structures and, moreover, to see development as policies through which state institutions also rehabilitate themselves and establish rule over people and places. Of course, such policing inherent in policies "may be more conspicuous in its effort than in its effect."[13]

Because, in discursive formulations of development's power, development is often cast as oppositional to the nonstate arena, especially with regard to peasants and other marginalized groups, collusion receives little attention. Instead, we see the familiar development of underdevelopment, popularized by dependency theorists.[14] Though insightful in many ways, these studies usually focus on development projects or case studies that delineate tensions or resistance between the state and a targeted population often in a time span so short that such tensions are magnified causing development to be understood conceptually and practically as a thing imposed by a monolithic apparatus. In short, a concrete thing leads invariably to the creation of subject populations. These are plausible arguments. Despite their rich Foucauldian insights about the production of certain kinds of knowledge and the devolution of control over constructed subjects, poststructuralists nonetheless hesitate to implicate some of development's target populations as participants in such discursive and material practices. Instead, they identify the emergence of cultural politics as informing the action of new social movements which offer hope not for alternative development, but for postdevelopment.[15] While such studies graphically portray the wrongful premises of development policies and the sometimes violent tensions thereby exacerbated, they tend to cast relationships between the state and the nonstate arenas in overly hostile terms, not auguring well for the transformation of such relationships. Furthermore, such studies tend unwittingly to support those antistate positions which find favor with advocates of current neoliberal policy. Despite mounting evidence of runaway privatization, and contradictorily, the visible hand of the state in the marketplace, such policy calls for the unmitigated unleashing of market forces in development. By advancing notions of the power of civil society, such an anti-state perspective blends well with a populism that champions the power or innate goodness or correctness of "ordinary people." Absent from this discussion, however, is the extent to which the power of development has incorporated ordinary people, so that in their lives the encounter with development creates a contradictory blend of support, resistance and transformation, presupposing advocacy of those policies which ultimately undermine the so-called civil position. Involvement with development is attractive for a variety of reasons, and people whose agencies seem to be eroding, oftentimes clamor for it.

Because modern societies like those in the Caribbean and in Latin America, as Anibal Quijano and Immanuel Wallerstein put it, incorporated resistance into their citizens' flight to modernity before and after emancipation, such societies are incomprehensible outside of that development context.[16] People from this region are the creatures of modernity despite the exclusionary humanistic traditions which imagine them as the detritus of history, a point made by a number of scholars working on the cultural dynamics of, for instance, the African Diaspora.[17] The politics of nationalism, and even postnationalism, involve a careful weaving of the promises of citizenship with a middle-class-dominated agenda of development acceptable to a wide cross-section of the population, namely, smallholders considered "backward" by their middle-class leaders, and even members of their own stratum.

Discussions of the strategies of power and the "tactics of the subjugated to resist and insinuate a virus against the vampire" (i.e., development), to use Steve Pile's language, might benefit from seeing development as mutually transformative of the state and nonstate arenas.[18] Actors from each arena seek to implement their agendas by strategically supporting or opposing projects, partially or entirely. The tale becomes not only one of mapping the terrain of resistance, nor of merely identifying different ways of seeing, but one of seeking ways to understand how relationships are forged between and among members of state and nonstate arenas, for the realization of development requires the modernization of national economies and a complex involvement with the market, incorporating many informal activities and requiring the acceptance of many of its promises, while creating spaces for the plotting of autonomous existences.

Postcolonial places like the Caribbean societies offer valuable data on development and the diverse socioeconomic representations which tend effectively to qualify less complicated approaches. The Caribbean represents a window and a site by which to understand the attractiveness of even that development which marginalizes, repels, and disenfranchises large numbers of citizens, and which structures peoples' relationships one to the other and to the political and governing elite. Consider the formation of the smallholder stratum. I use the term "stratum" because as will be discussed and shown diagrammatically (especially in chapter 6), (a) "it" has persisted and been reproduced for scores of years; (b) "it" has not been class-formed through a polarizing struggle having a definite historical trajectory (however interrupted historically); and (c) "it" persists in being, organizationally speaking, amorphous. Though "it" simply lacks structural organs (parties, unions, producer associations, consumer associations, etc.), there is nonetheless a consciousness of "itself" vis-a-vis other strata (such as merchants, big farmers, traders, etc.). Members do belong to various organizations, if only in an individual capacity, and they relate to development projects diversely, as all strata. Though smallholders were seen to be rooted in oppositional responses to the state and plantation, the postcolonial state, through a conjuncture of events and actions (borrowing late-colonial strategies), persuaded large numbers of them to see themselves as vital to and validators of development processes, since development offered *the* way out of their economic malaise.

By applying the Gramscian application[19] of the concept of hegemony as concerns the absorption of a subordinate agenda to fathom development's outcomes, we gain insights into how states insinuate their agendas into those of their citizens. When we consider collaboration between political elites and mobilized sections of the populace, however, we must transcend the confining aspects of that particular interpretation for another which highlights that consent, whether passive or active, marks moments in the relationship between government, state and citizen subjects. Active in the sense that working people believe that the leaders represent their aspirations, and passive as when they simply lack the cultural understanding of the reality of their situation—a loosely packed "false consciousness," perhaps. Joseph Femia insightfully interprets this paradox as relating to the inconsistency, and incoherences of ideas and values. Fleshing out this paradox further, he states:

> Hegemonic situations differ in intensity, and the degree of variation is rooted in the dynamics of historical development. In a paradigm case of hegemony, mass affiliation would approximate to unqualified commitment; but such a situation can persist only in those historical periods when the ruling class performs a progressive function in the productive process, and when well-organized radical oppostion is absent or discredited.[20]

Moreover it is doubtful that the modern bourgeois economic dominance neither translates into furthering or representing the nonelite's interest, nor commands absolute allegiance. Thus,

> The potential for social disintegration is ever-present; in the consciousness of the common man, elements of intellectual and moral

approbation coexist in unsteady equilibrium with elements of resignation and even hostility; his thinking is 'disjointed and episodic,'
but in all cases his responses are culturally conditioned.[21]

One of the strengths of Gramsci's work is the emphasis placed on the role of cultural socialization in shaping the ideas and values of the subaltern, and therefore
understanding the constitution of bourgeois rule. In other words reliance solely
on economic determinors was unlikely to lead to a deeper understanding of how
elites conduct their strategies and tactics of rule.

Ought we not to consider the social and cultural ways that knowledge production becomes conjoined between decolonizing elites and those outside formal
political structures, mobilized against the colonial state? To that end, I construe
the state's activity not only as economic, but also cultural. For instance, in discussions of the formation of the English state in *The Great Arch*, Phillip Corrigan and Derek Sayer warn that

> The exceedingly masculinist imagery—of states as objects or instru-
> ments, capable of being captured and used equally by different classes,
> needs jettisoning as much as the iconography of the momentary revolu-
> tion to which it is integral. What we have been dealing with, in this
> book, is the immensely long, complicated, laborious micro-construction
> and reconstruction of appropriate forms of power; forms fitted to ways
> in which a particular class, gender, race imposes its standards of life as
> the national interest and seeks their internalization as national character.
> The capacity of such groups to rule rests neither on some supposedly
> prior economic power—it is, on the contrary, above all through state
> forms and their cultural revolution that such power is made, consoli-
> dated, legitimated and normalized—not simply on their control of
> some neutral set of state instruments. Their political power resides rather
> in the routine regulative functioning of state forms themselves, in their
> day-to-day enforcing, as much by what they are as in any particular poli-
> cies they carry out, of a particular social order as normality, the bound-
> aries of the possible.[22]

I will apply these in discussing the strategies of a decolonizing elite embarked
upon the project of state capture and postcolonial/postnational state re-formation
as well as these elites' impact on the agricultural sector. I use the constructs of
postnational and postcolonial to "go beyond the binaries of colonial discourse."[23]
State formation, or the propagation of a culture to advance the idea of the state
as a supreme authority within particular institutionalized functions, contained the
seeds of consensus and discontent necessary to forge specific notions of the
Caribbean state, development, and citizenship. Like the formation of the English
state, and those of other nations, the Jamaican postcolonial state relied on elite

ideas about what might further the notion of sovereignty, or enable Jamaicans to respond to, and participate in, a kind of nation-building. My interpretation fits loosely into both Gramsci's framework of hegemony (which itself is loosely scripted), and that of the poststructural developmental theorists, which at some level presupposes oppositional relationships between the state and the non-state arena by virtue of the states' power to "label," i.e., produce the knowledge which controls the conduct of those so "labeled."

Though Corrigan and Sayer aptly refuse to apply their findings as regards English state formation to all states, their study invites some qualified generalizations about the cultural strategies or outcomes of state policies. Consider what they say about the kind of culture that state formation entails; consider also the mutually connective, even transformative, relationships between political elites and others; furthermore, the possibility of collaborative agendas, even when their aims appear at odds, and one must then ask, what happens when the cultures of subjects reflect the project of state formation or re-formation? Insofar as the relationship between state and subject is understood oppositionally, the former seeking to control the deviant powerless "in need of policing," the subordinate subject becomes a victim.[24] Distancing ourselves from this one-sided and partial reading calls for a Geertzian-thick interpretation of culture contextualized by changing socioeconomic arenas which implicate the subject variously. I shall not consider the full dimensions of this here.

Development is both the vehicle and the outcome of relationships formed within the state and the local nonstate arenas, though it does not occur in specific, politically designated places. Whencesoever development policy derives, its actors comprise populations inhabiting specific places, though unbounded, due to varying degrees of transnationalism. Indeed, reflecting on Caribbean histories, we can argue that development produces these unbounded spaces, structuring these lived experiences through which smallholders' responses are filtered. Though I will discuss the related methodology of inscribing place within a global source later, for the moment, I want to suggest that discussions of development policy are vital for the comprehension of state and society which exist in tense but highly connective relations. The state-in-society framework predicates state development on state and society's mutually transformative relationship, thereby enabling discussion of development's multidimensional character and moving beyond a priori assumptions of opposition. For, "in historical terms, the development of any state as an apparatus and as a hegemonic institution always takes place simultaneously, in conjunction with, and in relation to a non-state arena."[25]

The state-in-society approach eliminates a priori abstractions and generalizations about states though offering a middle-range conceptualization, that is, a more textured analysis of the complex relationship between state and society.

Such studies have demonstrated the "mutually transforming nature of state-society interactions."[26] Even so, this perspective, however, tends to analyze non-state arenas as separate, even oppositional spheres, since the state seems so much to hinge on coercive tendencies. Though interaction is assumed, it is one emanating from monolithic autonomous spheres.

Moreover, the importance of stressing such interaction and overlapping between these culturally and politically constituted spheres alludes to the ongoing processes of state and society (re)formation. Moreover the focus on policy mechanisms reinforces this processual approach. Consider that "states are never formed once and for all."[27] As George Steinmetz put it,

> Structural features of states involve the entire set of rules and institutions that are involved in making and implementing policies: the arrangement of ministries or departments, the set of rules for the allocation of individual positions within these departments, systems for generating revenues, legal codes and constitutions, electoral rules, forms of control over lower bodies of government, the nature and location of boundaries between state and society, and so forth.

People's relationship to governments and states is never fixed, so that relationships characterized as coercive, predatory, oppositional, etc., never quite capture the texture and possibilities inherent in these relationships—neither in the relationship of rule, nor in that of citizenship/subject.

Because the state-and-society analytic may recreate the notion of homogeneous spheres, I stress noncoercive situations in structuring my analysis of how political elites relate to various segments of the citizenry, and vice versa. This is not to suggest that this is a harmonious relationship. As will be demonstrated throughout the text, the narrative of development with its explicit gestures toward citizenship and self-realization, operationalized through a myriad of projects, created or reconstituted agricultural forms that for various reasons, dislocated the temporalities of those emancipatory claims. As such, therefore, relationships of citizens to the state undergo change as well. It is as David Nugent posited: "local people's relation to the nation-state and modernity has distinct spatial and temporal dimensions that shift through time according to complex changes in the organization and orchestration of power."[28]

If the relation between state and nonstate arenas is historically contingent, surely we ought to scrutinize those moments when, first, conditions allow citizens' agendas to coincide with those of leading segments of the state and, second, states' agendas overflow institutional boundaries to become embedded in society's private spaces; in other words, when the idea of state needs nary an institutional support to sustain it, or when citizens sustain state building without institutional prompting, when in anticipation of the brutal effects of new policy, citizens find comfort in reminding state elites of promises made by development policy instituted under different regimes of state or development.

That the state is rooted in an historically contingent relationship is the constitutive argument of this book. Witness how the state, or the idea of the state represented by national governments, has insinuated itself into the lives of smallholders via various bureaucratic interventions and development policies. Often though development's outcome may be pernicious, the state's reach is not imposed through a high energy, high modernist project, of which James Scott speaks, but emanates from a vision shared by ruling elites and ruling populace, at least that's what the picture looks like in the early nationalist phase of nation-state construction. Thus, as others suggest, albeit in different contexts, we ought to consider the cultural, ideological, and political accoutrements of power that constitute its "legitimating universes,"[29] which, considering this book's concerns, include symbols and ideas of development popularized for the similarities they bear to peoples' preexisting strategies to maximize life's rewards.

I argue that the relationship between state and nonstate be seen as dynamic, relying on the realization of local and global agendas in a fluctuating hegemonic fashion, that the fluidity of state-society relations depends on such conditions as local responses to global manifestations, not to mention the racial, gender, and class dynamics that regularly generate social relationships. This perspective therefore represents a new approach to the study of peasants, and rural-based working people, particularly in places which given their overall historical development, possess fragmented or absent strong independent nonpolitical (in the sense of connections to formal political parties and state institutions) spheres, or precapitalist traditions that reflect alternative ways of organizing community. Development therefore is implicated here as the crucial mechanism through which Caribbeans see themselves as citizens of nation-states, and more often than not transnational ones at that. As Lloyd Best put it, development created society, and I would add nation-state, and its ideology of nationalism.[30]

The book serves as a corrective to framing rural working people as fundamentally oppositional, or posing opposition as a relevant characteristic, a stand-in for proof of their agency. I contend that this represents a refusal to acknowledge the complexity of the negotiations smallholders made with those political elites who spearheaded the nationalist/postnationalist/postcolonial state project. Land-based working people saw themselves as evolving citizens able to capitalize on early gains of newly sovereign subjects, involved formally and informally in state projects. Although compliance with state agendas is more evident in the postcolonial period, it began in the late nineteenth century. Arguably, more obvious in the colonial period was a major clash of agendas. As will be demonstrated in chapter 2, smallholders and working people generally participated in the limited developmental programs late colonial governments were forced to implement in the face of global economic depression and the sugar industry's collapse. Later, during the protracted process of nation-building or as David Scott puts it, the "secular modernization" project,[31] in the Anglophone Caribbean, nationalistic discourses encouraged and fostered development projects in opposition to and in conformity with what the colonial authorities had offered. Thus, development both engendered opposition and found widespread support among smallholders, signaling a similar involvement under both colonial and postcolonial regimes.

Forged from systems of slavery and indentured labor, with complex histories of resistance, the formation of nation-states in the Anglophone Caribbean, a mid- to late-twentieth-century phenomenon, is inseparable from Western notions of freedom and sovereignty, the capacity of states to chart their own development. In a somewhat paradoxical manner, given the political models upon which national elites drew, individual freedoms were linked with those of the emergent postcolonial state. Mobilization for sovereignty was based on promises of national development. Cultural practices of citizenness were incorporated into or marginalized by this project, thus eliding forms of otherness that could ultimately pose challenges to the political inventions of national community. In the case of Jamaica, ideas about respectability masked notions of blackness that early national elites eschewed. Postnational elites incorporated cultural forms of the marginalized, but notwithstanding its populist rhetoric, routed through party and state institutions and statist development projects, whose rationalities envisaged backward, working peoples in need of redemption and leadership.[32] Marxist alternatives in the formative period of the PNP and later during the 1970s in its postnationalist populist statist phase, though operating from the same rationalities of the liberal democratic state, were nonetheless suppressed in various political party cleansings of the Peoples National Party.[33] Though I acknowledge such tactics of suppression and silencing, I am not so much interested in erasures per se, as in the role that development played as a silencer of alternatives and as a producer of specific ideas about "the national community," how development actually worked, what kinds of proclamations about citizenship it facilitated in the forging and reforging of nationness and statehood. The promise of development and of sovereignty, "to be our (Caribbeans') own masters," along with notions of respectability, convinced many West Indians of the possibility of a shared national identity. Such development carried with it certain ideas of citizenship. Therefore, the idea and practice of development cannot be extricated from the cultural constructs of citizenship and nationalism propagated by state elites and practiced by elements deemed societally respectable. Because of such links to citizenship, development was acceptable to the extent that it seemed the harbinger of citizenship's necessary conditions. Metropolitan nations served as models for West Indian nationalism, which provided the basis upon which the quest for citizenship was pursued.

While at the forefront of creating a postcolonial state, middle-class people neither invariably imposed their world view on a hapless, passive smallholder stratum, nor simply absorbed that stratum into their programs. Limited success usually met their attempt to do so, though working people had good reason to want to be included in these agendas, not necessarily understood as excluding them. Middle-class agendas promised life free of economic, social, and racial discrimination. This attracted lower-income Jamaicans to the middle-class-led nationalist movement (not always willingly) and drew support to middle-class political leaders like Norman Manley and Alexander Bustamante, from whom concrete benefits were expected. These alliances were made clearer during the 1970s, when leftist radicals projected what they thought were peoples' agendas.

Recognizing the insights provided by several authors on the rhetoric of development, my purpose is to examine historically the relationship between the Jamaican state and rural constituents in the production and practices of development. I am interested in the institutional expressions and social reproduction of development as effected by government authority. I argue that development projects undertaken by the state followed cultural as well as economic models and were aimed at the transformation of ordinary working people into self-sufficient subjects, though freighted by ideas of respectable citizenship. These programs provided the state with greater control over the lives of rural populations, who, in the earlier stages of the decolonization process, supported such programs though they undermined local control and practices.

Ultimately, the pact between the state and rural Jamaicans unraveled, resulting in the postcolonial crisis of legitimacy. To use Abraham's formulation, since the late 1970s, *the idea* of the state, and I might add of the nation, is now in a state of flux. The appropriateness of development's mediation between state and people is contested. This process's causes and effects are the subject of this text, the formation and shaping of a subject population of smallholders, whom most call peasants.

I focus on how a vital aspect of rural society was created and shaped by a developmental state and later, by that state's transformation, or its developmental demise. The attempt to create stable categories of small farmers whose lifestyles and communities conformed to various state concepts of subjects was a project of mixed success.[34]

Since 1944 the conditions for unraveling the idea of the state have been operative. I argue that the demands foisted on the state by the IMF and the World Bank since the 1980s propagated privatization as the vehicle for national economic growth and development. The partial dismantling of the developmentalist state did not necessarily undermine the concept of the state, though the state no longer represented the loci through which citizens might realize their socioeconomic potential. The coupling of privatization with the responsibilities and obligations of the humbled developmentalist postnationalist government did, however, result in the overt marginalization of the smallholder sector and in the scattering of its members among various income-earning activities outside of the purview of the state. One can therefore argue that state cultural, economic, and political development involved the creation and bureaucratization of smallholder production, as Ferguson did in observing that development in Lesotho resulted in more peasants standing in line for the promise of state largess. Nevertheless, both attempts at controlling this constituency and genuine elite efforts to eliminate rural poverty led, as smallholders manipulated the state for purposes of exploitation as well as escape, to a loss of control, that is, fluctuating hegemonies.

Early development, such as occurred during the nationalist era in Jamaica, was linked to notions of citizenship. Development was acceptable to the extent that it seemed the harbinger of citizenship's necessary conditions. This political rationale largely succeeded. When favorable conditions unraveled, however, development became a questionable proposition, as did to a lesser extent the state. Small wonder that middle-class Jamaicans conjure credible images of two societies, harking back to Philip Curtin's idea of early Jamaican society and Michael G. Smith's idea of a pluralist society inhabited by people belonging to distinct cultural worlds.[35]

This study treats Caribbean development policy differently than it has been treated in the past. The link between state culture, development, and smallholders has hitherto not been systematically and ideologically plumbed. The most notable, and most substantive attempts to formulate a Caribbean theory of underdevelopment belong to the New World theorists, who drew influence from modernization and dependency paradigms themselves limited by their stagist and statecentric view of development.[36] New World theorists account for the "blocked development" of the society and the "duality" of the agricultural sector in terms of the plantation's institutional presence. Disagreements aside, they contend that as "hinterlands" of exploitation, the plantation re-emerged, and identify the multinational corporation as a new form of plantation that stymies the independent development of Caribbean economies. Like dependency theory and the structural-institutional perspectives of the Economic Commission for Latin America (ECLA), New World theorists conceive the state as instrumental in eliminating economic backwardness.

Other studies speak obliquely to the issue of development. Take for instance Michel-Rolph Trouillot's investigation of the provenance of peasantry and its continued existence—an anthropological quest. In it he proposes that smallholders be regarded within the organization of labor and the "peasant labor process." He links smallholders' involvement in global capital accumulation to their own impoverishment, as well as that of the region.[37] In the "peasant labor process" institution, a household performs agricultural labor on a unit over which it exerts a form of control excluding similar groups. For Trouillot, peasants control the instruments of work, which generally represent less of an input than the labor they use. In other words, the Caribbean represents a space of capitalist production, heavily dependent on commodities, namely the bananas produced by peasants via a "peasant labor process."

Such an essentialized construction of smallholders' roles limits our understanding of the process whereby those roles are constituted. Too little emphasis is placed on the political and ideological ramifications of economic arrangements. Often, smallholders are treated as stable, timeless, tireless "independent" producers, beset by imaginary planters, state, and development, trapped "working for capital." Trouillot's brief discussion of how to rectify such egregious exploitation as the producers' marginalization implies a call for market disengagement. He favors a modern development which would break the current relationship producers have with capital and state via a "peasant labor process." In other words, the less marginalization implicit in a relationship, the better the ensuing development. Dependency theorists and plantation economy theorists would agree. The persistent structures which construed the "peasants'" involvement in a developing capitalist world economy remain today's more punitive neoliberal economic order.[38]

By the 1970s industrialization had affected employment in such a way as to cause plantation economy analysts to call for a disengagement from the world economy through autochthonous development.[39] Critical of state nationalizations, many New World theorists challenged the notion of state neutrality and opposed claims to a national development orientation, raising questions about Caribbean class structure, largely ignored by earlier plantation economy formulations.[40] Though questions about the character of the developmental state arose,[41] they nevertheless left unexamined the dialogic relationship between civil society and the state in decolonizing and in development, thereby fetishizing the state. Though they resembled dependency and postdependency formulations in their attention to the geographies of inequality created by capital, like most development theorists of that time, they were preoccupied with bringing about that development associated with modernization by accounting for Caribbean "underdevelopment" with obstacles implicit in an ever-ubiquitous plantation system. Smallholders and ordinary Caribbean people were accordingly victimized by the state and capital. There may be a romanticism underlying the New World paradigm, for it implies that in the absence of obstacles, smallholders would realize their true potential, a problematic claim at best, at worst, a rationalization of the naturalness of the terrifying structures and cultures of rulership in which working peoples were caught up. Such critiques, however sympathetic to a marginalized populace, reproduced the Western discourses of development which privileged notions of a feudal-like "peasant development" and nonpolitical neutral state relationships. The claim of the New World theorists that their ideas constituted an alternative approach to development hinges on modernist notions of development and conduct. Because the state is seen as critical to furthering development, nowhere does it come under scrutiny for its cultural impositions, nor for its bureaucratization of smallholders' lives, nor is the relationship between state and nonstate understood as formative and transformative. Indeed, New World theorists succeed in authorizing more bureaucracy, more control, more state power over the populace. They supported state control over the "commanding heights" of the economy albeit on behalf of Jamaican rural and urban working people. These ideas inform the 1970s, reputed to manifest a fuller flowering of Jamaican democracy and more certain purchase on citizenship for ordinary Jamaicans. Behind the calls for alternative forms of development lurks an eschatological constitution of the good life necessitating a vanguard role for the state and its political party.

However divergent such New World perspectives on development were, they offered a view of capitalist development that emphasized plasticity in the hands of the state. They presupposed an interventionist state within the context of development. Their solutions underscored the state's capacity to broker consensus between state officials and economic elites with the aim of modernization, that is, national development, a technocrat's nonpolitical program, as politically consequential as all that preceded it, however. Thus, these analysts were sold on the positive agency of the state, and a notion of capitalist development to which wage labor and formal enterprises obtained. In the Lewis model, deemed "Industrialization by Invitation," for example, an expanding industrial sector was ultimately to absorb members of the reserve labor pool, the unlimited labor supply factor, eventually negating their marginality.[42] This was not the case. Instead, informal activity defined the economic operations of rural and urban Jamaicans and served to provide a refuge, even in an oppositional fashion, from unliberating development projects.

How did a diverse middle-class influence the experience of rural and urban spaces and people, and how were smallholders implicated in these processes? Rethinking the link between the middle classes and the rural working people and that link's economic and cultural effect comprises this book's purpose. Such a constitutive context behooves any discussion of either the responses of working people to their lives' politicization or the nature of their continued involvement in global processes, outstripping the oppositional resistance paradigms which have prevented a frank appraisal of the structural dynamics of late colonial and postcolonial Jamaican society and its paternalistic nationalism.

Treating smallholders as victims, resistors, even accommodators oversimplifies their complex relationship to the state. I aim to illustrate the articulation of this relationship over time as this stratum's members worked skillfully to control the spaces of their production and social reproduction, and as the state hatched ways to rationalize its rulership. I intend to show how state governmentality, exercised through agricultural policy, established the domain through which the lives of smallholders were shaped and through which they subsequently made oppositional demands upon an increasingly incapacitated state, and conducted themselves accordingly. I mean by this that forms of protest engaged in by land-based working people oftentimes were conducted within the terrain of these development projects.

After the demise of the plantation system, the colonial and the postcolonial state demarcated the boundaries within which members of smallholder households engaged in agricultural production, thereby constructing their economic and cultural lives.[43] These boundaries, however, comprehend a powerful constitutive element resulting in highly contested politicized spaces capable of more than containment. As Ferguson noted in regard to the application and pursuit of development, the state has bureaucratized and governmentalized social and economic life in order to ensure the centrality of institutional apparatus as regards smallholders, provided smallholders conduct themselves in ways befitting of political and state support.[44] Similar processes exist in other parts of the postcolonial world.[45] Nevertheless, these processes do not necessarily lead to the formalization of socioeconomic life. Informalization seems to be the rule. One can argue that where capital has failed to formalize, the state has informalized in a way that cedes capital a dominant stake in commodity production, hence the emergence of a social stratum,[46] engaged in agricultural production and self-provisioning activities, so-called "informal sector activities." I illustrate the processes of development played out in the lives of individuals, both members of households and citizens of a decolonizing state. It is usually as members of households that individuals participate both in the wage labor associated with the spread of commodified relations and in the nonwage forms of labor[47] which include "informal sector activities."[48] Informalization is integral and complementary to formal-sector development.[49]

Outline of the Book

In chapter 2, the setting, *A Plantation Political Context: Of Peasants, State and Capital 1838–1938*, I use the demise of the plantation as a major historical marker representing on the one hand, the rise of global capitalism, and on the other, the end of slavery and the rise of various forms of contractual wage labor in the British empire, at least.[50] Focusing on the relation between colonial and the postcolonial states, my argument instances agrarian policies as vehicles and scripts of development, as well as sees their implementation as premised upon a pact between state and rural working peoples eager to participate in a new, independent Jamaica. Such an analysis de-emphasizes the plantation as the site of "original sin," "peasant" formation and wage labor, and takes a wider view of the development activities of the colonial and postcolonial state and smallholder, in a changing global economy.[51]

In Chapter 3, *Postcolonial Development 1938–1972: On the Backs of Blacks*, I argue that the early nationalist phase of nation-building, roughly from 1944 to 1972, evinced an understanding between the state and large sections of society, due to the association of political sovereignty with citizenship and with economic development. Sovereignty was vital for imparting citizenship and charting an independent path of economic development. Economic growth would generate the sort of development that would lead the individual to have a sense of belonging to a community and a nation. If Caribbeans were to be mobilized against colonialism, their sentiments and agendas had to be accommodated. Convincing Jamaicans of the connections between political sovereignty and economic well-being was the decolonizing task of political elites. The terrain had already been prepared, because Jamaicans, like most of the world's colonized people, were malcontent with colonialism. The nationalist movement was able to count on their support.

The collaboration of a brown middle-class state and a mostly black citizenry not only marked the beginning of small cultivators' incorporation into the state's process, but also shored up the state's and smallholders' belief in the desirability of development. While ethnically diverse societies like Trinidad and Tobago and Guyana used the communal politics of race, Jamaica, limited in ethnic and racial diversity, relied on a development linked vaguely to the notion of individual, communal, and national betterment, though steeped in classism and hidden fears and conceptions of race.[52]

During this period, though state culture came to prevail in rural communities, promises of transformation were never fulfilled, at least not in such ways as might strengthen smallholder communities and households. State elites strengthened the idea of the state as the principal arbiter of authority, effected the politicization of projects, the entrenchment of political tribalism, facilitated by the modernization of its institutional apparatus, and the ideological reflections on what constituted the nation. This may be referred to as the practice of stateness, that is, the way in which particular institutions of governance structure and influence social and economic relations with citizens.[53] Reflecting changes in state apparatus and the economy, agricultural policy linked smallholders to the state. For a large cross-section of society, however, while development meant the commodification of the farm plot and its produce, it also produced spaces which enabled the smallholder escape and incorporation into state projects.

Chapter 4, *In The Name of the 'Small Man': 'Heavy Manners' and the Creation of New Subjectivities,* examines the period 1972–1980, commonly portrayed as a time of social and economic experimentation under socialist leadership. I argue that this period sees a populist state seeking to redesign the consensus project of nationhood, by redefining participatory development as a strategy for reshaping community, reenergizing national development, and broadening the terrain of rights, albeit within the discursive paradigms of a bureaucratic state, reconstituted as socialist, and democratic. How could smallholders still considered "backward" be capable of redeeming themselves socially and culturally with the support of a vanguard state and its political party? Though the redefinition of development was crucial to the rectification of the pact between state and non-state, in the end, the Jamaican state could hardly afford to mobilize, in its own image, the kind of forces necessary to empower ordinary Jamaicans.[54]

I question the widely held view that a substantive attempt was made to devolve state functions onto small cultivators and working peoples, or the polis as a whole. More believable is the advocacy of "capitalism without capitalists," the expansion of stateness, through the increased state control of resources with no parallel distribution of power among targeted classes.[55]

In *Maneuvers of an Embattled State: Neoliberal Privatization and the Reconstitution of New Rural Subjects,* chapter 5, I address the dissolution of the decolonization project in the 1990s and the preparation via structural adjustment for full realization of neoliberal economic policy. Such policy defined the individual as responsible for her or his own welfare, obviating the state. The impulse to restrict Jamaican working people to their own resources becomes the dominant mark of the 1980s and 1990s. Smallholders were conceived less as people who could be supported, that is, controlled by the state, than as subjects culturally backward, overwhelmingly dependent on state resources. The state sought to rid itself of smallholders, that is to say, to redefine the state-society relationship. Issues of citizenship and participation wither with the resurgence of a doctrine of Jamaican self-amelioration. So disguised state patronage of local and foreign capitalists, as in the early 1950s, is a torch-bearer of economic growth. To explore these issues, I examine AGRO 21, a high-tech farming project, arguing that it epitomized the mechanisms whereby the state moved from targeting smallholders in terms of poverty alleviation or eradication undermining its own institutions, to establishing alternatives that result in securing private enterprises within the ambit of the state. AGRO 21 was superimposed on an agricultural sector, once a pivotal developmental concern. New agrarian strata consisting of merchants and local industrialists and encouraged by the state sought to explore new global markets in vegetables, fruits, and flowers. Such highly mechanized farms, in the context of entrenched, impoverished, rural classes and old-style large farm proprietors, soon sank into debt and mismanagement. I argue that AGRO 21 represented an open attempt of the declining developmentalist state to reassert itself within a neoliberal frame. Forged in the context of structural adjustment programs, state reformation involved the shedding of an old state-society identity for a new one, premised on an unhinging of the state from its old agricultural responsibilities.

Chapter 6, *Inseparable Autonomies: Of State Spaces and People Spaces*, focuses on the changing conditions of land-based working people. Over the years, rural households have been coopted into export agriculture with little control over the terms of compensation, and of costs and the conditions of production. Members of such households have been pushed out of the countryside into cities and towns, the "lucky" ones entering the world labor market via migration. I focus on factors such as occupational complexity, size of holdings, technological development, labor processes, land use, and tenure.

Smallholders' diverse strata reflect both the struggles and the strategies of accommodation, begun during the colonial period at the level of smallholder households, which sought to secure control over production and social reproduction, and the state, which attempted to control and manipulate those processes. Neither the smallholder nor the state wins outright, nor is the game inconsequential. Development begs a certain amount of consensus, albeit highly contested, necessarily resulting in more state power over smallholders' lives.[56] Since the formation of the postnational/postcolonial state, development has incorporated smallholders as commodity producers under its own terms, by linking their production rhythms to those of the market, now under neoliberal regulations. I posit that development has facilitated the formation of informal and formal relationships, the defining coordinates of rural land-based communities. These determine the spaces of survival, accommodation, and escape available to land-based working peoples.

Under these circumstances, questions of resistance, agency and development in a period marked by neoliberal economic imperatives need to be rethought. Therefore the Epilogue, *Re-making The State and Citizen: The Specter of Formal Exclusions*, constitutes a discussion of how globalization is facilitated locally. Working peoples are forced to create avenues for the realization of development, fully aware that the state cannot dispense development largesse, but nonetheless they clamor for such assistance. In the midst of economic decline, hope for development is rekindled. Adopting this perspective facilitates an opening up of questions related to land-based working peoples' agency, far more useful than the tired ones that address resistance as if it is still tied to a readily identifiable liberationist project. In this chapter I hope to demonstrate the constancy of a development framework, even amid the recognition of its ruinous nature, and against which to propose new strategies of community empowerment. The multiplex existence of smallholders has produced diverse responses to the postcolonial state's political and cultural projects, not least the thriving of informality, beyond the state's capability to control, but complementing its neo-modernist projects.

In postnational Jamaica, several ideas about self-improvement jostle with development's narrative, which is not the only one available, but which is hegemonic enough to silence others, deliberately. I elaborate why I believe that the countryside is no longer tenable as a metaphor of retreat or refuge against the unrelenting forces of various capital and development projects. The rise of technicist discourses on poverty reduction, the latest buzz phrase of development, promises to turn the countryside into a sea of small enterprises, grouped by economic interests. Such a policy heralds a severe alteration or the demise of the relationship of stewardship between the state and its rural constituents, a pivotal strategy of decolonization. Rural space in postcolonial Jamaica is comprehensible as a development project which enables its spatial and social reproduction through a constant negotiation of state and global economy, processes by which agendas are forged through a negotiable kind of resistance and accommodation.

Notes

1. Sidney Mintz, *Caribbean Transformations* (Chicago: Aldine Publishing Co., 1974), 37.

2. I am indebted to many ideas in the essays in David Scott's *Refashioning Futures: Criticism after Postcoloniality.* (Princeton: Princeton University Press, 1999).

3. Immanuel Wallerstein, *Unthinking Social Science: The Limits of Nineteenth-Century Paradigms* (Cambridge: Polity Press, 1991). Wallerstein deliberately avoids using the word "rethink," using instead "unthink," to highlight the misleading constructs and ideas of nineteenth-century social science paradigms.

4. William Demas, the general secretary of CARIFTA, in the mid- to late 1960s always spoke enthusiastically about the "new Caribbean man."

5. See for example the work of Wolfgang Sachs ed., *The Development Dictionary: A Guide to Knowledge as Power* (London: Zed Books, 1992); William A. Munroe, *The Moral Economy of the State* (Ohio: Ohio University Press, 1998).

6. See Michael Watts, "The Crisis of Development," in *Power of Development*, ed. Jonathan Crush (New York and London: Routledge, 1995): 44–62, 56.

7. Arturo Escobar, "Imagining a Post-Development Era" in Jonathan Crush ed. (1995), 211–227, 213.

8. See for example, James Ferguson, *The Anti-Politics Machine* (1994); Jonathan Crush ed. (1995).

9. James Scott, *Seeing Like a State: How Certain Schemes to Improve the Human Condition Have Failed* (New Haven and London: Yale University Press, 1998).

10. Michael G. Hanchard, *Orpheus and Power: The Movimento Negro of Rio de Janeiro and São Paolo, Brazil, 1945–1988* (Princeton: Princeton University Press, 1994).

11. Postdevelopment or alternatives to development have been discussed by a few. See Libia Grueso, Carlos Rosero, and Arturo Escobar, "The Process of Black Community Organizing in the Southern Pacific Coast Region of Colombia" in *Cultures of Politics: Politics of Cultures* (Boulder, Colorado: Westview Press, 1998), 196–219, and Arturo Escobar (1995). But see also Michael Watts' critique of the populist dimensions in this post-development debate. Michael Watts; "' A NEW DEAL IN EMOTIONS': Theory and practice and the crisis of development" in Jonathan Crush (1995), 44–62.

12. Immanuel Wallerstein, *The Capitalist World Economy* (Cambridge: Cambridge University Press, 1979).

13. A very useful point made by Nicholas Thomas in *Colonialism's Culture: Anthropology, Travel and Government* (Princeton: Princeton University Press, 1994), 45.

14. André Gunder Frank, *Latin America: Underdevelopment or Revolution* (New York: Monthly Review, 1969); Walter Rodney, *How Europe Underdeveloped Africa* (London: Paul Bogle Press, 1970).

15. See Arturo Escobar (1995, 1999); Ranjit Guha, "Domination without hegemony and its historiography," in *Subaltern Studies*, ed. R. Guha (Delhi: Oxford University Press, 1989).

16. Anibal Quijano and I. Wallerstein, "Americanity as a Concept, or the Americas in the Modern World-System," *International Social Science Journal* 44 (November 1992): 549–557, 549.

17. Paul Gilroy, *The Black Atlantic: Modernity and Double Consciousness* (Cambridge: Harvard University Press, 1994).

18. See Steve Pile, "Oppositions, Political Identity and Spaces of Resistance" in *Geographies of Resistance* ed. Steve Pile and Michael Keith (New York: Routledge, 1997).

19. Michael G. Hanchard, quoting Perry Anderson, concurs that the hegemony's geneology is attributed to G.V. Plekhanov, "the so-called father of Russian Marxism, was the first advocate of *gege moniya*, or hegemony, a a political struggle against tsarism coupled with economic and military advances against dominant, feudalist class." Michael Hanchard, (1994), 19.

20. Joseph Femia, "Hegemony and Consciousness in the Thought of Antonio Gramsci," *Political Studies*, Vol. XXIII, no. I (March 1975): 20–48, 31.

21. Idem, 34.

22. Phillip Corrigan and Derek Sayer, *The Great Arch: English State Formation as Cultural Revolution* (Oxford: Basil Blackwell, 1988), 205.

23. Akhil Gupta (1998), 22

24. Henrik Ronsbo, "State Formation and Property—Reflections on the Political Technologies of Space in Central America" *Journal of Historical Sociology* 1, no. 1 (1997): 56–73.

25. Resat Kasaba, "A Time and a Place for the Nonstate: Social Change in the Ottoman Empire during the 'long nineteenth century,'" in *State Power and Social Forces: Domination and Transformation in the Third World* ed. Joel Migdal, Atul Kohli, Vivienne Shue (Cambridge: Cambridge University Press, 1994), 207–230.

26. A. Kohli and V. Shue (1994), 294.

27. George Steinmetz, "Introduction: Culture and the State," in *State/Culture: State-Formation after the Cultural Turn*, ed. George Steinmetz (Ithaca: Cornell University Press, 1999), 9.

28. David Nugent, "Before History and Prior to Politics: Time, Space and Territory in the Modern Peruvian Nation-State," in Thomas Blom Hansen and Finn Stepputat eds., *States of Imagination: Ethnographic Explorations of the PostColonial State* (Durham: Duke University Press, 2001), 257–283.

29. Antonio Gramsci, *Selections from the Prison Notebooks of Antonio Gramsci*, trans. and ed. by Quintin Hoare and Geoffrey Nowell Smith (New York: International Publishers, 1971). Migdal (1994) defines "legitimating universes," as "the constellation of symbols in state-society relations that justify state domination,"15.

30. Lloyd Best, "The Mechanism of Plantation Type Economies: Outlines of a Model of Pure Plantation Economy," *Social and Economic Studies*, no. 17, no. 3 (June 1968): 283–326.

31. David Scott, "The Permanence of Pluralism" in *Without Guarantees: In Honour of Stuart Hall*, ed. Paul Gilroy et al. (London, NY: Verso, 2000), 282–299, 294. Scott's article locates M. G. Smith's theory of pluralism in the context of the collapse of the Jamaican nationalist middle-class project of secular modernization, and its similarity to the program of the Left from which it distanced itself, and vice versa.

32. D. Scott (2000a). Ibid.

33. Anthony Bogues, "Nationalism and Jamaican Political Thought" in *Jamaica in Slavery and Freedom*, ed. Verene Shepherd and Glen Richards (Kingston: Ian Randle Press, 2002), 363–385; Deborah Thomas, "What We Are and What We Hope to Be," *Small Axe*, no. 12 (September 2002): 25–48; Michaeline A. Crichlow and Fragano Ledgister, "Nationalists and Development: The Price of Citizenship in Jamaica," *Plantation Society of the Americas* VI, nos. 2 & 3 (Fall 1999): 191–222

34. This is also a point made by Munro in his discussions of the African state and rural citizens. See William A. Munro (1998).

35. Philip Curtin, *Two Jamaicas: The Role of Ideas in a Tropical Colony 1830–1865* (Harvard: Harvard University Press, 1955); Michael G. Smith, *The Plural Society in the British West Indies* (Berkeley: University of California Press, 1965).

36. Aspects of Plantation School theory can be traced back to Merivale's land/labor ratio analysis of the nineteenth-century (postemancipation) West Indian economy, which highlighted the dominant role of the plantation sector in the economy and which was subsequently translated into a general theory of "open" and "closed" resource systems by H. J. Nieboer. Nieboer's (1910) concept recurs in the work of Best and Beckford though Benn (1973, 250–251) argues that a more immediate source of it was probably Raymond Smith's sociological adaptation of Erving Goffman's notion of total institutions to the West Indian situation. There are also influences of Eric Williams' historical analysis in *Capitalism and Slavery* of the relationships between colonial slavery and the rise of industrialization in Britain in the eighteenth and nineteenth centuries. Other intellectual influences derive from orthodox economic sources such as Seers, Myrdal, Sweezy, and Baran. Of the Latin American dependency theorists which the New World/Plantation School shared affinities with were Prebisch, Sunkel, Gunder Frank, dos Santos, Cardoso, and Jaguribe. The historic conference on Plantation Systems in the world economy of 1959 had much influence on this school. A number of seminal papers were delivered, for example, Wagley's "Plantation Systems in the New World," where Wagley (1959) attempted to define "cultural spheres" in the New World, of which Plantation America was

but one. Padilla's paper on "Contemporary Social-Rural Types in the Caribbean Region" was another. She argues that there is a direct link between the socioeconomic organizations in plantation-dominated societies and in the existence of the plantation as an economic institution.

37. Trouillot explains the "peasant labor process," a middle-range construct, in the following way:

The peasant labor process is an institutional process through which a household performs agricultural labor on a unit over which it exerts a form of control that excludes similar groups with instruments of work which it also controls in an exclusive manner and which generally represent less of an input than the labor itself.

Michel-Rolph Trouillot, *Peasants and Capital: Dominica in the World Economy* (Baltimore: The Johns Hopkins University Press, 1988), 4.

38. Dale Tomich, *Slavery in the Circuit of Sugar: Martinique in the World Economy 1830–1848* (Baltimore: The Johns Hopkins University Press, 1990).

39. See for example the early work of André Gunder Frank, *Latin America: Underdevelopment or Revolution* (New York: Monthly Review, 1969); idem, *World Accumulation 1492–1789* (New York: Monthly Review, 1979); Theotonio Dos Santos, "The Structure of Dependency" in Fann and Hodges, *Readings in U.S. Imperialism* (Boston: Porter Sargent, 1971); also F. H. Cardoso and Enzo Faletto, *Dependency and Development in Latin America* (Berkeley: University of California Press, 1979). See also Philip J. O'Brien, "A Critique of Latin American Theories of Dependency" in Ivar Oxaal, Tony Barnett and David Booth ed., *Beyond the Sociology of Development: Economy and Society in Latin America and Africa* (London: Routledge and Kegan Paul, 1975).

40. According to Thomas, "the dominant social classes have historically developed and derived their ultimate support in the context of their relationship to imperialism. Their major contributions, therefore, are in the direction of a perpetuation of dependency relations. As such, they cannot in any objective sense be seen as the instruments of the international political and economic integration of these societies; indeed, a movement in this direction must have as a basis the downfall of all such classes." See Clive Thomas, *Dependence and Transformation: The Economics of the Transition to Socialism,* (New York: Monthly Review Press, 1974), 277.

41. For example, Thomas argued that the state was not class-neutral but was linked to the local class structure. In his framework, however, the state is perceived as engaged in a unidirectional relationship with society. It can be manipulated by various classes because, like them, it is fundamentally underdeveloped. C. Y. Thomas (1974).

42. W. Arthur Lewis, "The Industrialisation of the British West Indies," *Caribbean Economic Review,* no. 2 (1950): 1–61; idem, "An Economic Plan for Jamaica," *Agenda,* no. 3: 154–63.

43. This is very inspiringly captured in the typology of Lloyd Best (1968).

44. James Ferguson, *The Anti-Politics of Machine: "Development," Depoliticization, and Bureaucratic Power in Lesotho* (Cambridge: Cambridge University Press, 1994).

45. See for example, Catherine Boone, "States and ruling classes in postcolonial Africa: the enduring contradictions of power," in *State Power and Social Forces,* ed. Joel Migdal (Cambridge: Cambridge University Press, 1994), 108–140.

46. The analyst can identify similarities in the constitution of these classes, akin to the objective characteristics of this stratum, without assuming that members possess a unified vision of themselves as different from others.

47. Joan Smith et al., eds., *Households and the World Economy* (Beverly Hills: Sage, 1984).

48. See for example, Alejandro Portes, *The Informal Economy: Studies in Advanced and Less Developed Countries* (Baltimore and London: The Johns Hopkins University Press, 1989).

49. See Faruk Tabak and Michaeline A. Crichlow eds. *Informalization: Structure and Process* (Baltimore: The Johns Hopkins University Press, 2000)).

50. Hobsbawm cautions that the process was not uniform, and different forms of labor existed simultaneously in areas where capital bore through. Eric Hobsbawm, *The Age of Capital 1848–1875* (New York: Charles Scribner's Sons, 1974), 68

51. Dale Tomich (1990); Migdal et al. (1994).

52. Percy C. Hintzen, *The Costs of Regime Survival: Racial mobilization, elite domination and control of the state in Guyana and Trinidad* (Cambridge: Cambridge University Press, 1989). Also Ralph Premdas, *Ethnic Conflict and Development: The Case of Guyana* (London: Avebury Press, 1995).

53. See for example, Thomas Blom Hansen and Finn Stepputat eds. *States of Imagination: Ethnographic Explorations of the Postcolonial State* (Durham: Duke University Press, 2001), particularly the introduction.

54. Migdal makes a distinction between autonomy of the state and its capacity to effect change of any sort.

55. The phrase is Goran Djurfeldt's. Quoted in John Harris ed. *Rural Development: Theories of Peasant Economy and Agrarian Change*, (London: Hutchingson & Co. 1982), 146.

56. Arturo Escobar, *Encountering Development: The Making and Unmaking of the Third World*. New Jersey: Princeton University Press, 1994).

CHAPTER 2

A Plantation Political Context: Of Peasants, State and Capital 1838–1938

> From the family plots of the Jamaican hinterland, the Afro-religions of Brazil and Cuba, or the jazz music of Louisana to the vitality of Haitian painting and music and the historical awareness of Suriname's maroons, the cultural practices that typify various African American populations appear to us as the product of a repeated miracle. For those of us who keep mind the conditions of emergence and growth of ideas, patterns, and practices associated with African slaves and their descendants in the America, their very existence is a continuing puzzle. For they were born against all odds.[1]

Introduction

Between 1838 and 1938, colonial policy in Jamaica made a gradual shift from attempting to forcefully proletarianize free Jamaicans to accommodating and even facilitating their accession to land-ownership status. Diverse agendas of planters, colonial state, and land-based working peoples ensured the emergence of competing forms of sovereignty manifest in the unwillingness of land-based working peoples to continue their plantation dependence. Though the colonial project succeeded in thwarting the full-blown emergence of an independent smallholder stratum, the colonial state was unsuccessful as a hegemon, relying on force to achieve its ends. In this period, neither the colonial state, nor various working peoples, achieved their agendas in the ways in which they liked. The capture of the state was therefore key to a decolonization strategy. Considering the importance attached to land as a means whereby citizenship could be realized, land ownership became a key demand in the anticolonial struggle. The stage was set in the agricultural sector for an interdependence such as would thrust working people into a world whereby citizenship's realizations could be achieved "only" within and through the manipulation of parameters of state institutions at home and abroad. Colonialism was seen largely as an obstacle to the realization of sovereignties of place and self.

Many scholars share the perspective that in regards to agriculture, the colonial state implemented cosmetic flourishes to a planter-dominated society.[2] For example, they argue that neither planters nor the colonial government provided avenues for the upward social mobility of "peasants" who, undaunted by planter and state hostility (at times indistinguishable), asserted and carried out their agendas. Thus, during the postemancipation period and into the 1890s, laws and taxation policy worked to constrain any movement toward "improvement" on the part of the "peasantry." And the argument goes, the "peasantry" was never able to realize its potential as a result.

Historical data bear out the generality of this contention at least for that time. However, far too often the "peasantry" has been lifted out of its varied context and treated as the quintessential pole of resistance to plantation production and life, and as a marginalized stratum, although it solely advanced a "new" Afro-Caribbean culture.[3] The rise of the "peasantry" is proof that black West Indians resisted the designs of planters and their political control although they were not so successful in fashioning institutions that reflected their world view. I do not argue with the conclusions these analyses make about marginality, and the "miracle" of creolization as Trouillot put it, in the epigram above.

I believe that smallholders needs to be carefully qualified, as it alludes to (1) an unchanging set of colonial state relations, or a monolithic colonialism, (2) an undifferentiated essential smallholder sector, (3) somewhat predestined and predetermined (intended and expected) agendas of freed peoples and the colonial state, (4) undifferentiated smallholder demands, and (5) implicitly the notion that had land been more widely commodified, viable, independent family farms would have emerged leading automatically to a better life for its practitioners. Furthermore the discussion of the rise of a diverse smallholder stratum, although not usually framed as such, has been divorced from other developments of the postemancipation era, considering that the rise of a peasantry, was also the emergence of a wage worker, a tenant, and other mixed social strata, more often than not in the same person. This is crucial to apprehending the character and evolution of this stratum, and not least its politicization by colonial policies and later its postcolonial variant.

This chapter seeks to present a more historicized and textured picture of the varied and ambiguous origins of smallholder identity, linking them to a changing colonial state from one where planters dominated to a Crown Colony government that towards the end of its days pursued a kind of protodevelopmental economic program. Moreover, texturized and historicized are land-based workers, their evolution and character implicated within the colonial project not as passive subjects, but as agentive as well, influencing the actual operation of such policy. The idea is not to imagine these processes colonialism and labor formations, the struggle for citizenness if you will, as some sort of totality, but to explore the divergences, seeming contradictions and outcomes of the contact moments of colonial and free people. To draw upon Nicholas Thomas' insights on colonialism, I speak here of "projects." Thomas states that

> [Project] draws attention not towards a totality as a culture, nor to a period that can be defined independently of people's perceptions and strategies, but rather to a socially transformative endeavour that is localized, politicized and partial, yet also engendered by longer historical developments and ways of narrating them. Projects are of course often projected rather than realized; because of their confrontations with indigeneous interests, alternate civilizing missions and deflected, or enacted farcically and incompletely.[4]

Colonized and incorporated as a sugar plantation colony, Jamaica was an integral part of the British empire, in a developing capitalist global economy. Through production organized on large-scale plantations and the struggle to promote commodified relations in the colony, the colonial state underwent change, evidenced by the critical compromises that it had to make in its relations with smallholders and working peoples alike particularly from the 1890s. The outcome of these changes would forever stamp the character of capitalist development in this peripheral territory and lend to the agrarian sector a blend of unfixed, ever-shifting, overlapping class boundaries, within which members constantly struggled to carry out their agendas against or alongside government policy, and often in response to larger-sourced socioeconomic changes.

From 1838 to 1930, these tensions ultimately shifted the relational existence of smallholder households from the planter class to a more autonomous (relative to the planter class) colonial state. In this way, smallholders faced the state in their battles for social and economic space but only to become part of a broader development scheme. Against this background, I contend that until the late 1890s, the main concerns of a planter-sympathetic state made for a seemingly linear connection with early colonial policy. After that, the colonial state entered a transitional phase. It became a protodevelopmentalist state, from which later Jamaican nationalists would draw for their development policies.

The transformation of the colonial state was influenced by (1) the decline of sugar prices and commodity production globally, (2) the response by the Jamaican planter elite to salvage a declining industry, and (3) the unabated if transformed nature of struggles by working peoples (that is the, newly freed and smallholders) over the terms of their economic and social existence along "western" lines. In this context the meaning of Mintz's "Westernization"[5] is twofold. It means that freed people wanted independence from the rule of a planter class many of whom were bent on extracting their ounce of flesh from a people fatigued by enslavement, and later treacherous governmental policy. It also means a willingness to substitute or supplement land for other forms of livelihood and to be coopted and recomposed into the agenda of a protodevelopmentalist state. In short, it means the freedom to be a citizen, however diversely interpreted, within the politicized possibilities of the day.[6]

Ostensibly, like free labor whose freedom is premised on its autonomous capacity to dispose of its labor power to any employer anywhere (all things being equal), smallholders wanted to be free to own land, to earn higher wages, and above all to achieve respectability by any means beyond that. This diversity of demands, desires, and needs partially explains the rise of varied forms of labor and accounts for the limited battles fought over land, in the postcolonial period. Thus, besides farming, smallholders operated on several other fronts. Emphasis should therefore be placed on the varied forms of labor that emerged in the post-emancipation period, their relational positions, and the changing conditions of both state and economy.

Against this backdrop, one can characterize the transformed "peasantry" as a multi-identity sector under the influence of two (perhaps overlapping) tendencies. The first, is that under a hostile colonial, planter-dominated state, one can argue with some qualification,[7] that newly free people constituted themselves as smallholders as wage labor, own-account workers, migrant labor, against tremendous odds. In the context of changing global initiatives, many Jamaicans are themselves reconstituted as instruments of and for development, engaging in various forms of labor. The second tendency is that even while supporting plantation agriculture, the colonial state becomes less contained by planter agendas, and more development oriented (admittedly on a very limited scale) in spite of itself and its racialist biases. This is not to deny Jamaicans any sense of agency, but merely to emphasize the fact that from very early in their history, a point generally overlooked, free people as smallholders and others were quite implicated in development as a result of colonial policy. As I will show later, particularly in chapter 6, this has had serious implications for the multiple ways in which smallholders pursue their lives.

To unpack this argument I first situate the strategies of lived experiences (whether resistance, accommodation, or adaptation of both colonial state and working peoples), as part of responses to global developments. Since there is an enormous literature on the postemancipation period, I will summarize the tense relations between newly freed peoples and the planter dominated state. This first period concerns the constitution of the newly freed into smallholders and other forms producing or implicated in domestic and export production. The second part of the argument shows the implications of a dominating colonial state possessing little hegemony. It is unable to proletarianize the newly freed, but it seeks to do so nonetheless. It tries to heed global imperatives, but it does so datedly and so its strategies are superceded. In spite of itself, in response to the clamor for land from newly freed Jamaicans, the indifference to its existence by the British colonial authorities, and the failure of plantations, relatedly, it engages in perfunctory (proto)developmentalism. This is the evidence I present to show its changing form and substance. I discuss the rise of other forms of labor and their relation to the shifting terrain of smallholder identities. The limits of development and opportunity necessitate the redefinition of the boundaries of state and smallholder loyalties to any one source of livelihood.

A Trapped Colonial State in an Expanding Global Economy

Before and after 1838, free labor was seen as a clear alternative, more efficient between other precapitalist and noncapitalist forms of production. New forms of capital were emerging. As early as the 1890s, fifty-two years after the abolition of slavery, Jamaicans were welcoming the incursions of capital's new instrument of accumulation, the transnational enterprise, the Boston Fruit Company that would later expand into the United Fruit Company. Yet, ironically, both old planter capital and labor in the colony sought to resist modern capital in a world being reconstituted by the latter. Planters and laboring people each sought to pursue their own agenda at the expense of the other's. Though not a zero-sum game, planters behaved as if it were. In Jamaica, the politics of the colonial state would mediate, circumscribe and restructure developments. Modern capital was everywhere creating, sustaining and maintaining variants of commercial agriculture and forms of labor whether free, unfree or contractual, and using states to effect the necessary changes to preserve the social order.

By 1838, West Indian planters, "fattened on slavery and protectionism,"[8] once the toast of merchant capital and political power brokers, had their power trimmed when production and ideological systems that secured their profits and ostentatious lifestyles clashed in a global market dominated by new forms of accumulation. To be sure, scholars have noted that the economic and military rivalry among European states led to the development of substitutes for cane sugar, namely, beet sugar that ensured the decline of West Indian sugar. The impact of beet sugar on the world market was critical. Its rise within the mercantile system, meant that colonial powers were operating within a market based on "interstate rivalry" which required "force and exclusivity."[9] Also rising levels of productivity among newer sugar colonies, notably, Hawaii, Java, and Cuba, sealed the fate of the West Indians. One crucial result was that between 1883 and 1913, sugar prices fell 50%.[10]

Moreover, nineteenth-century industrialization sent Britain and other European powers foraying into Africa, Asia and Latin America for raw materials like minerals, grain, and fruit that supplanted older products in economic importance.[11] One measure of this was that as early as 1831, "cotton had supplanted sugar as Britain's leading import."[12] In the southern United States, cotton production had multiplied sixtyfold between 1790 and 1810, and accounted for two-thirds of U.S. exports by 1860. During this period Egypt, India and Latin America had also become major cotton producers.[13]

As preferential sugar duties crumbled in the onslaught of free trade, West Indian planters were forced to confront other sugar producers competitively.[14] For example, by 1825, the British market had opened its gates to other colonies, specifically, Mauritius and India. Industrialization on the world market, and the expansion of sugar production elsewhere, spelled the collapse of the West Indian sugar economy.[15] The unevenness of industrialization globally meant that agricultural prices in Western Europe were tied to ever-rising urban incomes so that between 1883 and 1913 temperate products rose in prices while those produced in the tropics fell.[16] Cane sugar prices had now become contingent on those for beet sugar.[17] When the price of beet sugar rose that of cane fell.[18]

These developments shaped the global sugar market and were at once cause and effect of a profound reorganization of the expanding world economy. After 1880, the reorganization of the world market also included the demise of Britain as a leading manufacturer, replaced by its successors, Germany and the USA. Again, these transformations included the decline of old commodities that had given the British Empire the edge. Cotton, textiles, pig iron, coal, steam engines and railways, gave way to new products and enterprises such as steel, engineering and chemicals that would transform the United States into the new industrial power.[19]

In this phase of world market expansion, agriculture became increasingly subject to the dominance of industry and its prospects less dependent on natural disasters than prices.[20] Of industry, Hobsbawm stated that

> Its demands multiplied the commercial market for agricultural products-mostly foodstuffs and the raw materials of the textile industry, as well as some industrial crops of lesser importance—both domestically, through the rapid growth of cities, and internationally. Its technology made it possible to bring hitherto unexploitable regions effectively

within the range of the world market by means of the railway and the steamer.[21]

West Indian sugar producers were too weak to compete. As it had done in Europe with precapitalist producers such as peasants, expanding industrial capitalism had "liquidated" the planter's economic,[22] if not social, base. Industrialization was not an option as foreign investment during the nineteenth century was concentrated on primary products. According to Lewis,

> Industrial countries took great pains to organise their tariffs so as to exclude manufactures from low-wage countries. Thus there were low tariffs on raw materials, with high tariffs on the processed version of these same materials—raw sugar, refined sugar; crude oil, gasoline, bauxite, aluminum; cotton cloth; oilseeds, soap; cocoa, cocoa butter; coffee, instant coffee; and so on.[23]

Given their declining power, West Indian planters were treated cavalierly and by 1833 were told the imminence of the end of slavery required that they try to make the best of a bad situation.[24] How to "minimize their losses"[25] in the face of their grim future, their increasing obsolescence and their imminent political demise, was the question facing the weakened planter-dominated colonial state.

The Planters' Agenda and the Politicization of Rural Jamaica

The reason planters continued to wield power over the social, economic and political life of Jamaica, and over its formerly enslaved labor force, is related to their continuous hold on the state machinery. As Lewis had reminded us, they were the social order.[26] Though there was substantial transformation of slaves into freedmen, from forced to wage labor and "peasantry," state power was still in the hands of those who had once been owners of human beings.[27] Thus, the preservation and manipulation of the state apparatus, if only for a generation or two (formally until 1866), guaranteed the survival of the planter class and their influence in the colony. It was the state machinery that was harnessed to create, however unsuccessfully, a wage labor force.

Though tensions between planters and colonial officials pervaded political life, planters dominated the state apparatus in the pre-1866 period. They exercised their control through representative government of which the main institution was the House of Assembly[28] comprising planters and merchants. The governor appointed a Legislative Council. Much tension and conflict existed between these two branches, as each strove to dominate the other. By 1832, the Assembly had captured the powers to initiate legislation and amend money bills from the Council. Assent of the Council was still necessary for a bill to be enacted into law.[29] The Assembly enjoyed a certain amount of autonomy. It had its own executive of permanent Boards, the Board of Public Accounts, the Board of Public Works and the Commissioners of Correspondence. Ultimate veto power lay with the Governor who was the chief executive and acted as viceroy, captain general, chancellor, and the agency through which the Imperial Parliament transmitted its orders to Jamaica by way of the Cabinet and the Colonial Office.[30] Executing the orders of the Colonial Office meant also that governors reserved the right to manipulate or block the passage of laws. Consequently, "the constitution of Jamaica was not suitable for efficient government unless home government and Assembly were in basic agreement."[31] De facto representative government meant rule by the planter class. Nevertheless, checks and balances by the Governor and the Home Office circumscribed its power. British opposition impeded its potential for full control and responsibility.

To bypass some of these checks, the Assembly depended on the judiciary for support. English central courts found their substitute in a system of central courts. These offices required "respectable" men, i.e., men of adequate social standing, and planters readily filled this qualification. It was perfectly logical that planters would use their legislative power to bolster their judicial powers. Faced with opposition from the executive, the planters planned to "increase the jurisdictional competence of the Justices of the Peace and the administrative powers of the Parish vestry."[32] Control over the vestry strengthened their hand.[33]

Debates between the Assembly and the Colonial Office reflected the obstinacy and determination of the old planter class to chart the course of life in the colony and prolong their sociopolitical and economic life. This intrastate wrangling led to the paradox of the Assembly gaining in influence, while the governor retained the final vote. Political and administrative stalemates were quite commonplace.

> While the power of the Crown was destroyed, no unity of administration was created in lieu; the executive authority was shared out between committees or commissions or officials whose responsibility to the Assembly was distinct and who were subject to no effective coordination and often were under very nominal control.[34]

With planters in control, they excluded black Jamaicans from the organized political process. Jews were allowed to vote in 1832, and a scattering of free colored voted. Usually, rule was oligarchical. This limited vote was one instrument by which planters sought to monopolize power:

In 1838, . . . the three members for Kingston represented 151 voters each, while members for three of the country parishes represented less than ten voters each. Thus the Assembly had a sprinkling of merchants and a few professional men, but a majority of attorneys, overseers, and small proprietors.[35]

Absenteeism[36] was an additional limitation to the number and quality of votes cast at any given time. For example, absenteeism presumably explains why in 1838, of the 13,000 individuals who qualified for compensation as former slave owners, only 2,199 were on the voters' list.[37] Another limitation followed from the eligibility of voters, as stated in the Act of 1840. Qualification depended on having a six pound annual income from a freehold, paying or receiving a rent charge of thirty pounds annually on property or paying three pounds in taxes annually. As if this were not enough, voters were severely restricted in selecting Assembly membership since the very process of doing so was highly discriminatory. The latter was restricted to individuals with an income of one hundred and eighty pounds from land or property worth approximately three thousand pounds. As one analyst put it, they designed the system to "preserve a tenuous balance not enough democracy to endanger their own political control, nor enough oligarchy to alarm the British Government."[38] Yet, Heuman shows that small landholders (owning less than 25 acres) were able to influence the outcome of elections in the two decades after emancipation.[39] Heuman states that "though the number of voters never exceeded 1 percent of the population, the small settlers who had moved off the estates made up a sizeable percentage of voters."[40] This so alarmed the colonials that in 1885 Crown Colony government made it difficult for blacks and coloreds to vote. For example, the provisions to assist illiterate voters were removed,[41] because the Crown felt that it needed to maintain control "where the Negro population enjoys so wide a franchise."[42]

Constituting the social order and secure politically, planters tried desperately to curtail the economic and social options of smallholders. They restricted their access to small-scale agricultural production and forced them to become dependent upon plantation work when required by the planters. Since alternative economic options were scarce in the colony, it was the availability of land that provided outlets and planters sought to restrict its access. They strove to foster a solid front to prevent land sales. However, the bankruptcy of many members limited their success. Additionally, churches, like the Baptists, bought land, and then sold it to members of their congregations. When they could not prevent outright land sales, planters restricted the amount of land that they could sell to newly freed persons.[43] Other measures employed included the destruction of the provision fields and plantation shacks of the smallholders, and the severe taxation of possessions owned by this class, such as donkeys, pigs, etc.[44]

Taxation as a Political Device That Deterred Smallholder Expansion

Since historians especially, have already detailed many of these measures, I will summarize only to show the extent to which social and economic options were politically circumscribed and affected by Crown Colony rule. Such state machinations, I am sure, contextualize the reach of Crown Colony rule, and I believe, the preoccupation with the state as a means to bring about change and development by anticolonialists, including smallholders and workers. For example, the thrust of pre-1866 taxation was crude and did not mask its antismallholder orientation. It was designed to protect the planter class and plantation production.

Duties were exceedingly high on foods consumed mainly by the poorer classes.[45] Objecting to the imposition of custom duties on food, but justifying the taxation of the poorer classes, Governor Grey pointed out its rationale:

> To make people work for wages, . . . taxation should be so designed as to stimulate the indolent. Imports should not be taxed, nor should tax fall heavily on the well-to-do and prosperous, but rather on those living above bare subsistence.[46]

And so it did.

> In a petition to the Governor, small settlers complained,
> Most of us, through much difficulties, have purchased land, and portions of these are in canes, others in coffee, cotton, and provisions; and we hope by these means to subscribe for the education of our children, and support the Public Institutions, as we hitherto have done. But there are some who lurk in secret places to plunder, when good men have gone to take their rest? too lazy to work for themselves. The law punishes them, however, when they are overtaken (sic) we are lacking a continuous and remunerative labour, and hence we have to pick out for ourselves such employment as will pay us best, looking for better days when our clothing and food will be reduced, as the present prices are intolerable. Your excellency, the difficulties to obtain land to cultivate extensively, and the overrunning by cattle, our provision fields?(sic) the owner having no fences to keep them from trespassing?(sic) fill the country with abandoned fields, and hereby want and destitution. The state of the by-roads which lead to the small freeholders and taxpayers' cottages, are uncared for, and in the most deplorable condition?some resembling goat tracks, and not ways for human beings. We speak out now, because we know Your Excellency will do all in your power.[47]

Although they shroud discontent in a general listing of causes of malaise and they make no reference to the specific deeds of the planters (and some of the misdeeds mentioned were committed by fellow smallholders), the plea does convey a general dissatisfaction with the state of life in the colony.

The first administration under Crown Colony government set about the task of overhauling the tax system. However, it was no more helpful than the earlier administrations to the struggling smallholder. The basic premise harked back to an untenable past, that being that plantation production would continue to be appropriate to the well-being of Jamaican society. The Governor, Sir John Peter Grant, declared that

> Sugar planters by the new customs law have been relieved from import duties on machinery, casks, and staves and other like imported stores required for the purpose of their cultivation and manufacture.[48]

Thus, under the Import Duties Law of 1867, the main source of revenue derived from the taxation of food and textiles consumed primarily by smallholders, laborers, and the poor. A regressive property tax raised the tax on cultivated lands. On the other hand, they applied a nominal tax to uncultivated land of which there was an abundance on plantations and estates. They levied three pence per acre on cultivated land. They taxed uncultivated land at three farthings per acre. The property of the small smallholder bore the brunt of this new policy. Tax returns for 1892/93 reveal its unfairness. Of the 2,594,276 acres that were taxable, approximately 77% was uncultivated, mainly on large plantations.[49] On these were levied the nominal tax of a farthing per acre. They estimated the cultivated area at 666,741 acres of which 75% was under guinea grass. They taxed this at one and a half pence per acre. Cultivated acreage under crop production, of which there was 167,677 acres, attracted the higher tax of three pence per acre. Fifty-two percent of this was in ground provisions, cultivated by smallholders. Another 21,450 acres were under coffee, and 32,466 in sugar production. Since the small settlers were the main producers of ground provisions and coffee, with a small number growing sugar cane, they paid the higher property tax rates.[50]

Another tax introduced in 1890 added insult to injury. Smallholdings were more heavily taxed than large ones. For example, holdings of less than 5 acres were taxed at five pence per acre; while larger properties of more than 1,000 acres were charged a quarter pence per acre. Meanwhile, they imposed load taxes on the carts and animals of smallholders and laborers; while those used by plantations went untaxed. Smallholders and laborers were ordered to pay rates of 3s.6d. for each ass and 6s. for each wheel of their carts, wagons, and/or drays.[51]

They expected that smallholders would pay for their resistance to plantation production and by extension (however reluctantly), succumb like their

English counterparts to the discipline of wage labor. Smallholders' responses, such as in the petition to Governor Eyre, and brief accounts of sporadic protests, support the contention that these strategies successfully impeded the commercial tendencies among smallholders. They succeeded however, in creating a stratum well versed in diversifying their economic options, constantly on the lookout for loopholes in the system, and many well acquainted with western forms of governance.

Incorporating Indentured Labor

Additionally, citing the shortage of labor as an obstacle to plantation production, planters aided by the colonial state supported immigration to bring cheap labor into the colony. In defense of the project to import East Indians into the island, the governor of Jamaica reasoned that "it is impossible . . . to obtain a regular and adequate supply of native labor. . . . There is that fact that the average Creole labourer has no desire to work for wages beyond what is necessary to supply his immediate needs."[52]

Immigration marked one type of policy which favored the survival of the old planter class. As I have shown before planters wanted cheap labor and the complete dependence of the ex-slave on plantation production.[53] They wanted a fixed unidimensional class of subordinates. Though a few planters had sought to reverse that decline, by using fertilizers, ploughs, etc. to reduce the cost of production, it seems that the vast majority continued to demand cheaper sources of labor to regenerate production on plantations. This was not only a planter vision. The theory of labor shortage coincided with the economic assumptions of the day. For, "official policy," Hall argued, "favoured the large agricultural establishment and special Parliamentary enactments facilitated the aggrandizement of private property."[54] In 1842, they formally accepted immigration as a policy designed to rejuvenate the sugar industry.

In the initial stages of the scheme, the West Indian colonial governments secured the importation of African labor. Still, African immigration was negligible within the general population and constituted only 2% of the population. Later, the planters requested an expansion of the scheme to Indians, and to Chinese. Toward the end of 1847, when the passage of the Sugar Duties Act eliminated preferential treatment for West Indian sugar, they retrenched it, but started it again in 1860 and ended in 1917. Indeed Roberts notes that by 1861 when most immigration had already taken place,

> only 18,000 of the total population of 441,300 were born outside of
> the island. . . . Natives of Africa formed the main groups of foreign-
> born population (10,500), but as they constituted only 2% of the

population it is evident that their contribution to population growth was of no consequence.[55]

Between 1845 and 1917 there were some 38,681 immigrants, of whom 30% (11,959) had returned home. This number however does not take into account the death toll considered high among the Indians, who formed the bulk of the immigrant labor force. By 1921 East Indians formed only 2.2% of the population.[56]

Indentured labor was a costly experiment. In theory, laborers under the scheme were offered conditions that matched or ostensibly were better than Creole labor (ex-slaves).

> Immigrants were to be paid the current daily wage of 1/6d for a day's labor of nine hours, or, the usual rates for job or task work, which brought about 2/for a good day's work. They were to be given free of rent, a cottage with garden attached; and they were also to be provided with free medicines and medical attendance.[57]

In practice, however, wages were likely to be a shilling or less per day,[58] and planters were slow in honoring their other obligations. They gave indentured laborers five-year contracts with the option to renew the lease and settle in Jamaica, or return to India. After having committed themselves to such expense[59] planters were reluctant to honor their obligations, especially the costly one of repatriation. Instead of that, they were willing to give laborers plots of land situated near plantations. These served the dual purpose of appeasing the laborers, giving them some semblance of independence, and ensuring a continuous supply of labor. But this stratum, though never slaves in the classic sense, nevertheless formed households, like ex-slaves straddling multiple forms of economic strategies.[60] They augmented that stratum of diverse subsistence producers, who were clearly more prevalent in the postemancipation period, as well as wage labor and other diverse forms of economic activity.

Other than to lower production costs and reduce the relative price of sugar, the direct effects of immigration were unclear. At least for the duration of the contract, the planters were sure of a steady but insufficient supply of labor. In estimating the effect of indentured labor during crop time when they needed labor, Hall contends that

> It is possible that by denying employment to some local workers during the off-season, the immigrants increased the willingness of these people to accept crop-season employment.[61]

Hall stresses that unless planters could find sufficient supplies of labor "the exclusive application of immigrants to crop-taking would inevitably lead to neglect of current cultivation work."[62]

The effectiveness of immigration as an instrument of labor replacement, as price reducer of sugar production, and as a savior for plantation agriculture over time was constrained by four basic factors. The first was its small scale and erratic application; the second, the ephemeral nature of the contract, and the fact that indentured laborers were just as eager as had been the ex-slaves to be free from complete dependence on plantation work; the third, a combination of the indigent state of the sugar industry itself, marked by the decline in the number of sugar plantations and the amalgamations; and the fourth, the spread of the less labor-intensive banana cultivation. Together these made plantation work seem as unfitting, unrewarding and therefore undesirable for indentured workers, as it had been for the ex-slaves.

The Rise of Variant Forms of Labor

In his Notebook III, Marx wrote,

> *The Times* of November 1857 contains an utterly delightful cry of outrage on the part of a West-Indian plantation owner. This advocate analyses with great moral indignation—as a plea for the re-introduction of Negro slavery—how the Quashees (the free blacks of Jamaica) content themselves with producing only what is strictly necessary for their own consumption, and alongside this 'use value', regard loafing (indulgence and idleness) as the real luxury good; how they do not care a damn for the sugar and the fixed capital invested in the plantations, but rather observe the planters' impending bankruptcy with an ironic grin of malicious pleasure, and even exploit their acquired Christianity as an embellishment for this mood of malicious glee and indolence. They have ceased to be slaves, but not in order to become wage labourers, but instead, self sustaining peasants working for their own consumption, because autonomous wealth as such can exist only either on the basis of direct forced labour, slavery, or indirect forced labour, wage labour.[63]

The reluctance of the ex-slaves to function as poorly paid wage labor for the plantations, the existence of significant supplies of abandoned lands, and the repressive measures adopted by the planter class to generate free labor, forged responses that ultimately led to the conception of new overlapping and interrelated forms of production. Emerging at a time when both the planter class and the British government sought to preserve the plantation as the mode of agricultural production, smallholders faced tremendous pressure in their varied quests to be independent of plantation capital. Under these conditions, how did they attempt to reorganize their households and their agricultural production to the existing social and economic order? An examination of the varied forms of labor and production provides generous clues to comprehending this process.

Unlike other Caribbean islands, such as St. Lucia where the decline of the sugar industry spawned new social relations such as metayage[64] (between the impoverished sugar planters and the ex-slaves), those in Jamaica, for the most part, entered multiple arrangements to strategize their multirelationship with the plantation. In the wake of emancipation three broad strata emerged:

> those who owned and worked freeholds, and were employers themselves, small freeholders who as well as cultivating subsistence depended on the plantations for employment and those who continued to labour on estates while renting cottages and provision grounds from estate owners.[65]

It is the first two strata identified by Hall and others that have been the focus of several works documenting the rise of an "independent" smallholder "class." They emerged through varied efforts of their own, by purchasing land despite the efforts of the planter class to interdict such sales. Others simply squatted on available unoccupied lands. Often, churches such as the Baptists purchased land for resale to members. The idea of the churches was not to create fully independent smallholders but to organize them so that one could "go to any estate he pleases to work and to return to his home and family when he has fulfilled as an hireling his day's employ."[66] Nevertheless, full independence, of production or reproduction and control over economic options, was exceptionally difficult to attain and the vast majority of the ex-slaves who fled the plantation continued to depend on it for their livelihood.[67]

The emergence of a substantial body of diverse subsistence cultivators producing for the domestic market was as, or perhaps far more, significant than the nascent development of a distinct urban working class or an "independent peasantry" during this period. The impact of this diverse stratum of smallholders was such that in 1890, 55% of all agricultural output was attributed to smallholder production.[68] Although Eisner's employment of the notion of the smallholder relies more on size than it does on qualitative relationships within and among households, and embraces holders with properties of fifty acres and more, table 2.1 should be valued for the general impression it gives of the agricultural pursuits of these new households in the Jamaican agricultural economy.

The consensus is that smallholders as main cultivators of ground provisions[69] produced for the domestic market. Table 2.1 highlights how this pattern of agricultural production evolved. The growing importance of ground provisions that accounted for 55% of total agricultural output reflects the niche that smallholder households occupied in the agricultural economy. Simultaneously, many were also involved in the manufacture of crude sugar for the domestic market.

Table 2.1.   The Pattern of Total Agricultural Output

	1832 %	1850 %	1870 %	1890 %	1910 %	1930 %
Ground Provisions	27	43	54	55	50	49
Animal Products	1	8	6	6	6	9
Retained Exports	1	2	3	4	4	3
Exports	71	47	37	35	40	39
Total	100	100	100	100	100	100

Source: G. Eisner, *Jamaica, 1830–1930. A Study in Economic Growth* (Manchester: Manchester University Press, 1961).[70]

In 1870 for example, the consumption of sugar on the local market reached 6,000 tons.

Smallholders were also known for their mixed cultivation practices. For example, they grew arrowroot, logwood, and coffee, the cultivation of which received a boost in the 1850s. Unlike the large agricultural enterprises, whose organization of production was highly rigid, these smallholders manipulated production in ways that exploited any market fluctuations in various crops. Thus, "the years which brought a decline of arrowroot also brought an increase in the production of lime juice and a new development in the growth of bananas."[71] I take this point up later.

The Response of the State to the Rise of Squatter Households

Restrictions placed on smallholder purchase of land in the mid- to late nineteenth century, compounded by the sparseness of employment outlets everywhere, invariably led to squatting. Colonial policy displayed a double standard in dealing with the issue. According to the Jamaica Blue Book, there were two categories of squatters, big and small.[72] State action was harsh toward the small squatter but protected and excused the big squatters. Policy was laid out in two laws, Law 37 of 1867 and the Land Settlement Law of 1897.

Under the provisions of these laws, District Courts were given jurisdiction over land disputes and power to remove all known squatters from land for which they could prove no ownership. Land for which neither quit-rent nor land taxes had been paid could be forfeited. The main effect was that thousands of acres of land reverted to the Crown. Between 1871 and 1912, more than 240,368 acres of forfeited land had become the property of the Crown.[73] Between 1870 and 1889, the Crown had repossessed 713 acres of land.[74] The assault against squatters discriminated against small squatters. The difference between the big squatter and the small one was that between a "Respectable Squatter" and a "Peasant Squatter." According to the Governor,

> The former is a squatter on a large scale and is generally a man of some position, who by some fortuitous circumstances, gets possession of some property, unrepresented and without heirs, and keeps it, works it, and uses it as his own accounting to no one; and in some instances goes so far as to sell portions to unsuspecting peasants. . . . The respectable squatter when he is attacked by government, generally contests the point.[75]

Presumably the "peasant squatter" was none of the above, and was an unwelcome social parasite in the agricultural economy.

Were squatters a transitory group sacrificed for the perpetuation of smallholders? For example did the squatter lands seized by the Crown go to larger smallholders or revert to squatters thereby augmenting the growth of smallholder households? Detailed accounts are not available. But we may speculate. The precise distribution of this Crown land is unclear. Eisner cites this period as the expansionary phase of smallholders; by implication therefore, much land was sold to this stratum. Two difficulties surface here. First, Eisner's notion of smallholder embraces plots of 50 acres and more; second, it has been shown elsewhere those holdings (i.e., the sum of various parcels) many of which one person or families held, had been bought by urban residents or by nonsmallholders.

Other research delineates two specific trends, which undermine Eisner's conclusions. In 1880s the practice of the Crown was to lease large parcels of land. For example, in 1879/80, of the eighteen leases made, twelve persons leased parcels of land between 100 and 1000 acres in size.[76] Another law enacted in 1878, designed to distribute state lands, revealed a preference to dispose of large and not small parcels of land. By these accounts, it seems that the colonial state seemed predisposed to distributing the land to those who could afford to invest in large amounts. Certainly they were not members of this stratum, at least not most of those who desperately needed land.

Furthermore this was underscored by the fact that the state, anxious to introduce new entrepreneurs into the moribund agricultural sector, passed Law 16 of 1871. This law eased the restrictions on the sale of land to foreign investors. The result was as intended the ownership of large tracts of land by foreign investors. One such investor, the Boston Fruit Company, in the space of only four years, 1881 to 1884, operated approximately 10,500 acres of prime lands in the parishes of St. Thomas and Portland.

That bias notwithstanding, roughly three decades after the colonial state had institutionalized support for large- and medium-scale agricultural enterprises, it was forced to make concessions to smallholders. A land settlement scheme designed for smallholders took shape. Instituted by the governor, Sir Henry Blake, the land settlement scheme of 1895 permitted the purchaser to deposit one-fifth of the total amount after which the land was surveyed and applicants given title. The remaining four-fifths plus the two pound cost of the survey was payable in ten yearly installments.[77] The cost of the land was below market price. The state sought to control agricultural land use through a government stipulation that one-fifth of the land should be reserved for permanent crops like coffee, citrus or cocoa.

But the name "land settlement" was a misnomer. Eisner believes that this was due to the quality of land being sold.[78] This is quite plausible, as much of forfeited lands were peripheral marginal lands in remote locations. The infrastructure was generally lacking. The governor himself alluded to this when he declared that unless roads accompanied plots offered for sale, purchasers would be few.[79] He was right. Part of the explanation for this was that the smallholder producing for the export and domestic markets required lands with adequate access to buying agents and central operations. It was little wonder there were so few takers of such cheap but isolated land. Yet placed under scrutiny, the state was indeed making concessions if only grudgingly.

Colonialism in Transition: Dominance, Hegemony and the Politicization of Social Life

Planter rule finally worked itself out in one of the most violent riots in Jamaican history, the Morant Bay Rebellion of 1865.[80] While still in shock and alarm over the loss of life and destruction of property, Governor Eyre, in one swooping stroke, abolished the constitution and instituted direct Crown Colony government, thus bringing to an abrupt end direct planter rule of the colony.

According to one historian,

> The constitution of 1866 gave the British political authority in an autocratic form. The governor was sure of his majority and the society was represented only by his nominees. The Order in Council of 1884 set limits to the extent that any governor could play the autocrat, by permitting the elected members when acting in concert to veto his bills and resolutions. But it did not modify the essentially autocratic character of the crown colony constitution.[81]

In this section, I examine very briefly some characteristics of the Crown Colony state, in order to contextualize the rise of a protodevelopmentalist state. Crown Colony government was a watershed marking these two distinct periods in the making of a smallholder stratum. I argue that while mediating between the two principal classes in the agricultural sector, namely the planters and smallholders, the colonial state, through its policies on taxation, land settlements and squatting, perhaps scored greater successes than had the planter class in shaping the explicit development of this stratum. Nevertheless, it was not a one-sided process.

Ostensibly, Crown Colony government claimed that it would arbitrate relations between the antagonistic Jamaican racial groupings and protect them from each other. For example, "looking after the interests of the blacks would protect them from the whites and from themselves."[82] But it would do so only in its own home-grown racist ways. Under the new form of government, old racialisms were reinforced, and new ones introduced. For example, high political and administrative offices were reserved for whites and the highest only for Europeans.[83] The practice of nonwhites of using these offices for assimilation into white society was no longer possible. The composition of the nominated element further underscored the falsehood of the humanitarian claims of Crown Colony government introduced into the executive. How could the Crown serve the interests of blacks when the entire nominated element comprised members of the propertied classes? Indeed, this created even greater dependence by blacks on the state and local white interests. As Augier stated,

> The imperial power to review colonial legislation had in the past been used to regulate the relations between the two societies, Jamaica and England; now after Emancipation it was being used to regulate the relations between two groups with the Jamaican society, ex-slaves and ex-masters. In the earlier period, the superior power of England had been exercised to maintain an economic relationship between Jamaica and herself according to the principles of political economy then in vogue. Now British power was being used to establish social relations between ex-slaves and ex-masters political expediency.[84]

Humanitarian claims aside, Crown Colony government was about the centralization and modernization of the state apparatus with the specific purpose of achieving maximum control over the economic, social and political development of the colony. They made old departments efficient; new ones like the Imperial Department of Agriculture and a local department of Agriculture were established. They introduced rational and accountable financial procedures.[85] New courts were established to dispense justice to the poor. All this was achieved by a concentration of power in the hands of the Colonial Secretary and his battalion of British heads of departments.

Events such as world depression and its specific repercussions throughout the British empire were to influence imperial policy and subsequently orient state policy to the more immediate needs of the colonies. For example the economic depressions of the 1890s and 1930s were the mitigating circumstances for the onset of loose welfare policy in Jamaica. For the smallholders, welfarism meant some space to operate, but not enough to climb out of the pit of deprivation and despair, and to move beyond hope.

The economic disarray of the 1890s, chronicled by the recommendations of the West India Royal Commission of 1897 (the Norman Commission), and the economically depressed conditions within the British economy heralded the coming of welfare policy in Jamaica. Though Jamaica was highly diversified as compared with other West Indian islands, the depression of the late 1890s alarmed officials and Jamaicans alike. Diversification aside, there was cause for alarm. Approximately 39,000 persons were directly dependent on sugar and many others were indirectly associated with shipping, cattle breeding, etc., all for the sugar industry. As shown earlier the bounty system employed by Britain's European rivals had led to the subsidization of beet sugar, sharp increases in production, a decline in production costs, and consequently an overabundance of sugar on the international market.[86]

The effect of this glut was a dramatic fall in sugar prices. The price of refined sugar fell from 29s.14d per hundredweight in 1882 to 14s.75d in 1896. Unrefined sugar also fell from 21s.09d to 10s.85d during that same period. The prices for molasses and rum also fell. Against this background, the Norman Commission was hard pressed to make appropriate recommendations to resolve the economic debacle in the sugar industry. Doubtful as to the effects of the European bounty system upon the West Indian sugar industry, the commission stated,

> Under any circumstances that can at present be foreseen, the days of very large or excessive profits from the sugar cane industry appear to us to have passed away; and in those portions of the West Indies which are unsuited for the establishment of large factories equipped with the best machinery, and which do not in soil, climate and the supply of labor possess special advantages for the production of sugar, even the abolition of the bounty system would probably fail to restore the industry to a condition of permanent prosperity.[87]

They explicitly denied West Indian planters the benefits of countervailing duties on beet sugar, arguing that the British market was large enough to accommodate all kinds of sugar. Instead, they recommended renewed efforts aimed at lowering the costs of sugar production and the settling of cane farmers on land near cane factories. Cane farmers could ostensibly support their subsistence practices, but also make themselves available for work in the factories when the necessity arose. The encouragement of smallholders seemed an adhoc response to the scarcity of employment opportunities in the economy, social policy masquerading as sound economic policy. Its approach to exploring alternative economic avenues was equally lukewarm:

> We have therefore no choice but to consider how means can be found to enable the mass of the population to support themselves in other ways than as labourers on estates. No large industry other than agriculture offers any prospect of success, except possibly the gold industry in British Guiana and when large estates cannot be profitably worked the adoption of the system of cultivation by petty proprietors is inevitable.[88]

It was not until the passage of the 1929 Act and later, its extension in the 1940 Act that the notion and practice of welfarism became entrenched in the politics of the colonial state. The passage of the earlier act was the precursor to the search for mechanisms to boost employment both in the colony and in Great Britain. They openly stated this in the terms of reference of the administering committee, the Colonial Development Advisory Committee.

> In accordance with section I of the Colonial Development Act, 1929, to consider and report on, in the manner to be prescribed in the regulations to be made by the Secretary of State under section I (9) of the Act, applications for assistance from the Colonial Development Fund, in furtherance of schemes likely to aid and develop agriculture and industry in the Colonies, Protectorates, and Mandated Territories, and thereby promote commerce with or industry in the United Kingdom by any of the means specified in section I (I) of the Act.[89]

To ease the committee's work, the Colonial Development Fund was established with a subscription of one million pounds voted annually. Fully aware of the novelty of this approach to development, the committee argued that it had operated within the letter of the Act and that "save in exceptional circumstances all orders for imported material should be placed in the United Kingdom manufacture and that, as far as possible, materials should be of Empire origin."[90] Yet they also felt that the colonies and the United Kingdom had been shortchanged particularly with respect to recurrent expenditures on schemes and projects. As they saw it,

> Their inability to consider applications for assistance towards long term recurrent expenditure has been a deterrent to the submission by

Colonial Governments of schemes which might have been of great value . . . (thus) This restriction has limited the value of the Act in those territories whose finances were weakest and where the need for assistance was therefore, the most felt.[91]

Thus it was, that the expenditure recommended under this scheme at least until the mid-1940s was primarily restricted to infrastructure, namely internal transport and communications, public health and water supplies and water power. Under the Colonial Development Fund, Jamaica received per head of the population a paltry 10d in loans and 2s.10d. in grants. For the whole British Empire only ten million pounds was granted for a decade of development.[92]

However, continued economically depressed conditions in the world forced the colonial state to extend the jurisdiction of the 1929 Colonial Development Act and increase its welfare component. How did this economic policy translate into the matrix of relations between state and smallholders? Was there sufficient change to occasion even a small rupturing of the agrarian order?

If they were committed to their promises there would be changes to agrarian policy of a planter-state era. Yet, whatever the promises, the moribund social order had to be maintained. Both the land and taxation policies sustained the thrust of their predecessors. It was directed against the expansion and consolidation of working peoples as small farmers, and gave disproportionate support to large agricultural enterprises. Thus, "the money spent on the crops of the small cultivator, the time and energy spent on his problems were as nothing compared with what was lavished on plantation agriculture."[93]

The agricultural policy of Crown Colony government was Janus faced, favoring large farmer entrepreneurs and disfavoring others. Take for example the treatment accorded to the Pringles and the Kerrs. In the early 1920s, the Pringles, owners of extensive properties totaling some 5,780 acres in St. Anne, St. Mary and St. Thomas besides 850 head of cattle, could avoid financial disaster when the banks refused to lend them more money. Governor Probyn made a special plea to Winston Churchill, Secretary of State for the Colonies, "asking that the government be permitted to make a special financial arrangement with the Pringles."[94]

Contrast this with the treatment accorded to Mr. Kerr, a tenant in perpetuity, and others like him. One argument is that they virtually ignored the needs of people like Mr. Kerr. Kerr had difficulty finding land to buy although he could afford it. They made no special intervention for him. Other tenants like Bertram Amos faced similar tensions.[95] Brodber concludes that

Young landless blacks who between 1923 and 1930 yearned for autonomy based upon own account farming, had to postpone their independence from the plantations and had instead to establish an in-

gratiating relationship with its owners and managers in the hope that
at some later stage in their lives they would offer to sell them lands.[96]

Unable to reverse the global tide moving steadily against the sugar industry, the
colonial state embarked on a futile effort to appease planters and save the plantations. The colonial state created the conditions for the planters to continue to thwart
the demand for land by black Jamaicans. So entrenched was antismallholder policy
that when dire need forced the state to grapple with the economically depressed
conditions obtaining in the colony they faced resistance from intransigent planters
whose efforts they had supported against smallholders.

A series of natural disasters combined with the excesses of land scarcity
forced the colonial state to shift gears and relax its rigid policies. Support for a
food production campaign required the willingness of the planter class to make
land available for smallholders. But penkeepers reacted with severe hostility and
warned against land settlement schemes aimed at providing land for land-starved
smallholders. They simply rented out land to the smallholders and then threw
them off after two years of land improvement. Commenting on the situation,
one administrator reported,

> (T)he people of St.Anne has our sympathy. The penkeepers have sim-
> ply outwitted the peasant. Rented them unproductive land which
> they cleared up and within two years the proprietors took it back
> shoving the peasant out of the parish.[97]

The critical issue here is that the colonial state was unable to pursue its foremost and primary project of revitalizing production by way of the plantation.
The series of contradictions engendered by plantation production and the depression within the sugar industry internationally were to be crucial barriers to
the ultimate pursuit of its economic policies. In fact one can argue, that the survival of the colonial state itself depended on its being able to make compromises
that would result in making land available to working peoples.

This ultimately led to a second phase of colonial policy—the establishment
of land settlement schemes. Recognizing that neither state nor private capital
could provide sufficient employment for the working peoples, or to complete the
process of proletarianization of the labor force, the colonial state set up several
land settlement schemes that expanded a stratum of smallholders. Additionally,
the steady decline of the fortunes of the sugar industry forced many landowners
to sell.

The perspective of some analysts, that land settlement programs contributed
tremendously to the consolidation of smallholders, has in recent times been disputed.[98] Satchell, for example, has ably shown that many middle-class persons
were the actual beneficiaries of these schemes. It is not my intention at this point

to engage this point per se. I am more immediately concerned with noting the shift in policy that led to a more favorable environment for the reconstitution of smallholder households that were simultaneously involved in subsistence and export production and could shift to other economic opportunities if and when circumstances permitted, and the link between state and individual well-being.

The weakened colonial state was continually forced to engage its constituents. Its path to revitalizing plantation agriculture was strewn with obstacles. Both the conditions obtaining within the colony and the depression in the sugar industry internationally were crucial barriers to the ultimate reinstatement of dated and unworkable economic prescriptions. For example, with the falling price of sugar, a number of estates converted from sugar to bananas. In 1900 alone, 191 former sugar estates registered as banana estates.[99] Yet while more smallholders benefitted from land settlement schemes and (in general) small plots of land, these were inadequate to sustain their households.

As Bryan stated,

> The growth of the smallholder as a class was therefore constrained by a number of factors, some legal, some associated with the continued land monopoly, high rentals—in 1897 it was reported that rents in St. Mary varied from 20/- through 24/-and 28/-per acre and reluctance of planters to lease land (it was noted that the Pringle banana combine refused to lease land because peasant proprietors would compete with it). In 1897, it was concluded that 'considering the class of lands that can be got and all the conditions attached, of taxes, fencing, certain reserved rights of proprietors, and the rentals charged, the people can hardly avail themselves of even such land as may be said to be in the market for rent or sale'. There had been some access to land it is true, but not necessarily on the basis of firm, secure titles, or on the basis of secure tenancy.[100]

Under these conditions, land for most smallholders remained scarce. Although some smallholders had access to land and therefore, altered the structure of land use, the skewed land ownership pattern remained mostly intact.[101] In short there were real limitations to the "reforms" of the colonial state even as it was forced to come to terms with the reality that nonplantation labor presented. The meaning of this reform was that it severely limited the emergence of small commercial farms, but led to new and reconstituted social strata that would reflect and constitute the thrust of protodevelopment. This should not be ignored. As Brodber argued,

> The development of the plot with its interdependence between farming, trades and commerce, continued through the 20th century to 1923 to be a distinctly discernible form. But neither as a set of re-

lationships nor as lands owned by black peasants was the plot a discrete system. In both senses it was surrounded by the plantation and
crossed its arc at key points. The administration of the island still lay
in the hands of the larger plantation interests: such matters as the
percentage of its income to be paid to the general upkeep of the island was not decided in the plot. In addition, the majority of land
in the island was owned by the planting interests so that the plot's
expansion to include a new generation depended on the willingness
of the large landowners to sell. How to engineer this increased space
was a constant question for young blacks, who saw making a living
from own-account farming as the way to independence from the
plantations.[102]

One of its enduring results is, part-time agriculture, conditioned by the rise of
occupational multiplicity among rural smallholder households and the fluidity
of social class, became a defining feature of the agricultural sector of the colony.
It still is.

Trying to Make an Export Tradition Work: The Rise of Contract Small Farmers

It will be remembered that in Marx's statement, noted earlier, about "Quashees"
(freed persons) resisting capital, Marx did not specify that "Quashees" were only
resisting one form of capital, the plantations and even then not all of them. It is
clear that newly freed labor wanted to confront capital not as subordinate un-
derpaid wage labor, but as its equal or nearly so, in any case, from a position of
strength, perforce as "independent farmers." It should be recalled that the Jamaican smallholders, were not precapitalist or even noncapitalist, building alternative social, cultural and economic institutions beyond the boundaries of the
plantation. They might have known alternative social, economic, and cultural
practices, but they did so within the plantations' boundaries. That is to say that
responses to capital were shaped by what in all appearances were the "masters'"
tools. But these tools had long been forged and appropriated by those who considered themselves torn and tattered but equal. Even analysts at pains to prove
the existence of a "sub-culture" among church-created "peasantries" in the post-
emancipation have to admit that

> In order for new freedmen to become independent farmers, certain
> conditions were necessary. First, they would have to be able to grow
> subsistence crops successfully. . . . Second the freedmen would require
> outlets for surpluses which could be exchanged for cash to buy the

things which were not part of his consumption patterns. Here, too, success had also been partly assured by Jamaican slavery itself, since slaves had been permitted, even encouraged, to market their surplus at island markets. These markets continued in strength after Emancipation, even increasing in number. Moreover, there grew up a brisk export trade in agricultural staples, many items formerly produced on estates becoming peasant products.[103]

The issue of resisting one form of capital and not another, is forcefully brought in relief with the rise of Jamaican contract farmers in the late nineteenth century. Less than twenty-two years after emancipation, smallholders were moving beyond the production of ground provisions. Indeed, many had become contract farmers of bananas.[104] This was possible because the late eighteenth century witnessed the decline of the planter class and the rapidly diminishing hegemony of Britain globally. The rise of the United States as a dominant economic and political power created a new environment for the flourishing of new or reconstituted forms of labor in agriculture.

One could argue that the emergence of the banana trade signaled the maturation of working peoples as producers of export crops. To be sure, it was the persistence of smallholders and the financial backing of new entrepreneurs that resulted in the establishment of bananas as a major export crop by the turn of the century.[105] But as a group they would suffer losses associated with fierce US competition as well as the prevailing economic policies. Members of smallholder households cultivated 80% of the trade intended for the United States on plots of land less than ten acres.[106] Such households experienced much prosperity during those times. According to Holt,

> The surge of depositors and savings in its government savings bank suggests both the impact of the fruit trade on the town and the role of the peasant class in the trade. The number of bank depositors and their total savings increased from 238 with £5,000 in 1880 to 778 with £10,155 in 1889, representing a 100 percent increase in the value of the deposits and better than 200 percent in depositors. Much of that growth came from small depositors, which suggests a more prosperous peasant class.[107]

But though most smallholders cultivated freeholds, tenant farmers existed among them and there was considerable overlap besides constant shifts between and among them.

> On properties he owned or leased Baker also maintained tenants, to whom in some cases he apparently made advanced commit-

ments at the beginning of a growing season to purchase their produce. On one such estate, BoundBrook, he actually received more
in rents than from bananas grown. Indeed, one result of the increased demand by estates for property suitable for bananas was
that buying or renting their own plots became more difficult for
peasant growers. *By the 1890s land rental rates in Portland soared to
twenty to twenty-four shillings per acre per year, driving many peasant producers to become tenants to Baker or some other estate
owner.*[108] (My emphasis)

However, consolidation of smallholder households in those parishes was short-
lived as larger planters competing for land squeezed out the smallholders, forc-
ing them to become workers on banana properties or as labor elsewhere in the
colony or outside.

For the colonial government, small-scale agriculture rendered agricultural
production and productivity uncompetitive. For the most part the economic activities of smallholders endeared them neither to the planter class nor to the colonial government. Planters and colonials were united in their belief that the improvement of the colony lay in large-scale agriculture. This was why they
attempted to bring the full force of the state that they controlled at different periods to interdict the proliferation of small producers. This "open war" did not
abate until after the Morant Bay rebellion of 1865 and the institution of Crown
Colony government in 1866. Then the sharpness of the attack against smallholders became less overt and less physical, but the domination of their options
nonetheless continued unabated under the new form of colonial state now existing in a changed and changing world economy.

"Open war" on households of small producers which raged before 1866
and plateaued thereafter, effectively ruptured the basis for the existence of
households solely dependent on agricultural production. Effectively the stage
had been set for a critical feature of capitalist development on the island, the
straddling of multiple sources of income among members of the households of
small producers, and other working peoples, the fragmentation and the *muta-
tion* of identities, but also a fusion of protodevelopment tendencies into the
agendas of smallholders. Some had indeed been recomposed especially in the
second phase of the colonial state. In this scenario, land would always be a critical resource, but not always the only desirable avenue for gaining respect and
earning a livelihood. Thus, while planter and state policy had smallholders and
working peoples on the defensive, and made life extremely difficult for them,
there were limits to the hegemony that they, or the colonial state, commanded.
There were clear limits to effectively controlling the directions and path of capital, globally.

Diversifying Beyond the Boundaries of the State

Toward the end of the nineteenth and the early twentieth centuries, these developments clearly took their toll on the availability of employment within that sector, and in the economy as a whole. The island's economy was becoming more diversified, but its overwhelming dependence on sugar meant that with the negative shift in the terms of trade against tropical products overall, the economy was "caught in the collapse of the sugar."[109] Also, the hurricanes of 1912, 1915, and 1917, and the distress occasioned by the First World War, led to smallholder disaffection within agriculture. The concentration of properties in both the sugar and the banana industry[110] too circumscribed the economic choices of smallholders during this period.

Thus, smallholders were forced to seek their livelihood in alternative ways. Migration was one outlet that smallholders felt pulled toward.[111] Roberts and others[112] record considerable movement from rural parishes to developing urban centers and to overseas locations at this time. That smallholders were constantly being reconstituted along wage and other forms of labor is noted by a colonial committee:

> We find that there is a tendency amongst portions of the rural population to gravitate towards the towns and Kingston especially. The class to which we refer are moved by a desire to obtain their livelihood by other means than agricultural labour, and by the hope of that casual employment at high rates which is often to be obtained in towns.[113]

While urban migration was mostly a female phenomenon, migration within and between rural parishes and overseas occurred largely among males, and was associated with the developing banana industry, as wage labor, tenants or small farmers or all or some.[114]

The female departure from the rural areas to Kingston and other urban centers coincided with their transformation from agricultural labor of various sorts to their absorption into urban employment mainly as domestic workers but also as commercial workers, notably traders, known as higglers. This was particularly evident after 1921. The decline of women as agricultural workers had been in evidence since 1891. It was dramatic. In 1891, 74.5% were employed and in 1943, 34%. Their participation in domestic occupations jumped from 11% in 1891 to 31% in 1943.[115] Males too were leaving agriculture, but not in such large numbers. During that time, male participation in agriculture fell from 68% in 1891 to 46% in 1943.

The reorganization of the global economy, now increasingly under the growing hegemony of the United States, occasioned the vast movements of populations worldwide. For example, between 1871 and 1915, approximately thirty-six
million people migrated from Europe, two-thirds of whom went to the United
States.[116] With factoral terms of trade moving against tropical products, and the
disarray in the agricultural sector on the island, the growing U.S. involvement in
Latin America facilitated the much-needed outlet for male smallholders. Between 1881 and 1921, coinciding also with the displacement of smallholders in
the growing banana industry on the island, and the expansion of the cultivation
of that fruit elsewhere, e.g., Costa Rica, emigration reached its peak. Approximately 146,000 Jamaicans, mostly males, left the island for the USA, Panama,
Cuba and other areas.

Perhaps we can date the origins of the demise of smallholders referred to
misleadingly as "depeasantization"[117] around this time or as early as 1844, since
those so engaged began to opt out of it.[118] Under these conditions, the household organization of smallholders and their members' identities necessarily
would have undergone dramatic transformation as smallholders, in adapting to
a changing world scenario, redefined their forms of livelihood.

Conclusions

The charge that planters and colonials used the powerful instruments of taxation
policy, antisquatting legislation, land-sales practices and general physical harass-
ment with the intention of eliminating whatever controls that smallholders
wanted to exercise over their own reproduction, cannot be denied. Nor can we
ignore the evident desire of smallholders to pursue as many choices as possible,
once it became evident that agricultural pursuits were no guarantee to their survival. As they negotiated the stakes of their claims, neither planter, colonial state
nor smallholders achieved its precise objective. For smallholders if theirs was a
victory, it was Pyrrhic. The emergence of smallholder households attested to a
limited victory of control over their own social reproduction but there were limits to such control as the reach of state policy and their responses to it prepared
for a world not of their own making, nor that devised by the colonial state. For
the colonial state and planters, who still dominated the social order, the aim was
to preserve the status quo at any cost. But the status quo could only be maintained if they made certain compromises with working peoples and within the
possibilities of the transition to a world being reconstituted by new forms of capital. The planters' limited control over the critical resource of land and the stagnation of tropical products internationally would in the future lead to the characteristic feature of Caribbean agrarian social structure, versatile smallholder

households, and an authoritarian state with the semblance of hegemonic rule. The successes of the state lay with its relative success at manipulating the local options and conditions of smallholder production and work in the context of development.

In this chapter, the argument has focused on the emergence of the multiple resistance strategies of state, planters, and smallholders and the shifting boundaries between and among identities. Tensions revolved around issues related to production, e.g., for cheap labor, and reproduction, the desire to carve respectable and self-sufficient patterns of existence, that would make the plantation only one option, perhaps (under the circumstances of low wages) the least desirable. One of the main results of this strategy has been the emergence of diverse forms of subsistence and export production ranging from the rare independent smallholder households, principally dependent upon cultivation of the plot, to the more common occurrence of households straddling multiple sectors, and those that occupied the seams of subsectors.

In this scenario, the colonial state becomes a casualty of change as well, and in this continuing struggle to redefine roles and statuses, it experiences limited moments of hegemony, relying for the most part on coercion. Seen in this light, between 1838 and 1930 neither the state nor the smallholder stratum carved its living space in exactly the way either wanted, yet in a vastly changing world, the social order remained remarkably intact.

Notes

1. Michel-Rolph Trouillot, "Culture on the Edges: Caribbean Creolization in Historical Context," in *Historical Anthropology and its Futures: From the Margins,* ed. Brian Keith Axel (Durham and London: Duke University Press, 2002), 189–210.

2. Roy Augier, "Before and After 1865," *New World Quarterly* 2, 1 (1965): 21–40.

3. See for example, the perspective carried in George Beckford and Michael Witter, *Small Garden . . . Bitter Weed, The Political Economy of Struggle and Change in Jamaica* (Morant Bay: Maroon Publishing House, 1980).

4. Nicholas Thomas, *Colonialism's Culture: Anthropology, Travel and Government* (Princeton: Princeton University Press, 1994), 105–106

5. Refer to discussion in chapter 1.

6. I treat this as an elaboration of Trouillot's point regarding the interpretation of freedom in the postemancipation period. Trouillot was writing in relation to the overgeneralized reasons about the relation of slaves to the plantations after slavery. See Michel-Rolph Trouillot, "Labour and Emancipation in Dominica: Contribution to a Debate," *Caribbean Quarterly* 30, nos. 3 & 4 (1984): 73–84.

7. I am thinking of the influence of the Baptist church.

8. Sidney Mintz, *Caribbean Transformations* (Baltimore: The Johns Hopkins University Press, 1975), 155.

9. Dale Tomich, *Slavery in the Circuit of Sugar: Martinique in the World Economy* (Baltimore: The Johns Hopkins University Press, 1990), 14.

10. W. Arthur Lewis, *Growth and Fluctuations 1870–1913* (London: George Allen & Unwin, 1978), 209.

11. Tomich (1990), 22.

12. Ibid.

13. Ibid.

14. Ibid.

15. Between 1883 and 1913, "industrial production grew about 10 percent faster than tropical agricultural exports, whereas from 1929 to 1937 agricultural exports were growing much faster than industrial production (but) Prices of exports fell." See W. Arthur Lewis, *Growth and Fluctuations 1870–1913* (London: George Allen & Unwin, 1978), 227.

16. Paul Bairoch, *The Economic Development of the Third World since 1900* (California: University of California Press, 1975), 132; Lewis (1978), 189.

17. Lewis (1978), 191.

18. P. Bairoch (1975), 132.

19. Lewis argues that U.S. manufacturing exploded between 1891 and 1899, registering a growth rate of 11.7 percent. W. A. Lewis (1978), 123.

20. Eric J. Hobsbawm, *The Age of Capital 1848–1875* (New York: Charles Scribner's Sons, 1975), 176–177.

21. E. J. Hobsbawm (1975), 174.

22. See Hobsbawm's description of how capitalism undermined various agrarian bases in Western Europe, the USA and some parts of Latin America and Asia. See Eric J. Hobsbawm (1975), 183.

23. Lewis (1978), 230.

24. Thomas J. Holt, *The Problem of Freedom* (Baltimore: The Johns Hopkins University Press, 1992), 29.

25. Ibid.

26. W. A. Lewis (1978), 215.

27. Philip Curtin, *Two Jamaicas: The Role of Ideas in a Tropical Colony 1830–1865* (Cambridge: Harvard University Press, 1955).

28. The Assembly was the body that gained at the expense of the Privy (or Executive) Council of the Governor, the upper House of the Colonial Legislature. The Assembly was, thus, the equivalent of the House of Commons. While in constitutional theory direct intervention by the legislature was considered improper and a usurpation of the powers of the Crown, in Jamaica and other West Indian colonies, the Assemblies fought with the Governors for greater autonomy: "Colonial Assemblies tended to arrogate to themselves executive as well as legislative power because the executive represented an outside interest not responsible to their constituents." Thus the Assembly constantly attempted, and often succeeded in usurping the power of the Crown or Royal prerogative such as "the power to make and control appointments." C. V. Gocking, "Early Constitutional History of Jamaica: with special reference to the period 1838–1866," *Caribbean Quarterly* 6, nos. 3 & 4 (1960): 113–133.

29. Philip Curtin (1955), 72.

30. Ibid.

31. Ibid., 73.

32. Ibid.

33. Since that office assessed various local tax rates and their appropriation for the maintenance of roads, the jail and parish works allowed them to appear as distinct enemies of working peoples.

34. Ibid.

35. Philip Curtin (1955), 75.

36. That is to say the absence of many planters from the island mainly in England.

37. Ibid.

38. Ibid., 181.

39. Gad Heuman, "The Struggle for the Settler Vote: Politics and the Franchise in Post-Emancipation Jamaica," in *Peasants, Plantations and Rural Communities in the Caribbean*, ed. Malcolm Cross & Arnaud Marks (Leiden: Department of Sociology/Caribbean Studies, Royal Institute of Linguistics and Anthropology, 1979), 1–28.

40. Ibid., 4.

41. Patrick Bryan, *The Jamaican People 1880–1902* (London: Macmillan, 1991), 14–15.

42. Ibid., 15.

43. For a discussion of this see Douglas Hall, *Free Jamaica 1865 -1865. An Economic History* (New Haven: Yale University Press, 1959), especially chapter 3; G. Eisner (1961), especially chapter 12.

44. Taxation by the colonial state was not introduced for the first time after emancipation. In the mid-eighteenth century, the central colonial government imposed taxes on rum, imported goods from North America and other foreign countries. Each slave owned by planters was also taxed. However, it would seem that the abolition of slavery in 1834 gave renewed vigor and license to the state to impose heavy taxes upon the newly freed slaves.

45. G. Eisner grants that duties added on the average 15 per cent to the c.i.f. value of imports in 1850, but for certain commodities the increase was even greater: for codfish and herrings it was 20 per cent, for flour 24 percent, for rice 31 per cent and for beef as much as 42 per cent. See Eisner (1961), 366.

46. Ibid.

47. D. Hall (1959), 195.

48. Sir John Peter Grant in C/O 137 424 #90/1867. Section 27.

49. Governor's Report 1894, p. XVI, quoted in Veront Satchell, "The Jamaican Peasantry 1866–1900. The Relationship between Economic Growth of the Peasant Sector and Government Policies" (Mona: Dept. of History, U.W.I. mimeo, 1982), 24. Idem, *From Plots to Plantations* (Mona: Institute of Social and Economic Research, 1990).

50. V. Satchell (1982), 25.

51. Ibid.

52. George W. Roberts, *The Population of Jamaica* (New York: Kraus Reprint Co., 1979), 126–127.

53. Apprenticeship defined the transition between 1834 and 1838. It was so called because it was ostensibly designed to "prepare" ex-slaves for freedom. However, planters squeezed out every bit of labor they could during this period.

54. Douglas Hall (1959), 256.

55. Roberts (1979), 111.

56. Ibid.

57. Ibid., 53.

58. Ibid.

59. G. Eisner (1961), 144.

60. See Verene Shepherd (1991).

61. D. Hall (1959), 58.

62. Ibid.

63. Karl Marx, *Grundrisse* (New York: Random House, 1973), 325–326.

64. According to Marshall, planters saw the system of metayage as a "desperate expedient which enabled them to retain ownership of their estates and secure some profits during a period of depression. They adopted a system which would allow them to pay wages in kind rather than in cash; the labourer now in 'partnership' rather than on wages, shared with the planter the risks, expenses and profits of sugar production. The labourer supplied all the manual labour necessary for the cultivation, reaping and manufacture of the canes grown on a plot of land loaned to him by the planter; the planter supplied carts, stock and machinery for the manufacture of the sugar; and the sugar produced was shared between them." See Woodville Marshall, "Metayage in the Sugar Industry of the British Windward Islands 1838–1865," *Jamaican Historical Review* V (1965): 28–29.

65. D. Hall (1959), 158.

66. J. W. Hinton, *Memoir of William Knibb* (1849), quoted in G. Eisner (1961), 211.

67. Douglas Hall, "The Flight From the Estates Reconsidered: The British West Indies 1838–1842," *Journal of Caribbean History*, nos. 10 and 11 (1978): 16–24.

68. G. Eisner (1961), 171.

69. The cultivation of ground provisions served a dual purpose. In the first place, it supplemented the household income as it lowered the cost of production; secondly, it covered those areas of nourishment where wages fell short.

70. Ibid., 168.

71. Douglas Hall (1959), 192.

72. *The Blue Book of Jamaica 1874* (Kingston: Government Printery), Section W3.

73. G. Eisner (1961), 222.

74. Veront Satchell (1982), 18.

75. Ibid. As the Jamaican proverb has it, "When nagga tief, him tief likkle bit, when backra tief, him tief whole estate." Trans.: When the black poor man steals, he steals a little but when the white boss steals, he steals the whole estate.

76. V. Satchell (1982), 19.

77. S. H. Olivier (1930), 317.

78. G. Eisner (1961), 224.

79. "Governor's" *Blue Book of Jamaica, 1899–1900* (Kingston: Government Printery), 324.

80. Chapter 7 entails a fuller discussion of this phenomenon.

81. Roy Augier (1965), 33.

82. Ibid.

83. Douglas Hall (1959), 233.

84. R. Augier (1965), 24.

85. Ibid., 35.

86. The Commissioners felt that despite the increase of sugar production from 2,016,084 to 3,437,774 tons, beet sugar producers capitalizing on the rapid accumulation of capital had increased beet sugar production by phenomenal rates. Between 1882 to 1894, beet sugar production rose from 1,783,200 to 3,840,256 tons and was expected to increase accordingly. *West India Royal Commission Report 1897* (Cmnd. 8655, London: HMSO 1898), 5.

87. Ibid., 9.

88. Ibid., 17.

89. This Act applied to all non-self governing colonies, protectorates, protected states and mandated Territories for whose affairs the Secretary of State for the colonies is responsible. See *The Colonial Development Advisory Committee. Eleventh and Final Report covering the period 1st April 1939–17th July 1940* (Cmnd. 6298. London: HMSO 1941).

90. Ibid., 7.

91. Ibid., 9.

92. In its full eleven years of existence, the committee approved five hundred and ninety-six schemes and projects amounting to £8,875,883 of a total estimated expenditure of £19,284,536. Of this amount £5,671,656 had been for free grants; another £3,203,427 pounds were loaned.

93. R. Augier (1965), 38.

94. Erna Brodber, "Making a Living in Jamaica 1923–1980" (Ph.D diss. University of the West Indies, Mona, Jamaica, 1987), 152.

95. Ibid., 156

96. Ibid.

97. Copy of the report by Hon. and Rev. A. A. Barclay and Mr. William Cradwick-CO.137/742 dispatch 711 Probyn to Viscount Milner 27/9/20. End. Copy of report by Hon. & Rev. A.A. Barclay and Mr. William Cradwick, cited in Erna Brodber (1987), 158.

98. Eisner and Marshall are the leading proponents of this interpretation.

99. Veront Satchell, "Pattern of abandonment of sugar estates in Jamaica during the 19th century," paper delivered at the 21st Caribbean History Association conference in Guadeloupe, Basse-terre, 19–24 March 1989), 11.

100. Patrick Bryan, *The Jamaican People 1880–1902* (MacMillan: Warwick University Caribbean Studies, 1991), 141.

101. See Patrick Bryan (1991); V. Satchell (1982, 1990).

102. Erna Brodber (1987), 147.

103. Sidney Mintz, "The Historical Sociology of Jamaican Villages," in Charles Carnegie ed. *Afro-Caribbean Villages in Historical Perspective* (Kingston: African-Caribbean Institute of Jamaica, 1987), 1–19, 2.

104. Roberts states that banana cultivation was responsible for significant internal migration of working people to the Eastern parishes of St. Thomas, Portland and St. Mary and also for tremendous infrastructural development of those areas.

105. G. Eisner (1961), 234–235.

106. See Holt (1992), 349.

107. Ibid.

108. Holt (1992), 353.

109. See Lewis, (1978), 214.

110. See for example, George Cumper (1954) on the sugar industry; and on bananas, see Holt (1992), especially chapter 10, for a summation of these developments.

111. W. A. Lewis noted that the terms "pull" and "push" were unfortunate terms since they allude to separate and distinct rationales when in reality they exist coterminously. Lewis (1978), 183.

112. See Elsa Chaney, "Migration from the Caribbean Region: Determinants and Effects of Current Movements," mss. (Georgetown University Center for Immigration Policy and Refugee Assistance, 1985).

113. Roberts (1979), 142.

114. Roberts (1979), 162–164.

115. Roberts (1979), 86.

116. Lewis (1978), 181.

117. See for example, Ramon Grosfuguel, "Depeasantization and Agrarian Decline in the Caribbean" in *Food and Agrarian Orders in the World Economy,* ed. Philip McMichael (Connecticut: Praeger, 1995),

118. "Despite their many limitations, the data on agricultural employment suffice to show the declining dependence on agriculture since 1844." Roberts (1979), 90.

CHAPTER 3

Forging Nationals out of Rural Working Peoples

We have managed to avoid the feeling in our work that we come down from above and do things for the people. You move among the people in a spirit of partnership with full knowledge of their desires, hopes and ambitions, and with a desire to foster in them initiative and self-help. I have an abounding faith in the people of this country. They are a great people to lead in any field of activity, in any sort of life. They have faults, but these are the faults of the economic and social condition under which they live, and the fruit of the historical legacy they suffer from. They have endured all these things and are enduring today with the great potentialities which they possess. . . . You have only to move among our people of the poorest classes today to know what ambitions they possess (and you see it most markedly among the young) to know what a power there is in the spirit of this country when we can harness it and mould it into one whole. It is this strength of character which it will be your duty to temper and mould in the direction that will conduce to the greatest good for the country in the difficult years ahead of *us*.[1]

Since independence? Is hard for me to see it. I can't see any difference. It appears to me it worse today. Everything is so expensive and you can't get anything to do. Things are much dearer. This government giving we hell. Definitely worse. The economic standard has deteriorated. You may run a little more but inflation of prices, no comparison. Independence mash we up a lot. The things them are rather harder to get and it is dearer. Some are in no position to carry on ourself or run our situation.[2]

61

Introduction

The twin projects of nationalism and modernization were instrumental in forging a consensus of sorts between political leaders and their political followers. The quest for state sovereignty, linked to that of citizenship, offered hope and promise of a new dawn to the working people of Jamaica. In that sense, decolonization was not simply something which resided in the imaginaries of leadership but was also interpreted variously by working peoples within the context of citizenship and individual well-being. Working people were to a large extent convinced that they needed to be brought into the light of modernity. This was not surprising considering the pervasiveness of perspectives on the linearity of modernization that underpinned the ideology of the world states. In that sense, the agendas of national elites and working peoples intersected in terms of national and personal development. Modernization policies which defined agricultural policy brought more land-based working people into the ambit of state bureaucracy, creating in the process linked structures of production, avenues for export production and a myriad of smallholder plots. It also grounded the relationship of clientilism which has been a defining feature of Jamaican and Caribbean party politics. Yet, the unrealization of those promises of economic and personal development set in train the unravelment of the state/citizen pact. Modernization's failure to compensate for the occupation of people's spaces by state institutions reflected by the inadequacy of development assistance, and the growing dependence on clientilism, resulted in the entrenchment of informalization within the economy generally. Hardly only a functionalist derivative, informalization also reflected the desire of working people to escape the radar of bureaucratization, and to establish limited modes of personal sovereignty as they grappled with the betrayed promises of politicians and their agents of development.

I would like to discuss the relationships facilitated by the emergent developmentalist state between political elites and rural land-based working peoples from the 1940s to 1972. The mechanisms of rulership extant at that time presage and follow the demise of formal colonial rule, and later, the destabilization of the nationalist developmental agenda, not through a struggle against development per se but, and this may seem contradictory, its marginalizing outcomes. Objectively, large numbers of Jamaican working people questioned the efficacy of projects as well as the nationalist ideologies of rulership. Much has been written about this and while it is not my intention to replough this material, I want to draw attention to the narrowness of its constructions, demonstrating the contradictory processes that attend the making and sustenance of a land-based working people. These contradictions involve, on the one hand, the production of certain social strata and their link to domestic and export production of agricultural commodities, and on the other, the policy formulations of a developmentalist state, practicing control of the countryside. I may state an obvious point when I claim that the interests of the elite, state and working peoples jibed at times fairly harmoniously in relating development to sovereignty and sovereignty to personal well-being, but the needs of the nation, as perceived by nationalists, oftentimes disturbed the social locations of working peoples. This was particularly evident in the developments attending the onset of mining in Jamaica.

This chapter underscores the multilinearity of Jamaicans' pursuit of modernity. The ambivalent or multivalent zig-zag gestures of agrarian policy, or development philosophy, at once target "backwardness," seeking to undo it, and the conditions through which it differentiates itself. Targeting "backwardness" means bringing working people out of darkness, formalizing agrarian social relations, i.e., making the presence of nationalists and the state felt, and controlling land-based activities. These policies incorporated highly bureaucratic forms, unable to survey successfully rural space. Given the state's limited resources, because the state could not accommodate or formalize all such space, it succeeded in generating the spaces where informality flourished. However impoverished working peoples are, they still retain elements of autonomy. Paradoxically, the continued existence of land-based working peoples problematizes the development agenda, though confirming its endurance.

I would like to identify the nature of the relationship working peoples forged with national elites, and vice versa, as elites became the *man-ners* of the early postcolonial state. I would like to do so against the postcolonialists' interpretation of contemporary events as representative of a severe rupture between state and nonstate, given the weak purchase of the developmental state in the era of neoliberal globalization. I would like to read backwards, nonteleologically, to identify the particularities of the modern project in agriculture, and to argue that the community activities of these national elites, in and outside their capacity as state officials, crafted agricultural policies that delineated the arenas of production, that allowed rural working people to feel connected to the project of state sovereignty and to imagine themselves part of the making of such a national community. Agricultural policies generated particular lifestyles constituting the means through which rural working people reinforced the state in their lives, even as they understood the limitations of its institutional power. How better to understand the ways in which rural working people clamored for development even as many withdrew, than to explore the ways in which community, state and development came to resonate (and continue to resonate) with hopeful possibilities for a very large, though diminishing, rural constituency.

Such an exploration disputes the literature that speaks to the oppositional lifestyle of working people and to that oppositionalism as the sole content of their relationship with elites in the late colonial and early postcolonial state. Much of the literature on smallholders concerns their oppositional lifestyle and the marginalization attending their incorporation into the world market as commodity producers. The pluralist framework goes so far as to champion the idea of a cultural-institutional divide separating "folk" and "elite."[3] Critics of the pluralist paradigm have not sought to discount the paradigm itself, however; they have simply challenged cultural-institutional premises from the vantage point of class, whence abstractions are perceived as history. Both positions ignore the universal currency of "ruling class" ideas among the oppressed and exploited and the ways in which this currency predisposes working peoples to accept and to believe ideas about development and the intersection of the nation and their lives. The desire for development crisscrossed class lines, as pervasive as the idea that the Jamaican small farmer was ignorant, and in need of education.

The administrative ascendance of Jamaican middle-class nationalists via the political party machinery, beginning in the mid-1940s, signaled the formal dismantling of the colonial state, a critical watershed in decolonization. Linking decolonization and sovereignty with development, even within the restraining bureaucratic framework of the colonial state, nationalists were able to implement programs that broadened the state's role in the Jamaican economy, not to mention its class base. Those institutional arms fashioned a Jamaican society and culture, in which the lives of smallholders were increasingly politicized and governmentalized. Though the direction of development was state-led, it was secondarily supported by significant sections of the oppressed and exploited. Small cultivators were not always victims, as alleged. Their incorporation into the state, formally and informally, implicated them in their own transformation.

The link between citizenship and development which originated before 1944 has remained dynamic. The development of Jamaica's early modernization phase was challenged variously, culturally by the Rastafarians, socioeconomically by a small intelligentsia based at the erstwhile University College of the West Indies, as well as by groups like the Young Socialist League. The rise of the Black Power Movement in Jamaica in the late 1960s highlighted the unraveling of much of the pact between state and citizenry.[4] Despite such critiques a shared culture presupposed progress based on the application of correct state policy. In the agricultural sector, that culture registered in the belief that the mere possession of land was a prerequisite to progress and independence, the strategy of early nationalists. Without vital credit and technological assistance, people with small plots of land were destined to remain subsistence export producers. But state-led modernization was not without real consequence. It made credible a notion of the state among the very radicals who challenged its policies. Those who opposed development and sociocultural policy found themselves unable to imagine alternatives to the structures through which the state had legitimated itself, evident especially in the Democratic Socialist period of the Jamaican government.

Modernization spawned significant developments in the agricultural sector. Between 1894 and 1944, years of transition from colonial to self-government, agriculture policy was three-pronged, consisting simultaneously of land settlements, modernization and conservation schemes, at once welfaristic (employment creation) and capitalistic (capital generating). These programs persisted as the foundations of agropolicy for the nationalist, postcolonial state. Other schemes to subsidize and modernize smallholder agricultural production, executed through conservation and farm improvement, served to regulate smallholder production, at least for the scheme's duration.

Beginning in the mid-1940s, attempts to transform the Jamaican economy from a primary agricultural producer to an industrial one prolonged the viability of the small plot as the site of subsistence export production.[5] Where the direct needs of capital prevailed, e.g., land for bauxite companies, smallholders shifted to other livelihoods. Discussions about this period stress the failures of government policy (PNP and JLP) to challenge the social order and permanently relieve "peasant production." They focus on the false assumptions of prevailing economic models, chronicling "failures," attributed to the nationalists' class origins. By treating only policy failures and the attendant victimization of small cultivators, however real and insidious patterns of ownership and land access are, these studies obscure other facets of development. Though this approach has yielded some important information apropos the gap between policy and its implementation, it is strange to analyze what did not happen, thereby disregarding the actual circumstances of agriculture and of small farmers during this period. What happened involved the politicization and governmentalization of social life, no small point, as such a process resurfaces later, that is, continues throughout the Democratic Socialist era of 1972 to 1980. Only the writings of Carl Stone call attention to this point; also ignored is the rise and consolidation of the informalization of social life, accompanying its bureaucratization.[6]

To trace how development incorporated the smallholder, I examine the ideas of community in 1944, during the transition from the colonial to early postcolonial state. These ideas assumed the state's importance in transforming Jamaican society and the Jamaican economy from agriculture to industry. Popularly the smallholder was considered a burden, a "traditional sector," hence an undesirable stratum. Smallholders had to be reeducated through demonstration models, extolling the benefits of modernization. This widely held belief coincided with the experience of nationalists confronting a colonial state. Decolonization was not only about a constitutional divorce from colonial connections, but was also about guiding citizens, morally and economically, into a modern world, where they could develop their potential and their national community. Agricultural projects implanted this vision into rural Jamaica, among its working people.

Forging Rural Ground

The labor revolt of 1938 produced two leaders who consequently played a major role in shaping the island's politics. Alexander Bustamante carved a niche for himself as the head of the labor movement, a messianic populist who found favor among Jamaican working peoples. His cousin, Norman Manley, on the other hand, the colony's leading lawyer, was invited to take the leadership of the Peoples National Party (PNP), the first successful organization of middle-class activists in Jamaican politics.[7] Though associated at the start of this tumultuous period, the two leaders had separated within five years. By the 1940s, Jamaica had not only two political parties, but also two affiliated trade union blocs, each linked to one of the parties. The Peoples National Party (PNP) and the Jamaica Labour Party (JLP) headed almost without exception the postwar evolution and transformation of the Jamaican state. Differences in composition and class appeal, especially obvious in the postwar period, belied the general similarity of their visions of island development. However, for a sense of the Jamaican nationalist agenda, we look to Norman Manley since Bustamante relied on a charismatic populist leadership, which led to his electoral successes.[8] By 1964, the convergence of the parties' policies was apparent enough to cast doubt on the PNP's portrayal as an opposition party in the 1965 elections.[9]

The PNP equated self-government with economic independence and linked that independence rhetorically to the quest for social justice on the island. The PNP's conception of change asserted "no dichotomy between the cry for nationhood and the cry for bread," a widely circulated notion that affected members of all classes.[10] To make "bread" available to a wider cross section of the Jamaican populace, the pursuit of a "political kingdom" seemed paramount. Politics seemed development's natural vehicle. Manley declared that his "generation had a distinct mission to perform to create a national spirit with which we could identify ourselves as a people for the purpose of achieving independence on the political plane."[11] This national spirit was preoccupied by societal rifts. Spurred by the events of 1938, Manley sought to rectify inequalities based on color, particularly the link between race and resource ownership. Intermittent flirtations with socialism, advocating the state's strong role in public ownership, showed that Manley, like Bustamante, favored a paternalistic approach to the Jamaican masses. Since the "Empire and British rule had rested on a carefully nurtured sense of inferiority in the governed,"[12] both men believed a period of political tutelage necessary for Jamaica's masses. Small farmers had to be reeducated as responsible citizens. The state's enlightened leadership would bear that torch, along with teachers, visible in rural Jamaican communities, and "bring it home to the masses of the people in this country that there is a new discipline of service that is wanted such as has never been known in this country before."[13]

Manley was concerned about social development, but also about economic development. Economic development was about success. The creation of a nation and a community would only be realized if national economic resources could be meaningfully harnessed. Whether in office or leading the opposition, Manley championed the state as the instrument enabling economic development. Rational planning under the management of civil servants was critical for state and societal (re)production.

After winning the 1955 parliamentary election, Manley announced his intention to outfit a Planning Department "for development purposes in all its aspects."[14]

> We intend to set up an Economic Advisory Council to work in conjunction with the Minister of Production, and the Planning department will be under his charge. This council must be made up of men of experience and talent who combine practical knowledge and know-how with goodwill and devotion to the interests of Jamaica as a whole. . . . What I want to find is a person to be Standing Chairman and Consultant Adviser to the Planning Department itself. I am looking first of all for a man with *economic* training and preferably, indeed almost essentially, one who believes that Government must take a major role in planning in countries with *backward economic situations like ours in Jamaica.* Then he must have practical business and industrial experience, if possible in an international way. . . . He should have actual experience in working in a country that started to raise itself out of depression and misery by actively planning the development of its resources and economy. Finally, I would like him to have close contacts with the United Nations Special Organizations, for I look for a lot of help in that quarter.[15]

The nationalists who sought to remedy Jamaica's *backward economic* situation pursued a strategy that relied on increasing capital accumulation and industrialization, the supposed foundations of developed economies and the vehicles to carry "underdeveloped" societies into modernity.

Competing visions of development within the PNP were silenced, specifically the left-leaning section of the PNP whose socialist platform between 1938 and 1952 called for more state ownership, cooperatives for workers and peasants, producer ownership in agriculture and an enlarged definition of democracy in the society. Although Stone argues that such ideological differences were symbolic, since neither leftists nor centrists could effect changes under a colonial state, one cannot help but imagine an alternate version of Jamaica's political history in which such ideas are allowed to run a democratic course. After all, the leftists controlled the Trade Union Congress, taking it with them, when they left the PNP.

Planning Communities, Executing Development

During the period 1938 to 1972, the height of decolonization and nationalism, one witnesses the insinuation of a nationalist state agenda onto the polity. It is apparent that large numbers of rural working people (in the context of an emerging, politically independent state) supported the ruling elites, shifting later much of this support to the state (from roughly 1938 into the 1950s) as part of an informal contract in the search for better socioeconomic existences. The reception that smallholders, and rural working peoples in general, gave to programs like Jamaica Welfare, trade unionism, and the closely related clientilistic politics spawned by the two dominant political parties manifested this trend.

Such promises heightened the socioeconomic expectations of working peoples, shaping the quality of smallholder participation (and their discontents/resistance) in a society that was, on the one hand, fast coalescing and, on the other, pulling apart according to middle-class notions of respectability and development. While the middle classes were certainly at the forefront of state formation, they did not always impose their world view on hapless, passive smallholder strata or simply absorb them into social programs, try though they might. Working peoples had good reason to want to be implicated in these agendas, which they did not necessarily see as different from theirs. Middle-class agendas promised a better life, free of economic, social and racial discrimination.

I would like to highlight a process that is overlooked, underresearched and at best only hinted at by most analysts, one that remains a silent aspect of smallholder existence, namely the extent to which the diverse middle class influenced the lived experience of rural and urban spaces and peoples. To that end, I will analyze how this influence was wielded and how smallholders were implicated in these development and cultural agendas, thus how their experiences were shaped. The reconceptualization of the link between the middle classes and the rural working people in the context of development projects is this chapter's aim. This approach goes beyond the enduring oppositional framework that marks specifically the discussion of culture and "peasantry" or "folk" and, more generally, of development's oppositional status vis-à-vis the experience of working peoples.[16] The search for authenticity pays no particular attention to how fluid social relationships were restructured in colonial, nationalist, and postnationalist or postcolonial eras, each with its distinctive *geiste*.

I would like to suggest that institutional appeals to character had been made before along with programs aimed at modernizing agriculture, pivotal to anticolonial struggles. The discourses about economic development and community building or character building, advanced in the main by PNP nationalists, were hard to translate materially, for agricultural development entailed a faith in an encompassing state vision of modernization that left little room for alternative community vision, or for the individual sociocultural economic practices of smallholders. The nationalists required that working peoples see along with the State, to adapt the title of James Scott's eponymous work. Yet the realities of community life, including unequal access to resources, meant that working peoples would interpret this vision variously.

The Jamaica Agricultural Society

Middle-class individuals and institutions succeeded in reaching deep into the quotidian life of rural working people to impart values regarded as important for state, nation and community building. One such institution was the Jamaica Agricultural Society (JAS). In its early days, JAS served the interest of the state and of the planter class in promoting the sugar industry. Like the colonial state, the JAS was preoccupied with the fortunes of the sugar industry, and expressed a specific bias toward the planter class. Against the backdrop of the West India Royal Commission of 1897 and the institution of bounties by European governments, which had an adverse effect upon sugar production in the West Indies, Sir Henry Blake addressed the Society to point out the importance of the sugar industry and its relation to the small cultivator, declaring:

> That a Great Industry planted by England created by the investment
> of millions of English capital and employing hundreds of thousands of
> the people of the West Indian Islands is rapidly being crushed out
> of existence by the operation of foreign bounties. . . . If a large pro-
> portion of the sugar Estates of Jamaica were or could be placed under
> regular cultivation it would mean an expenditure of hundreds of
> thousands of pounds alone in this country. These wages go directly to
> the agricultural labourer. But much of the money is then gradually
> distributed among the people in the surrounding localities, largely
> because this class of the wage earning people is the only one that can
> become purchasers from the small producers . . . on account of that
> alone, we can see how largely the interests of the small settlers and the
> small producers are bound up in the existence of the prosperity of the
> sugar estates.[17]

The significance of this statement lies in the fact that, in spite of the production of alternative crops such as ground provisions and bananas by smallholders and the flagging fortunes of the sugar industry, the JAS president was still prepared to render full support to the sugar industry, even calling for its expansion,

noting its importance to the livelihood of tens of thousands of agricultural laborers. In this scheme of things, the smallholder was important only as this enterprise's facilitator. Later in its evolution, from about 1940 onwards, the Society
broadened its base, becoming the ally of medium-scale farmers. Its link with Jamaica Welfare, subsequently renamed Jamaica Welfare, Ltd. in 1943, gave it substantial influence in smallholder communities. Its national reach was facilitated by
the many branch offices established with state support throughout the island.[18]

Launched in 1895, the JAS suffered from an "illogical duality of role." In
Marshall's words, "it was a paternalistic creation, it was voluntary, government
subsidized, and expected to work closely with the government's Department of
Agriculture."[19] Its objectives were multifold:

> teaching the people in their districts; teaching better cultivation; en-
> couraging the development of new agricultural industries and assist-
> ing in the improvement of livestock and poultry by judicious impor-
> tation.[20]

Its board of management reflected the composition of the Jamaican elite. At
its formation, Sir Henry Blake, the Governor of the island, became its first president. Other members of the board included prominent planters, all members of
the upper echelons of Jamaican society, like Dr. Pringle, G. McGrath, H. E. Cox,
and Messrs. R. Craig, W. Fawcett, H. Cork, Capt. Baker, and Geo. Douet, the
Secretary. The association readily gained the favor of large planters, but it failed
to expend much effort to reach smallholders. The Association's 75th Anniversary
issue recalled that "The large land owners seemed ready to understand how the
Society could help farming, but it took some effort by the Board to secure the
confidence of the small farmers."[21]

The JAS comprised the main or parent body as well as a number of autonomously operated Branch Societies. These societies elected their own committees and had local agendas, which complemented the agenda of the parent
body. In a sense, the branches operated like Parish Councils, party to a similar
range of community issues and eager to decentralize the main office's agendas.
Members discussed agricultural issues, road works, transportation, health, and
water supplies, etc.[22] Thus, the organization was "a major instrument of rural development, as well as a representational and lobbying organisation."[23]

Though the increase in the membership of farmers of medium-sized acreage
and teachers in the late 1930s and early 1940s imbued the JAS with a decidedly
middle-class outlook, its members were genuinely interested in uplifting the
masses of Jamaicans. The JAS sought to spur working peoples to social and economic heights that would allow them to contribute to the emergent sovereign
state. To this end its leadership stimulated among small farmers discussions of
major government policies. One of its leaders, Chair D. T. M. Girvan, who had

served as an officer of Jamaica Welfare, urged that "in all the branch societies, and particularly those in the pilot areas for farm development, regular discussions should be conducted."[24] He recommended the election of leaders who would be responsible for particular readings and interpretations of the organization's articles.[25]

The JAS was part of the Jamaican middle class's efforts to convert and to convince "peasants" of the need for community improvement. An example of the underlying outlook of the effort came in 1975 with the passage of the Minimum Wage Law by the Manley government. After discussing the pros and cons, JAS leadership appealed to the government to fix wage rates so that farmers employing labor in the production of coffee, bananas and citrus might afford it.[26]

The Society was prepared to disavow publicly the interests of its members, many of whom comprised the hybrid laborers, and who stood to lose most if wages were fixed. This was not surprising given their underrepresentation in the organization's executive. Moreover, the large discrepancy between the total membership and those who had actually paid their dues represented the financial difficulties experienced by many of its low-income members. Under these conditions, it is little wonder that middle-level farmers and teachers were able to consolidate their hold over the organization, cornering leadership positions.

The trend is hardly unique to the JAS. In her study of the issue of social change and social mobility in rural Jamaica, Foner found that at the very least it was the middle class which was assured of positions of leadership in such bodies.[27] According to Foner, "leadership in the party branches is based on high status in the community so that position in them is not an independent source of prestige."[28] Furthermore, the smallness of the communities ensured that the class background of individuals and families was known and mobility was assured. Foner's study demonstrated that persons of high status in the rural areas were more likely to become leaders in such organizations as the JAS than were low-status smallholders.[29]

Building Communities and Selling Them Development

Early constitutive links between rural working peoples and the middle classes provided a basis on which a middle-class-led nationalist movement could take root, incorporating large sections of rural and urban working people into its image of community. Nationalism relied on such a link to consolidate a development program synchronized with a worldwide development process and to effect a local cultural persuasion under the motto "Out of many one."[30] The motto reflected a notion of community that was pervasive among middle classes and aspirants to that status. By linking notions of individual welfare, community development and national development, middle-class elites were able to mobilize large sections of urban and rural working peoples. This was very evident in the operations of Jamaica Welfare. Because the vast majority of Jamaican people relied on wages, at one level, unionism became integral to this mobilization, resulting in the characteristic phenomenon of political unionism, that is to say, political parties strategically affiliated with or indistinguishable from their trade unions. Political unionism provided the critical mass needed to control the state. The effect of this was twofold. First, it made middle-class status a desirable, if not ideal social position. Secondly, wage struggles received more play than land reform struggles, perhaps because they represented politically less difficult terrain, and might have been more easily settled.

Nationalism, its associate movement, political unionism, and the trade union movement were pursued primarily on an urban front, but also on sugar estates as part of agricultural reforms, and along with reforms associated with farm operations. In other words, the ideals of citizenship were channeled through these various reforms, most carried out on behalf of the Jamaican working peoples, though in compliance with a middle-class agenda. When the cause was taken up again in the 1970s, a new situation had developed on the island. Social relations had congealed, Jamaica's position in the world economy became even more tenuous, and the middle classes championed democratic participation by the institutionalization of worker/farmer representation. In many ways the middle classes succeeded in reviving the bureaucracy's legitimacy and resuscitating its meaning in the lives of Jamaican working peoples. They also lowered their expectations of the state's developmental capacity, however.

Middle Classes and Rural Masses: The Jamaica Welfare

The idea of building a better Jamaica, and redefining the notion of citizenship, was epitomized in the work of a body known variously as Jamaica Welfare Ltd. (1937–1943), Jamaica Welfare (1943) Ltd. (1943–1949), Jamaica Social Welfare Commission (1949–1965), and subsequently the Social Development Commission. Jamaica Welfare had its beginning in 1937, when it was run by a select group of middle-class Jamaicans. By the late 1940s, it had become increasingly an instrument of the state, and subject therefore to party politics.

Jamaica Welfare was born in the wake of severe discontent between Jamaican banana farmers and the monopoly corporation of United Fruit. As a result of negotiations with the company in the United States, Norman Manley, representing the Jamaican Banana cooperative, set up Jamaica Welfare with funds of one cent on each bunch of bananas shipped.[31] Subsequently, as it was divested of its middle-class nongovernmental autonomy, Jamaica Welfare received its funding by way of grants from the Colonial Welfare and Development Fund and, later, from the postcolonial state. Its objectives were:

> To promote, manage and control schemes for and to do any act or thing which may directly or indirectly serve the general interests and the social or economic betterment and aid of the agricultural or working peasantry, small settlers, farmers, labourers and working people of and in Jamaica. To engage in any work or activity directly or indirectly relating to the health, cultural improvement, education, recreation, agriculture, industry, finances, trade, justice and morals of or for the persons described.[32]

To staff the organization Manley handpicked people whom he felt shared the ideals of his organization. Many who were handpicked recalled that they were selected by Manley or had been recommended by his trusted friends and colleagues.[33] Both Girvan, who became the coordinator of Jamaica Welfare, and Pansy Hart, who was very active in the agency, spoke openly of their recruitment.[34] This made for a middle-class-led organization. Its first board of directors, chaired by Norman Manley, consisted of eleven persons recruited from agriculture, the civil service, business and law, anthropology, land surveying, medicine and education.[35] In Manley's words, "Welfare tapped a deep stream of middle-class interests in Jamaica. We had no trouble building a good staff. School teachers were anxious to come in and were prepared to do so on terms that meant no financial benefit to them but answered a deep feeling that rural Jamaica needed special help."[36] As perceived, rural Jamaica needed many things before the colony could "call itself civilized"[37] and, as a precondition for the island's modern national status, Jamaica Welfare hoped to instill a national pride among Jamaicans and create a positive attitude toward development as conceptualized by the decolonizing elites. It would do this by using volunteers convinced of the need to "build a new Jamaica." Translated, this meant building a more responsible and self-reliant community, discovering ways and means by which *men*[38] might better their lives.

Sometimes working in concert with the JAS (on whose board, incidently, a number of its leaders served), or with the Lands Department and, later, with the Ministry of Agriculture, Jamaica Welfare targeted the rural population for a number of projects. The organization promoted cooperatives, built community councils, and created cottage industries, savings clubs, adult literacy programs and instructions in home improvement. Its reach throughout the island was extensive. In 1948/49, its programs covered 236 villages throughout the island.

There were 77 Village Committees and 51 constituted Village Community Councils, together co-ordinating the activities of 343 groups. The total number of organised groups was 1,180 made up of 127 Pioneer Clubs, 57 Handcrafts Groups, 261 Cooperative groups, 110 3 F groups and 725 groups organised by other bodies and assisted by Jamaica Welfare. In 1948 Leadership Training was carried out in 149 Zone Training Days, 1,570 Leadership classes, 308 Demonstrations, 41 Observations visits, 17 Training camps and by a "Moveable school" method—first developed in St. Mary. In the Co-operative programme there were 185 Savings Unions, 30 Buying Clubs, 432 Poultry groups, 158 groups for mutual help. The Commission undertook the organisation of Fishermen Co-operatives which eventually led to the registration of 17 Fishermen Co-operatives and the establishment of a Fishermen's Federation.[39]

Jamaica Welfare spread quickly from 10 villages in 1938, to 16 in 1944. By 1949, the organization had reached 229 villages with a population of roughly 200,000.[40] By 1955, the agency had trained hundreds of leaders and affected the lives of thousands of rural working peoples. Its far-reaching operations were unprecedented, as was its public relations propaganda. In the pages of its print organ, *The Welfare Reporter*, images appeared of working peoples swayed by and convinced of the program's genuine benefits. One such "Village Leader" was Ambrosine Wehbley, a mother of twelve, who, after the storm of August 1944, became active in the program. The report of the 'Welfare Reporter' speaks for itself.

Before the storm of August, 1944, Ambrosine Wehbley, a resident of the Ragsville section of Guys Hill, decided that she should throw in her lot with the other progressive residents of Guys Hill. She discussed it with her husband Erasmus Wehbley, a cultivator and occasional trader in tobacco. But she did nothing. The storm came. Sheets of zinc, roofs, garments, etc. all flew away. Houses, trees, roads were destroyed, families were wrecked, and among them were the Wehbleys. When Mrs. Mary Kelly and Mrs. Leila James Tomlinson (Field Officers of Jamaica Welfare [1943] Ltd.) went around offering consolation and preaching co-perating, Amrboisine listened and ACTED. She became a foundation member of the Ragsville Traders Pioneer Club, the group which in Jamaica has pioneered the way for co-ops, of unlimited liability. The 3–F Campaign came in 1945 and found the Ragsville Pioneers eager for new projects. President Ambrosine was keen on it from its inception. In fact she became known as one of the three 3–F experts of Guys Hill . . . and Guys Hill is tops in 3–F!![41]

Despite its distinct notions of "character," or respectability, and development, construing such a middle-class operation, Jamaica Welfare volunteers invited participation from the working people whom they served seeking to generate leaders from within the communities they served. This was a lesson learned from earlier strategies which had targeted the building of community centers. The community center approach deterred participation. Because people felt that the centers belonged to Jamaica Welfare, participation in the activities within was low. In the words of one leading participant and chronicler of that era, they were prepared to learn from their errors.

> Whilst recognising that the Centres had undoubtedly brought many benefits to areas which had hitherto had no facilities for culture or recognition, Jamaica Welfare Ltd. admitted that the basic purpose was not being achieved, as "the people were not being sufficiently involved, participation was superficial, and the qualities of self-help and responsibility were not being developed." It was therefore decided that no further Centres of this kind should be erected. Instead a new approach was adopted by which villages were encouraged to form Community Associations and Councils, and to utilise existing facilities, such as school buildings, or where necessary to erect modest halls on a self-help basis, as Community Centres. These Centres were affiliated to the Jamaica Welfare Ltd., and received small grants towards furniture and equipment, and had the services of the Company's officers, but the emphasis was clearly on local initiative.[42]

Sybil Francis, one of the agency's officers in the 1940s, recalls that it was an exciting period, that everyone involved was enthusiastic and highly motivated.[43] The idea of becoming citizens in an independent state, though still many years away, enlivened participation. Folk and Christian songs spurred the volunteers and staff on in their mission and mobilized community members to want to belong and participate in the agency's programs. The 3–F campaign—Food, Fitness and Family—was especially successful, linking family with agricultural development and better living.

> The campaign focused the attention of both men and women on the home and family, and highlighted the link between agriculture and better living. It successfully involved the local village community in attacking a national problem. Finally in stimulating an action programme based on a need of which the community had hitherto been unaware—whilst still maintaining local initiative—the campaign represented an advance from the "felt needs" approach in Community Development to that of "persuaded" or "counseled" needs—a concept which is now being internationally advocated and discussed in current Community Development literature.[44]

The JW might be considered the only agency in Jamaica's history to advance a notion of "protodevelopment" that distinguished economic space from sociocultural space, a peculiarly current concern.

From 1949 on, the direct, systematic influence that the middle classes exercised over significant sections of rural, and later, urban populations through the Jamaica Welfare, as individuals in a nongovernmental organization, was phased out. The Jamaica Welfare became a statutory body, renamed the Jamaica Social Welfare Commission, fully financed by the state.[45] Its board came to consist of fifteen members, five representing the government ex officio, five others appointed by the Governor, and the rest representing affiliated organizations. In 1958, upon the devolution of a Ministerial system government, the Commission was made a corporate body with the Minister responsible for appointments to its Board.[46]

This shift from direct middle-class control over the Jamaica Welfare to state control occasioned a severe decline in the programs and projects which had been central to its operations. The Community Councils, Parish Welfare Councils and Village Committees critical to Jamaica Welfare declined significantly. Whereas Jamaica Welfare had always operated as an autonomous body, even when it associated with other agencies like the JAS and land settlements, in the post-1955 era, the government propelled it toward new vistas. When the government implemented its pivotal program, the Farm Development Scheme, discussed earlier, it called upon the renamed Jamaica Social Welfare Commission (now under the Ministry of Education and Social Welfare), to be part of a team effort to create the Co-ordinated Extension Services and to implement the Farm Development Scheme. Others involved in the effort included the Ministry of Agriculture, the JAS (Jamaica Agricultural Society), the 4-H clubs and the Agricultural Loan Societies Board.[47] Under this arrangement, the Welfare Commission was severely dwarfed by the JAS and the Ministry, and rather than play the leading role to which it had grown accustomed, it succumbed to servicing the Scheme.[48]

In short, the new government policy undermined the work of the Commission. According to the Commission's Report for 1957/58:

> The design set for the operation of the Farm Development areas gave to Jamaica Agricultural Society and the 4-H organisation the responsibility of organising communities to receive the services afforded by the Commission. This meant that quite a different approach from the normal pattern had to be instituted in the Farm Development Areas. Concentration by way of planning, visiting training and attendance at meetings was most heavily on them. As a result the number of Community Councils decreased by 101 to nineteen while the project activities thrown up by voluntary leaders themselves could barely be maintained.[49]

In 1963 and 1965, sole control over the now renamed Social Development Commission lay with the Minister of Development and Social Welfare, Edward Seaga, who furnished his own ideas about community development. A detailed project document, entitled *Manual of Community Development*, elaborated the new approach, focused on building community centers, and strengthening the role of a resident village officer, who was to ensure the implementation of government plans. The approach was highly centralized, instructions coming from the command center of the Ministry, and its staff was expected to follow closely the minutiae set forth in the *Manual*. Seaga's address to new trainees signaled the new direction:

> Your first effort and interest in a village is to win the co-operation of the villager; and I have gone to great lengths to explain to you how this should be done. Your next interest is to take the rein of leadership in the village in your hand; to begin to organize projects, to teach the craft work, to carry out home economics instruction and to organize the use of the Community Centre. Your next job will be to see who are the most interested persons—those who are showing themselves as the potential leaders. . . . At some point before you leave the village it will be necessary for you to establish what will be known as a village Council or a Community Council.[50]

This address revealed a new kind of state centralization in the postcolonial era.[51] The centralization differed from the colonial state in terms of its Jamaican personnel and its pursuit of a systematic project of community development. It was similar to the colonial state in its constrained release of its vital constituency. Known as the Jamaica Social Welfare Commission, both the agency's functions and methods veered sharply away from its predecessor, Jamaica Welfare. For example, the main plank of Jamaica Welfare's program, citizenship-building, sought to incorporate rural participation by inculcating local leadership as far as possible. Because it was nongovernmental, it could not dictate and draw upon the relatively vast resources of government. Neither was it formally linked to a political party, though its chief officer, Manley, was leader of the opposition party. It could neither scare, nor coerce. The agency's incorporation into the state introduced a new, sinister force, one that favored a cosmetic paternalism as it regarded the problems and prospects affecting rural and urban working peoples. Unlike the agency administered by Manley and friends, the JLP government divined what Jamaicans needed in a way that afforded little discursive input from the communities involved.

State centralization appeared to narrow the range of responsibilities undertaken by the JW. Projects became ends in themselves and not aimed at building a better Jamaica through community development and by empowering local people. The Ministry of Development undertook many activities once the sole domain of the JW. As a result the SWC had to link its activities to those of the Ministry, the government and the state. In the context of shrinking economic benefits, most of the programs were now geared toward employment generation. A variety of programs promoted by the Jamaica Social Welfare Commission, had historical precedents. For example, the "Home and Family Week" project was an outgrowth of the earlier "Better Homes Campaign." Similarly, health, education, recreation and cleanliness programs remained intact. The Craft workshops were expanded to include the Corporate Area, i.e., Kingston and its environs. With the Ministry of Youth as its partner, the SWC taught metal, needle and straw work to young men for sixteen weeks.[52] The Community Cooperative programs of 1965 were similar to those of the 1940s. They sought to "harness the human resources of the villages" and "to organise residents within the framework of a Central Purpose Cooperative Society the principal function being (a) the preservation of the democratic life of the community, (b) integrating the villagers as a whole with the motto (Out of Many, One People)."[53] During the 1960s, more programs emerged that targeted social decay in the Corporate Area. For example, craft programs and food preservation provided employment, and The Urban Development Project created a new constituency, namely, the urban underprivileged. What distinguished the earlier period from the 1960s was the centralized state approach to welfare and the direct intrusion of party politics in the programs' execution. In short, it was believed that citizens could not be counted on to reform themselves, but had to be led directly by right-thinking state officials. In a way the early postcolonial state itself was actively inviting a dependency that marginalized the individual and community initiatives that marked the nationalists' strategy. This is not, however to suggest that diminished agency was all-pervasive.

These mechanisms of reform were readily displayed in agricultural policy and in the governmental pronouncements of that time. I would like to spend the rest of this chapter delineating the particular agricultural projects and policies which shaped rural spaces, allowing rural Jamaicans to see themselves as integral to development, and to consider relations with national elites inside and outside of the government bureaucracy strategic and hence important.

"Every Acre Has a Use, Every Acre Needs a Man":[54] The Modernization of Space

Apropos development, Jamaica nationalists construed the world as highly competitive, dominated by fighters. Accordingly, Jamaica needed to demonstrate its mettle internationally. It was a war of sorts.

> The future and safety of Jamaica depends upon our raising our standards of production, and increasing our skill and knowledge in the use of our land in the use of our hands. . . . It takes a new vitality to reach into the will and heart of the people, to raise standards of production, to face the competition of the world. Now, before it is too late, go out as a crusade to let the people know that hard work is demanded. Everybody is fighting his way in this competitive world. Let us show the world how Jamaica can fight for itself under good party leadership.[55]

The agricultural plan included government intervention in land titling to ensure the land's vitality for commodity production. Arrangements made between owner and government resulted in the mobilization of idle land for not only export but also food crops. So-called food forests were proposed to bring easier-accessed land under production. The government would help by providing credit, infrastructures, and technical assistance to improve crops and methods, and would fund these through taxation, thus stimulating agricultural as well as industrial development.[56] These ideas, although enumerated by the oppositional PNP, even from its oppositional location were readily implemented by the governing JLP.

Planning for Progress

Though the mainstay of the economy, agriculture epitomized backwardness, modernism's despised opposite. According to theory, rational planning would rectify this sad state of affairs. The first ten-year plan (1946–1957) was the product of the Report of the Economic Policy Committee and the Agricultural Policy Committee. Revised in 1951, it articulated the infrastructural development of agriculture: irrigation, credit to small farmers, erosion conservation measures, and the provision of marketing facilities for the smallholder. The establishment of the Agricultural Development Corporation meant research into and the development of traditional and nontraditional crops, such as rice.[57] Following closely the provisions of the Welfare Acts of 1940 and 1945, general infrastructural development, such as communications, roads, and water supplies, received much support.

While the original plan did not allow for the establishment of capital-generating projects, its 1951 revision did, overriding earlier doubts about the inappropriateness of industry in the West Indies. Because plans reveal the government and state's intentions as much as expenditures detail their implementation, it is useful to note the priorities of government plans. The twinning of socioeconomic and agricultural or economic space that epitomized the operations of the JW came to an abrupt end with the attainment of self-government. Rural space underwent a reshaping that undermined earlier types of consensuses between rural working peoples and the protoindependent state. Ideas about industrialization merited a different consideration of the smallholders' more or less moral economy. Consider the state's new relationship to the bauxite companies. Mining rearranged agricultural space and contributed to the delinking of economic and social space I referred to above. Mining relations exposed as mere rhetoric the government's claim of agriculture's national importance, much less the welfare of smallholders' well-being in those communities and elsewhere on the island.

Before I enter into this discussion, I would like to summarize the major economic trends of this period in order to cast the heritage of state-led agricultural development.

Of note here is the significant difference between original and actual expenditures in Social Welfare, Health and Education as compared with those for Trade/Industry and Agriculture. Expenditures allocated for Trade and Industry, and for Communications and Works showed the administration's attempts to build infrastructure to attract capital accumulation in nonagricultural areas. Given its conception of development, the postwar colonial state, operated by Jamaicans, entered a new relationship with private capital.

Seeking to Move up in the World

The strengthening of Jamaica's economic base, as understood in the 1940 Statement of Policy, necessitated the economy's industrialization. This required substantial capital of an economy characterized by the scarcity of its resources.

Table 3.1.   Original, Revised (1951) and Actual Plan Expenditure in Pounds and Percentages

Sector	Expend. in pounds £000			Percentage Total		
	1.*	2.*	3.*	1.*	2.*	3.*
Agriculture	6030	6616	6632	31	36	36
Communicat./works	1742	1611	2931	9	9	16
Trade/Industry	400	400	1114	2	2	6
Education	3302	2093	1744	17	11	9
Public Health	5563	6117	4418	28	33	24
Social Welfare	1774	1011	683	9	5	4
Miscellaneous	724	337	701	4	2	4
Total Expend. on Schemes	19,536	18,163	18,327	100%	100%	100%

*Note: 1. Original 2. Revised 3. Actual.
Adapted from: N. Girvan, *Foreign Capital and Economic Underdevelopment in Jamaica* (Kingston: Institute of Social and Economic Research, 1971), 102.

New relations between the state and national and foreign capital were therefore proposed.

Relations with foreign capital had existed since the turn of the century. By 1938 Barclays Bank dominated banking, and the United Fruit Company controlled banana industry marketing and production. While companies like United Fruit had initiated investments during the eighteenth century, significant advances had been made to promote, for example, secondary industry with the passage of the Pioneer Industry (Encouragement) Law and the establishment of the Industrial Development Corporation in 1949 and 1950, respectively. Such institutional arrangements primed the emergence of a "corporate economy" although many Jamaica-controlled corporate enterprises were in fact branch plants of multinational corporations.[58]

Coincident to the state's own activities were the national capitalist class's attempts to link foreign and local investors to the state, thereby consolidating its base.[59] The state's association with bauxite companies exemplifies best the relations between the state and foreign capital which resulted in foreign companies gaining economic concessions.

The Mining Law of 1947 made it possible for bauxite companies to own thousands of acres of land by stipulating land ownership as the basis for mining. In 1957 the law was amended to permit the companies to lease. Between 1944 and 1957, Reynolds and Alcan, the primary bauxite companies, purchased 5% of the total land area of Jamaica, roughly 135,000 acres. Furthermore, the enactment of the Bauxite and Alumina Industries (Encouragement) Law made "the remission of tonnage tax and customs duty on plant, machinery and building materials necessary for the mining, treating and transportation of bauxite."[60] The nominal returns to the economy brought by this legislation were used to justify further concessions. According to a government pronouncement:

> in a country which depends for a large proportion of its investments from overseas the influence of Government on the direction of investment in the private sector cannot be very great. Indeed the mainspring of Government's action is to offer as many inducements as are reasonable to attract as much capital as possible. We are not in the situation where there is a large amount of capital all eager to be invested and which has to be regulated and controlled. (Thus) it is intended to lay a special emphasis on attracting foreign capital to Jamaica and the provision of incentives by way of tax concessions, tariff protection and industrial space will be continued. Government will also ensure that basic facilities such as water, roads and communications are provided whether by itself or by private enterprise.[61]

To this end, several laws were passed and/or amended, such as the Pioneer Industries (Encouragement) Law, the revision of the customs tariff to encourage imports of machinery (capital goods) and basic raw materials, the establishment of an Industrial Estate and the Industrial Incentives Law and the Export Industry (Encouragement) Law, designed to stimulate the local manufacture and re-export of articles. Additionally, joint Industrial Councils and other conciliation facilities were added to the industrial relations machinery.[62]

Despite changes of government, this period's industrialization program remained fairly constant. The JLP's accession to office resulted in an administration that carried out PNP-formulated policy. In its independence plan the JLP administration stated that "the Government sector must be large enough to act as a lever in the economy and as a balancing factor as policy dictates."[63] The new administration projected that no less than 65% of the financing for the Independence plan would come from foreign contributions, whether loans or investments, an estimate they eventually scaled down.[64]

Between 1950 and 1956, agriculture grew incrementally, becoming increasingly lethargic, declining from 2.3 percent from 1950 to 1954 (roughly .6% per year) to 1.7% from 1954 to 1955 to .2% from 1955 to 1956.[65] During this period the fastest growing sectors were manufacturing, mining, construction, transportation, wholesale/retail, and miscellaneous services, including tourism. In 1950, agriculture's contribution to the GDP (at factor cost) was 36.2%; by 1957, it had fallen to 13.8%.[66]

The emergence of new relations between foreign capital and the state was evident in the expansion of the mining and construction sectors, which in turn affected the expansion of the manufacturing and commercial sectors. While the political elite continued to stress the importance of agriculture, they focused on mobilizing resources for trade and industrial development. The factory building program of the Industrial Development corporation alone was allocated £1,210,000.[67]

Fixing the Agricultural Sector

Both the colonial and the colonial/nationalist administrations construed smallholders as inhabiting a metaphorical area of darkness. In their bind to sustain welfare and "industry," land settlement schemes became welfaristic, while modernization and rehabilitation schemes advanced the industrial project. Both sets of programs became instruments through which governing regimes attempted to stabilize agrarian relationships. The more the state appeared to exercise control, the more the sector seemed unviable economically, even as agrarian class relations stabilized. It was clear that industrialization as well as the more viable agricultural units needed a smallholder sector, regardless of its fragmentation. A key agricultural strategy continued to be, therefore, the establishment of land settlement schemes, providing rural working peoples and others with small plots of land.

To this end, agricultural policy after 1946 continued to be influenced by the 1897 commissions of enquiry, as well as by the 1938 Wakefield Report, and the Moyne Commission report, not to mention the Agricultural Policy Committee. In the late colonial period, policy was also influenced by the recommendations of the International Bank for Reconstruction and Development (IBRD).

In response to the chronic unemployment experienced in the West Indies, the 1897 commission apologetically proposed the settling of rural working peoples as small farmers. The Moyne Commission of 1938 recommended that land be cultivated more intensively in order to increase food production and support a growing population. As the commissioners stated, "the most urgent need is the development of *peasant* agriculture, but substantial progress between both peasants and estates is dependent upon far reaching reforms of the basic methods now in vogue."[68] Considering the 1897 commission, the Moyne Commission cautioned colonial administrations to seek first the improvement of the husbandry of smallholders, that is, ameliorate existing land settlements before establishing others. To that end, the Commission advocated "that governments should undertake powers for the compulsory acquisition of agricultural land needed for land settlement and similar purposes."[69] They also recommended upgrading the techniques used by smallholders to include mixed farming on both small and large agricultural holdings.

The Wakefield Report of 1942 recommended the revitalization and expansion of government service in agriculture, via such institutions as the Jamaica Agricultural Society, the Agricultural Department, the 4-H clubs, the practical training centers and the Forestry and Lands department. The Agricultural Policy Committee (APC) of 1944 outlined three uses appropriate for agricultural land: 1) the production of food; 2) the maintenance and extension of the principal export crops and the pursuit of new export crops; and 3) the production of raw materials for industrial development. The APC also emphasized the need for soil conservation, intensification of land use and good husbandry methods. The program was predicated on the committees' standards of correctness as regards all West Indian agricultural producers. For the agricultural committee, the civilian arm of the colonial state, incorrectness meant the persistence of "traditional" agriculture and the use of archaic technologies in the smallholder sector. According to the committee, these problems could be remedied by improved agricultural techniques, such as the adoption of proper planting practices, extended and improved use of fertilizers, and intensified research into both land management and land use. As in the earlier colonial period, when there was public concern over the *plight* of the smallholder, the policies adopted in the post–Moyne Commission era privileged export production and the stability of large-scale plantation producers and medium farmers.[70] Modernization of the labor process of the smallholders would take place only to the extent that it stabilized the social order predicated on the coexistence of the small mixed-crop agricultural plot that facilitated a multiprong technology of survival, that is to say, a set of techniques performed to transform rural Jamaicans into smallholders, while enabling them to participate in a number of income-generating activities, outside of the state's purview, though in league with the state.

While many researchers cite the inadequacy of the plot for farming and focus on the state's failure to sustain viable farming, they overlook the ways in which smallholders operating these small plots actually became entrenched in rural areas as labor for others like themselves and medium- and large-scale farmers. Before I address this oversight, I summarize the key features of land settlement schemes, suggesting that we reconsider the role land settlements played, outside both their abject failures to resuscitate the smallholder sector, and their conceptualization as palliatives for political clients. Land settlements were also spaces from which working peoples launched themselves beyond and further into agriculture. They bespeak the fact that national governments unintentionally enabled socioeconomic flexibility. They must be construed as spaces which demonstrate the state's failed attempt to patrol and to control rural production.

The New Land Settlements

Land settlements as part of the state's official agrarian policy were organized on either a freehold or a leasehold system, and were not only stopgap unemployment measures. For instance, areas considered hazardous by natural or man-made disasters were often organized into land settlements called Authorities. Land settlement schemes were particularly abundant during the period of 1929–1971. A total of 269 properties was acquired during this time, amounting to 234,041 acres.[71] Of this, the available acreage was 173,835, divided into 39,381 allotments, an average of 4.5 acres per household. As table 3.2 below shows, though land settlements increased the number of farmers, the average size of the plot remained more or less constant, often decreasing. Between 1951 and 1962, each allottee received roughly 3.93 acres.[72]

Between 1938 and 1949, land settlements flourished on the island and in many West Indian Islands. These plots had characteristic features:

1. the average size of the allotment was not to exceed 5 acres in size, though no minimum acreage was stipulated;
2. subletting and subdivisions were prohibited;
3. allottees were required to be bona fide farmers;

Table 3.2.   Land Acquisition Settlement Programme, Jamaica, 1929–1971

Years	No. of Properties	Acres Acquired	Acres Allotted	No. of Allotments
'29–50;	140	149,165	122,928	26,859
'51–62;	55	30,430	23,896	6,082
'63–71;	74	54,446	27,911	6,440
Total	269	234,041	173,835	39,381

Adapted from: I. Johnson, M. Strachan and J. Johnson, "A Review of Land Settlement in Jamaica." *Proceedings of the 7th West Indian Agricultural Economics Conference, Grand Anse
Grenada, April 9–15* (U.W.I. St. Augustine: Trinidad, 1972), 4.

4. transfers could be made only with the permission of the land commissioner and
   no title could be issued earlier than five years from the date of land possession;
5. allottees had to use approved agricultural practices, such as soil conservation
   measures, and to have pasture land (1/5 of the plot size during the first year,
   2/5 thereafter).[73]

To the extent that these criteria were followed, they might have assured state
officials more control over smallholders' cultivation. But, as we will see later,
many provisions were flouted, and the conditions created on the settlements
yoked settlers to income-generating activities not necessarily agricultural. Take
for example the St. Mary Land Settlement Scheme.

The St. Mary Land Settlement Scheme: Modernity in Shackles

The St. Mary land settlement scheme was instituted in 1947, the peak of land
settlement programs. As with other land settlement schemes, the typical participant was male, forty-six years old, in a family of six, with roughly ten years of
farming experience, often involved in income-supplementing occupations such
as prison warden, milkman, carpenter, even banana purchasing agent.[74]

The scheme was usually freehold tenure. Comprising about 257 acres, oc-
cupants owned approximately 223, though the lack of control over the terms of
purchase resulted in multiple plot ownership. Single ownership of three holdings
or plots of land was normal. For example, twenty-seven allottees owned forty-
nine holdings, averaging 1.8 holdings each.[75]

Most of the farms averaged between 5 and 10 acres. Twenty-one farms were
less than 15 acres, and three were as large as 27 acres. Some 72% of the scheme
was cultivated, and 50% was devoted to banana production. As was national

practice, small cultivators engaged in mixed-crop cultivation. Settlers grew a combination of food and export crops, export crops accounting for roughly 51.12% of total cultivation. Crops grown in pure stands accounted for 20.55% of acreage, while mixed crops occupied 51.12%.[76] Traditional export crops prevailed; 61% of the total gross output on farms consisted of bananas and coconuts. By comparison, the cultivation of tree and ground provisions and livestock was meager.

The value of the gross output per farm ranged from £64.6s to £687.9s, on average of £263. Smaller holdings generally recorded a higher value of gross output than larger farms. Holdings of less than 5 acres earned an average £42.5s and 3d per acre, while holdings of more than 20 acres, when assessed by acreage, averaged only £14.8s and 2d per acre though their total gross output was of course higher.[77] Two factors partially explain this. Because much has been written about the causes of this phenomenon, I mention them in brief. First, settlements tended to be on marginal land. Second, the sheer inadequacy of resources forced the smallholder to adopt more intensive cultivation practices to eke as much out of the land as possible.

Data on investment by acreage reveals this impoverishment, where investment ranged from £500 to £3000 per farm, though as table 3.3 shows, most holdings recorded total capital investments of about £1,500.

According to a survey of land settlements, farmers with larger acreage were more selective in their cultivation practices, less inclined to cultivate the least arable parts of their farms. When capital investment is treated in relation to farm size, an interesting picture emerges. The total capital investment per acre evinces an inverse relationship to farm size. That is, the larger the farm, the smaller the investment per acre. Land improvements accounted for 91% of capital investment. But what constituted "land improvements?" According to a 1962 government survey,

Table 3.3.   Frequency Distribution of Farms by Total Capital Investment

Total Capital Investment of pounds	No. of Farms	Percentage
Under 500	2	7.4
500 to under 1,000	10	37.0
1,000 to under 1,500	–	25.9
1,500 to under 2,000	3	11.1
2,000 to under 2,500	2	7.5
2,500 to under 3,000	–	–
3,000 and over	3	11.1
All Farms Total	27	100.0

Source: "Survey of Government Land Settlements." (Ministry of Agriculture Kingston: Govt. Printery), 49.

Table 3.4.   Relationship of Cash Expenses to Size of Farm in Pounds, Shillings and Pence

Size Farm Acres	No. of Farms	Total Per Farm	Cash Expenses	
			Per Acre in pounds	
<5 acres	5	311.14.8	62.7.0	16.17.0
5–<10	14	1266.13.9	90.9.7	13.6.3
10–<15	2	316.17.3	158.8.8	12.18.8
15–<20	4	1382.10.6	345.12.8	20.18.11
20–>	2	434.12.0	217.6.0	8.5.7
All Farms	27	3712.18.2	137.10.4	14.9.4

Source: Ministry of Agricultural Report. "The Economic Organisation of Small Scale Farming, based on Banana, Coconut and Cocoa-Highgate Area. St. Mary, 1958–1959." (Kingston: Govt. Printer, n.d.), 66.

"attractive" dwellings accounted for much of this percentage. Small farmers had devoted the largest portion of total capital investment to building houses. Investment in machinery and equipment was only 2% of total capital investment. The scarcity of machinery and equipment is perhaps related to the substantial amount expended on labor. Capital invested in livestock was only 4% of the total £62 per farm.[78] Investment in machinery for all twenty-seven farms was only £135 pounds, an average of £5 pounds per farm household. The three lowest investments made on the farm averaged only 7s. per farm, while the three highest amounted to £25 pounds. Investment was highly skewed as six of the larger farms had invested 83% of the total amount.[79] Although government officials hailed the investment in machinery as evidence of both modernization and the move from subsistence to commercial farming, they failed to consider the quality of this machinery. Much of it consisted of basic manual tools: machetes, forks, shovels. While numbers are not available, it was reported that much hired labor used on farms engaged in work on an hourly, daily or per task basis. One can therefore speculate that small cultivators had to supplement their income, often seeking employment on other plots of land. Modernization was not exclusively about raising incomes, though this was of course considered desirable. Only those with substantial agricultural properties were able to do so. The highest annual farm income, £242, was achieved by two 10- to 15-acre farms. Not surprising is that the lowest farm income, £94 pounds per annum, belonged to farms of less than 5 acres. Also, the amount of profit was proportional to farm size.[80] The bigger the farm, the higher the returns, despite the intensive cultivation practices of smallholders. Moreover, cash expenses were far greater on smaller farms.

As table 3.4 above shows, excluding the 15- to 20-acre category, larger farms spent much less per acre than smaller farms. Holdings under 5 acres spent an average of £17 per acre, while those over 20 acres spent only £8. Perhaps these expenditures represent economies of scale. In any case, there were other issues at stake. One of these was building or capitalizing on the level of informal economic activity that was always a part of the agricultural sector. An intrinsic aspect of modernization therefore was the institutionalization of differential spatial temporalities. That is to say, while instituting goals is considered to be THE criteria by which modernity is measured, all forms of labor, income earning activity, etc., are harnessed to generalized commodified relationships. (I want to take this issue up in chapter 6 to show these tendencies' spatial expressions and their rootedness.) So are formal spaces locations where informality flourishes. I locate processes of informalization in the colonial and early postcolonial period, and I question the accuracy of the literature that posits informality as oppositional to the state sector. As I have stated elsewhere, "often the informal economy stands mockingly in relation to the state, the gatekeeper of formalized institutional and societal relations."[81]

Masking the Informal Tendencies of State and Development

Though the extant informal-sector literature tends to focus exclusively on urban and industrial developments, agriculture also warrants consideration.[82] Clearly the formalization of rural social life was accompanied by a simultaneous informalization. Though land settlements like St. Mary formalized rural life, because land granted was accompanied by inadequate capital, or none at all, working people tending farms had to find other means to supplement their incomes, thus negotiating, sustaining alternative types of social relationships. Agriculture became a part-time activity. Bureaucratization succeeded in undermining the very processes it sought to generate. And those processes existed as a condition of formalization not unique to St. Mary. Land settlements could not of course be completely surveyed by the state, allowing therefore for a certain amount of autonomy, and compounding the fluid social relations common in the countryside.

A descriptive survey of 116 land settlement schemes confirmed these patterns of labor and the looseness of state control in areas lacking proper infrastructure such as roads, water, and basic amenities.[83] When Sir John Huggins claimed, as governor in 1949, that the government not only provided infrastructure—water, roads, bridle paths, marketing depots, recreation facilities, social amenities—but was a generous land agent as well, he could not have lacked evidence to the contrary. Furthermore, it was not all that clear that actual or prospective smallholders were being settled on these properties.

Though several official claims asserted that most settlers were farmers, the Agricultural Committee of 1945 cited cases of persons appropriating such land for purposes other than farming, in the name of friends and relatives under secret trusts.[84] Indeed, Redwood noted that "most purchasers of land on the settlements were neither the unemployed in need of relief, nor land hungry would-be farmers."[85] Furthermore, he concluded that "many purchasers had neither the aptitude for the experience nor the intention to engage in farming."[86]

People were sold land without verification of farming ability. No strict stipulation on residential location existed.[87] Considering a sample of 104 of a total of 116 land settlers, occupying a total of 80,961 acres, resident purchasers held 29% of the land, while nonresidents held 70%.[88] Furthermore, nonresident cultivators produced more export crops than did resident farmers. Interestingly, agricultural laborers accounted for the bulk of resident purchases: 2,851 out of 4,380 acres (65%). Though the occupations of nonresident purchasers are not recorded, the location of the land settlements most often near large private plantations might account for the following effects:

71% of all settlers supplemented their income by working on nearby properties.

13% of resident purchasers on all settlements regularly did seasonal work off their holdings.

4% of resident purchasers on settlements with properties within five miles regularly performed seasonal work off their holdings.

12% of resident purchasers on settlements without properties within five miles regularly did seasonal work.

24% of resident purchasers on settlements with properties within five miles regularly did part-time work off their holdings.

24% of resident purchasers on settlements without properties regularly did part-time work off their holdings.[89]

Though land settlement schemes provided land to smallholders, its ownership drove smallholders to alternatives, if not self-supporting activities. It would be difficult to argue that land settlements resulted in the amelioration of smallholders' and working peoples' economic conditions. No wonder Le Franc concluded that "[L]and policies were never intended to alter to any significant degree the existing distribution of property."[90] Governor Wakefield was correct in contending, however, "that land settlements had tided the country over a very difficult period, and had proved to be a stabilizing influence with the people."[91] At some level they performed a useful function, not least to the economy's formal sectors.

These features notwithstanding, the colonial state also benefitted from these schemes. In spite of frequent tax arrears, land settlements generated government revenue in terms of both monies used to purchase property and taxes subsequently imposed on smallholders. The selling price per acre ranged from £2 to £27, though the modal price was between £2 and £5. Unfortunately data regarding resultant state revenue are unavailable. These revenues might not have been high overall, but land settlement schemes were clearly palliatives designed to augment state control over agricultural production, in particular that of the smallholders' production, if not smallholders' lives. In the cases in which such schemes created owners of land with no capital, they gave something to fall back on, something to bide time while they searched for income elsewhere. There were also cases in which smallholders entered the domestic and international market.

Production for export became a way of life for many, along with the constant search for alternative employment on nearby properties in the towns or even overseas. Smallholders turned to nearby large plantation owners. They became proletarians, independent workers, subsistence farmers or a combination of all of these. When outside work was sufficiently remunerative, they sometimes hired labor on a piecework basis to oversee their small properties, and moved, or did something else.

Working to the Rhythm of Capital

In addition to providing access to land, projects sought to impress upon smallholders the need for new technology. The Farm Improvement Scheme (FIS) and the Farm Development Scheme (FDS) sought to replace "backward" techniques with modern ones. Established in the 1940s and 1950s, and designed to improve the fertility of soils through subsidies of limestone and fertilizers, the FIS and the FDS required farmers to have resources to implement the complex practices required in farm maintenance. These expensive ventures cost roughly 560,000 pounds. Land clearing, drainage, improvement of water supplies and the project administration comprised the bulk of expenditures.[92]

Soil Conservation, barriers	25,000	Contour drains	33,000
Run Off Trenches	8,000	Planting Materials	2,000
Liming	5,000	Phosphates	5,000
Holding improvment/farm bldg	40,000	Water Supplies	70,000

Source: *The Farm Improvement Scheme* (Kingston Ministry of Agriculture, n.d.).
Figures listed are in pounds sterling.

The schemes opened 26,000 acres of partly used and unused land to production of crops such as sugar, bananas, rice and grass; roughly 5,000 of these acres had been fully conserved. In addition, the project provided for the construction of tanks with a combined water holding capacity of 7,000,000 gallons and for 2,150 miles of internal fencing.

Such technology better suited English farms than their Jamaican counterparts. The Jamaican countryside contrasted sharply with that of England. The alkaline composition of Jamaican soil, for example, rendered lime less necessary. Jamaican smallholders did not possess the financial resources required for the scheme's success, and the application was done on an ad hoc basis. When fertilizer could be afforded, it was applied with inadequate soil preparation, due to financial and temporal constraints.[93] Though these schemes ignored land-based working peoples' lack of resources, the FIS laid the basis for similar schemes that would further entrench new technologies the agricultural sector. Six years into the scheme's operation, only 7,259 agricultural holdings (3% of the total) had been issued grants. In 1951 the scheme was phased out, and similar schemes were introduced.

The FDS was implemented from 1955 to 1960 as part of a broader five-year national plan. This scheme intruded more deeply into the lives of smallholders than the FIS. FDS's objective was to help individual farmers with grants, loans and free planting material. It was designed to maintain and expand the production of export crops, to encourage food production and proper land use, to provide sufficient capital for farm financing, to raise productivity and to introduce novel farming techniques.[94] Its accomplishments included land clearing, soil conservation, pasture improvement, the construction and/or repair of farm buildings, the provision of water supplies, the planting of permanent and food crops as well as reforestation.[95]

Bureaucratic in its operation, the implementation of the FDS relied on discussion groups to draw farmers and households into its ambit. D. T. M. Girvan encouraged discussion leaders to study their subjects, to encourage shy participants, and limit the contributions of domineering members; in short he encouraged FDS leaders to do their best "to keep a cheerful and friendly atmosphere where all may feel completely free to express their views or to ask for information."[96] In this way, the FDS linked several agencies to the smallholders' households, and ultimately to state policies. Extension services formulated individual plans and supervised the farm work and subsidy distribution. Parish Development Boards approved the applications of prospective participants. The Agricultural Loan Societies Board and People's Cooperative Banks issued loans to qualified candidates. To ensure loan eligibility, the government passed in 1955 the Facilities for Title Law,[97] enabling farmers to secure title-deeds, a requirement for loans and general assistance. In order to qualify for development funds, farmers' land had to be commodified.

The Scheme aimed first to establish cores of development, and then to extend those cores nationally into a network of modern farms. To this effect, twenty-two pilot areas were established under identical plans. At the end of two years, only about one-third of smallholders were actively involved in the FDS. As a result, the scheme's planners worked only with those farmers determined to "progress," many of them outside of the original pilot areas.

Although development projects touted the elimination of "backwardness," particularly that of small farmers, those granted subsidies were not necessarily of this stratum. Assistance under the scheme was phased out after a "sufficient level of development" had been reached. Due to financial constraints, the comprehensive farm planning was scaled down and redesigned to assist those farmers capable of independent development, granting partial assistance to those who could satisfy the agricultural bureaucracy's requirements.[98] As a result, larger farmers were the scheme's main beneficiaries. Even if such schemes did not co-opt the full support of all targeted smallholders, the institutionalization of modern technologies in the agricultural sector and the introduction of office personnel entailed by such institutions limited the options smallholders could generate autonomously. I do not want to give the impression that the creation of spaces for smallholders to effect their agendas, so-called informality, was a conscious state policy. It may have been one of the unintended consequences of a policy that sought, above all, to modernize agricultural spaces. Ruling elites held steadfastly to the idea that modernization must eliminate backwardness, further evidenced in Rehabilitation and Recovery schemes.

Recovery and Rehabilitation Schemes

Farmers participating in Recovery/Rehabilitation Schemes were encouraged to sustain production with the help of subsidies for soil conservation works and bush clearing. Designated areas of assistance were termed Land Authorities, originally short-term rehabilitating schemes targeting areas considered environmental hazards. While reducing short-term erosion of land through specific cultivation practices, the state further insinuated itself into the production practices of the smallholder.

The Yallahs Valley Land Authority (YVLA) was one such scheme. The YVLA had over 57% smallholders, although together they occupied only 10.5% of total acreage. Participating large farms, on average 317.85 acres, held over 55% of total acreage.[99] But not all participating units were land owners. Two-thirds of all farmers owned the land they farmed, and one-third rented idle or underused land from the owners of properties often several hundred acres in size.

A Board of Directors managed the Yallahs Valley Land Authority Project, regulating land use. Accordingly, "a strong measure of authority was legally feasible with expedient *compulsory reforms* to accomplish a swift improvement of the physical and human degradation existing in 1951."[100] One section of the reforms bound the Land Authority to prepare provisional compulsory improvement schemes for lands within the relevant area. To get people to abide by the regulations, the project offered freehold tenure. Freehold tenure was an interesting contradiction, for, whereas freehold facilitated some degree of small farmer control over the terms of production, the project sought to regulate such autonomy. Indeed, regulation could not have been assured without land ownership or other contractual arrangements. The Facilities for Title Law, passed earlier, did just that, making freehold ownership more accessible to larger numbers of people. Given title deeds to their holdings, they were "encouraged" to cultivate food crops for the domestic market.[101]

The YVLA served as a model for another such scheme, The Christiana Area Land Authority (CALA), established in 1955, and servicing some 10,000 farmers. Like its predecessor, CALA had its beginning in an area dominated by smallholders, 68% of whom were scheme participants. Located on roughly 6,240 acres, the scheme targeted the poorest smallholders, most of whom (40%) had incomes far below the poverty line of 50 pounds per annum.[102]

The project linked state and farmer contractually. The state undertook large-scale tasks such as river training, stream control, grassing, afforestation, and road and water line construction. In return the farmer was expected to follow a set of procedures that guaranteed farm development:

> For each farm to be developed a land capability map is [sic] prepared by the Authority, which forms the basis of a full and comprehensive plan embodying a farming programme for a number of years. Incentives in money, materials and fertilizers are given for establishment of pastures, for soil conservation measures for farm buildings, farm water supplies (tanks) afforestation and establishment of permanent crops. For soil conservation work contour trenches, stone walls, vegetative barriers etc. the subsidy amounts to 75% approved cost with a maximum of 10 pounds per acre. For afforestation 5 pounds per acre plus free planting material is given as a subsidy.[103]

Attempts to reorganize and regulate agricultural production were followed by similar efforts to channel commodities through a state-managed Agricultural Marketing Corporation (A.M.C.). Participating farmers on settlements and schemes had little choice in the matter. When introduced, the A.M.C. was expected to stimulate production throughout shortages and to protect the consumer from high prices and speculators. In times of normal supply, the A.M.C. hoped to maximize farm income and, in times of surplus, to buy and store agricultural commodities.

The A.M.C. had limited credibility among smallholders, as the prices it offered were usually below the market. Later, I show in greater detail that, as a result, smallholders sought to escape the corporation's scrutiny, preferring to sell their produce to higglers (i.e., market women), who sold primarily on the domestic market.

The Other Side of National Development

Attempts to modernize agriculture via new technologies, rehabilitation, and land settlement schemes reinforced a division of labor, through which smallholders maneuvered. By 1968, small holdings had become more numerous, and their properties, less substantial. Conversely, large holdings decreased in number, but increased their share of acreage. Another phenomenon, no less important, was the large-scale migration of smallholders. Jamaica experienced large-scale migration between the early 1940s and early 1970s. Of the 150,000 migrating males 34% (51,000) were formerly engaged in agricultural work.[104] Internal rural-urban migration kept pace with overseas migration, and during this period, the population of the capital city, Kingston, and its environs grew by 12%. The growth of the urban parish of St. Andrew was estimated at 72%.[105] This rural departure was felt in the rural labor markets, insofar as wage laborers became scarce.

Agriculture's share of the labor force contracted in 1960. It dropped from 45% in 1943 to 39% in 1960. The farming population decreased from 900,000 in 1961 to 740,000 in 1968, representing a loss of 18% or roughly 160,000 persons. Reputedly, the number of agricultural workers fell by 37%, or from 262,000 in 1961 to 165,000 in 1968.[106] The contraction was uneven, however. Small farms tended to suffer more from the loss of labor.

The sort of agribusiness seen in Latin America was largely absent, though industrialization, in the form of mining operations, contributed in no small way to the countryside's dislocations and transformations.

Land ownership as a prerequisite of mining operations caused bauxite companies to purchase land feverishly, causing issues in agricultural acreage. Alcan and Reynolds, the two largest bauxite companies, acquired some 136,472 acres from large landowners, most of whom were former penkeepers, representing 5.7% of Jamaica's agricultural land. The average size of these holdings was 291 acres, though many were well above the average. Late comers like Kaiser and Alcan also purchased land from smallholders (detailed elsewhere). The government often reappropriated land from land settlements in order to sell it to such companies. One study posits that nearly all government land settlement schemes released to settlers within the main bauxite region were affected by the bauxite land acquisitions.[107]

One such property in the parish of St. Anne, Tobolski, a leading bauxite site, lost more than 68% of a total of 1,960 acres settlement land by 1959. In the parish of Manchester, another leading bauxite area, on the Chudleigh property approximately 57% of agricultural acreage formerly allotted to smallholders passed to bauxite companies.[108] These acquisitions were of particular import to actual and prospective smallholders, who were compensated by cash and relocation to other parts of the parish. In some cases companies bought land for which they had no immediate mining plans, instead intending to engage tenants in specific types of farming. Sometimes, land formerly held by smallholders was leased back to them, the terms of such leases varying from company to company. According to one researcher:

> Some companies are more lenient in terms of leasing agricultural lands; however, their land use policies are more strict, as well as enforceable. At least one company requires tenants to fully utilize the acreage leased, and the crops planted must be short term. The planting of tree crops . . . is strictly forbidden. . . . The lease-price is usually competitive and the installments must be paid on the due date.[109]

In other words, smallholders held land until the bauxite companies needed it. By 1962, 30% of all lands owned by the Alcan company had such leases. The company supervised land use, but tenants were free to make marketing arrangements.[110]

Smallholders were neither altogether hostile to nor mere victims of these practices. They benefitted from these arrangements in several ways:

> Those farmers who received payments in cash from their transactions invested their money in a variety of ways. The more popular types of investments were house purchase, children's education, farm purchase and improvement, assisting members of families to migrate to England and elsewhere, and especially in the case of small farmers, saving in the local commercial Bank.[111]

Bauxite mining operations displaced many former smallholders. With the exception of those who bought back and/or improved their farms, many were often forced to relocate. In a few cases, resettlement meant moving from agriculture to some other sector. In the community of Schwallenburg, according to one observer, "[T]he lifestyle of the people has shifted from a rural-oriented agricultural one to an urban oriented, semi-proletarian and commercial one."[112]

Most at issue in such developments is not necessarily the unfair situation forced on smallholders, but rather the state's complicity in practices which undermined the very economic stratum it sought to modernize. Though the state created space for smallholders' existence, it did not guarantee that space's existence, nor one's ability to pursue the activities for which that space was intended. Government stipulations led directly to bauxite companies' acquisitions. Regulation attended neither the manner of acquisition, nor subsequent land use. The Bauxite and Alumina (Encouragement) Law of 1950 gave the companies a veritable carte blanche. Section 2 of a subsection stated:

> Mining subject to such condition (that) the total area and fertility and the productivity of the land available in Jamaica for agricultural and pastoral purposes shall not be diminished to any greater extent or for any longer period than can in the opinion of the Commissioner of Mines economically be avoided by the companies for the speedy and full development of the Bauxite/Alumina Industry.[113]

Free from enforceable guidelines, companies applied liberal interpretation to such laws.

The concessions such policies have couched have led some analysts to assume the necessary marginalization of smallholders. Yet marginalization so construed may obscure a crucial point of class transformation, not to mention the state's greater presence in the rural and the agricultural sectors. Many smallholders were transformed from farmers to proletarians, or from a farmer producing mixed crops to one producing pure stands of cash crops. Insofar as they became company tenants, they engaged in new social relations involving capitalist landlords, interested mainly in mining. Far from being marginal, smallholders acceded to new social roles: proletarian, subsistence farmers, even tenants operating on bauxite properties. They could hardly be said to have been marginalized. They had a hand in their own transformation, and their existence was important to the idea of the state. They were central to its vision of a sovereign modern community, considered at once dispensable and indispensable.

Conclusions

How do we comprehend land-based working people in the light of literature that locates them as a separate culture, an authentic folk with rich histories of resistance? Interesting from an academic perspective, this question leads to another: can we talk about ruptures, discontinuities, breaks, or resistance without attempting to understand how social spaces were made and people's experiences, constituted? Can we address fluid historical tendencies without falling into lures of abstractions? Can we discuss the relationship between state and land-based working peoples, without falling prey to oppositional notions, historically and empirically inaccurate? Can we address policies in terms that speak of their productive aspects, using a Foucauldian perspective?

The insinuation of export production and modernization into society's "backward" sectors characterizes Jamaica's late-colonial and early postcolonial eras. It was a critical process that fostered a deep penetration of the state into the lives of smallholders, and one that disturbed the ways in which smallholders eked out livelihoods. Processes of informalization attended this formalization. Consequently, land settlement projects and modernization schemes invited their own failures. In the colonial period, land settlements were implemented reluctantly, in lieu of state and plantation employment. During the protonationalist and nationalist phase, such settlements were linked to the development part of decolonization. In the age of industrialization, smallholders were seen as needing the tutelage of the state, and, under state leadership, were forced to produce in ways which officials argued could benefit all involved. Insufficient land without capital frequently led to part-time agriculture. Modernization schemes co-opted small-farm production, bringing smallholder operations within the purview of the state. The shortcomings of such schemes forced smallholders to seek supplemental employment. As aspects of smallholders' lives became governmentalized, as a result of informalization, others became more free, perhaps more negotiable. Formalization and informalization are dual tendencies of a single process, that of "modernization" and "developmentalism."

The political-economic elite were not the only members of society to consider development beneficial. As many have shown, industrialization's power to draw third world countries into the West's idea of the modern world is indeed persuasive.[114] As elitist as such development may appear in practice, its advocates were widespread among members of the incipient black middle classes and intelligentsia. So politicized had life become under late-colonial rule, that the eradication of that rule was linked not only to the capture of state power, but also to development, prosperity and nation-building. Protonationalists equated colonial rule with the stunting of the island's development potential. Judging from the general desire for development, many shared the notion. Even radicals who wanted things differently, advocated state-led development, though of a socialist type.

Although development models were propagated by international agencies, they found ready support among a political and economic elite forged in the fires of anticolonialism with masters' tools. Bryan argues that the late nineteenth century saw both the masses and its leaders joined in support of the empire. The Jamaican people supported the empire, even as they resisted its instruments, namely Crown Colony rule. They believed, like Manley, that they were masters of a destiny linked inextricably to the empire. Jamaica's independence was necessary. As Manley formulated it in one of many speeches on the importance of self-government:

> And since that empire is still the depository of ideas which admit the
> rights of subject peoples we may be glad of the connection. That is the

loyalty of commonsense. If the current idealism of colonial political
thought in England is sincere, then we are by our policy merely translating into working terms in which to express our own duties and responsibilities the ideas which on the side of our rulers are summed up
in the phrase, 'colonies are a trust,' and in the often repeated assertion
that the aim of British rule is to assist *backward* peoples to achieve self-
government and a national status as quickly as can be.[115]

To the extent that the Jamaican populace was sold on ideas of decolonization and
development, this period represents a hegemonic phase of nationalists' rule. According to Stone:

> The party leaders allocated patronage benefits to all classes and guar-
> anteed mass legitimacy to the state through party support and welfare
> pork barrel politics. They mystified the masses with charismatic ma-
> nipulation and outpourings of propaganda which played on their ex-
> pectations while constantly promising to administer the system on
> their behalf. These symbolic assurances (millenarian and utopian in
> the case of the PNP and pragmatic in the case of the JLP), comple-
> mented by the use of revenue to allocate marginal benefits to the
> poor, incorporated the masses into the state system.[116]

Stone's somewhat narrow notion of false consciousness and ideological mystifi-
cation aside, the pact between state and society (or at least significant sections of
it) was severely strained by the late 1960s. New ideas about sovereignty, culture,
and development surfaced in the 1970s. The Jamaican people reaped the bitter
fruits of development by benevolent edict. Manley's statement that his generation's mission was to attain self-government was a truism, which highlighted that
generation's complicity in development. There was little to separate processes of
decolonization from development. They were but two sides of the same coin,
and they shared a common space in the collective imagination. "Backwardness"
had been reconstituted, under different conditions, and the working peoples'
plight would be taken up by the next generation of political leaders.

Between 1940 and 1972 the smallholder sector was often being remade,
through dislocation and transformation, and despite the plots many acquired.[117]
Development and decolonization did not seriously disturb the social order, but
preserved it. Under the nationalists, both smallholder production and smallholders' lives became woven into the imperatives of export production, surrounded by the bureaucracy. Even as a multidirectional stratum of multiple origins, smallholders were involved with development policy. Jamaican
smallholders discovered that the state's reach was binding. If many land-based
working people straddled different temporalities occasioned by responses to capitalist production, so did the state, though its managers strived for uniformity.

Political elites had to respond to these divergent structures, emerged as a result of modernization policies. As we shall see in the following chapter, the governing regime continued to reconstitute smallholder production in the context of an advanced notion of citizenship, and in a postnationalist era, seeking to recover the project of decolonization, though in a changed world, where the decoupling of state and nation, the most abiding feature of postcoloniality, was rapidly becoming the norm.

Notes

1. Norman Manley in his final address, "Farewell to Jamaica Welfare (1943) Ltd.," on the occasion of the transition of the Jamaica Welfare to the JLP government-managed Jamaica Social Welfare Commission. In Norman Girvan ed., *Working Together For Development: D. T.M. Girvan on Cooperatives and Community Development 1939–1968* (Kingston: Institute of Jamaica Publications Limited, 1993).

2. Nancy Foner, *Status and Power in Rural Jamaica: A Study of Educational and Political Change* (New York and London: Teachers College Press, 1973), 125–126.

3. Michael G. Smith, *The Plural Society in the British West Indies* (Berkeley: University of California Press, 1965).

4. Obika Gray, *Radicalism and Social Change in Jamaica, 1960–1972* (Tennessee: University of Tennessee Press, 1991).

5. What I am referring to here is the fact that small farmers, those owning less than 5 acres, produced export crops, but with paltry resources. I do not want to refer to them as petty commodity producers, because I think the latter is an analytical concept that marks a kind of transitory phase to capitalist farmer.

6. I make reference to these various writings throughout the text.

7. Rex Nettleford, *Manley and the Politics of Jamaica: Towards and Analysis of Political Change in Jamaica, 1938–1968* (Kingston: Institute of Social and Economic Research, University of the West Indies, 1971), 1.

8. Bustamante won the 1944 and the 1949 elections. Manley won the 1955 election, but lost the election that would have made him the first postcolonial leader of Jamaica in 1962, when the island attained independence.

9. Nettleford (1971) comments that "By 1964, the PNP in opposition was forced to contemplate a new look so as to present to the country a real alternative to the JLP, so close had the policies of both parties become." 324.

10. Nettleford op. cit., xliv.

11. Ibid., 365.

12. Ibid., 98.

13. Ibid., 107.

14. Ibid., 197.

15. Ibid.

16. The search for "working class" agency cannot be underrated, but when it is construed so narrowly deals abstractly with the notion of experience, insofar as it overlooks

experience as social process, the changing terrain upon which such processes are grounded and ends up obscuring the influences that development orientations advanced by the state, had on shaping working peoples' experiences, shaping their responses to them.

17. Governor Sir Henry Blake's presentation in *Journal of the Agricultural Society*, 2 (December 28, 1895), 45.

18. For example in 1910, there were 500 direct members, 63 branches with 3,500 members and 11 instructors. In 1935, just 25 years later, there were 727 direct members, 298 branches with 6,841 members and 21 instructors. See C. Hoyte, *History of the Jamaica Agricultural Society 1895 to 1960* (Kingston: Jamaica Agricultural Society, n.d.).

19. W. Marshall, "Peasant Movements and Agricultural problems in the West Indies," *Caribbean Quarterly* (1972), 1.

20. Stated in the Association's 75th Anniversary Issue. *Journal of the Agricultural Society?The 75th Anniversary*, 20.

21. Ibid.

22. Ibid., 28. Also Norman Girvan compiler and ed., *Working Together for Development D.T.M. Girvan* (Kingston Jamaica: Institute of Jamaica Publications, 1993), 304.

23. Norman Girvan (1993), 304.

24. Ibid., 312.

25. Ibid.

26. *Journal of the Agricultural Society* (May 1975), 28.

27. Nancy Foner, *Status and Power in Rural Jamaica: A Study of Educational and Political Change* (New York: Teachers College Press, 1973). For example, Foner cites the case of the head of the PNP office, a medium farmer with 25 acres of land inherited from his father, who had been considered a big farmer. Not only was this medium farmer well placed as head of various schemes and societies, such as the J.A.S. and the Burial Scheme society, but so too were the rest of his family; his brothers and his children were also respectable members of the rural middle class. On the other hand, the head of the JLP branch was a small unsuccessful farmer, unable to command the respect of his political and social colleagues.

28. Foner (1973), 114.

29. Ibid. See especially chapter 11.

30. Jamaica's motto since 1962.

31. In Manley's words: "The proposal was that the United Fruit Co. Would set aside one cent per stem exported from Jamaica to form a fund to be administered by an organization to be created by me for the good and welfare of the people of Jamaica, with emphasis on the rural people. This would mean, as things then stood, some 25,000,000 cents or 250,000 dollars nearly £80,000 annually."

32. Pansy Rae Hart, "To build a new Jamaica," *Jamaica Journal* 25, 1 (1993): 30–33, 31.

33. In Pansy Rae Hart's account. She herself was handpicked as was D. T. M. Girvan.

34. Hart (1993) writes, "Many years later, the Secretary of Jamaica Welfare, R.H. Fletcher, passed on to me recommendations of which I had been unaware. Handwritten on a compliments slip from the law firm Manton & Hart were the words: 'Dear Norman: What do you think of Pansy for one of the jobs that seem to arise in J.W. Ltd? She seems so efficient that it seems a pity her services can't be used. Yrs. Ansell.' Below this

appears in another handwriting, 'Have told Fletcher long ago that she should have next vacancy. She will do I feel sure v. well and take a live interest. NWM,'" 30.

35. Sybil Francis, "The Evolution of Community Development in Jamaica (1937–1962). *Caribbean Quarterly* 5, 2 & 3 (1969): 40–58, 44.

36. Ibid.

37. The notion of civilized and civilizing Jamaica was a constant refrain uttered from Welfare's leadership and volunteer service people.

38. Welfare Reporter 1942, quoted in Pansy Rae Hart (1993), 32.

39. Norman Girvan (1993), 230.

40. Sybil Francis (1969), 49.

41. "The Welfare Reporter" circa 1947, quoted in Norman Girvan (1993), 261.

42. Sybil Francis (1969) and from personal interview of Ms. Francis on July 22nd, 1997, 46.

43. Ibid.

44. Interview and Francis (1969), 52.

45. There was a good deal of rancor over this. As the chief minister, Alexander Busta-mante accused the organization of being strongly influenced by the politics of its chair, Norman Manley, then leader of the opposition party, the Peoples National Party. See Manley's response to this in the *Welfare Reporter* which carried his farewell speech, "Farewell to Jamaica Welfare" in Norman Girvan (1993), 240.

46. Sybil Francis (1969), 50, 51.

47. Sybil Francis (1969), 53.

48. Ibid., 54.

49. Ibid.

50. Horace Levy, "Jamaica Welfare Growth and Decline," *Social and Economic Studies* 44, nos. 2 & 3 (1995): 349–357.

51. Given the social decay that was then rampant in inner-city communities, urban Jamaica received consideration as well,.

52. *Social Development Commission: Programmes for Social Growth 1943–1981*, n.d., 148.

53. Ibid., 152.

54. Said Manley in a speech on the night of his election to office, in 1955, announcing agricultural plans for agriculture which entailed this slogan. Nettleford op. cit., 198.

55. Nettleford, 206.

56. Ibid., 199.

57. Norman Girvan, *Foreign Capital and Economic Underdevelopment in Jamaica* (Kingston: Institute of Social and Economic Research, 1971), 101. Also G. Eisner, *Jamaica 1830–1930. A Study in Economic Growth* (Manchester: Manchester University Press, 1961), 287.

58. Stanley Reid, "An Introductory Approach to the Concentration of Power in the Jamaican Corporate Economy," *Essays on Power and Change in Jamaica* (Kingston: Herald Press, 1976), 15–44, 28, 29.

59. Ibid.

60. O. Jefferson (1972), 151.

61. *A National Plan for Jamaica 1957–1967* (Kingston: Government Printer), 118.

62. Ibid.

63. *A National Plan for Jamaica 1957–67*, 220.

64. N. Girvan, (1971), 117.

65. Ibid.

66. *Economic and Social Survey of Jamaica* (Ministry of Planning: Govt. Printer), 102.

67. Ibid.

68. *West India Royal Commission. Report and Recommendations 1938–1939*, 20.

69. Ibid., 24.

70. For a more detailed discussion see *Report of the Agricultural Policy Committee 1945*. (Kingston: Government Printer).

71. Irving Johnson, M. Strachan, Joseph Johnson, "A Review of Land Settlement in Jamaica," In *Proceedings of the 7th West Indian Agricultural Economics Conference*, Grand Anse, Grenada, April 9–15. (St. Augustine: Trinidad, 1972), 4.

72. Ibid.

73. Government of Jamaica, "Land Reform in Jamaica with emphasis on Land Settlement" (Kingston: Ministry of Agricultural and Lands, 1962).

74. The Economic Organisation of Small Scale Farming, based on Banana, Coconut and Cocoa-Highgate Area, St. Mary, 1958–1959, ii.

75. Ibid.

76. *The Economic Organisation of Small Scale Farming*, 53–54.

77. Ibid., 54–55.

78. Ibid., 49–50.

79. Ibid., 60.

80. Ibid., 69.

81. Discussion of aspects of this paradox are seen in Michaeline A. Crichlow, "Reconfiguring the "Informal Economy" Divide: State, Capitalism, and Struggle in Trinidad and Tobago," *Latin American Perspectives* 99, 25 no. 2, (March 1998): 62–83.

82. See for example, Dipak Mazumdar, "The Urban Informal Economy," *World Development* 4, 8 (1976): 655–679; Alejandro Portes, "The Informal Sector: Definition, Controversy and Relation to National Development," Review VII, 1 (Summer 1983): 151–174. Also Alejandro Portes and L. Benton, "Industrial Development and Labor Absorption: A Reinterpretation," *Population and Development Review* 10, 4 (December 1984): 589–611. I review much of this literature in M. Crichlow (1998).

83. Paul Redwood, *A Statistical Survey of Government Land Settlements in Jamaica B.W.I. 1929–1949* (Kingston: Government Printer, 1945).

84. *Agricultural Policy Committee of Jamaica 1945* (Kingston: Government Printer), 9.

85. P. Redwood (1945), 8.

86. Ibid., 10.

87. Ibid., 11.

88. Or 57,255 acres. Ibid., 13.

89. Ibid.

90. E. Le Franc, "Peasants and Community in Jamaica," (Ph.D. diss., Yale University, 1974).

91. *The Wakefield Report* (London: HMSO, 1941).

92. Administration   17,000 [pounds] Land Clearing   80,000

93. Ibid.

94. G. J. Kruijer and A. Nuis, *Farm Development Scheme 1955–1960. A Report on an Evaluation.First Plan* (Kingston: Ministry of Agriculture, 1955).

95. The estimated total expenditure of the scheme was 850,000 pounds contributed by the Colonial development and Welfare Fund; the remaining 102,300 was provided by the local administration.

96. Norman Girvan (1993) D. T. M. Girvan, 313.

97. Manley elaborates on this process whereby land becomes commodified. See Nettleford (1971), 208.

98. Ibid.

99. G. J. Kruijer and A. Nuis (1955), 12–14.

100. Barry N. Floyd, *Agricultural Innovation in Jamaica: The Yallahs Valley Land Authority.* Occasional Publication No.4 (University of the West Indies, Jamaica: Department of Geography, 1969), 14.

101. The YVLA regularized tenurial patterns by recognizing leaseholders and offering them the prospect of becoming freeholders of land, providing they adhered to the practices of improved land husbandry being promoted by the Authority. See Floyd (1969), *Agricultural Innovation in Jamaica*, 12.

102. G. J. Kruijer, *Sociological Report on the Christiana Area* (Kingston: Ministry of Agriculture and Fisheries, 1969), vii.

103. Ibid., viii.

104. O. Jefferson (1972), 14.

105. Ibid.

106. Ibid.

107. Michael Salmon, "The impact of Bauxite Alumina: Land Utilization within Jamaica's Bauxite Land Economy after the emergence of the Bauxite Alumina Industry," mss. (Mona: Institute of Social and Economic Research, 1983), 47–48. Subsequently published as "Land Utilization within Jamaica's Bauxite Land Economy," *Social and Economic Studies* 36, no.1 (March 1987): 57–92.

108. Ibid.

109. Roy Russell, "The impact of the Bauxite Alumina Multinational Corporations on Rural Economy and Society in Jamaica: A Survey of Farmers in Five selected Bauxite Mining Areas," mss. (Mona: Institute of Social and Economic Research, 1982), 24.

110. Ibid.

111. Ibid.

112. Michael Salmon (1983), 74.

113. Noel Cowell, "The Impact of the Bauxite Mining on Peasant and Community Relations in Jamaica," *Social and Economic Studies* 36, no.1 (March 1987): 171–216, 208

114. Michael Salmon (1983), 51.

115. Nettleford (1971), 101.

116. Carl Stone (1983a), 53.

117. Carl Stone (1983a), 55.

CHAPTER 4

In the Name of the "Small Man": "Heavy Manners" and the Creation of New Subjectivities

Even those who opposed the prevailing capitalist strategies were obliged to couch their critique in terms of the need for development, through concepts such as "another development," "participatory development," "socialist development," and the like. In short, one could criticize a given approach and propose modifications or improvements accordingly, but the fact of development itself, and the need for it, could not be doubted. Development had achieved the status of a certainty in the social imaginary.[1]

It seems to me, then, that from the point of view of the postcolonial present there is a more important story to be told than the story of the *ideological* rivalry between the Left and the liberals in the Jamaican nationalist movement. This would be a story in which the Left and the liberals constitute not the irreconcilable polarities that they appear to be in Robotham's betrayal narrative, but rather competing ideological moments in what is in fact a *common* secular-modernization project. If in the Left's betrayal narrative the imagined community of the nation is pictured as an embattled space of class interests, class struggle, class conflict, and class complicities, in the story of the making (and unmaking) of the secular-modernization project what is at stake is the *rationality* through which the construction of the moral and political order of the postcolonial state was imagined and pursued. The Left and the liberals shared the *ground* of this rationality.[2]

Introduction

During the 1970s, it appeared that a new project of reconstituting the idea of the independent citizen got underway in Jamaica, with the ascension to office of the Democratic Socialist Michael Manley. New laws instituted sought to unsilence and recognize the sociocultural practices of the ordinary citizen, or the "small man," as he/she was referred to. Both the state and citizens sought to renew the pact that they had more or less made about development and its benefits for realizing democratic citizenship. Under a generalized land reform project, members of the Democratic Socialist state sought ostensibly to undo the exploitative conditions affecting land-based working people and others, including the unemployed and youth. Land-reform policy entailed the establishment of sugar cooperatives, state farms and land-lease programs. Implemented on behalf of the "small man," the rhetoric accompanying these efforts belied the authoritarian approach that marked their operationalization. Though of a leftist bent, these strategies linked the left and the right in the assumptions which they made about modernization and development, marking the extent to which the development imaginary pervaded the policies and politics of many of different ideological persuasions, as Arturo Escobar and David Scott observed. In Jamaica both the left and right were agreed on the need to operate on behalf of the "underprivileged," and that development would provide a better future. Both underestimated the ability of "suffers," or "backward" working people to forge strategies of their own making. Both the left and the right believed in modernization's claims toward the inevitability of a brighter tomorrow. Moreover, the Democratic Socialist state laid the foundations for even more informalization within the time-spaces of the agricultural sector and the economy as a whole, the effect of which was the subversion of the very institutional structures by those who were its targets, even as reform policies secured more state leverage in the countryside.

The 1972 election was crucial for the JLP ruling administration and the opposition PNP, for by the late 1960s, the island's socioeconomic crisis had deepened. The most popular song of 1968, "Everything Crash," ridiculed the breakdown of social services, as well as the strikes that followed. In response to such public sentiment the JLP's 1972 electoral campaign emphasized the administration's many accomplishments, though the need for land and agricultural reform, in the face of declining agricultural production, had already unglued the pact between the state and significant elements within the nonstate arena. Compared to the JLP, the PNP offered a new kind of economic and social development, state acknowledgment and promotion of popular culture, the promise of a moral renewal and people's participation in the affairs of the state.[3]

Citizenship in a "new Jamaica" entailed an open relationship with the state and participation in development initiatives. Such self-reliance was a touchstone of the new policy, not merely autarchy, as Manley wrote, but "a matter of emphasis; it calls for bending every effort of will, ingenuity and planning into, first, doing everything for ourselves that we possibly can; and second, getting maximum benefit from what we can do by doing it as efficiently as possible."[4] Such initiatives made a new kind of subjectivity possible—one through which the State could impart a technology of rule and culture.

Scott's text on the tragedy of state-planned development highlights the aesthetics of orderliness involved in such policy. He shows that these projects emanate from ideas developed outside of the context of the local populations' customs, desires and rationales. Scott sees large-scale state efforts at transformation as an "attempt at domestication, a kind of social gardening devised to make the countryside, its products, and its inhabitants more readily identifiable and accessible to the center."[5] Scott sees state-devised projects as coercive strategies designed to bring about order and to implement controls, sometimes in areas where none such existed before. The Tanzanian Ujamaa village experiment that lasted from 1973 to 1976, one such scheme, succeeded in displacing large numbers of peasants through compulsory villagization. The scheme emanated from anticapitalist, pro-communal ideology and promoted African traditions considered beneficial, but on the decline. The Ujamaa project was the result, in Scott's words, of a "benevolent, poor and weak state" seeking to inculcate cooperative values into the rural sector. The difference between the Tanzanian situation and the Jamaican one, was that the Jamaican targets were not settled populations of landowners herded into planned spaces; also the vocabulary or desire of social change was not propounded only by political and state elites. The concept of "heavy manners," referring to "discipline," was espoused in popular song and interwoven in everyday oral expressions, suggesting a tacit agreement between state and working peoples.[6] At some level Jamaican working peoples willingly submitted to the state's institution of "heavy manners" as the price for securing jobs and for other socioeconomic benefits. The people saw themselves as inflictors of "heavy manners" on the opposition. It cannot be said that any of the four elements, which Scott cites as necessary combinations for "full-fledged disaster" (the administrative ordering of nature and society, a high modernist ideology, an authoritarian state, and a prostrate civil society lacking resistant capacity), obtained in Jamaica.[7] Gathering popular opinion and the setting up of task forces proved to be efforts ostensibly to include but which in their application, mask the state's authoritarian approach to socioeconomic reforms.

Though the envisaged development required state leadership, regular consultation with the people from relevant sectors was to guarantee the public "a part to play in the decision-making processes of government."[8] Manley's elaboration of the interplay between institutions and government elucidated the strategy's operation. Dialogue with private sector leaders was one effective safeguard against derailing government programs. Such dialogue was to prevent misunderstanding and confusion. Manley's ideas deserve to be quoted at length, for they emphasize how state authority needs to address development:

> [O]ne must build into all the planning mechanisms of government an element of institutional participation. For example, an economic planning council must be supported by advisory committees in which the politician, the government technician and the relevant institutional leadership meet regularly to discuss and plan. This gives to a government the opportunity to explain to sectoral leaders problems that arise from a total view of the nation's situation as well as the part which a particular sector is expected to play in the drive for overall national objectives. Equally, the leaders of a sector have an opportunity to explain their particular difficulties and to feel that their worth as contributors to the total national effort is recognized. An important by-product of the entire process is that it challenges sectoral leadership to focus its attention upon creative initiatives as well as immediate problems. This, then, is the method of involvement which must extend to education and teachers, health services and doctors and so on throughout the system.[']

To Scott's discussion of high modernist projects implemented by authoritarian states could be added those projects of development that arise out of popular electoral consent, but are implemented in a high-handed fashion that undermines the very processes of consensus that they seek. In more democratic postcolonial polities like Jamaica, authoritarianism, a colonial condition still pervasive throughout state institutions, like the large civil service, gains new life in people's everyday interactions, and so is always present, but masks itself within discourses of the right and left, which project both state and nonstate (e.g., nongovernmental organizations) as acting on behalf of downtrodden "sufferers." "Seeing like a state" is not only a symptom of the states Scott describes. The sharing of authoritarian identities between people and state works largely against "sufferers," who are usually on its receiving end, and who invariably expect higher levels of inclusion. One may, like many poststructuralists writing on development, question the extent to which development emerging from within a certain ideological context can escape that context, to allow for exceptional reforms. Consider Scott's statement that the high modernist project was not in itself dangerous: "where it animated plans in liberal parliamentary societies and where planners therefore had to negotiate with organized citizens, it could spur reform."[10]

In liberal parliamentary societies, such as Jamaica, even well-intentioned leftist academics assumed authoritarian postures in submission to the popular state's demands. The abstract assumptions of development plans took prominence over the search for local knowledge, though the rhetoric assumed a connection with the "small man." Though not overtly guided by a high modernist ideology, the social engineering that underlaid these projects involved a material cultural transformation of a low modernist kind, designed to reorder working peoples' lifestyles and reconstitute subjectivities in ways that agreed with the transition to Democratic Socialism, as the state and its well-meaning advisors saw fit. Consider the rationale that underlay the "Peoples Production Plan" a technique devised by Jamaican leftist academics in response to the crisis of the Jamaican state in the 1970s. The planners sought to link what they identified as the immediate needs of the country with strategies for returning "power to the people" at the level of the community in accordance with the principles of Democratic Socialism, the ideology through which the needs of the country and citizens' responsibilities were identified:

> [I]t should be clear that this plan is informed and guided by a particular ideological orientation. [T]his orientation is the government's commitment to the principles embraced by the ideology of democratic socialism. To write a plan under the guidance of an ideology means that by definition the planners themselves could not adopt the traditional bureaucratic posture of neutrality and non-commitment. Their own orientation has to be positively in tune with that of the government whose directives they are trying to concretise.[11]

The idea was to incorporate popular opinion into the national plan. The plan determined the importance and place of such opinion according to the principles of Democratic Socialism. Essentially the work of academics, and technocrats, the Plan's critical subtext lay in strengthening the role of the state in people's lives. To do so, it placed a lot of emphasis on Community Enterprise Organizations (CEOs) seeing them as pivotal to the implementation of projects. In other words, the CEOs were the designated brokers between capital, the state and the populace.

Participatory politics necessitated a rehabilitated state with renewed links to those many Jamaicans who had registered their discontent about the social order and the state's role in its perpetuation.

Edwards notes that in the "roots and culture" genre of reggae:

> [E]lite notions about the nation, nationality, citizen-ship, and democracy, are undermined by reggae critiques that are grounded in the unresolved questions of race, class, colour, slavery, imperialism, colonialism and neocolonialism. In these reggae songs, the state is not a liberal democratic entity but rather an oppressive regime: a Babylon system, a state of emergency, and a product of crisis that also produces crises for the poor and oppressed who are described as living in

an embattled state of siege, harassed and brutalized by the representatives of Babylon (the police and the military), subjected to road-
blocks, curfews, imprisonment, and myriad forms of daily dehuman-
ization.[12]

Against the backdrop of social disorder and discontent, the PNP received an
unprecedented mandate in the 1972 election. The party won 37 seats of 53 contested seats, giving it 53% of the vote. The PNP's mandate was passed on in its
promise to restructure the state's relationship to the discontented, underprivileged, expectant Jamaicans, as stated by Manley, the PNP's leader, "to make government the beneficiary of institutional advice and responsive to the popular
need."[13] This politics of participation had as its strategy, "communication and
dialogue, its methods involvement, its purpose mobilization."[14] The goal of the
"politics of change" was an egalitarian society, that is a restructuring of class relations, land reform, a revision of the meaning of citizenship, and the incorporation of certain popular cultural practices, particularly those associated with Jamaica's African heritage. The PNP electoral strategy had already incorporated a
number of symbolisms connected with Afro-Jamaicans, the largest segment of
Jamaican society. Effecting such broad social agendas necessitated the creation of
wealth. Manley noted that the pursuit of a more equitable distribution of wealth
required the development of society's productive forces. That the production of
wealth depended on economic production made no less necessary the transformation of the "major institutions of democracy."

Participatory politics required that the state expand and assume responsibility for and control of the "commanding heights" of the economy. Declaring itself "Democratic Socialist," the regime rationalized the nationalization of foreign
companies and joint public ownership with private enterprise, thereby restructuring agreements with foreign companies doing business on the island. Land reform policy received immediate attention, with smallholders as its primary beneficiaries. Enterprises designed to increase food production implemented
agricultural policy, often creating new problems without having solved old ones.

The new agricultural enterprises were forced to operate beset by both the
rhetoric of democratization as enunciated variously by leftists within and outside
of the PNP and the resistance of an entrenched civil service. Within this fray,
new sets of social relations brought elements of the state into closer, tense contact with the rural working peoples. It could be argued that both national government and working peoples shared a common perspective about development,
however alternative. As Escobar argued in the epigraph above, "Development
had achieved the status of a certainty in the social imaginary.[15] Even so, divisions
between ideologues and administrators and technocrats, between clientilistic
(patron-client) politics and the growing economic crisis threatened the fragile,
new social pact.

Much literature has been generated about the politics of the 1970s. Several analysts have commented upon the appropriateness or inappropriateness of the government's ideological "swing to the left,"[16] judged according to the analyst's support for a certain political format of developmental change. I am interested in exploring the "common secular-modernization project," which the left and the liberals shared in the 1970s. In this instance, the modernization project imagined working people participating fully in agricultural projects not of their own making, but formulated and activated by the state, manned for the most part by left-leaning technocrats, who believed Democratic Socialism to be the path to Socialism. Many have treated these first-time programs as sufficient evidence of state radicalism. Yet those who have analyzed these schemes stress their failures and mismanagement and chronicle the nature and frequency of participants' discontent.[17] Rarely discussed is how these schemes, radical in form, nonetheless assumed a liberal approach that viewed the agricultural sector, including its working people, as backward and in need of leadership. Despite their radicalism, development projects were cut from the same cloth as those of previous regimes. It was no wonder that left-leaning officials were unable to undermine the elitist way in which resources were distributed, ultimately succeeding in reinforcing the view that working peoples of Jamaica lacked appropriate agency or, in more popular parlance, organic socialist initiative.

Having said this, I would like to reiterate that the agricultural enterprises of the 1970s were a radical break from earlier schemes and programs of the colonial and early postcolonial periods, for they fostered a new kind of subjectivity. Mired in bureaucracy, like their 1960s predecessors, smallholder production was regulated in ways affording greater control to a state whose leaders promised substantive independence and an alternative kind of socialist development, guaranteeing more high-quality benefits to a larger number of underprivileged Jamaican working peoples. The government delivered neither, but succeeded, as Ferguson observed for Lesotho, in extending the lines of rural and urban Jamaicans beholden to a weakened state for their well-being, citizens who became in time even more resistant to the state's middle-class value system.

Domestic Background of New State Policy

Domestic economic and social crises precipitated the PNP's victory. Unemployment had risen from 13% in 1962 to 24% in 1972. Income distribution had grown increasingly skewed. The share of income of the poorest 40% of the population dropped from 7.2% to 5.4% between 1958 and 1968.[18] The income of the poorest 30% of the population fell from J$32 to J$25 per capita in constant 1958 dollars. In 1962, some 60% of the labor force was earning less than J$20 per week.[19]

Class and racial inequality had also sharpened, exacerbated by the racial turmoil of 1965, which resulted in the looting and burning of several Chinese businesses in the city. In 1968, the government banning of Walter Rodney, a University lecturer,[20] precipitated another series of riots. Violent crimes increased from 152 in 1964 to 457 in 1967.[21]

The rise of nationalist groups and movements such as the Rastafarians, or the radical Marxist bent of the intelligentsia comprising faculty and students at the University of the West Indies (UWI), illustrated the extent of the discontent and the need for change. The kind of development promoted by "Industrialization by Invitation" had already disillusioned large segments of the poor. The cry for Black Power was not simply an echo of the Civil Rights movement in the U.S., but rather it illuminated the racial basis of an ineffective, derailed decolonization process. As Lewis recalls, the black consciousness movement had already gained momentum by the time the PNP was ushered into office. Urban Kingston was alive with the presence of various leftist groups, espousing nationalist or socialist sentiments.[22] A political space for something different from the Norman Manley form of Nationalism was opening up for such collectives as *Abeng*, a loose grouping of more or less leftist people, including a significant number of those once with the PNP. According to Lewis, *Abeng* with its disparate leftist elements fed into the PNP via many currents: Rastafarianism, Socialism, and Jamesian (C.L.R. James) perspectives. But, "the dominant current in *Abeng* was a Jamaican nationalist radicalism. It wasn't *black* nationalism, because it involved the Rousseaus, it involved Dennis Sloley, people who were involved in the effort to come to grips with how Jamaica could be renovated, how Jamaica could be changed, and these broad groups were all part of it."[23] As Lewis put it, "Michael Manley feeds into this as he feeds into every aspect and every area of Jamaican social and political life to renew the People's National Party. So at the time that you are discussing the future of *Abeng*, the People's National Party's leader-to-be and the person who becomes the leader, is seeking new blood, and goes after it aggressively for the People's National Party."[24]

Riding this wave of protest, disenchantment and political optimism, the populist PNP entered office on the slogan "Better must come," aiming to place the state in the employ of ordinary Jamaicans. Like the nationalist appeal of the previous era its populism did not conjure images of a deadly backward oligarchy as did populist regimes of Latin America.[25] Instead, its populism emerged in the context of the nationalist dream's fracturing, linking sovereignty and a certain regime of development with the well-being of the Jamaican working people. In the spirit of Laclau's understanding of populism, the PNP was a populist multiclass movement that sought to exert its hegemony "not so much to the extent that it is able to impose a uniform conception of the world on the rest of society, but to the extent that it can articulate different visions of the world in such a way that their potential antagonism is neutralized."[26]

The PNP party leadership aimed to make the state work on behalf of ordinary Jamaicans. Democratic Socialism, the anti-imperialist movement, and the language of Third World nationalism legitimized its program of social and economic reform. 1972–1980 contained a phase of classic reformism, in which the national government strengthened its bureaucratic structures, even as it endeavored to create the perception of incorporating the marginalized in its corridors. Public institutions (e.g., parastatal agencies) oversaw the process of capital accumulation. What were the main economic forms through which the state led the capital accumulation process? What new cultural forms emerged in the agricultural sector, and how did they in turn affect or reinforce the state's presence there? First, let me review the general thrust of socioeconomic change, for it provides a useful context for analyzing specific agricultural and land reforms undertaken during the 1970s, and illustrates the ways in which state officials were able to incorporate the wishes of the Jamaican working peoples, giving the impression that power was being shared with them, when in fact this was hardly the case.

Between 1972 and 1980 the PNP administration instituted a series of popular reforms designed to alleviate glaring social problems. Both these programs and the zeal with which they were carried out rehabilitated the national government, if not the state, as an instrument and arbiter of development. As never before, ordinary Jamaicans felt themselves participants in the process of change.

Table 4.1 illustrates a sense of the enormity and character of the reforms implemented by the government. The intended beneficiary was, as Beckford would say, the "small man."

Table 4.1.   Programs Initiated under, or Expanded between 1972–1980

Programme	Target
Special Employment Programme	Unemployed
Operation Grow	Landless
Food Subsidies	Landless
Free Secondary and University Education	Poor
Establishment of Women's Bureau; Equal Pay Act	Women
Farmers Development Programme	Small Farmers
Enactment of a National Minimum Wage	Menial Labour
Establishment of Sugar Cooperatives	Sugar Workers
Nationalisation of Bauxite Companies	All Classes
Establishment of a State Trading Corporation	National
Establishment of a Literacy Programme	Illiterate
Establishment of a National Commercial Bank	National
Construction of Small Industries Complexes	Small Business
Establishment of Worker Participation	All Workers

Source: Adapted from N. Girvan et al, "The IMF and the Third World: The Case of Jamaica, 1974–1980," *Development Dialogue* no. 2 (reprint from 1980), 117.

In 1974 and 1975, the government acquired 75% of the local telephone company, the capital, Kingston's, bus company, Barclays Bank and about 30% of resort hotel capacity. A public fund was instituted for housing construction.[27] These programs, particularly those associated with state ownership, along with statements of the party's far left-wing elements, earned for the PNP its communist label. In response the PNP argued that it favored a mixed economy whereby:

> Certain sectors are owned and controlled by the State; other sectors are owned and dominated by the traditional private sector, small businesses and cooperatives; and others are shared between the State and private organisations. Such an economic organisation implies that the State will provide opportunities for private enterprises to earn profits and rewards which are equitable and reasonable and where appropriate, provide incentives and government support to encourage desirable enterprises.[28]

This pursuit of greater political sovereignty was best exemplified by the government's relations with bauxite companies. Upon the recommendations of the National Bauxite Commission the PNP government sought to repatriate idle lands owned by the companies, acquire 51% ownership in the companies' mining operations, establish the Jamaica Bauxite Institute (JBI), use the JBI's influence in the nonaligned bauxite-producing world to support the formation of a cartel, the International Bauxite Association (IBA), and develop a smelter complex in cooperation with Mexico and Venezuela. Except the proposed smelter complex, all proposals were realized.[29]

> The repatriation of land from the bauxite companies placed some 22,232 acres of land back into the hands of the State, but there were other important implications. The repatriation of the lands, for instance was not just aimed at bringing the land back into local ownership and bringing idle land into food production. The land ownership question was tied to the control of reserves: some companies had 150 years of reserves under their control at their then rate of extraction. Together the companies controlled 1.5 billion tons of bauxite but were mining only 12 million tons annually. Thus land ownership was related to control of reserves and, in turn, to the rate of extraction and therefore revenue.[30]

The bauxite levy that accrued from this policy resulted in an increase in tax revenues from J$25 million to J$200 million in just one year. Control of the land was multivalent. It provided the state a commanding control over developments within the Jamaican economy, and renewed assertions about sovereignty. It renewed the meaning of citizenship and the mechanisms to create wealth directly.

Another government policy established the State Trading Corporation (STC). The STC comprised many subsidiaries, which included Jamaica Nutrition Holdings, the Jamaica Building Materials Ltd., Jamaica Pharmaceuticals and Equipment Supplies Ltd., and the Jamaica Textiles Import Ltd. It was believed that these would grant the State greater economic control, especially as regarded trade diversification.[31] In controlling trade, it was felt imports would be rationalized.

Re-articulated Agriculture

Just as the reorganization of bauxite companies was seen as the ultimate control of national resources, the rationalization of agricultural production was perceived as necessary for the government's rearticulation of the economy. Agriculture in the hands of individual Jamaicans had to be synchronized with the public's needs, however defined. To this end, the agricultural sectoral plan was far more comprehensive than any of its predecessors. It called for large-scale production of domestic food, adequate nutritional levels for the population, agro-industrial development and the expansion of export markets. Reducing the overwhelming reliance on exports required the following: (1) ensuring efficient and proper use of agricultural land; (2) improving rural amenities and raising the standard of living; (3) increasing rural, especially farm, incomes; and (4) ensuring readily available credit and marketing facilities. Three main programs formed the substance of land reform. They were Project Food Farms, Project Land Lease, and the Sugar Cooperatives. A guaranteed price system, as well as land reform, would ensure the efficacy of these programs.

Project Food Farms

An umbrella scheme divided among several properties, Project Food Farms (PFF) was created by the state to manage the unemployment crisis and to mobilize food production. The scheme's objectives were:

1. To develop approximately 25,000 acres during the first year of operation and a similar amount within the second and third years of the project's operation.
2. Operate each property as a single unit in the first instance.
3. Encourage group and cooperative activities.
4. Develop a system of long-term leasehold tenure.
5. Increase production of food in the island.[32]

Instituted in 1973 at a cost of J$748,651, the cost of operating Project Food Farms escalated eight months later. A training ground for young farmers for the cultivation of food crops, Food Farms were expected eventually to become self-reliant cooperatives through the sale of their produce to the state-owned Agricultural Marketing Corporation (AMC).

Project Food Farms began operating in January 1973 on one property, though within a year it had incorporated eight properties, namely Hounslow, Truro, Silver Spring, Serge Island, Shrewsbury, Shettlewood, Hopewell, and Cape Clear,[33] tapping into various sections of the State bureaucracy for their operation. Farms were coordinated by one regional coordinator, two assistant regional coordinators, five temporary managers, one assistant manager, and five recorders, albeit operated under the central offices of the Ministry of Agriculture. They were supervised by the Social Development Commission (SDC), a government agency (the evolved JW), also responsible for youth programs island-wide. The Deputy Chief Technical Officer in the Ministry of Agriculture had full executive responsibilities for the project and was advised by a Coordinating Committee, comprising sixteen technical and administrative officers, also Ministry of Agriculture officers. This committee met monthly and was chaired by the Deputy Chief Technical Officer. Although operating directly in the field, the managers were expected neither to attend meetings nor to submit reports.[34]

A closer look at the operation of the Nyerere Farm reveals how programs designed to make citizenship more inclusive, instead subverted that objective, thanks to the resilience of civil service-type administrators, for whom an individual's social location was fixed and immutable. The politics of participation looked less and less like a fair exchange, with administrators giving instructions to farmers rather than heeding their feedback. Inadequate farm resources further exacerbated project tensions.

The Nyerere Farm

It was evening when we arrived at the Nyerere Community Farm, a fellow student, his nephew and I. We had been intrigued by the stories about the farm and in awe of Nyerere's Ujamaa experimentation in Tanzania, we decided to collaborate on a final-year term paper on the farm. Our arrival on the farm was greeted with expectation and scepticism. Having spent several hours on the road, I expected to find somewhere to purchase food. The farmers had plenty of ground provisions, but there was no "meat kind." My response was that fish would be fine. But "meat kind" meant all kinds of flesh, including fish. They knew where we could purchase a chicken, and so pooling our resources, we purchased a small chicken. That night the small chicken was shared among seven of us. After the meal, the farmers smoked stashes of ganja. Except my colleague and his nephew, we all shared in this ritual too. That night, sated and comfortable, we spoke with farmers about the Nyerere. They were keen on talking. Things were not going well. They were idle for most of the time. Resources were scarce, and there were abiding "quarrels" between the managing committee and the farmers. There were generational problems too. Some farmers were young but many were forty or older. Their farming skills had been tested in this area. The villagers around were not cooperating. They were not even impressed. Some were jealous of those farmers who had houses. They withheld information about the soil. They told us stories about the class conflict between them and the managing committee. Settlers pointed to withered crops, which had done well for several weeks only to wither, as if burnt, soon after. No one had warned them about the soil. They were not consulted. They expected the Food Farms would be their ticket to better lives. They were despondent, but they were not giving up, like many others had done.

The Nyerere Community Farm was part of the Community Youth and Development Project that embraced the Montpelier group of properties, former sugar plantations, of approximately 12,000 acres. There were three Project Food Farms: Cacoon Castle (where the Nyerere Farm was situated), which had 2,009 acres, of which 800 were considered arable; Haughton Grove, a 950-acre farm, of which 800 acres were fertile, and the Mafoota farm with 1,800 acres, of which 800 were arable.

Modeled on the Israeli Moshav Agricultural Project, the Nyerere Community Farm was established in 1974. Its specific aims were to:

1. arrest rural-urban drift;
2. diversify and increase agricultural production;
3. mobilize the youth toward agricultural production.[35]

The project targeted youth between 18 and 30 years of age, laying out specific guidelines for their involvement. Members were expected to be self-reliant, honest, resourceful and willing to work and to learn new techniques in agricultural production. They were expected to participate in management and to assume eventual responsibility for the project. Lands were to be leased for a minimum of 49 years with contractual hereditary rights for successful farmers. Farmers' homes were expected to be within two miles of the farms. Any farmer dishonoring his/her contractual obligations could be dispossessed of farms and farm equipment. Unlike settlements of early administrations, participants received farm-based accommodations. The idea was to create model farming communities about 110 houses built on the property in staggered fashion, which would be linked and integrated into the older surrounding communities.[36] The project's targeted ages, 18 to 35, received preferential treatment, such as superior facilities (farms established on fertile land) and all possible services (tractors, ploughs, etc.). These farmers, most from urban areas, were in the scheme's Phase III division. Participating farmers were not unlike "common" farmers in that most were primary school dropouts. Most Phase I and II participants had prior experience as farmers and many had held second jobs, whereas among the younger farmers only 25% had ever held second jobs.

Management of Farms

Nyerere farms were government-leased. Each farmer operated under a 49-year agreement with a hereditary option, though in reality only the younger farmers, those of Phase III, qualified for the option.

In addition to farming households a Social Worker, an Extension Officer and a few administrative clerks resided on the farms. The farm's daily management was coordinated by the Farm Managing Committee. This Committee represented all farmers, influential in the recruitment and housing of project members. In addition to officials from the Social Development Commission and the Ministry of Agriculture, 13 farmers sat on this committee, whose functions were:

1. the maintenance of a continuous supply of water;
2. the eviction of some nonproductive farmers and squatters;
3. the provision of street lights;
4. the sorting of farmers for continued financial and other general assistance.[37]

The Jamaica Development Bank provided farmers with credit facilities on an individual basis, as each farmer had to prove her/his ability to repay any loans. In the formative years of the scheme, however, the Project had been allotted a budget by the Ministry of Agriculture, from which farmers received funds after loan approval, a practice discontinued due to abuses in patron-client relationships.[38]

Farm produce marketing was arranged by the Agricultural Marketing Corporation, a parastatal agency through which each farmer was expected to channel her/his produce.

Organization and Production of Farms

Each farm on the Project was considered a discrete unit. Each household made its own decisions regarding the cultivation of crops and the hiring of labor. However taboo the hiring of labor on such farms may have been per se, a combination of the systems of hired labor and partnership or individual farming became the norm.[39]

The three levels of the project corresponded to land quality, the farmers' ages and the services such units could receive. Phase III farmers lived in concrete houses and farmed fertile lower lands, enjoying the available services. The more elderly Phase I farmers lived in wooden houses, and farmed on the drier hillsides without such services as ploughing. In general, younger farmers were better provided. Because the Nyerere Farm Project was but one part of a broad scheme, farm equipment had to be shared among the farming units. Nyerere had therefore to share equipment with farms such as Haughton Grove located more than seven miles away.

Performing Food Farms

Difficult to ascertain, the financial performance of Project Food Farms provides a critical measure of their success, as well as the tenor of state relations toward smallholders. The pricing system and the official marketing agency, the AMC, occasioned such dissatisfaction among farmers that it became difficult to assess the volume of food produced and produce sales, due to the prevalence of informal or unofficial transactions.

A Ministerial report of Project Food Farms' first-year performance concluded that the scheme's production outstripped the national averages only in certain food crops. In Hounslow, a farm with credible records, 70 acres yielded an average of 1.35 tons per acre. Compare this with Truro, with an average 0.18 tons per acre on 65 acres. During this period, the national yield for corn was 0.4 tons per acre. On Hounslow farms yields were six times that of Project Land Lease, and three times that of the national average. Table 4.2 shows the general production trends.

As table 4.2 below shows, PFF rivaled the national production average in only cabbage, corn, and peanuts, while outperforming Project Land Lease in four crops.

Despite scanty records, the PFF's inefficiency likely resulted from high production costs. According to one analyst:

> A total of 1,152 acres were (sic) put under cultivation. Of this, 949 acres were planted in short term crops, 251 acres in medium term crops (plantain and pineapple), and 352 acres in permanent crops. Of the total planting approximately 363 acres were reaped. The total cost of production and reaping was $612,925, the average per acre cost was $395. The total value of returns from reaping was $51,999. The average per acre return was $143.24.[40]

Table 4.2.   Comparison of Yields between Project Food Farms, Project Land Lease and Island Average

	YIELD	PER	ACRE
Crop	Project Food Farms s. ton	Project Land s. ton	Island Avg. 1973 (s. ton)
Cabbage	3.30	0.40	3.10
Carrot	0.20	3.30	3.50
Corn	0.79	0.20	0.40
Cow Pea	0.04	0.01	0.37
Peanut	0.51	0.50	0.40
Pumpkin	2.78	1.80	4.20
Sweet Potato	2.80	3.60	3.30
Yam	2.50	3.90	5.10

Source: *Ministry of Agriculture Report* (Kingston: Govt. Printery, 1974)

Production far exceeded returns and ranged from J$130 per acre at the Serge Island Farm, to as much as J$813 per acre at the Truro farm. Labor costs were also high, comprising 88% of total expenditure and ranging from J$89 to J$621 per acre. Costs varied even when farms were under the same management, as were Truro and Shrewsbury, where costs were J$507 and J$445, respectively, or Shettlewood and Hopewell, both of which were relatively mechanized and produced similar crops (cow peas), J$89 and J$215 respectively.[41] Farms' varied production levels can be attributed to variations in the intensity and cost of labor.

Project Food Farms was an expensive venture. In the light of discrepancies produced by the absence of reliable farm records, it is difficult to assess the farms'

Table 4.3.   Expenditure of Project Food Farms from January 1973 to January 31, 1974, in Jamaican Dollars

Personal Emoluments	$338,874.10
Traveling & Subsistence	6,926.96
Supplies and Material	135,222.42
Rental of Property	14.00
Hiring of Heavy Equipment	4,022.00
Public Utility Service	48.05
Other Operating Maintenance Expenses	55,571.87
Grants and Contribution	528.52
Awards and Indemnities	2,350.00
Equipment	169,657.75
Livestock	50.20
Land Structures	35,385.10
TOTAL	$748,651.10

Source: *Ministry of Agriculture Report* (Kingston: Govt. Printery, 1974), 25.

efficiency, profitability, and the national benefits. The records on the project's actual expenditure reveal the extent to which the project had become mired in bureaucracy, benefitting the project's administrators, rather than smallholders.

As table 4.3 above shows, personal emoluments comprised 55% of farm expenditures. Only 9% (J$55,572) was spent on operating and maintenance expenses, but 23% on equipment from which farms seem not to have benefitted. Unfortunately, records fail to indicate the actual percentage garnered by both management and workers/producers. Despite high labor costs, even at minimum wages, the necessity compelled the expenditure. Excepting Shrewsbury and Hopewell, whose labor costs per acre were below 50% of acreage costs, all other farms exceeded 50%, and some were even as high as 123%.[42]

This scheme's costly bureaucracy represented not the least of its internal problems. For example, farmers adamantly rejected the state stipulation that they sell their crops to the AMC. Many crops found their way into the better-paying outlets offered by higglers and other traders. A 1976 Ministerial brief noted that, while 195,000 lbs. was recorded as having been sold to the AMC, it was an unreliable indicator of production levels, as much was being sold to higglers; according to the report, "there is a resistance to selling to the AMC because of the low prices."[43]

Although scheme participants had access to tractors for land preparation, disorganization and poor planning often rendered impossible their use. One farmer told me that, in anticipation of tractor services, he often prepared his land, only to wait a very long time for the tractor to arrive or to return from being repaired. No training was given to farmers in the operation of certain farming equipment, so that fields remained unploughed whenever trained personnel were absent.

Another major complaint was farmers' lack of input into project decision making.[44] Though free to plant crops, farmers had no say in the hiring and firing of staff. As a result, they bitterly opposed information and advice supplied by the Managing Committee, often circumventing the stipulated arrangements, as in the case of the AMC. Rivalry between older and younger farmers underscored the uneven allocation of resources, and resulted in the jealous hoarding of such vital information as might have prevented waste.

According to its objectives, the PFF was to serve as a model for surrounding rural communities, though, except for the clinic, no other services were exchanged between the villagers and the farmers. Because many farm participants were from urban areas, villagers kept their distance, resenting urban (St. Andrew) farmers for their "town" habits.

PFF may have boosted food production, though at high social and financial costs. Its overheads were exceptionally high, and many of its management practices, questionable. While it succeeded in strengthening the influence of the state bureaucracy in the agricultural sector, its relief to the smallholder was not significantly different from that of the 1940s land settlement. Perhaps the PFF's origins in concern for island unemployment caused it to resemble too much other welfare schemes. But not to be underestimated is the fillip which it gave to the state's presence, deepening the seductiveness of clientilistic politics, though such state largesse could not be long sustained given the IMF's coming structural adjustment reforms. Such politics infused the state with a sense of its own importance, renewing Jamaican nationalism. The PFF was instituted amid clamor for social and economic reforms as well as the state officials' determination to redefine a national culture in a way that rendered the state indispensable.

Project Land Lease

Established in 1973 at a cost of J$507,491, Project Land Lease (PLL) settled tenants on leased land. Aptly summarized by Stone, the objectives of Project Land Lease were:

1. The provision by government of the credit, working capital, technical assistance, and marketing facilities to individual tenant farmers to complement their labor inputs.
2. The provision of land on a leasehold rather than a freehold basis on conditions of tenure that ensure government controls over land use and productivity.
3. Detailed and comprehensive planning of land use, credit control, and overall production on the farms.
4. Careful selection of project participants on criteria reflecting both the need for land and potential for productive land use and careful observation, monitoring, and control of tenant farmers as regards productivity.
5. Close working relationships between technical extension staff and tenant farmers that allow for a maximum diffusion of technical knowledge among tenant farmers.[45]

By the time the project ended, its costs had skyrocketed. Costs were apportioned as follows:

1. Cost of Acquisition.................................. $J 11,877,076
2. Cost of Rentals......................................$J 800,000
3. Infrastructure...$J 25,349,412
4. Houses for PL III....................................$J 2,940,000
5. Recoverable Loans less repayments...........$J 10,820,297
   Total...$J 50,986,794

Source: M. S. Perera, "Project Land Lease I–III" (Kingston: Ministry of Agriculture: mimeo, 1982).

Patterned after the Alcan tenant scheme, the PLL was established under the assumption that land access would lead to a better standard of living for smallholders and the landless, resolving land scarcity in the agricultural sector. There were three types of Land Lease projects. Under the first two, the government leased land from private owners and rented supplemental tenancies to farmers living within two miles of the property. The third type of Land Lease project, the most elaborate, and least developed of the three with which it had much in common, included a housing provision. Credit expenses for land preparation, planting material, and fertilizer, were provided by the government through the Public Enterprise Organization and were expected to be repaid by produce sales contracts with the AMC. Highlights of the Land Lease project were:

1. The tailoring of holdings to achieve the difference between what the farmer could earn from his own land and what was considered to be an adequate income per unit of land (estimated at J$1500–2000).
2. Provision made for the landless plots, largely considered to be full economic units. Emphasis was placed on youth.
3. Hereditary rights, compensation for capital improvements, and termination from the lease would be based on nonperformance.
4. Domestic food production, and long-term development of the farm were components of the land use policy.[46]

Hailed as one of the most successful agropolicies, by the end of 1980, over 39,000 farmers had been settled on 74,760 acres of land. Among the three schemes, land was apportioned as follows: 71% of all beneficiaries received land under Phase I of the program and 3% under Phase III; the remainder, 26%, received land under Phase II. As its name suggests, Land Lease resulted in the leasing of 483 properties (from private landholders) constituting some 124,070 acres, of which 56.6% or 70,254 was arable.

As can be seen from table 4.4 below, the most popular project was PLL I, the oldest and most established Phase. Land Lease incorporated many farmers

Table 4.4.   Subscription of Tenants on State Farms

	No. of Tenants Placed	Acreage Distributed
PLL I	28,829	48115
PLL II	9,934	22,123
PLL III	1,006	4,522
TOTAL	39,769	74,760

Adapted from: C. Stone, "Tenant farming under State capitalism." (Kingston: U.W.I. unpub. mss., 1976)

at a pace that made settlement, rather than alternative production, the objective. In 1979, Homer Preston, an USAID official, described it as a "practical approach to developing viable small farm units and at the same time increase agricultural productivity." Preston felt that, unlike the Alcan scheme which was self-sustaining, emphasizing intensive production, the major concern for PLL was farm settlement,[47] which was certainly true. Between 1972 and 1981, 11,000 farmers were placed on PLL I,. remarkable when compared with the earlier resettlement schemes of the late nineteenth and early twentieth centuries, which had settled 37,000 persons in 43 years.

Organization of Project Land Lease

Recalling earlier land settlement schemes, PLL differed from them in attempting to recruit people from farming backgrounds. Eighty-one percent of tenants were either smallholders or farm laborers prior to PLL recruitment. 34% leased between .6 and 1 acre; 25% leased between 1.6 and .3 acres; 3% leased between .1 and .25 acre; and 5.1% leased .3.1 acres and above. Approximately 40% of the sample occupied one acre or less. According to a Ministry paper:

> When this is linked with the fact that 56% of the farmers had no land
> of their own, and that 41% of those who had operated on less than
> one acre of land, indications are that these parcels of land provided
> by Project Land Lease are much too small.[48]

Performances and Constraints

Project Land Lease was successful at two levels. First, it increased food production; second, it made land available to those who would not have otherwise had any. Between April 1973 and the end of March 1981, PLL properties produced 387,900 tons of food crops (mainly tubers, vegetables, and pulses), valued at $J232.74 million. In 1980, such properties produced as much as 12% of total food crop production in the country (that is to say, 50,000 out of a total 410,760 tons). The Project's contribution to domestic food production was staggering. Overall production in 1976 jumped from 4.6% to 19.5% in 1980, stated in pounds (lbs.), from 29 million to 150 million pounds.[49] This was no small feat, for only 23% of the land was deemed to be ideal for profitable production; 32% ranged from poor to very poor, and 45.3% was considered fair. Though suitable for cultivation, the land considered fair was far from ideal in terms of drainage, soil condition, or rainfalls. Of a total of 70,584 acres of arable land on the scheme, only 22,033 were under cultivation.

Contrary to officials' claims, PLL settlers came from varied backgrounds. About 55% of a sample owned no land previously. Another 40% did not even operate under any of the more commonly recognized systems of tenure, namely, family land, individual, or rented. On PLL I, 32% had in the past owned land; 51% claimed they had no previous access to land; 5% rented land, 8% leased land, and 4% had been squatters. Of those fortunate enough to have had access to land in one way or another, 82% had less than five acres, and only 8%, more than eight acres. Stone correctly concluded that the scheme rescued smallholders from downward mobility, raising them into the "displaced peasants" category, while the "displaced peasants" became "small peasants."[50]

But PLL also fell short of its plan to make families central to production via the primacy of family labor. Over 67% of the PLL farmers hired labor. Several explanations were posited for this:

1. Farmers worked other plots of land besides the Land Lease allotment.
2. The unavailability of adult family labor;
3. The relatively low level of exchange labor or "day for day" labor arrangements on the farms;
4. The advanced age of some tenant farmers;
5. The poor quality of some land, requiring extensive preparation;
6. Farmers hired labor for status purposes.[51]

The prevalence of hired labor belied the reliability and sufficiency of household labor, which consisted for the most part of children. Due to the smallness and inferiority of the plot, the cultivator had to supplement household income, necessitating more farm maintenance. At the same time, the absence and/or inadequacy of government funding forced the smallholder to employment off the farm.

The absence of basic infrastructure was regularly cited as a shortcoming of the PLL, which failed to maintain or create water supplies, farm roads, and drainage systems. The smallness of land allotments was another popular complaint. Seventy-four percent of those interviewed in the Stone survey considered land allotments too small to ensure a decent livelihood. And many microholdings were infertile, the effect of which was to further "limit the income potential and productivity of these tenant farmers."[52] Without government financial support, smallholders had to rely on their own efforts to treat soil infertility, cultivating at "higher rates than normal." Delays in the delivery of fertilizers and other products proved detrimental to PLL production. That smallholders achieved such successes in spite of deficiencies was remarkable.

While the PLL stipulated that the AMC be the only outlet for the sale of produce, the AMC's low prices forced PLL farmers to seek private traders.[53] Though the bulk of crops, 27,170 lbs., or 70%, was sold to the AMC, roughly 29%, or 11,540 lbs., to higglers and 1% to others.[54] Roughly 77.6% of tenants who sold produce to the AMC believed its prices unreasonably low. Smallholders complained incessantly of the under pricing policies, as prices received from AMC were often far below those of, for example, higglers. It was noted that,

> Although the A.M.C purchased 70% of the volume, the amount paid farmers for this volume (sic) was 60% of the total value of the crops sold, while the higglers who bought 29% of the volume paid 33% of the total value. The highest volume/value ratio was recorded by the Other purchasers, who bought 1% of the volume sold but paid 7% of total paid for purchases.[55]

Confusion over patterns of crop production were compounded by ambiguous policy, resulting in Extension Officers privileging crops grown in pure stand, though the former preferred mixed stand acreage.

Since loans were tied in with AMC purchases, resistance to AMC led to a breakdown in loan transactions. Up to 1974, monies lent to PLL farmers consisted of more than 50% ($J286,714) of the scheme's total expenditure. Of a sample of farmers, 404 owed $33,820; 53% was owed for land preparation, 20% for planting materials, 15% for fertilizer, and 10% for rental.[56] Only 5% ($J1,783) of the total amount had been repaid. In other words, 95% of the loans were outstanding. Debt repayment was estimated at less than 10% of the outstanding loans.[57]

According to table 4.5, 32% of the PLL tenants paid between 26% and 50% of the gross value of their crops to Land Lease for credit extended to them, while 31% paid out between 51% and 100% of their crops and 36% paid less than 25%. However high the rate of loan returns may seem, these figures serve to underscore farmers' indebtedness. Smallholders blamed the situation on the low returns they got from the AMC, claiming that their earned income was insufficient to lower their debts.[58]

Table 4.5.   Credit Repayment by Tenant Farmers at Last Crop Sale

Of Gross Revenue used to Repay Debt(s)	% Of Tenant Farmers
Less than 25%	36
26% to 50%	32
51% to 75%	13
76% to 100%	18
Total	100

Source: Carl Stone, "A Sociological Survey of Tenant Farmers on Project Land Lease," (Kingston: Dept. of Govt. U.W.I: mimeo, 1974).[59]

Many dispossessed or displaced smallholders were able to upgrade their standard of living at a heavy price. Provided with access to land, integrated into agricultural commodity production as a result, smallholders were saddled with unmanageable debts, as even Stone would have agreed. The conditions under which they worked such marginal land represented no significant improvement in their social and economic condition. According to Stone's survey, many seemed content with their status, particularly as landowners and employees. 51% felt that they were better off because of their involvement in PLL; 49% believed that they were not, 13% commenting that nothing had changed; 36% felt that they were actually worse off.[60]

Pioneer Youth Farms

Smaller in scale and focused on rural unemployed, the project Pioneer Youth Farms (PYF) was instituted in 1978. In 1978 nine PYF farms employed 193 workers. By 1980, a total of 11 farms employed 120 young farmers. Cultivation increased from 307 in 1978 to 706 in 1980. Like the Project Land Lease and Project Food Farms, PYF contributed to the production of domestic food crops, from 193,276 lbs. in 1978 to 545,713 lbs. in 1980, though the farms were costly and the repayment on loans, low. By 1980, the cost of these schemes amounted to J$39.1 million, of which J$13.7 million was recoverable, though only J$2.8 million had yet been recovered.[61] It was estimated that the average cost to the government of one scheme participant was approximately J$960.00.[62] Between 1978 and 1980, costs amounted to J$2 million, of which J$1.2 million was deemed redeemable, though only J$0.08 million had been repaid.

Considering the program's expense, its successes seem scanty. Austerity measures adopted in the face of the economic decline, along with the demands of the IMF, effectively curtailed recruitment. Between 1978 and 1980, during the IMF and government agreement, only 3,459 acquired land under both Phase I and II, none under Phase III.

The Sugar Cooperatives

The establishment of sugar cooperatives was one of the most far-reaching land reform measures, pivotal to the kind of socialism that would transform the ordinary worker into the sovereign, self-reliant subject of a new postcolonial Jamaica, heralded by Manley. More than any other social and economic program, cooperativization served to reorganize class status, transforming wage-workers to owner/producers on the former sugar plantations.

When the PNP assumed office, the three largest cane farming properties, Frome, Monymusk and Bernard Lodge, approximately 48,000 acres each, had already been sold by their foreign owners and belonged to government. Pressured by the Social Action Center (SAC), a nongovernmental organization (NGO), the Manley administration altered its plans for marketing/purchasing cooperatives with individual leaseholds in favor of producer cooperatives collectively managed and operated.

Cooperativization entailed the mobilization of 4,600 agricultural workers for sugar production on 23 farms nationwide, each estate comprising 2,000 acres of land, and containing 200 members. Initially three pilot farms of 6,000 each had been established: Barham, Salt Pond and Morelands, on which 500 workers signed 49-year sugar production leases. Throughout the process of establishing cooperatives, the Sugar Workers Cooperative Council (SWCC), an NGO both linked to the cooperatives' operation and engaged in worker mobilization, formed steering committees on farms.

Structure and Organization

The principal organization administering the cooperatives between 1974 and 1976 was the Frome Monymusk Land Company (FMLCo.), comprised of the Governor of the Bank of Jamaica and middle- and upper-level civil servants. Because FMLCo was established during the JLP administration, which favored individual land purchases, the organization reflected these preferences.[63] During the first two years of its tenure, FMLCo. was distinctly anticooperative. In 1974, faced with opposition from the workers and the SWCC, the organizing body of the SAC, the membership of the FMLCo. expanded to include worker and union delegates. At the end of 1976, the FMLCO's authority had been entirely undermined, and, as a result, the USWCC, a body representing workers, was created to assume management of the cooperatives. The formation of management committees which included workers heralded the cooperatives' novel restructuring.

In reality the cooperative farm structure pertained only to farm operations, leaving unaltered an estate structure which, even in harmonious times operated autonomously and often in antagonistic relation to field/farm cooperatives. Because the government was interested only in the organization of the farm cooperatives, other areas, such as the estate clerical staff at the factory and the Tractor and Transportation department, remained isolated from the object of its regulation.

GOVERNING BOARDS

|

USWCC CENTRAL BOARD

|

ESTATE BOARD (CHAIRMEN OF 10 farms of T&T* and 2 members at large)

|

|

FARM MANAGING COMMITTEE [11 Members each on 10 farms]

|

COOPERATIVE MEMBERSHIP

*T&T= Tractors and Transport Department.

Source: Adapted from, U.L.F. Frolander and Frank Linderfeld, "A New Earth: The Jamaican Sugar Workers Cooperatives, 1975–1981." Unpublished mss., n.d., circa 1975.

State Bureaucracy and Sugar Cooperatives

No single governmental institution oversaw the cooperatives' operations and development, though the state continued to exercise much control via various, overlapping institutions.[64] Until 1976, before its replacement, FLMCo oversaw the cooperatives, functioning mainly to provide technical and managerial services over a period of three years. After 1976, unlike the FMLCo with its links to the political directorate and the sugar technocracy, the USWCC courted co-operators, largely severing links to state sectors. Only through its General Secretary, the chief executive of the USWCC, were links forged with the state bureaucracy, as he was in a position to influence decisions of the Central Board.

Influential with the sugar industry in general,[65] the Sugar Industry Authority (SIA) served to connect co-ops with the state. The SIA became "the financial overlord of the sugar cooperatives guaranteeing their bank loans, providing separate loans of its own, collecting cane sale revenues, and in general attempting to oversee their financial activities and budget preparation."[66] The SIA's functions included the domestic pricing of sugar, the paying of cane farmers, and the settling of a time frame for receipt of these earnings. Without the SIA's assistance, therefore, it would have been well-nigh impossible for the cooperatives to obtain credit, much needed for its operations. Nevertheless, the Ministry of Agriculture assumed

ultimate authority over the cooperatives, establishing a desk to supervise cooperative affairs. It also provided an advisor to the USWCC board and "through its Parliamentary Secretary, was a major conduit for political inputs and interaction."[67]

Organization of Work

Despite the sugar workers' change of status from wage laborers to part-owners, work
was organized in much the same way as it had been prior to cooperativation. The
overseer provided task-oriented work. Some workers ingratiated themselves with the
overseer in order to be given fewer menial tasks. Favoritism prevailed. At the Frome
cooperative, it was well known that certain members received better task-work in return for loyalty to the Project Manager. Efforts to eliminate favoritism failed to receive support from the staff, hostile to the very idea of cooperatives and workers'
control.[68] On farms like Monymusk and Bernard Lodge, workers were most successful at eliminating it because they chose their supervisors. Feuer stated that:

> While field staff now formally derived their authority and power
> from the workers themselves, and hence were restrained from em-
> ploying their traditional autocratic patterns, the basic system of work
> organization with its hierarchy, its task work pattern, its irregularity
> and dependence on favours and good relations with overseers re-
> mained. All this contributed to the reinforcement of dependency pat-
> terns and the maintaining of existing social relations of production
> (despite their nominal transformation).[69]

Workers/owners felt very little if any change in field work relationships.
Changes such as security of tenure failed to reduce the pertinacity of prior work
practices.

The organization of the sugar estate remained as entrenched as the work organization, characterized by the separation of its various operational areas, field
operations being separate from factory, and factory from clerical, etc. Within the
context of the twin association of class and color, this meant that, although
workers had become part-owners of the newly formed cooperatives, they continued to occupy the lowest rungs in the power hierarchy.

Incongruity between the Co-ops' Organization and How They Worked

The decision to maintain factory operations as before, separate, if linked by the
continued production of sugar, ensured management by the state-owned Na-

tional Sugar Company, rather than worker committees. These estates' incomplete cooperativization caused much tension between clerical staff, factory/estate workers, and the cooperators. These tensions highlighted the extent to which the bureaucracy had strengthened its position over the workers/owners, the cooperators, even as bureaucrats pursued new enterprises, as well as the reluctance of key elements in the state to allow workers/smallholders too much agency, despite the lip service paid freedom.

The separation of factory and cooperatives was an injudicious decision. Because factory workers were more skilled and received higher pay than field workers, they considered themselves better off, resulting in a systematic reinforcement of this division of labor, thereby increasing the likelihood of conflict, such as that which erupted during harvesting.

In the past, because the companies owned both factories and estates, they were able to manipulate cane supplies in the event of cane farmers being incapable of or unwilling to supply. They were also able to reduce the costs of their weekend production by accepting small farmers' canes, eradicating higher production costs and enabling them to keep factories continuously supplied with cane.[70] Though these companies' continued administration of the factory did not change such practices, the cooperatives were forced to bear the extra costs of their weekend production. The cooperators shortsightedly agreed to this since they earned additional income during the weekends. However:

> the factories over which the cooperators had no control, severely limited the revenues of the co-ops by frequent late starts of the crop, by slow-downs and strikes, by breakdowns and general inefficiency. Large amounts of cane were left standing in the fields and stale cane, delivered too late after burning, brought a lower price. Furthermore it was clear that the need to supply the factories with cane profitably or not also had applied to the cultivation of marginal lands, unsuitable for the cultivation of sugar cane.[71]

This ambivalence toward the cooperative movement intensified class struggles between clerical staff and workers/cooperators, leading Feuer to observe that:

> The Project Managers, overseers and assistant overseers who composed the field staff, together with other technical and middle management elements among factory and estate administrative staff, [sic] were part of a heterogeneous agrarian bourgeoisie. This class also included larger farmers, contractors, (for example, owners of heavy agricultural equipment) and local merchants. The linkages between the estate staff, who did not directly exploit labor, and the bourgeoisie who did were based mainly on the fact that most of the staff had worked long years managing and controlling workers for foreign capital, in

particular Tate and Lyle (Frome and Monymusk) and the United Fruit Company (Bernard Lodge). It was not, however, uncommon for staff members also to have local business interests including interests in farms, shops and contracting operations.[72]

Though cooperativization had left intact the division of labor on the estates, operations had inflamed extant antagonisms, resulting in hostility between the factory and the field workers. Factory workers and clerical staff found it difficult to accept the class transitions underway. Repeated clashes with workers disrupted the cooperatives' operation.

Expressed Resentments

Because staff members never accepted the idea of cooperatives, the fight was not simply to put workers in their place, but also to undermine the very cooperatives. In their endeavor to destabilize cooperativization, staff members allied themselves with, for instance, trade unions, whose influence had declined vis-à-vis worker/owner structures. Conservative government officials and anti-co-op sugar industry elites represented groups with vested interests in the co-ops' failure.[73]

The Bustamante Industrial Trade Union (BITU, JLP affiliated) and the National Workers' Union (NWU, PNP affiliated) opposed the cooperatives' formation. Because the BITU represented in the past between two-thirds to three-quarters of sugar workers, their ill will was particularly pronounced. Like other antico-op groups, the BITU did everything in its power to undermine the credibility of the cooperatives among creditors, as well as worker/owner participants.

Lack of Worker Control

Worker dissatisfaction with and distrust of the staff/clerical workers was compounded by the workers' powerlessness to dismiss them, able neither to hire, nor to fire. Attempts by the SWCC to restructure relations between workers/owners and staff failed in the face of a bureaucracy which had enough power to guarantee itself job security for at least one year. Eventually, a resolution was arrived at, a compromise of sorts, which in exchange for workers/owners' control of hiring and firing policies guaranteed the bureaucracy at least two years of employment, promising severance pay often before severance.[74]

When the SWCC tried to instruct education to instruct the worker/owners of their rights, sections of the establishment were able to erect immense bureaucratic obstacles. While the SWCC established committees to address workers/owners' grievances, the bureaucracy was able to dog their operations. The SWCC was but an NGO linked to the PNP, itself a heterogeneous group containing many members displeased by the party's leftist swing. The SWCC's mobilizational and educational activities among sugar workers were often viewed as a usurpation of civil service workers' authority, a viewpoint which predated the cooperatives' establishment. Unable to prevent their formation, these various bureaucratic bodies sought to control their development.[75] Managers resisted SWCC worker education on the grounds that it hobbled production. Disobedient workers who attended SWCC education sessions were punished. One worker lamented:

> when we needed to go into Kingston, (for SWCC business) and I came back down, my boss would tell me that I couldn't work on a Saturday or a Sunday and those days were the premium days when you would earn most money. So I would have to be contented with three days or four days per week pay and that time I was getting $1.85 per day.[76]

According to Frolander and Lindfeld:

> Under pressure from the SWCC, the PNP political directorate finally agreed to expand the cooperatives. At the same time the government tried to insure that its bureaucracies would contain and control them. The government favored cooperatives, but only if they were implemented by its officials, and was suspicious of any independent organizing efforts that were not sponsored by the Cooperative Department or the Land Company.[77]

Performance and Decline

These problems hindered the cooperatives, contributing to their demise. Although the drought of 1977 has been seen as the factor leading to the decline of production on the cooperatives, in reality, other phenomena were at work when production dropped by almost 30% at Bernard Lodge and, at Monymusk, by 38%. Between 1974 and 1976, combined losses from the Frome Estate and the Monymusk estate were approximately $J5,133 million.[78]

The 1977 drought sent production to levels below anything experienced before. Almost 300 acres had to be abandoned because of drought's effects on water quality. Drought conditions, along with the maturation of the large debt, dealt cooperatives a blow in the late 1970s. The crisis that affected cooperatives is best described by Feuer:

> The financial scissors caused primarily by production declines on the one hand and cost increases, on the other, forced the cooperatives to cut back on certain inputs and activities. For example, the cultivation of the crop lagged and fertilizer usage dropped.[79]

Cooperatives, such as Morelands, which had performed remarkably well in the pre-1975 period, could not sustain their level of performance, as many production costs had been absorbed by the land company (FMLCo), thereby causing the overestimation of cooperatives' pre-1975 performance. When the FMLCo ceased to exist, the Morelands and other cooperatives were forced to contend with huge debts.

Losses between 1976 and 1979 were estimated at roughly J$1.8 million, J$10,000 per member on the Morelands cooperative.[80] Cutbacks on the use of certain vital sugar production inputs, such as fertilizer and manual weeding, further weakened the cooperatives' foundations.[81]

Other cooperatives which had performed well up until 1975, like Springfield, suffered a combination of natural and man-made disasters. In 1978, a dispute centering on cooperators and management conflict, and the inefficiency of the Tractor and Transport Department, which lacked vehicles to transport punctually the reaped crop, forced the Springfield cooperative to leave 200 acres of cane unharvested.[82]

Large increases in the sugar workers' wages, based on the sharp rise in sugar prices between 1973 and 1975, served to associate the cooperative movement with a soaring wage expectation, mirrored by real production costs, thereby reducing the surplus the industry was able to generate, when the sugar price declined as suddenly as it had increased. Also, staff and workers' entitlement to severance pay and the transformation of the sugar estates to cooperatives proved too heavy a financial burden, not to mention that the salaries of clerical staff, supervisors, and chairpersons proved to be additional strains on the cooperatives' finances.[83] Incomes of this group doubled and tripled those of the cooperative workers during the farm's operations, creating major income disparities:

> At Springfield, the lowest only averaged 43% of the supervisors' incomes, and Morelands 53% in 1977, a year of generally lower incomes average incomes of the supervisory group actually continued to increase the chairpersons were averaging $5,778 in gross income, or over three times the average general cultivation worker's income.[84]

All such inefficient management practices as excessive overtime pay, disorganized transportation, especially during harvest time, and the extensive cultivation of marginal lands contributed to the upward spiraling of production costs.[85]

To assess validly the crisis in the 1970s, one must consider conditions prior to the cooperatives' establishment, characterized by estates' poor condition and an increase in worker participation, due to the promise of severance pay.

On its assumption to office in 1972, the PNP government was faced with a fait accompli. The three estates previously owned by the multinational companies Tate and Lyle and the United Fruit Co. had been purchased by the JLP, the government which preceded them. It was public knowledge that the main reason for the estates' sale had been their lack of profitability. A subsidiary of Tate and Lyle, the West Indies Sugar Corporation (WISCO), had reputedly lost some J$5.5 million on all of its operations at both Frome and Monymusk between 1967 and 1970.

At the time of the government purchase, production and sugar yields were very low. In the two years prior to the establishment of the Morelands farm cooperatives, cane yields were less than 29 tons per acre. At another farm, Springfield, in the five years before Springfield became a cooperative (1976), an average of 28 tons per acre was reaped annually.[86] One reason for low yields was that much marginal land had been under cultivation. In cases such as Monymusk, production was sustained on lands considered to have a high concentration of salinity and little water. In order to keep the price of labor down, management retained a surplus labor force, despite the mechanization of operations, common practice at the Monymusk farm.

The strategy by which workers were mobilized to become cooperators greatly influenced the cooperatives' development. Severance pay and the promise of profits enticed workers into participating. As the primary NGO mobilizing sugar workers, the SWCC milked the attraction of severance pay to legitimize the idea of cooperativization, reasoning that, unless the workers associated financial profitability with participation in collective farms/cooperatives, mobilization would prove onerous.

Three developments in particular lent credence to the SWCC claims. First, the success of the three pilot farms, Barham at Frome, Morelands at Monymusk, and Great Salt Pond at Bernard Lodge,[87] doubled the mobilization efforts of the SWCC and hastened the pace of cooperativization at the expense of such precautions as economic feasibility assessments. Second, severance pay awarded soon after cooperativization became an unsubstantiated symbol of bountiful harvests to come.[88] Third, the price of sugar on the global market rocketed. The future of cooperatives appeared auspicious.

Jamaica's economic recessions, the state's attendant fiscal crisis, and shortfalls in the industrial sectors' foreign exchange earnings placed tremendous pressure on the cooperatives' sugar production.[89] Crop diversification came under severe attack. The cultivation of food crops, and rice and poultry rearing, which had proceeded incrementally on cooperatives, was discouraged. Sugar cane was still king.

Such difficulties led the workers/owners to question the financial viability of the cooperatives, quickly reverting to wage-earner mentality.

> When they (the workers) came to "paybill" every Thursday after 1976, it was still as proletarians. When earnings appeared low or the system unjust, they complained just as bitterly as they always had, often in the same manner and with the same single mindedness of purpose. They did not see, nor were they adequately supported in seeing that with the cooperatives they had more constructive avenues to achieve justice.[90]

Between the IMF and the demobilization of the SWCC, there was little room for cooperatives to flourish. The economic disorganization caused in part by the severe austerity measures imposed by the IMF forced the curtailment of funds for critical items such as machinery, fuel and computer processing. The Crop Lien program, for example, instituted in 1977 under the Emergency Production Plan, could no longer come to the aid of co-ops, as IMF conditions prohibited state guarantees of private loans even for productive sectors. Access to credit was effectively blocked.

The effective elimination of the SWCC's educational programs deepened the co-op workers' demoralization, along with low production levels and low international prices. When the state appealed for "belt-tightening" measures, workers felt that financial sacrifice was unjustified and contrary to the preservation of the cooperatives. In returning to office, the JLP made clear its preference for private enterprise initiatives, as well as its intention to eliminate cooperatives, despite a last-minute attempt by the SWCC to reorganize and diversify production. The JLP cited as justification for its intention the cooperatives' decadent conditions, the financial crisis, and chronic low productivity. In 1981 the cooperatives were disbanded.

Conclusions

Cooperatives differed radically from previous land settlement schemes and state tenant farms, defining new relationships between workers and management, smallholders, workers, and the state. Like Project Land Lease, Project Food Farms, and Pioneer Youth Farms, their emergence was instrumental in forging new agrarian subjectivities, starting with the transformation of impoverished wage earners, even unemployed, into part-owners of sugar estates, or farm owners. But cooperatives remained hostage to key contradictions of the postcolonial condition. The continuities of colonial traditions of civil service "rule," and the class and development bias within them, led to ideological excesses. Cooperativization, however, like Project Food Farms and Project Land Lease, resulted in the strengthening of bureaucracy, which in its various mutations, often undermined itself. Workers lacked control, and organizations like the cooperatives and SWCC, were severely hampered by a solid front of establishment including traditional unions, the employees of the workers themselves, and the farms' clerical staff. In other words, power never seemed to leave its original moorings, nor to surface among cooperators.

What certain elements and/or institutions within the postcolonial state allowed, others took away. Worker confidence was particularly undermined by ambivalent strategies. In the twilight years of the PNP regime, smallholders were still ensconced within traditional agrarian structural relations. If anything, the cooperative experience may have taught them to know their rightful station, somewhere at the bottom of the economic and social ladder, as laborers, nothing more.

The trajectory of reform implemented by the Democratic Socialist state to enable the development of new subjectivities, ranged from state land settlement projects to farm cooperatives in the agricultural sector, backed up by official employment, appreciation of various forms of popular culture, and a recognition of the social structural specificities of Jamaican life. I have traced agricultural reforms, the rhetoric of transformation in which these reforms were shrouded, and the conflicts that attended their incipient institutionalization.

In the specific case of the cooperatives, the contradictions inherent in the state's development policy to nurture collectivism and to develop viable structures for protecting the cooperative initiative (both within and outside of the agricultural sector) were a vital factor contributing to their eventual demise. The preservation of hierarchy within the workforce along traditional lines stymied democratic forms of work organization. The cooperatives therefore represented reform measures advanced by the leftist elements of the PNP party and government operating with a liberal sensibility that afforded little independence and power to those whom its development policy and rhetoric targeted. Nor did they ameliorate people's life conditions. Though little changed, materially, people's beliefs in the inability of the state to effect structural changes in their lives were altered. They continued to frame their demands in terms of the state's societal obligations, nevertheless. Herein lies one postcolonial contradiction.

The discourse of rural society's democratization, making citizenship more inclusive through socialist development, ended up strengthening the state bureaucracy, creating new forms of state dependency, ultimately undermining or paralyzing working peoples' initiative. Championing new state/worker relationships the Manley Administration embraced "Quashie," but State administrators were generally unwilling to grant "Quashie" too much initiative, or to incorporate variant views into plans. The efforts to transform "the institutions of a free society," part of the democratic socialist plan to effect participatory development, whereby the institutional inhabitants would "work in concert with the government" to "accelerate the pace of change," as well as to "mobilize people to enthusiastic participation in the processes of change and even help to fashion the shape of change," aimed at creating a new Jamaican citizen, a subject capable of responding to development by balancing individual needs with those of the nation, a new form of nationalism and collectivism, impossible to produce.

Development of the sort imagined carried with it a belief in the ultimate efficacy of the state bureaucracy, planning officials, technocrats and even civil servants. It required working people to position themselves within its imperatives, a type of "high modernism." Cooperation was important in this transition, but cooperation required the tacit support of a new regime of political power holders eager to bestow "power" on "sufferers," in this instance, smallholders and the landless, persons recognized as the marginalized under the old order.

Reforms enabled the pervasiveness of state bureaucracy islandwide, not least among smallholders. A popular government had succeeded in incorporating the concerns and the cultural forms of the marginalized, translating them to further capacitate a weakened state bureaucracy, thus ensuring (perhaps at best), at least for a few more years, belief in the durability of development and the state's role in development. At the same time, even as the state agents occupied people's spaces within the agrarian sector or attempted to create them, they ended up creating state spaces which fostered resentments and escape routes by working people leading to their manipulation of state projects, and state officials, and vice versa. Agendas were linked in different self-interested ways.

Notes

1. Arturo Escobar, *Encountering Development*, 5.

2. Scott was addressing Don Robotham's critique of the pluralist paradigm, as advanced by Michael G. Smith. See David Scott, "The Permanence of Pluralism," in *Without Guarantees: In Honour of Stuart Hall* ed. Paul Gilroy (London and New York: Verso Press, 2000), 282–301, 293–294.

3. For a general descriptive account of the 1972 electoral campaign, see Olive Senior, *The Message is Change* (Kingston: Kingston Publishers Limited, 1975).

4. Michael Manley, *Up The Down Escalator* (London: Andre Deutsch, 1987), 225.

5. James Scott, *Seeing Like a State: How Certain Schemes to Improve the Human Condition Failed* (New Haven: Yale University Press, 1998), 184.

6. The lyrics to the song "Heavy Manners."

7. See especially James Scott (1998).

8. Michael Manley, *The Politics of Change: A Jamaican Testament* (Washington: Howard University Press, 1974, 1990).

9. Ibid., 70.

10. James Scott (1998), 5

11. George Beckford, Norman Girvan, Louis Lindsay, and Michael Witter, *Pathways to Progress: The People's Plan for Socialist Transformation, 1977–1978* (Morant Bay: Maroon Publishing House, 1985), 24–25.

12. Nadi Edwards, "States of Emergency: Reggae Representations of the Jamaican Nation State," in *Social and Economic Studies* (Special Issue on Reggae Studies) 47, no. 1 (March 1998): 21–32, 22.

13. Michael Manley, *The Politics of Change* (1990), 75. During the election campaign leading up to the 1972 election, the PNP held islandwide meetings, inviting people from all walks of life to "tell it like it is." This was early indication of the party's image as one fostering participation. For a general description of the 1972 electoral campaign, see Olive Senior (1972).

14. Ibid.

15. Arturo Escobar (1995), 5.

16. See for example Obika Gray, *Radicalism and Social Change in Jamaica, 1960–1972* (Tennessee: University of Tennessee Press, 1991); Evelyn Huber Stephens and John D. Stephens, *Democratic Socialism in Jamaica: The Political Movement and Social Transformation in Dependent Capitalism* (Princeton: Princeton University Press, 1986); Olive Senior (1972).

17. Practically all those writing on this period focus on the failure of projects, accept their modernization assumptions, and target mismanagement as the main problem affecting their implementation and operation.

18. Norman Girvan, Richard Bernal and Wesley Hughes, "The IMF and The Third World: The Case of Jamaica, 1974–1980," *Development Dialogue reprint from 1980:* no. 2: 113–155.

19. Ibid.

20. Thomas Lacey, *Violence and Politics in Jamaica 1960–1970* (Manchester: Manchester University Press, 1977), 69.

21. See David Scott, "The Dialectic of Defeat: An Interview with Rupert Lewis" in *Small Axe* no. 10 (September 2001): 85–117.

22. Ibid., 101.

23. Ibid., 102. Also, Trevor Munroe, *Jamaican Politics: A Marxist Perspective in Transition* (Kingston and Colorado: Hienemann Publishers and Lynne Reinner Publishers, 1990). Munroe also makes a similar point arguing that the PNP's shift to the Left between 1970 and 1980 "was conditioned first and foremost by the growth of black consciousness and popular militancy in the late 1960s" (276).

24. Ibid.

25. Ernesto Laclau, *Politics and Ideology in Marxist Theory* (London: Verso, 1977). I also acknowledge Akhil Gupta's reading of Laclau in *Postcolonial Developments: Agriculture in the Making of Modern India* (London, North Carolina: Duke University Press, 1998).

26. Ibid

27. White Paper, quoted in Stephens and Stephens (1989).

28. Michael Manley, *Jamaica: Struggle in the Periphery* (London: Third World Media Limited/Writers and Readers Publishing Cooperative Society Limited, 1982). Idem, *Up the Down Escalator*, (London: Andre Deutsch), esp. ch. 2. Evelyn Huber Stephens and J. D. (1986), 77–78.

29. Ibid.,

30. Ibid., 164–165.

31. M. S. Perera, *Project Land Lease I-III* (Kingston: Ministry of Agriculture Report, 1982).

32. Michaeline A. Crichlow and Trevor Spence, "The Case for Land Reform in the Third World: A Look at the Jamaican Procedure," mss. (Department of Sociology, University of the West Indies, Mona, 1978), 30.

33. Ibid.

34. Ibid.

35. For an outline of these plans, see Government of Jamaica, *Annual Report of the Nyerere Managing Committee*, (Kingston: Social Development Commission, 1976).

36. M. Crichlow and T. Spence (1978), 62–63.

37. Ministry of Agriculture, *An Evaluation of Project Land Lease and Project Food Farms*, n.d., 29.

38. Ibid.

39. Ibid.

40. Ibid., 25–26.

41. M. S. Perera (1982).

42. Ministry of Agriculture, *An Evaluation of Project Land Lease and Project Food Farms*, 30–31.

43. Interviews with farmers on the Nyerere Farm in 1978.

44. M. S. Perera (1982).

45. Carl Stone, *A Sociological Survey of Tenant Farmers on Project Land Lease* (University of the West Indies, Mona, 1976), 3.

46. Ministry of Agriculture, *An Evaluation of Project Land Lease and Project Food Farms*, 17.

47. According to the Ministry paper, "When this is linked with the fact that 56% of the farmers had no land of their own, and that 41% of those who had operated on less than one acre of land, indications are that these parcels of land provided by Project Land Lease are much too small."

48. Ibid.

49. Ibid.

50. Carl Stone (1976), 4; Using hired labor revealed aspects of the real conditions obtaining on the plot and in the household. First household labor was not reliable, since for the most part it consisted of younger children. Second, the smallness of the plot, and its infertility made it incumbent on the cultivator to supplement household income and employ labor just to maintain the farm. On the other hand, soil infertility and the absence and/or inadequacy of government funding forced the smallholder to seek hired la-

bor, as well as employment off the farm. Ministry of Agriculture, *An Evaluation of Project Land Lease*, 16–17.

51. Ibid.

52. Ibid., 19.

53. Ibid., 18

54. Carl Stone, *A Sociological Survey*, 13.

55. Ministry of Agriculture, *An Evaluation of Project Land Lease and Project Food Farms*, 19.

56. Ibid.

57. Carl Stone, *A Sociological Survey*, 22.

58. Ibid., 28–29.

59. Ibid., 22

60. E. Huber Stephens and John D. Stephens (1986), 277.

61. Ibid.

62. As Carl Feuer noted: "Despite these limitations, FMLCo maintained its authority, personnel and structure under the new Manley regime. Its central position was in fact confirmed and reinforced by the 1972 planning committee report." See C. Feuer, "Jamaica and Sugar Workers Cooperatives: The Politics of Reform." (Ph.D. diss., Cornell University, 1983), 38.

63. C. Feuer, 228.

64. Ibid., 228–229.

65. Ibid., 231–232.

66. Ibid., 229.

67. For further discussion of this conflict, see M. Frolander and F. Lindfeld, "A New Earth: The Jamaican Sugar Workers' Cooperatives, 1975–1981," mimeo, n.d., 47–49.

68. C. Feuer, 276

69. Ibid.

70. C. Feuer, 266.

71. Ibid.

72. Ibid.

73. C. Feuer, especially chapter 9, 266–280.

74. Opposition came from Labor unions, political parties and entrenched sugar interests such as the Land Company.

75. M. Frolander and F. Lindfeld, 49.

76. Ibid.

77. M. Frolander and F. Lindfeld, 69–70.

78. Feuer, 345–346.

79. Ibid., 343–345.

80. Ibid., 345.

81. Ibid., 347.

82. C. Stone, *An Appraisal of the Cooperative Process*, 14.

83. C. Feuer, 324–325.

84. In 1974, the Frome Monymusk Land Company estimated that 2000 acres of its land ought to be phased out of cane in the short run. Two years later WISCO's managing director estimated that up to 4000 acres mainly at Monymusk (but also at Frome)

were not yielding and could not yield the minimum necessary for reliable profits. Most of this land was taken over and utilized by the cooperatives. C. Feuer, 158.

85. For a detailed assessment of the performance of the cooperatives see C. Feuer, 342–353.

86. Stone attributes this success to the fact that "the cost of production for most of the cane reaped was based on cost levels prior to the massive wage and salary increases while income and revenue reflected increases mirroring the increased foreign exchange being earned by the industry." Carl Stone, *An Appraisal of the Cooperative Process*, 13.

87. Ibid.

88. M. Frolander and F. Lindenfeld, 93–94.

89. C. Feuer, 294.

90. For a deeper discussion of the effects of the IMF on Jamaica, see Norman Girvan et al, "The IMF and The Third World: The Case of Jamaica, 1974–1980," *Development Dialogue*: 113–155. Also, Jennifer Sharpley, "Economic Management and the IMF in Jamaica: 1972–1980," *DERAP Working Papers A235* (September 1981)

CHAPTER 5

Maneuvers of an Embattled State: Neoliberal Privatization and the Reconstitution of New Rural Subjects

If the widespread consensus of the 1950s and 1960s was that the future belonged to a capitalism without losers, securely managed by national government acting in concert, then the late 1980s and 1990s have been dominated by a consensus based on the opposite set of assumptions: namely that global markets are basically uncontrollable and that the only way to avoid becoming a loser—whether as a nation, or organization, or an individual—is to be as competitive as possible.[1]

It is tempting for political parties eager to show results to create new governmental institutions or programs instead of reforming or terminating those in existence because of the web of entitlements, resources, and institutional routines surrounding a given sector. New programs and discourses are believed to be able to bypass and displace older and existing structures by virtue of the energy and hegemonic strategies pursued by a new regime.[2]

Introduction

Up until the 1980s, the rhetoric of agricultural development tied the well-being of the agricultural sector to that of the smallholder. The health of one was contingent on the other. With the onset of neoliberal economic globalization, that relationship was seen as untenable. In other words the project of decolonization that enabled smallholders to identify more or less with certain expressed national development projects, was no longer deemed necessary nor desirable. Nowhere was this more evident than in the showpiece AGRO 21 that defined the 1980s and shaped the new rationalities of government in the agricultural sector. AGRO 21 signified the extent of the state's willingness to facilitate the neoliberal agenda at the expense of the state's coffers and by the articulation of rhetoric that relegated the "peasant" citizen to the role of secondary partner in this new economic order. Hitherto, smallholders were considered the quintessential historical citizens, upon whom the agricultural sector, even the nation depended. Underscoring this relegation was the institution of a new organization that replaced the traditional Ministry of Agriculture as the vanguard agricultural institution. The AGRO 21 organization was the new nerve center, headed by the Prime Minister himself. Personalized privatization notwithstanding, the attempt to facilitate globalization came up against the expectations of development fostered during an earlier era of smallholder prominence. But these fairly desperate attempts to thwart the neoliberal impetus stood little chance. The sea change in economic policy set the stage for the entrenchment of an agenda that would underscore the demise of smallholder as critical to economic strategy on the island. A new subject was in the making, underscoring the transformation of states globally. In vulnerable small places like Jamaica, there would be loud, deep and lasting implications.

In this chapter, I examine the state's role under an emerging neoliberal globalization project. I would like to shift the discussion of the 1980s, particularly the role of AGRO 21, away from the focus on failure and inappropriateness of technology, to which it has been subjected, but rather to recast the 1980s as the start of a sea change in the policy orientation of the Jamaican state. In other words, I discuss the rise of a new kind of government conduct designed to reconstitute its relationship with a smallholding stratum now considered backward enough to be left alone, and outside of the dominant policy of the period. This was a different rationality than that which characterized the 1960s. Backward as they were construed then, the sentiment was that they were redeemable. Policies of the 1980s differed also from that of the 1970s which as I have shown sought to expand the reach of state institutions deeper into rural space, but within the strictures of government-led low modernist projects.

Following the creditors' guidelines, the Jamaican state attempted to ensure capital a leading role in the agricultural sector. It did so in many ways, reminiscent of the 1960s, but with marked differences. Smallholders were forced to settle for domestic production, while large-scale firms continued to dominate export markets. A new class of entrepreneurs was introduced into the agricultural sector, many from old commercial houses, many connected with other domestic or international private-sector operations. Some were professionals, interested in cashing in on high-demand crops like coffee.

I will first discuss the AGRO 21 investment farming project and examine its agricultural consequences, then I will discuss formal and substantive changes since the 1980s, analyzing their meaning for the development and well-being of the state's relationship to land-based working people—up until then, a pivotal focus of its policies. My central concern is to show how a new kind of agricultural policy became institutionalized making it possible to unhinge smallholder agriculture from the concept and practice of development and to redefine national development, more or less independent of their contributions. In doing so, I would like to frame the discussion in terms of the more productive perspectives that delineate state maneuvers under neoliberal globalization. These perspectives shun the idea of state demise, focusing instead on the transformation of state institutions, the emergence of new actors, and the mechanisms through which neoliberal global economic policy is facilitated.

By focusing also on a project designed to placate smallholders, the chapter seeks to identify the political dimensions of state maneuvers which influence the ways in which such policy is carried out. By political dimensions I refer to the ways in which pivotal actors of the past, those no longer considered salient to current economic accumulation measures, by virtue of their political capital, the vote factor, have still to be appeased.

I would like to suggest that the relationship between political/state elites and constituents/various publics, is critical to understanding how state policies even when they overwhelmingly favor new actors may still hold out promises to groups considered marginal to new accumulation processes. Even so, programs implemented still necessitate close ethnographic scrutiny. For example, as I will show in this chapter, projects targeting smallholders were still highly ineffective materially. They held out discursive promises which allowed for the continuation of a patron-client relationship to the state, but with little impact on those conditions marked for improvement. Moreover, smallholder policies during this time were clearly subjugated to those favoring the new class.

AGRO 21 was the start of the neoliberal agenda's operation, which commenced after the PNP had agreed to bring the country under 1977 terms and conditions of the IMF. Referred to as a "betrayal" by architects of an alternative plan, the IMF agreement, in the words of Beckford, called for the placement of the PNP under "heavy manners." As he recalls:

> The first IMF agreement was signed in July 1977, and at annual party conference in September, Manley took to himself tasks in both party and state, that had been the main responsibility of the leader of the left wing, Dr. D. K. Duncan—thereby forcing Duncan's resignation from his dual role as general secretary of the PNP and minister of national mobilization and human resource development.[3]

With the assumption to office of the JLP, ideologically to the right of the PNP, the government was eager to follow the economic path being laid down by the

IMF, believing in its appropriateness for the Jamaican economy and people, but also to signal its cooperation to the U.S. primarily.

Such policies called for the repositioning of the place of the Jamaican working peoples in a reforming polity. Those of them involved in agriculture were no longer upheld as the sector's saviors, but as hindrances. A new level of intolerance began to pervade the Jamaican polity, one that delinked poverty from the sphere of collective concern back onto the body and personal agenda of the individual. Concerns about production, privatization and investment led to a new style of governance. In the agricultural sector, the Ministry of Agriculture, the institution that traditionally formulated and implemented agricultural policy, was seen as a hindrance, bypassed for a governing style where privilege is a badge of honor, and support for the haves, linked to the restabilization of the economy and the country's sovereignty, is imperative.

Munroe reminds us that in a Parliamentary democracy such as Jamaica, the Prime Minister has absolute clout, and his views and actions are seen as a measure of the direction of the country.[4] The setting up of a parallel institution as the center of the new agricultural initiative, AGRO 21, with the Prime Minister, Edward Seaga, as its patron so to speak, was a clear message about the kind of path that the administration would pursue. It was privatization to be sure, but a personalized statist one— and supervised in great detail by the Prime Minister and his office. AGRO 21 was a manifestation of the transformation of the developmentalist state, hardly diminishing the role of the state itself, nor the responsibilities of those who "manned" it.

The decline of the state's developmental role vis-à-vis agriculture and its command over domestic space are often cited as critical effects of structural adjustment policies. Important components of such a decline are market liberalization and the state's lack of substantive autonomy in generating resources to control production and policy within transnational capital circuits.[5] It is believed that while the state plays at least a supporting role in the incorporation of the economy by transnational capital, in the process, it loses its capacity to shape and regulate domestic agriculture.

Many studies demonstrate that structural adjustment policies (SAPs), divestment and privatization spell the demise of state institutions.[6] The argument claims that states are no longer key players in development projects and domestic policy, as they were in the postwar period. Instead, multilateral agencies originating in overly industrialized countries assume greater control over national economies, transforming states into hollow vessels through which transnational directives flow. Transnational entities, multilateral agencies, and capital usurp state function, despite its persistence, and state officials become servants of transnational entities. In the mid-1980s, a senior Jamaican government official lamented this state of affairs, arguing that the government had been reduced to playing primarily a regulatory role.[7]

Because many of these directives limit states' participation in the economy, and because states cooperated in these actions, they enabled their own undermining and more broadly, their transformation. Though no longer vital economic agents (though disputed[8]) within their political boundaries, states, however, have neither "bowed off the stage apologizing for their egregious errors of rule," nor been wholly pushed off, however contracted their roles, however eroded their institutions.[9] A systematic study of states' maneuvering within these global constraints might ascertain how globalized economic/cultural dynamics have disrupted and transformed the conditions of political rule, how the notion of citizen has undergone change, giving rise to new expectations, definitions, and reconstituted social relations, particularly between state and people. Knowledge of spatial social histories is needed to understand, for example, how states, as a particular set of hegemonic relationships, operate in citizens' lives. After all, local institutions and their cultural imperatives filter the global dynamics which influence people's personal lives and cultural practices.

The intensity whereby state functions are replaced by their privatized counterparts varies across global landscapes. The privatization of state enterprises, as others have pointed out, enables the emergence of practices formerly rare, nonexistent or incipient. Nevertheless, states both core and peripheral continue to contribute to changing international spaces, as well as to undergo transformation.[10]

That the state is a terrain of contradiction and contestation is well known. The seemingly opposite processes of a state's transnationalization and the preservation of its national prerogatives guarantee a constitutive tension, in which internationalization occurs. States no more play a passive role in this process than simply collapse before the logic of transnational capital.[11] Southern states, like Jamaica, redefined their responsibilities within the confines of structural adjustment policy, neoliberal globalization, and the "logic" of capital, according to an historically active role in domestic development and traditional ties with constituencies such as urban and rural working peoples. In other words, political elites whose survival is tied to their ability, both symbolic and real, to deliver goods to a populace attempt to find loopholes in the system of market liberalization even as they pay lip service to the "fairness" and "efficiency" of global economic realities. This tendency is particularly marked in postcolonial states where political terrain is violently guarded, as in Jamaica whose political culture is defined by rivalry, political clientelism, and violent partisanship.[12] The loopholes found within this particular period involved for the first time a cutting loose from the earlier focus on smallholders to a development policy based on commercial farming of a scale that, by definition, excluded key rural elements. It was, as Akhil Gupta notes of the effects of the Green Revolution in India, a "betting on the strong," those with sufficient resources.[13] Such a policy also excluded the institutions that administered to them. Rural society was being conceptually and developmentally rearranged. Smallholders' production mattered in so far as it complimented that of commercial firms. A new kind of agriculture was underway, whereby land-based working peoples were considered liabilities. And the traditional institutions of state that served them, primarily located within the Ministry of Agriculture, were backgrounded. These developments, it may be argued, constitute a dismantling of the developmental state, but hardly register the disempowerment of state officials, or the decline of relationships defining the state. Rather it shows as other analysts have argued, the globalization of the state, which refers to "state restructuring in which states adopt policies that are increasingly attuned to the imperatives of global capital accumulation."[14]

While the institutionalization of investment agriculture in the early 1980s was a direct outcome of market liberalization policies via increasing privatization, it represented a bid by the state to reestablish some direct political control over a different kind of agricultural production process. The state likewise sought to redefine agricultural development by shifting its attention away from smallholders and their concerns and, to a lesser extent, the traditional agricultural classes, seeking to create or reconstitute a class of local and foreign capitalist farmers. This shift in focus marked a new path but one which bore elements of the earlier era of "Industrialization by Invitation." Whereas previous regimes had remained harnessed to earlier practices of placating the smallholder sector, the 1980s witnessed the severing of this connection. As always, lip service was paid to the contribution of the smallholders and programs were targeted to specific areas of their concentration, but a disproportionate amount of resources was channeled into the AGRO 21 program. I would like to suggest that AGRO 21 be perceived as a neoliberal modernist elitist project, insofar as it emanated from a neoliberal perspective or ideology proclaiming the virtues of privatization and the market. It was a high modernist project both in its ideology, scale and target. Unlike the Democratic Socialist Plan, which targeted Jamaican youth and "sufferers," i.e., landless and urban employed, AGRO 21 deliberately bypassed this stratum focusing instead on new social strata, identified as pivotal to the development of the agricultural sector. My analysis therefore of 1980s agricultural policy shifts the focus away from the chronicling of the failures of the schemes and projects introduced, to one which highlights the new state/nonstate arenas that got restructured, and how the agricultural sector served as the key arena through which state elites marked their turn away from earlier policies.

Notwithstanding a debt crisis and the highly conditional structural adjustment loans, the Jamaican state leveraged privatization policy for political gain. Both the favoritism accorded new entrepreneurs and the Prime Minister's direct control over the AGRO 21 program suggest the state's unwillingness to relinquish control to the so-called imperatives of the market, as well as the emergence of a personalization of an important bureaucracy. Privatization should have undermined the government's control over the economy and over large segments of the society. However, the organization responsible for implementation was highly politicized, thereby ensuring the state an economic role which lasted until the collapse of most investment farming projects in 1989. What remained was a new approach to agriculture enunciated in language that advocated efficiency and profit and spoke of globalization's demands. What officials meant, in the words of an economic planner, was a shift of resources away from "inefficient" smallholders to large farms that have the potential to compete globally.[15] This became the common language marking the turn in agricultural policy.

By 1989, the Jamaican state's role as an instrument of/for development had eroded. As multilateral agencies expanded their roles in such an indebted economy, national institutions seemingly became mere forms for their directives. In the years since 1989, state elites have become increasingly constrained in their ability to act, even as mediators. Even so, operated between 1983 and 1987, as the foremost instrument of investment farming, the AGRO 21 program calls into question the assumptions regarding the automatic loss of state autonomy through liberalization and privatization. Concurrently, World Bank structural adjustment policies penetrated the agricultural sector, as well as the larger economy, with unprecedented ease.

Since 1977, the Jamaican state has had to follow policy guidelines set by the IMF, World Bank, IDB, and USAID, more or less concurrently.[16] Since 1987 the World Bank has ensured that painstaking scrutiny be applied to the implementation of the policies for which loans are secured. Given the country's indebtedness and its balance of payment crisis, Jamaica was forced to follow a program of deregulation through divestment, strict regulation of public spending, and increasing foreign exchange earnings through export production.[17] These reforms included:

1. The reform of Export Marketing Organizations (EMOs) to allow private organizations to export traditional crops.
2. The leasing and/or selling of idle or underutilized land.
3. The establishment of the Agricultural Credit Bank in 1982 in order to increase the efficiency of agricultural credit markets.
4. The creation of the AGRO 21 Corporation Limited, an agricultural company for promoting private-sector agricultural development.
5. The reorganization of the Ministry of Agriculture, emphasizing downsizing, integration and privatizing.[18]

After 1987, the Agricultural Sector Adjustment Loan assured the increased presence of the World Bank in the island's agricultural policy. As a result, the policies on land use which involved restoring productivity to thousands of acres of agricultural land prompted a status report by the President of the World Bank, stating:

> Under SAL I, an inventory of Govt.-owned land was carried out and a policy was formulated to transfer these lands to the private sector. Under SAL II, the transfer of Govt. land got under way, with about 7,000 acres having been either sold or leased by September 1983.[19]

The report also outlined the condition for certain loans:

> Under SAL III, there were a dated covenant and a condition of second tranche release related to these four EMOS. The dated covenant stated that the GOJ was to adopt no later than February 28, 1985, efficient pricing formulas to set the farm gate prices to be paid by the coffee, cocoa and pimento EMOS. The condition of second tranche release was that satisfactory progress should have been made in the GOJ's program to restructure these four EMOs along the following lines: (I) exclusion of research, extension and other non-marketing activities from the areas of competence of the EMOs; and (ii) deregulation of the external marketing activities of these organizations.[20]

USAID's concerns likewise fitted into the Bank's strategic scrutiny.[21] Three years into the agricultural "reform" program, USAID commissioned a report[22] to determine the nature of problems in the agricultural sector in order to make recommendations to speed up reparation and divestment, as well as to examine the compatibility of Jamaica's agriculture with that of the United States.[23] In addressing the issue of government and private-sector control, the USAID consultant pointed out that examples of successful government agricultural enterprises were practically nonexistent worldwide. He advised that "The GOJ (*Government of Jamaica*) is far too involved in most segments of Jamaican agriculture. Use of management contracts is a good start. They should accomplish complete divestment as rapidly as feasible."[24]

The Government of Jamaica followed these loan conditions, although not always willingly.[25] Still, in keeping with the loan guidelines of international agencies, the Seaga government set in place the policies of the IMF and the World Bank. While constrained by external directives, the perfunctory one-upmanship characteristic of Jamaican politics marked most policy shifts. For example, the Government rationalized the abolition and dismantling of the policies of the 1970s by arguing that they had abruptly halted the attempts made during the 1960s to eradicate the distortions of a colonially inherited economy.[26] The link between the programs of the 1960s and those of the 1980s lay in promoting the expansion of exports through "the growth of non-traditional agricultural and industrial export production."[27]

The political and economic context is important. The JLP's turn at governing Jamaica came when foreign investment seemed to have deserted the island. The Jamaica National Investment Promotions Limited (JNIP),[28] an autonomous state enterprise, had been unable to attract foreign investment. Commenting on this dilemma, a Ministry paper opined:

> The majority of proposals which both JNIP and JNIC had assessed were from individuals or companies offering technical and/or managerial services but no investment. This was also despite the Caribbean Basin Initiative (CBI) and the establishment of the joint US/Jamaica Investment Committee chaired by Mr. David Rockefeller. In the final analysis the capital inflows from foreign investment expected as a result of the initiatives by the Government of Jamaica (GOJ) were not materializing.[29] In addition, both major economic sectors bauxite and agriculture, were in decline. Agriculture, a large employer, was making only a nominal contribution to the Gross Domestic Product.[30] Beginning in 1980, earnings from major crops such as bananas and sugar had declined, and the economy was still highly unstable, "showing few signs of growth and though the initial inflows of loans and aid in various forms had replenished stocks of goods on supermarket shelves there were few other positive, particularly long-term benefits, in evidence."[31]

Economically crippled by this enduring downturn, Jamaicans welcomed the JLP government, headed by Edward Seaga.[32] While the Manley government's Democratic Socialist policies of the 1970s focused on alleviating the socioeconomic conditions of the "small man" through state control of the economic "commanding heights," the Seaga government came into office touting the free market and a philosophy rhetorically grounded in antistatism.[33] Seaga's victory attracted a tremendous inflow of funds from international agencies, and encouraged U.S. support to authorize softer, larger loans.[34] Characterizing himself as the man[35] who could fix economic distortion and provide for the well-being of the Jamaican peoples bound Seaga to promises difficult to keep, considering the strict structural adjustment policies of the International Monetary Fund (IMF). Seaga's rhetoric soon lost any claim to realization, considering the economic and social realities.[36] Furthermore, his attempts at repairing the structural warp of the Jamaican economy were illusory.[37] Several analysts document the Seaga government's contradictory actions in the face of structural adjustment policies and IMF imperatives. It has been shown that Seaga's government neither cut its expenditures, nor divested as quickly as was proposed by the IMF. Also, his government resisted devaluation until they found themselves in bitter contention with the IMF. Huber and Stephens attribute this foot-dragging to the political realities of the day and conclude that such a model was not viable since it did not "contain both a coherent long-run program for economic development and a viable strategy for maintaining political support."[38]

Whatever his concessions to the working peoples, the policies of Seaga's JLP sought to deepen the economic role of private-sector capitalism, even as this was accomplished by state involvement under the Prime Minister's personal guidance.

Agricultural Distortions and New Creations: AGRO 21

The language which cast agricultural problems in terms of modernization theory ostensibly permitted the state no definitive role.[39] This was mere rhetoric. The entire agricultural sector was depicted as laboring under the burden of traditional methods that made it uncompetitive in the world marketplace. The new government was interested in agrarian transformation à la the U.S.: commercial, large-scale farms producing for export. If fundamental change was to be realized, the economy would have to increase its foreign exchange earnings by attracting investors and improving agricultural yields via high modernist methods.

Against the backdrop of economic disarray, a weak foreign exchange market, and the enduring structural defects of the agricultural sector, not to mention the pressures of USAID, the IMF and the World Bank, the government of Jamaica touted commercial agriculture as the means to economic rehabilitation. According to Seaga, AGRO 21 epitomized "the true quest for independence in the 21st year of Jamaica's independence," in both name and design.[40] An investment program for the recovery of the agricultural sector, AGRO 21 affected the entire economy. Among its objectives were:

(A) Improvement of the investment climate in Jamaica and development of the country's investment capability (in public and private sectors) to achieve the fastest possible expansion of the country's ability to produce goods and services for export and for domestic consumption;

(B) Deregulation of the economy to encourage more private sector participation in the production and distribution of goods and services and to facilitate the creation of a more competitive economy;

(C) Enhancement of the country's ability to earn foreign exchange through the rehabilitation and expansion of the traditional export industries, tourism and agriculture and the reorganization and refurbishing of the industrial sector;

(D) Development and adequate manpower policies and programmes to increase the number of skilled workers in the country.[41]

During the 1980s, AGRO 21 was the major force in the government's planning, analysis and coordination of agricultural policy.[42] It was perceived as the vehicle for imposing modern, commercial agricultural standards. Emphasis was placed on developing new export markets and instilling in the minds of prospective farmer-entrepreneurs the need for a major technological overhauling of the labor process. What was at stake was:

>   (1) The transformation and modernization of the agricultural sector beginning with the sub-sectors/projects targeted for AGRO 21 and the creation of a major conduit through which private and institutional capital and technology can be mobilized for further development and growth of the Jamaican economy
>   (2) The achievement of strong annual growth in the gross foreign exchange contribution of the agricultural sector during the next four years in order to bolster current efforts aimed at achieving a positive net international reserves position within the shortest possible time frame.[43]

AGRO 21's financial backers shared a similar perspective. The primary backer, the USAID, believed that the establishment of new commercial farms would lead to a new export market and "demonstrate to investors with access to private land the potential for profit and open a new market and source of technical help for small farmers."[44] It was presented as the future of the country, a veritable revolution.[45]

As in the earlier "Industrialization by Invitation" of the 1950s and 1960s, and much to the chagrin of USAID officials, the state was actively involved in procuring and rewarding investors, as well as mediating between credit agencies and investors.[46] It was able to do this because of the reorganization of government statutory bodies, the restructuring of the Ministry of Agriculture and the devolving of new, enhanced responsibilities to state institutions. Ostensibly, the government sought to end its involvement in development, by stimulating the participation of private entrepreneurs in its ventures. Even so, the government was carving out a niche for itself and for a "new" class of commercial farmers, by overseeing the establishment and operation of AGRO 21. The state was prepared to do so at the expense of those older agencies which had filled a similar role in the past. During this time, government participation in the economy was reconstituted but certainly not diminished. The office of the Prime Minister began to issue the directives that would signal a new era of facilitated globalization.

AGRO 21 grew out of neither the traditional structure of agricultural production, nor existing state institutions. High-technology farming brought new organizations, leading directly to the Office of the Prime Minister. Seaga's multidepartmental steering committee was answerable to him through the Secretariat. This arrangement effectively excluded the Ministry of Agriculture, whose offices had historically been responsible for all aspects of agriculture. Even when certain responsibilities or special programs/projects were assigned to statutory bodies, the final decisions belonged to the Ministry. AGRO 21 changed the structure of governance.[47] In addition to the Secretariat of the Office of the Prime Minister,[48] supportive agencies were the Ministry of Agriculture, the National Planning Agency (NPA), Jamaica National Investment Company (JNIC), Jamaica National Investment Promotions Ltd. (JNIP),[49] the Agricultural Credit Bank, the Department of Statistics, the Scientific Research Council and USAID.[50] During the 1970s, all structures created to facilitate the operation of Project Land Lease, Project Food Farms and the sugar worker cooperatives remained under the Ministry of Agriculture's jurisdiction, restructured as a result of AGRO 21, their redundant responsibilities often confusing.

Among the Ministry's reconstituted responsibilities were:

(A) The development of a land resource and capability plan for the entire country, prioritized in terms of the requirements of AGRO 21.

(B) The provision of technical support in animal and plant protection and quarantine; and livestock development;

(C) Reorientation of the extension services to: disseminate the new technologies to the small farmer community; to assist farmers in the process of applying the new technologies in high-yielding varieties and crops best suited to their environment and having prospects for export;

(D) The development and documentation of existing farm locations, cropping and production patterns in order to facilitate the development of an orderly collection and marketing system;

(E) The establishment of standards for farm produce and educating the farmer in regard to the use of the inspection and grading stations.[51]

The government had succeeded in creating new structures, bypassing old ones and, no less important, reconstituting or resuscitating its instrumental effects within a key sector of the economy. Though old institutions had been stripped of their traditional responsibilities, the state had been invested with new agencies which assured its continuing role in reform and development. This political maneuvering sought to replace old farmers, particularly smallholders, with new entrepreneurs and marginalize small farming by privileging modern export-oriented "agribusiness." Perhaps, as stated by Mr. Pinella, the first USAID-appointed director of AGRO 21, this was a "revolution" of sorts.

Other Reforms

AGRO 21 required not only new organizations, but also a new environment, which the dismantling of Export Marketing Organizations (EMOs) facilitated, ostensibly to reduce monopolistic controls over export sales.[52] During the 1970s[53] EMO policy distorted prices, leading to differentials that favored domestic production by creating severe disincentives for export production.[54] To bring them more in line with new expectations, EMOs were stripped of their nonmarketing functions. The Ministry of Agriculture took over research and extension services, and the private sector assumed the supply of farming inputs. Additionally, projects on growing crops were shifted to the JNIP, which sold them to private investors. These projects were relieved of their marketing functions, so that by 1990 prices were set by predetermined formulae.[55]

The decision to close the operations of the sugar workers' cooperatives followed from the desire to eliminate old agricultural structures, and erase ideas about worker participation which had dominated policy rhetoric of the 1970s. The economic argument was that the sugar workers' cooperatives experienced operational difficulties as waste, inefficiency and declining sugar production.[56] The government dismantled the sugar cooperatives, erecting in their stead the National Sugar Company.[57] A new company was later formed to handle the operations of the Frome and Monymusk sugar properties, assisted by Tate and Lyle. Meanwhile, the government changed the structure of the Sugar Industry Authority (SIA), the company that oversaw the sugar industry, and reduced the latter's presence on that board to one member. When the Grays Inn sugar factory closed at the end of the 1983/84 sugar harvest, approximately 1,000 acres of its land were made available to the Jamaica Banana Producers' Association for high-technology banana production in keeping with the investment initiatives of AGRO 21 on the Bernard Lodge sugar properties. Investors cultivated winter vegetables, as well as cane for ethanol production.[58]

A new culture of privatization was set in motion, but one effected by the Jamaican government. Project feasibility studies used terms outlining economies of scale, competitiveness in the world market, universal standardization of produce, high technology, etc.[59] Studies were designed to ascertain the feasibility of expanded production of foods such as yams, sweet potatoes, cocoa, pumpkins and okra.[60] The traditional smallholder crops of sweet and hot peppers and tomatoes were also included. Raising productivity levels required intensive technology and capital outlays, impossible for small farmers. For example, 50-acre plots of hot peppers, once a traditional smallholder crop, were considered "the minimum size from the point of view of viability, but the optimum from the point of view of present market size."[61] Mixed farming or intercropping, a mainstay of smallholder farming on plots of (usually) less than 5 acres, according to the AGRO 21 feasibility studies, was best practiced on a *minimum* of 76 acres, the *recommended* size being 785 acres. Crops of sweet peppers, tomatoes, cucumbers and cantaloupes were considered solely in relation to agribusiness concerns, i.e., "maximization of investment in equipment for cultivation and packaging."[62] Other traditional smallholder crops, such as hot peppers and cucumbers, were deemed viable on plots of no less than 50 acres, requiring high levels of technology. Under these circumstances, traditional smallholders and farmers owning medium-sized farms had difficulty competing with state-supported entrepreneurs.

The Rise in Capitalized Agrarian Properties

These new agricultural enterprises were heavily capitalized. At the start of the program, government sources estimated the cost of total fixed capital through 1986/87 at J$958 million. Approximately "J$898 million would cover on-farm establishment, including land costs, and J$60 million for machinery and equipment."[63] This was required to bring properties up to a high level of modernization and to make them attractive to investors.

One major property, Spring Plain Project, of approximately 3,000 acres was made up of ten sections, an investment totaling J$288 million.[64] Its technologies included drip and microjet irrigation and earth reservoirs for water storage. Regarding the cultivation of winter vegetables on the Spring Plain project, one analyst stated:

> A network of perforated plastic tubing, manufactured in a J$2 million, purpose-built factory on site, has been laid in the fields and filtered water, containing dissolved plant nutrients, is distributed through the system. The technique is called drip feed irrigation; separate nozzles direct water onto the roots of individual plants. Sensors buried in the soil continually monitor soil moisture, and relay data back to a micro-processor located at the side of the field, and which supervises the distribution of water to plants. Thus the amount of water needed for irrigation is minimal, and it is possible to achieve high plant densities.[65]

The Victoria Banana Company, operated by Israeli management, cultivated an Israeli-adapted version, "a clone of the Great Cavendish type."[66] It had a drip irrigation/fertilization system "controlled by a central computer which can apply water, fertilizers, pesticides and other chemicals."[67] It used a cableway system to move bananas from field to packaging center and, rather than the traditional pole support, boasted an overhead support system for banana-laden trees.[68]

Its itemized valuation was estimated as follows:

Banana Cultivation	$J30,000,000
Infrastructure	8,000,000
Equipment	5,000,000
Assignment of Lease	6,000,000
	$J49,000,000[69]

When this property was converted from winter vegetables to orchard crop production, its entire assets were valued at $J10 million above original costs.

Privatization and export-led strategy led to the emergence of a new class of agricultural entrepreneurs. They were neither old-style estate owners, undercapitalized small farmers, nor the foreign assembly operations investors of the 1960s. A sense of this new stratum emerges by examining the lessees on new commercial farms.

International Rice Corporation leased 2,400 acres from the Agricultural Development Corporation for fifteen years. Equity was distributed among two private shareholders (80%) and the National Investment Bank of Jamaica (NIBJ), which held the rest. Agro-export Development Company Limited, its two shareholders being a businessperson and banking clerk, leased and subdivided Caymanas Horticulture Park, a fertile property of 4,500 acres.

Sunleaf Foliage had a 25-year lease on 30 acres. Its shareholders consisted of two business executives, one dermatologist, and one company director from Florida. Inter-Grow Limited's shareholders likewise represented a sampling from the largest merchants/traders/manufacturers operating through the following companies in Jamaica: Grace Kennedy & Company Ltd., Mussons Limited and House of Issa.[70] Each of these shareholders subscribed J$800,000 to the enterprise.

Under AGRO 21 leases were generous. The annual rentals of seven properties averaged roughly J$7,500.00. One lessee paid J$92,970, and another, J$16,000. One leased a property for J$9,077.85 and another, the parastatal company Urban Development Corporation, leased for only J$1,500.00.

Agricultural Incentives for New Entrepreneurs

Several lessees were allowed to lower and reschedule their rents, and they could get credit from the National Investment Bank of Jamaica when in arrears. The International Rice Corporation of Jamaica was able to escape NIBJ scouting for two years before its financial and operating difficulties came to light. The annual base rent of its property was J$168,000. That company borrowed J$4,000,000 from the Agricultural Bank at an interest rate of 25% per annum, considered generous at the time.

Political favoritism was particularly evident in the Spring Plain Project (SPP). The SPP consisted (eventually) of ten separate schemes.[71] It received more incentives than any other AGRO 21 project. Because lease arrangements were never signed, the SPP had free access to land and its loans were guaranteed by various state agencies:[72]

> Under the blessings of the Office of the Prime Minister, the project received full and active support—in terms of licences, permits, other authorization, concessions and discretionary treatment—of the government bureaucracy; in Customs, at the Trade Board, Ministry of Agriculture, the Airports Authority, the Ministry of Health, the Bank of Jamaica, the Ministry of Finance, the Revenue Board, Air Jamaica and the JNIP. It appears that the rules with respect to documentation and timely reporting were often stretched to accommodate the exigencies of the project throughout its four years of active existence.[73]

Restructuring the Traditional Export Sector

While diversification was tantamount to agricultural reforms of the AGRO 21 variety, structural adjustment directives aimed at deregulation and privatization were also felt in the traditional export sector. A joint agreement between the government of Jamaica and the IBRD (World Bank) to rehabilitate the sugar industry hinged on a management contract with the British-based company Tate and Lyle. That company assisted in introducing high-yield sugar and more advanced technology into the labor process.[74] The coconut industry was also rehabilitated with the introduction of disease-resistant and high-yield varieties.[75]

The Banana Board was divested "of its existing growing projects, and of the functions of buying and selling bananas and inputs for production."[76] Growers' organizations assumed control. As if to punctuate this decision, the government signed an agreement with United Brands, Jamaica Banana Producers and the Commonwealth Development Corporation to manage 2,500 acres of pure-stand bananas in the parish of St. Thomas, as well as an additional 4,500 acres elsewhere.[77] Once a statutory organization of the Ministry of Agriculture, the Banana Company was reorganized as a grower-managed trading company responsible for the purchasing, shipping and selling of bananas to the United Kingdom. The All Island Banana Growers' Association (AIBGA) was accountable for the servicing of the industry.[78]

The sugar industry operated similarly. An emphasis on privatization, underscored by the highly publicized contention that sugar declined under cooperative management, led to the dismantling of cooperatives and a reduction in sugar acreage. It was announced that approximately "20,100 acres would be withdrawn from sugar cane and used for the production of winter vegetables and other crops for import substitution."[79] Once a major sugar producer on the island, Tate and Lyle was recalled to provide technical management and assistance to the Frome, Monymusk and Bernard Lodge estates. The assets of these factories were subsequently transferred to a new company, Jamaica Sugar Holdings Limited, whose shares were held jointly by the Sugar Industry Authority and The Jamaica National Investment Bank.[80]

The structural adjustment program also affected the coffee industry. As with the banana and the sugar industries, the government reached an agreement with the OECF Japan to cultivate 3,500 acres in Portland and St. Thomas and also deregulated the Coffee Industry Board. According to agricultural minister Percival Broderick:[81]

> The Government is satisfied that in order to induce significant expansion to these commodities (cocoa, coffee, citrus, pimento) it is necessary to give both growers and processors an opportunity to become directly involved in exporting their products to lucrative foreign markets. It is equally important however, that the commodity organizations retain a sufficient degree of control over the export transactions of individual growers and processors in order to ensure proper quality of the commodities to be exported and the maximization of foreign exchange returns to Jamaica.[82]

Echoing popular island sentiment one *Gleaner* columnist faulted deregulation for excluding the small grower, regardless of product quality.[83] A grower organizing her or his own marketing had to supply a certain amount of coffee to qualify for consideration by the Board. Approved growers were licensed by the board after meeting certain conditions, leaving some people to wonder whether the board had any right to regulate the export of coffee.

The Collapse of Projects But the Survival of Investment Farming

By the mid-1980s, key projects in the agricultural restructuring showed signs of imminent collapse. By focusing on two such investment farms—Grace Kennedy and Co.'s (a Jamaican trading cooperation) Halse Hall Properties and Spring Plain—we can discover how it was that despite such generous incentives and political favoritism, AGRO 21 investors registered such colossal failures. Consider the fact that the Grace Kennedy and Co.'s Halse Properties, cultivated in the period before AGRO 21 and benefitting from incentives provided under the latter, throughout the 1980s, did not save the company from ruin. Even as the Seaga government's grand showpiece, Spring Plain could not survive.[84]

Grace Kennedy and Co. started cultivating vegetables in 1980,[85] using such technology as improved seeds, irrigation and full fertilization, disease control, mechanical cultivation and crop specialization.[86] As Grace Kennedy and Co. hoped to reap maximum profit from farming, it chose vegetables for quick turnover. The company also hoped to develop crops that "would contribute to the improvement of the Jamaican trade balance such as export crops, or import replacing crops for the local food processing industry and fresh market."[87]

Agronomically production exceeded expectations, but costs were high enough to prevent full cultivation expansion. Although the company had leased 1500 acres, only 800 were deemed cultivable, and of these only 115 acres were under vegetable production that first year.[88] During 1981/82 net loss exceeded J$.5 million.[89] However, bolstered by the crop yields of 1982/1983, the company expanded production to 260 acres and invested J$7.5 million more. A shift from sprinkler irrigation technology to drip technology improved yields, but inflation and further devaluation of the Jamaican dollar pushed production costs well beyond those projected compounding the project's economic difficulties. Its demise was attributed alternately to such factors as the world's trading companies, the nature of production and export marketing of agricultural products, the rising costs of production, problems with the irrigation system, postharvest difficulties or lack of relief.[90] In 1986, Grace Kennedy and Co. closed down its operations at Halse Hall.

The collapse of Spring Plain in 1986 alarmed the public, who attributed its failure primarily to mismanagement and political "footballism." Farm leaders in the traditional export crops of sugar, bananas and citrus expressed outrage at the lack of official information on the project's 1986 collapse, calling it a "laugh and debacle," referring to the "Spring Plain Fiasco."[91] Problems cited included poor communication between high-tech operators and local agronomists apropos soil conditions, the incompetence of Israeli "experts," and alleged lower produce sale prices than those originally quoted to dealers.[92] It was also claimed that the Agricultural Credit Bank (ACB) lent the project J$12 million without the necessary loan documents.[93] The public's belief that the ACB had suffered colossal losses prompted the release of a statement from the project's principal lending agency, the National Investment Bank of Jamaica.[94] In this statement the directors[95] attributed the difficulties and final collapse of the project to unprecedented wet weather in 1986, and a fall in the winter vegetables' prices in the U.S. and world markets. The board defended the bank's decision to offer generous loans to the company, citing three features that had attracted investment: (1) production under drip irrigation, (2) air transportation at reasonable cost and (3) Israeli expertise.[96]

Because of disappointing winter vegetable yields, Spring Plain diversified its operations to include a freshwater fish farm, a nursery, a factory to manufacture drip irrigation tubes and a banana growing project.[97] Like the NIBJ's directors, Prime Minister Seaga denied any wrongdoing at Spring Plain, and attributed mistakes to errors of judgment and lack of information. He declared the government's continuing interest in vegetable production and opined that losses accompanied risk taking. Seaga pointed out that the nation had benefitted from high-technology farming at a time when traditional export crops were scarcely exportable and prospects for new products seemed grim. Some additional benefits were: (1) foreign exchange earnings or savings of US\$36 million; (2) employment for 27,000 workers; (3) the utilization of 50,000 acres of previously idle land; and (4) the use of high technology increasing farm productivity.[98]

Despite the Prime Minister's buoyant optimism, it was clear by 1987 that this high modernist investment farming had failed to achieve its objectives. Visiting several properties only three years after Spring Plain's cessation, one columnist wrote wryly of ruin:

> The impression I got on a visit to Thetford is of a poem "The Deserted Village." Not only is the land left idle but valuable equipment lies strewn around as if in a haphazard grave yard. Seeing Spring Plain today, overgrown with scrub, equipment and very expensive equipment left to the mood of the elements one could never believe that so much had been squandered there in such a short time ago. One gets an urge to get a spade and dig to find out if some of the money was in treasure buried beneath the scrub and brush. Ditto for Bernard Lodge where the burial ground is of even more recent vintage. And ditto as well for many of the other projects in which our recent government had a hand. The "brown thumb" is everywhere in evidence.[99]

An Act of Development: Managing Old Clients

Aware of criticism that AGRO 21 was "fe big man,"[100] the Minister of Agriculture announced that large-scale agricultural investment "must not replace our concern for the small farmer; that it must set an example for, and assist him with developing his own technology by seeing something working."[101]

The Ministry of Agriculture, which had in the past borne responsibility for the entire agricultural sector, as noted earlier, and which had occupied a peripheral position in this new investment agriculture scheme, was nevertheless responsible for apprizing small farmers of technological developments on commercial AGRO 21 farms. In short, the future of small farmers not directly involved in AGRO 21 lay in their full support of the program. While elites staked their belief in the saving graces of large-scale, highly technologized agriculture, small farmers felt that the "government's policies were taking the country back to the years of large estates in which the small farmer would scarcely be able to own his bit of land," and would have "to give up his fork, machete and spade to take up higglering (informal marketing) to feed himself and his family."[102]

To save face among small farmers, who were one of the JLP's key political constituents, the government advanced two strategies. First, it gave smallholders greater access to credit by streamlining the operations of financial institutions. Peoples' Cooperative Banks (PCBs) were established to disburse credit to farmers. PCBs relied on the Agricultural Credit Bank (ACB), which had emerged from the phasing out of the Jamaica Development Bank. The ACB was to become a viable enterprise providing credit to farmers "on a timely, cost-effective and relevant basis." It also operated as a wholesaler of credit on-lending funds to commercial banks, PCBs and other institutions which retailed to farmers.[103]

In the past, reluctant to make loans available to agriculture, commercial banks were incorporated into schemes as suppliers of credit.[104] What differentiated this approach from the pre-1970s sort of agricultural development was the marginal amount of credit assumed for small farmers.[105] These were truly small loans. In 1991 73% of loans disbursed to each small farmer were less than $J10,000. Commercial banks and approved financial institutions lent generously to large farms. One analyst estimated that "54% of these loans were between J$100,000 and J$500,000."[106] As was the case before 1972, farmers were expected to produce according to what was needed both domestically and externally. Now they were required to conform to AGRO 21 guidelines, which abolished such relief as subsidy or discounted credit.

The government's second strategy was based on the notion of the "mother farm," quite common in many parts of the Third World, ostensibly allowing for the association of geographically related small farms with a central, large, high-technology farm.[107] Thus could smallholders benefit from modern technology and be further drawn into commercial farming through "mother farms" contracts. This was never realized. According to reports, small farmers could not be forced to abide by any contract and those deemed capable of "mothering" did not feel secure enough to teach small farmers.[108]

Given this backdrop, it was difficult to agree with Seaga's sentiment that small farmers were benefitting widely from technology introduced on large estates, and that these high-technology farms complemented smallholder production.[109] Seaga's optimism failed to infect such associations as the Jamaica Agricultural Society, comprising many sorts of farmers but having most contact with small farmers. Society President Senator Courtney Fletcher called the Spring Plain situation "a colossal national economic let down" and accused the government of abandoning the small farmer "who for many years had sustained the economy" and now "had been starved of support."[110] Fletcher underlined these charges by pointing to the decline in resources allocated to the smallholder sector:

> The resources allocated to the servicing of this sector called economic service to agriculture in 1983/84 was 1.97% of the Budget. In 1984/85 it was 1.61% of the Budget; and in 1985/86 it was 1.5% of the Budget.[111]

Stanching a Hemorrhaging Smallholder Sector: Hillside Agricultural Project

During the operation of AGRO 21—and the economic thrust toward greater privatization—the government facilitated the Hillside Agricultural Project (HAP) under the auspices of IFAD,[112] the government of the Netherlands and other government and farmer contributors. Like the many modernization projects of the past, HAP's objective was to increase productivity, expand acreage under tree crops (primarily cocoa and coffee), as well as raise levels of productive employment and income for small farmers and other residents of hillside communities.[113] The introduction of sound environmental practices was also integral to the project.[114]

HAP operated on the eastern section of the island in St. Thomas, St. Catherine, Manchester and Clarendon, where hillside farming predominated, targeting the full-time smallholder.[115] In areas such as Rio Minho and Rio Cobre 75% of farms were less than 5 acres, occupying roughly 32% of total land and producing for domestic as well as export markets.[116] Small farmers who operated at least half an acre were eligible, but had been cultivating tree crops with food grown primarily for domestic markets.[117]

The scheme operated through thirty-two subprojects, each with an independent management team. HAP participants received grants from the Ministry of Agriculture and agricultural inputs such as training and technical assistance. Unlike earlier agricultural projects, the Hillsides project was tightly supervised. Small farmers (with less than 10 acres) received loans for farm tools, seedlings, fertilizer, chemicals, organic manure and 80% of the first year's labor.[118] Coffee farmers were categorized by the type of coffee grown, e.g., Blue Mountain coffee received J$4,992 per acre and High Mountain coffee, J$5,052.[119] Cocoa farmers received roughly J$1,518 per acre. Advances were provided to some farmers on a crop lien basis, 10% for coffee, 20% for cocoa. To qualify for loans small farmers had to satisfy the development officer's assessment of their needs and resources, as well as accept practical recommendations. There were strict guidelines regarding loan qualifications. Although the intention was to grant 75% of credit to farmers cultivating or rehabilitating tree crops on less than 2 acres, farmers were still expected to provide collateral, often acquired on a crop lien basis.

Projects were to be monitored often, as mature tree crops warranted a certain amount of scrutiny. In the case of coffee, "the Coffee Industry Development Company (CIDCO) would be responsible for monitoring and evaluating coffee development at the farm level, including numbers of borrowers contacted, total acreage planted/rehabilitated, compliance with recommended practices (including soil conservation) impacts on production and the status of loan repayment through the CIDCO deduction order."[120] This close monitoring presumably eliminated the incidence of loan rescheduling and debt delinquency, the bane of previous smallholder projects.

Several institutions connected with the project provided support services, including the Ministry of Agriculture, the project's principal coordinator, and credit agencies, such as the Agricultural Credit Bank, the Peoples' Cooperative Banks, the National Development Foundation of Jamaica, the Coffee Industry Board and the Coffee Development Company. These institutions ensured that HAP operated as a credit scheme aimed to stabilize the small-farm sector.

One study confirmed the success of the project as regards the expansion of tree crops.[121] Indeed farmers benefitted from the distribution of seedlings, fertilizers, herbicides and pesticides. Yet the spread of correct technical practices resulted only when small farmers received free inputs and the market guaranteed fair crop prices. It was noted that

> Under the project, these inputs were given free to the farmers who started using these at a higher level than when they had to purchase them. It is thus expected that along with the increased prices of all inputs and low prices for their output, if the perceived gain is marginal or less, then many of these farmers would have reverted to their former practices.[122]

To be sure HAP had a demonstrable effect. Participants adopted at least one of several HAP-advocated farming techniques; the most common, pruning, increased plant density and increased fertilizer use. Nevertheless, one study contends that HAP was "preaching to the converted,"[123] that the project's loci did not include worst-case scenarios, nor were the participants non-tree crop farmers. The project was preventive in orientation and benefitted only a few farmers in its area of operation. The project lent to a mere 200 farmers. Out of roughly 22,000 cocoa farmers, only about 74 actually benefitted.[124]

New Class Alliances Amid an Old Division of Labor

While earlier governments relied on the old Ministry of Agriculture to implement agricultural policy, the Seaga government bypassed it and partially dismantled such institutional structures. New entrepreneurs were welcomed into an agribusiness venture, and their investment protected by the state. This agrarian transformation did not resemble the commercialization of family farms in Chile, Venezuela and Mexico (as Llambi and others writing on Latin America have documented).[125] Investment agriculture relied on investors with sufficient capital to commercialize properties. Many investors were not even agriculturalists. As we have seen earlier, some were traders. One of the biggest investors, Eli Tisona of Israel, had made his capital from hamburgers, and subsequently invested in a 5,000-acre farm producing vegetables for the UK market.[126]

The sentiment among the elite and middle classes was that the high-technology farm was the wave of the future and that small farmers should continue producing for the domestic market, since commercial farming lay beyond their financial reach. Seeking to account for Jamaica's decline in exports, one columnist argued that

> the traditional range of banana farmers has been trying to do a job which has been impossible for them to do. They haven't the flat land, they haven't the high-tech capacity and beyond all, they haven't the money. Can you imagine what would face a Jamaican farmer were he to try to borrow $35,000 per acre at 23% per annum for only 5 years? High-tech is now for the very big boys. It is they who must now revive Jamaica's banana industry, if it is to be revived at all. The future of Jamaica's banana industry is now firmly in the hands of the high-tech operators—two or perhaps at the most three. All that is needed to give Jamaica a valuable and flourishing export trade of 120,000 tons a year are 6 or 7 thousand high-tech acres, with a capital which though it makes the mind of the traditional farmer boggle, is available to them for long terms and at reasonable interest rates.[127]

With the entry of commercial farmers and entrepreneurs, the agrarian social structure experienced "high modernist" technological shifts. Given the ruinous results of AGRO 21, agriculture reverted in large part to its pre-1970s structure but with new concerns spurred by the demands of the globalization project. Democratic Socialism of the 1970s and the neoliberalism of the 1980s and 1990s shared a common belief about the type of development that would boost agricultural accumulation. Neither strategy yielded positive results to commercial farms, small farmers, or large-scale entrepreneurial farms. Both regimes attempted to secure political control over socioeconomic developments in the agrarian sector, despite the rhetoric of, on the one hand, worker control and, on the other, privatization and market liberalism.[128]

The imposition of high-technology farms in the agricultural sector spelled disaster for smallholders and others operating within traditional frameworks as producers of both domestic and export crops. Whereas, under the Democratic Socialist regime of Michael Manley in the aftermath of so-called worker-controlled farming, the agricultural sector quickly reverted to the structural norms of the pre-1970s era, the shift to high-technology farming assured its continued persistence, despite AGRO 21's failures. Moreover, the PNP government's leader, P. J. Patterson, followed Manley into "relentless" support for neoliberal globalization policy. The regime was coopted into the imperatives of the structural adjustment programs, particularly the 1990 agricultural sector adjustment loan (ASAL), which demanded the steady dismantling of state-controlled enterprises, the divestment of government properties and economic responsibilities and the "downsizing" of agencies serving the public sector.[129] Thus, since the return to office of a PNP government, the policies which guided the JLP government have not changed substantively. Then in opposition, the PNP called for the resignation of the government over the winter vegetable disaster epitomized by Spring Plain and other properties' colossal losses. In office since 1989, the PNP[130] announced that AGRO 21 would be phased out within a year and that its functions would be limited to managing government's land divestment program.[131] In a similar turnaround in 1989, Manley announced that the market logic had been "pursued relentlessly" since the PNP had regained the reins of government. Investment farming continued, only this time as the responsibility of the Agricultural Development Corporation (ADC), of which AGRO 21 was once a subsidiary. The institutions at the helm of the economic globalizing project, the IMF, IDB and USAID, and now the World Trade Organization (WTO), have now emerged as key shapers of the state's agenda. As Levitt put it, "the government is increasingly transformed into the local executing authority of programmes designed by the Washington-based agencies."[132] But even this statement hardly captures the mechanisms through which these new directives are instituted, and how they introduce different actors into the state structures, nor how these changes effect a new kind of ideology that asserts individualized privatization.

Continuities of the 1980s and 1990s

When the JLP government assumed office in the late 1980s, buoyed by external and domestic support for market liberalization, it ended the reformist and redistributive policies of the past, particularly of the 1970s,[133] thereby (arguably) fore-stalling the sustained impact of the agrarian enterprises that emerged between 1972 and 1980.[134]

Moreover, the globalization project has linked the agendas of multilateral agencies facilitated by the imposition of IMF guidelines and, since 1987, by the World Bank.[135] Thus, state policy has differed little during the 1990s.[136] Notwithstanding the project failures of AGRO 21, the sort of ideas that investment farming instituted continue to thrive. AGRO 21 was indeed a successful instrument which facilitated the new culture of privatization, now underway on the island. The skepticism toward the smallholder's role in this new culture has become entrenched, fueled by concerns about the country's ability to compete in the globalized arena. An FAO report confirmed the continuing trend:

> The SAP has attracted a new type of producer and marketing agent to the agricultural export sector. In the case of the production level these have been high income entrepreneurs, often a professional who works fulltime in another sector, has capital for large-scale production, and is able to hire management and labor services. In the case of marketing, it is an enterprising person who has been a trader in the non-agricultural sector and who sees an opportunity to earn foreign exchange through the agricultural sector to promote the general trading business. New entrants to the "Blue Mountain" coffee sector provide examples of these changes.[137]

Developments in coffee and banana production evince the changing division of agricultural labor. I refer specifically to the marginalization of smallholders and the encouragement of such "new" entrants as medium or large-sized farming enterprises.

Such marginalization can be tracked by noting the early contributions of agro-working peoples, from around 1900, when smallholders contributed 80% of the bananas destined for the United States. The Agricultural census of 1978/79 and the Farmers' Register of 1982 attributed 98% of all export production, and banana production specifically, to farms of less than 25 acres in size. Thus, smallholders not only held significant stakes in domestic crop production, but they were also seriously involved in production for export.[138] Until the mid-1990s, three high-technology farms, namely, Eastern Banana Estates Limited, Victoria Banana Estates in Clarendon and St. Mary Bananas, produced 73% of all banana production on the island.[139] Between 1985 and 1995, these AGRO 21–established farms saw productivity rise from 10 to 25 tons per hectare, more than 9 tons per acre. Exports likewise increased from 12,000 to 76,000 tons in that ten-year period. The contribution of other growers fell roughly from 97% in 1984 to 21% in 1995.[140]

There has been increased regional and social disparity and greater inequity. In 1986, small farmers in the parish of St. Mary complained about the decline of banana production in that parish. While banana output increased overall, its production in traditional areas declined. According to one account of a small farmer meeting in St. Mary, "farmers were reminded of the time when the parish produced 7,000 tons a week. Now the parish can only muster 1,200 tons a week."[141] These farmers attributed their shifting fortunes to the following causes: the hurricane ravages, the change in government policy, including the replacement of the Banana Board by the grower-controlled Banana Export Company (BECO),[142] high interest rates on loans charged by the Peoples' Cooperative Banks (PCBs) and the closure of several boxing plants.[143] St. Mary's small farmers now face severe transportation problems. They must travel with their fruit over a longer distance, resulting in a higher incidence of spoilage and deterioration. Faced with these frustrations, some resorted to selling small quantities to higglers, opting out of export agriculture.[144]

Like bananas, until the 1970s, coffee production was the domain of smallholders. During that time, 85 percent of production came from farms of less than 2 acres in size. As forest and pine gave way to intensive coffee production in the 1990s,[145] 55% of production, particularly of the highest quality (Blue Mountain), was being cultivated on medium and large holdings.[146] Coffee production and productivity have increased substantially. Yields grew from 398 boxes per hectare in 1985 to 529 boxes in 1995.[147] At the same time, the export of Blue Mountain Coffee increased by 739% between 1989 and 1993.[148] Nevertheless, the downsizing of extension services and difficulties in accessing credit, despite public announcements, have effectively stalled small farmers' entry or restricted their advancement.

Large farms' penetration of areas previously dominated by small farmers characterizes also the sugar and the citrus industries. Not only did government sell its sugar concerns, notably the factories of Bernard Lodge, Long Pond, Frome and Monymusk, but it relinquished its position in marketing and regulation. Crop marketing was placed in the hands of a grower-dominated company, Jamaica Cane Product Sales (JCPS).[149] Since 1978, the acreage operated by non-estate sugar farmers has declined significantly from 114,000 in 1976 to 19,000 in 1991. On the other hand, estates have increased their share of acreage cultivated from 24,000 acres in 1978 to 47,000 acres in 1984.[150] Employment figures in table 5.1 below reflect the contraction in the number of small farmers, and the acreage they controlled. With the decline of 1970s programs such as the sugar cooperatives, and divestment of public lands to private enterprise, notably high-technology farms, the number of small farmers decreased by 12% (10% men and 2% women).[151]

Table 5.1.   The Share of Employment by Labor Market Sector, 1977–1989

Peasant agriculture	1977	1985	1989	1977–85	1985–89
Both sexes	25.5	27.7	22.5	2.2	−5.2
Female	4.9	5.6	4.9	0.7	−0.7
Male	20.6	22.1	17.6	1.5	−4.5
Wage agriculture					
Both sexes	10.4	8.4	5.9	−2.0	−2.5
Female	4.7	3.2	2.1	−1.5	−1.1
Male	5.7	5.2	3.8	−0.5	−1.4

Source: Adapted from P. Anderson and M. Witter (1994), "Crisis Adjustment and Social Change," 30.

Conclusions

Agrarian developments since the 1980s underscore significant transformation in the social relations obtaining in the agricultural sector specifically and within the Jamaican state generally. The transformation represents not a reversion to the old plantation days, as small farmers rhetorically contend, but a new development unprecedented in Jamaica, though commonplace globally, namely, the redefinition of the state's role in light of the demands of multilateral agencies in pursuing a neoliberal economic agenda. In Jamaica, as elsewhere, this has resulted in maneuvering to balance the traditional relationships that the state bureaucracy has had with certain social strata.[152] The shift in emphasis from the sort of worker/smallfarmer control of the 1970s large-scale commercial farms supposedly better able to compete on the world market has led to the decentering of smallholder agricultural production. Negotiating multilateral agencies' agendas necessitated consideration of political consequences, so that, even as the state operated within a debt regime, it was not always a conspirator in its supposed demise, nor a willing, acquiescent actor, and often tried to explore the loopholes of such programs and in doing so facilitated globalization. Current discussions of globalization overlook such state resistance or maneuvering, masked as it is in statements about states making the terrain safe for capital, to focus on the strategies whereby states accommodate and facilitate globalization. Examination of the state's historical role in globalization requires analyses of the different circumstances, the new forms of accumulation that are needed, and the situations that institutions find themselves in and also, the changing nature of the relationships between state and nonstate arenas.

AGRO 21 is a pivotal example of how beleaguered states attempt to 1) create new institutions to prepare the terrain for the demands of a neoliberal economic agenda, and 2) accommodate the agendas of new actors selected to lead and engage the neoliberal accumulation process. The exploration of historical contingencies is as important as that of the operations and impact of global forces. Since the 1990s, the Jamaican state's developmental role has changed somewhat, insofar as it cannot produce development along its "own" lines, but must act as the vehicle through which global policy and its implementation proceeds. The PNP's replacement of the JLP in 1989 witnessed continued conformity to IMF, IDB, and USAID policies.[153] This policy supports large-scale agricultural enterprises, the undercutting of agricultural subsidies to land-based working people, and the reduction of support services, unless sustained by farmers themselves. Some argue that the structural adjustment programs of the 1980s and, by extension, the neoliberal policies of the 1990s will have little effect on a stratum long accustomed to being jostled around by development policy. A study of one small farming community concludes that small farmers manipulate residency, responsibility and reciprocity and, to the extent of their effectiveness, end up winners or losers.[154] Therefore they state, "SA (structural adjustment) is then just another in the series of difficulties and that the small farmer simply continues in the trajectories of strategic flexibility and limping survival."[155] True, but the changes since the mid-1980s have been unprecedented and fundamental, and the developmentalist state, which bolstered patron-client relations with land-based working peoples, has more or less reached its limits since the 1980s. Surely this means that smallholders are no longer the subject of development, rhetoric notwithstanding. Nor is the state the same. So immense change has been effected on the island, which reverberates within the agricultural sector resulting in dramatic shifts in strategies for survival of both state and working peoples.

I have attempted to place the changes that have taken place in agriculture in the context of the sort of globalization expressed in Jamaica. It looks like a zero sum game. Large-scale, often local farmer/capitalists gain at the expense of land-based working peoples. How these tensions will develop amid the targeting of a different constituency, and the declining role of land-based working peoples, is hard to say. It need be recalled, however, that smallholders have agency. They are not passive, accommodating and powerless against change. Mythologized as resisting peasants, they are seldom seen as development's creations, sustained and undermined by state policies, maneuvering within them to effect agendas and ensure their survival, however tenuous. It is imperative that we also discuss the political maneuvers of smallholders, given their multidirectional location and existence, as they attempt to influence state policy. For they must, given their past centrality to the policies of the development state. But they come up against state institutions with a different set of economic imperatives, and political elites conscious of global institutions and actors, which circumscribe and determine their agendas.

Notes

1. Hirst and Thompson 1996: 6; see also Krugman 1996, quoted in Paul du Gay, "Representing Globalization: Notes on the Discursive Orderings of Economic Life" in *Without Guarantees: In Honour of Stuart Hall*, ed. Paul Gilroy et al. (London: Verso, 2000), 113–123.

2. Thomas Blom Hansen and Finn Stepputat, "INTRODUCTION: States of Imagination," in Idem, *States of Imagination: Ethnographic Explorations of the Postcolonial State* (Durham: Duke University Press, 2001), 30.

3. "Small Garden, Bitter Weed: A Postscript: The IMF, Democratic Socialism and Zig-Zag Politics: Jamaica, 1976–1977," in Kari Levitt Kingston (Canoe Press, The University of the West Indies 2000), 349.

4. Trevor Munroe, *Jamaican Politics: A Marxist Perspective in Transition* (Colorado and Kingston: Lynne Rienner Publishers, and Heinemann Publishers, 1990).

5. See for example, David Barkin, "The End to Food Self-Sufficiency in Mexico." *Latin American Perspectives* 14, 3 (1987): 271–297.

6. Philip McMichael and David Myhre, "Global Regulations vs the Nation State: Agro-food Systems and the New Politics of Capital," *Capital and Class* no. 43 (Spring 1991): 83–105.

7. Omar Davies, "An Analysis of the Management of the Jamaican Economy: 1972–1985," *Social and Economic Studies* 35, no.1 (March 1986)

8. Giovanni Arrighi (1998). Arrighi posits that states never had the powers that they have reputedly lost.

9. Stuart Hall (1996).

10. Stuart Hall, "The Local and the Global: Globalization and Ethnicity." in *Culture, Globalization and the World System* edited by Anthony D. King. (Minneapolis: University of Minnesota Press, 1997); Linda Weiss, *The Myth of the Powerless State* (Ithaca: Cornell University Press, 1998)

11. Laura T. Raynolds et al., "The "New" Internationalization of Agriculture: A Reformulation," *World Development* Vol. 21, no.7 (1993): 1101–1121. Here the authors delineate substantive differences in the responses and capacities of Mexico, Dominican Republic and Puerto Rico. The latter two resemble more the Jamaican case.

12. I have adapted the phrase used by Weiss in her discussion of the role of the state and the creation of an informal sector.

13. Akhil Gupta, *Postcolonial Developments: Agriculture in the Making of Modern India* (Durham, London: Duke University Press, 1998), especially chap. 1, 60.

14. Hilbourne Watson, "When the Liberalist Solution is Part of the Problem: Capitalist Globalization and Contradictions of the Liberal Democratic State." Paper delivered at the Conference on "Interrogating the Globalization Project," University of Iowa, Iowa City, November 1–4, 2001), 9.

15. Interview with an economic planner in the Ministry of Agriculture, June 2000.

16. How this intriguing development occurred under Democratic Socialism is the subject of several texts. For example, George L. Beckford and Michael Witter, *Small Garden Bitter Weed* (London: Zed Press, 1982); Trevor Munroe, *Jamaican Politics* (Heinemann and Lynne Rienner Publishers, 1990); Nelson Keith and Novella Z. Keith, *The Social Origins of Democratic Socialism in Jamaica* (Philadelphia: Temple University Press, 1992).

17. Jamaica's total external debt then was estimated at US$4.5 billion dollars; or every person on the island owes US$1,800.00. See Kari Polyani Levitt, *The Origins and Consequences of Jamaica's Debt Crisis, 1970–1990* (UWI Mona: Consortium School of School Sciences, 1991). In March 2002 the debt stood at J$494 billion or 133.1% of GDP. For more on this issue see the Epilogue.

18. "Assessment of the Effects of Structural Adjustment on the Agricultural Sector, Jamaica Technical Report" (Rome: FAO, 1995), 14.

19. Report of the President of the World Bank to the Executive Directors for an Agricultural Sector Adjustment Loan for Jamaica, Feb. 9, 1990, Annex IV, 46 (page 1 of 8).

20. Report of the President of the World Bank to the Executive Director for an Agricultural Sector Adjustment Loan to Jamaica, Feb. 9, 1990. 48–49 (Pages 3 and 4 of 8).

21. See Table 25 in AGRO 21 Master Plan. Table 25 AGRO 21: Fixed capital demand/supply, 3.6.

22. William R. Furtnick, "Jamaica Agricultural Sector Analysis prepared for the Jamaica U.S. Mission during March-April, 1986," mss. Consultant report—USDA/OICD.

23. It was agreed that, except in the case of Florida, which in any case suffers from not infrequent freezes, the development of Jamaica's AGRO 21 with its large winter vegetable component was not incompatible with US agricultural schemes.

24. Jamaica Agricultural Sector Analysis (1986), 18.

25. See Kari Polyani Levitt (1991), for a discussion of the problems which the Jamaican state had with the Fund and the Bank. Also Patricia Anderson and Michael Witter, "Crisis, Adjustment and Social Change A Case Study of Jamaica," In *Consequences of Structural Adjustment A Review of the Jamaican Experience*, ed. Elsie Le Franc (UWI Mona: Canoe Press, 1994), 1–55; and Margaret Newman and E. Le Franc, "The Small-Farm Sub Sector Is There Life After Structural Adjustment?" in E. Le Franc (1994): 118–210.

26. Some of these structural defects cited were, "the widening gap between the demand for investment resources and domestic savings and the underdevelopment of the local capital market, the inadequate ratio of fixed investment to gross domestic product, the severity of pressures of development on the balance of payments, the relatively high rate of growth of imports per unit of domestic output, and the rise in the level and rate of unemployment." For a more detailed characterization of the economy see *Structural Adjustment of the Jamaican Economy (SAJE) 1982–1987*, 1.

27. Ibid.

28. The JNIP had its early beginnings as a division within the Jamaica National Investment Company Limited (JNIC).

29. Ministry paper no. 56, 2.

30. In 1981 agriculture's share of employment in the productive sectors amounted to 70%. In the economy as a whole, it accounted for 36%.

31. *Structural Adjustment of the Jamaican Economy (SAJE) 1982–1987*, 2.

32. No further information on paper no. 56 is supplied, except that it was signed by P. J. Patterson, Q.C. Deputy Prime Minister and Minister of Development, Planning and Production, 21 November 1989.

33. See Evelyn H. Stephens and John D. Stephens, "The Political Economy of Structural Adjustment: The Seaga Government of Jamaica," unpub. mss. Paper delivered at the Caribbean Studies Association XIV annual conference Barbados, May, 1989.

34. Levitt argues that the Jamaican government was massively financed by multilateral and bilateral loans and suggests that there was something suspiciously political about this. K. Levitt (1991), *The Origins and Consequences of Jamaica's Debt Crisis 1970–1990*.

35. Seaga (and his supporters) derided Mr. Manley, punning on the word mis(s)management of the economy and referring to himself as the capable and macho "Mr. Management."

36. Several analysts document the Seaga government's contradictory actions even in the face of structural adjustment policies and IMF imperatives. For example, in an examination of its general economic policies, Huber and Stephens (1992) argue that Seaga resisted many of these guidelines, e.g., his government did not immediately cut government expenditures, neither did it divest as quickly as was proposed by the IMF. Also, his government resisted devaluation so much that they found themselves in bitter contention with the IMF. Huber and Stephens attribute this foot dragging to the political realities of the day. They argue that "The free market capitalist model is not a viable politico-economic model, at the very least in a democracy with relatively high degrees of mobilization. To be a viable politico-economic model, a model must contain both a coherent long-run program for economic development and a viable strategy for maintaining political support. Thus, one reason why the IMF model is not viable is that the economic policies cannot be applied without provoking resistance and thus inconsistent application of the policies." See Evelyn Huber and John D. Stephens, "Changing Development Models in Small Economies: The Case of Jamaica From the 1950s to the 1990s," *Studies in Comparative International Development* 27, no. 2 (1992): 57–92.

37. For a fuller discussion of the politics and economics of the Seaga government see Evelyn Stephens and John D. Stephens, "Political economy of structural Adjustment: The Seaga Government in Jamaica," unpub. mss. (Paper presented at the Caribbean Studies Association XIV Annual Conference, Bridgetown, Barbados 23–26 May 1989).

38. E. Huber and J. D. Stephens, (1992), and E. Stephens and J. D. Stephens (1989).

39. Some agricultural problems included the absence and/or inadequacy of inputs, the existence of massive acreage of underutilized or idle land, the destruction of critical areas, e.g., watersheds, through indiscriminate farming, inadequate extension services, lack of sufficient water resources, difficulties of titling, inaccessible credit or marketing inefficiencies.

40. Statement from the Prime Minister and Minister of Finance and Planning, *AGRO 21—Making Agriculture Jamaica's Business* (Kingston: National Planning Agency, 1983).

41. See introduction in *AGRO 21 Making Agriculture Jamaica's Business.* (Kingston: National Planning Agency).

42. *Status Report on AGRO 21 Corporation & Affiliated Companies* n.d., 2.

43. *Master Plan: Agro 21 Making Agriculture Jamaica's Business,* 2.1.

44. Jamaica Agricultural Sector Analysis (1986), 15.

45. The first director of AGRO 21 was made available under a contract with the US-AID. Upon his departure at the end of his term in April, 1985, he was credited by a Minister of State in the Ministry of Agriculture as having been among those "who had led the Revolution in the minds of the people." Mr. Pinella replied he felt he had been part of a peaceful revolution. *The Daily Gleaner,* Sat., April 13, 1985.

46. A plausible argument is that the Jamaican state evolved in conditions of relative autonomy and political liberalism. Ledgister, for example, argues that the state in the recently decolonized Caribbean possesses a significant degree of autonomy from the local ruling class. This is because of its roots in the Crown Colony of the late colonial period which was the agent not of the colonial, but of the metropolitan ruling class. Not only was it autonomous, it operated on twin principles of nineteenth-century liberalism and authoritarianism, that is to say, it guaranteed rights, but also privileged social control. The emergence of democracy meant that it was taken over by middle-class political aspirants on the basis of mass support; in order to sustain that support it had to play a significant distributive role. See Jorge Dominguez' introduction in *Democracy in the Caribbean*; also Fragano Ledgister, *Class Alliances and the Liberal-Authoritarian State* (Trenton, New Jersey: Africa World Press, 1999).

47. See Appendix 1, showing diagram of the AGRO 21 organization.

48. The argument for its location was that investors would stand a better chance of cutting through bureaucratic red tape and expediting the implementation of projects. As we will see later, the secretariat soon metamorphosed into a fully fledged government-owned corporation controlled from the Prime Minister's office.

49. One *Gleaner* columnist, lauding the government's new policies in reference to investment, argued that the government felt that the JNIP would "capture and purify these (investment) enquires before allowing them to enter into the pipeline of economic activity." "JNIP Success or Failure," *The Sunday Gleaner,* August 7, 1983.

50. According to Dr. Broderick, Minister of Agriculture, USAID, one of the program's major external supporters, sat on the committee in an ex-officio capacity. See *The Daily Gleaner,* Saturday, May 28, 1983, 10.

51. *Master Plan: AGRO 21* (1983), 5.3.

52. Notably, cocoa, citrus, coffee and pimento.

53. Two reasons were cited for this distortion, firstly, "the foreign exchange rationing that led to reduced food imports, creating incentives for import substitution in the agricultural sector," secondly, "the differences in marketing arrangements for export and domestic crops." See *Structural Adjustment of the Jamaica Economy 1982,* 7.

54. Although the External Marketing Organizations (EMOs) still have a part to play in assuring a maximum return to small farmers, these organizations seem to have grown beyond their optimal size, and their dominant role over export crops is not consistent with an export-led development strategy based on greater reliance on the private sector. *Structural Adjustment of the Jamaican Economy 1982,* 7.

55. Report of the President of the World Bank to the Executive Directors for an Agricultural Sector Adjustment Loan for Jamaica, February 9, 1990. See ANNEX IV, 48 (page 3 of 8) 5.3.

56. Explaining how it would treat with the sugar cane workers' cooperatives under the structural adjustment programme, it was stated that "Sugar production has declined

steadily over the last decade. As a result, output in 1980 was nearly 40 per cent below the 1970 level. This decline is a reflection on the inefficient operation of the nationalised sugar factories as well as falling production in the fields, resulting from dismemberment of the sugar estates and the creation of sugar cane workers' co-operatives that never functioned satisfactorily. Sugar is a major employer of labour as well as a source of foreign exchange earnings, hence immediate actions have to be taken to restore its viability and expand production." See *Structural Adjustment of the Jamaica Economy 1983,* 8. The Monymusk factory lost $J51 million since 1977 and was projected to lose another $J14.3 million in 1983 and 1984. Since 1977 Gray's Inn Factory has lost $J29 million. Cited in *The Daily Gleaner,* Saturday, Sept. 17, 1983, 12. The closure of the Sugar Workers' Co-operatives was not a passive operation. Certainly workers/settlers protested. Through their attorneys six co-ops appealed against their rapid closure. Their case was that the decline of the sugar industry was not a function of the operation of the sugar cooperatives, since sugar production had been in decline since 1965. Citing the report that came out of the Drummond enquiry of 1981, they argued that Bernard Lodge had been viable. They were of the opinion that the sugar cooperatives had not been given sufficient time to prove themselves. For the details of this argument, see "Govt. Said To Have Erred in Scrapping Sugar Co-ops," *The Daily Gleaner,* Thursday, September 1, 1983, 12.

57. For the debate on this issue, see Norman Girvan and Owen Jefferson, *Readings in the Political Economy of the Caribbean* (Kingston: New World Group, 1971).

58. *Economic and Social Survey of Jamaica 1983* (Kingston: The Planning Institute of Jamaica, c 1983), 7.9.

59. See "Investment Potential in Commercial Agriculture vol.1 Winter Vegetables" Also "Ethnic Foods Cost of Production per acre (small farmer) (Kingston: Strategic Planning Department, AGRO 21, 1987). Also, Elaine Smith, "Ethnic Foods Farmgate to Florida Market Cost/Return Models" (update) (Kingston: Strategic Planning Department, 1988).

60. Although operating in Jamaica, foreign consultants still had a US frame of reference, referring to these crops as "Ethnic Foods"!

61. *Investment Potentials in Commercial Agriculture Vol.1. Winter Vegetables.* Strategic Planning and Monitoring Unit AGRO 21 Jamaica Conference Center, Landell Mills Associates (Caribbean Ltd.), No date, 61.

62. Ibid.

63. *Economic and Social Survey of Jamaica 1983.* Section: 3.1.

64. It was broken down as follows: (000) Jamaica AGRO products J$113, 600.3, St. Jago/Spring Plain Farms, J$15,023.9, Packing House, J$12,024.5, Jamaican Aqualapia Limited J$31,738.3, Farm Machinery Centre, J$26,724.3, Floraculture JA. Ltd., J$9,190.0, JA. Drip Irrigation, J$1,853.6, JA. Tissue Culture Ltd., J$25. Vegetable growing J$33.6 and Victoria Banana JA. Agrosystems Halse Hall, J$77,636.

65. David Barker in "Recent Developments in Agricultural Planning in Jamaica: The AGRO 21 Programme," unpub. conference paper, Caribbean Studies Association, Caracas, Venezuela, May 1985, 6. This article was subsequently published as David Barker, "The changing Caribbean: New directions for Jamaican Agriculture," *Caribbean Geography* 2, no. 1 (1985): 56–66. Barker concluded that the early results reported in *The Daily Gleaner* pointed to success and that, in light of that, Jamaicans would welcome AGRO 21. Both the success and the welcome were short lived.

66. *Status Report on AGRO 21 Corporation & Affiliated Companies,* mss., 27.

67. Ibid., 28.

68. Ibid.

69. Status Report, 34.

70. Incidently, Inter-Grow was set up after the closing of Halse Hall, Grace Kennedy's vegetable farm, in 1986.

71. The Spring Plains Project consisted of Jamaica Agro Products, Jamaica Aqualapia Ltd., Jamaica Drip Irrigation Ltd., Floraculture Jamaica Ltd., Victoria Banana Co. Ltd., Spring Plain Property (Clarendon) St. Jago Property (Clarendon), St. Jago Packing House (St. Jago Property), Farm Machinery Center (St. Jago Property).

72. Faye U. Sampson, "Report" (submitted to AGRO 21 Corporation Limited, Making Agriculture Jamaica's Business, June 2, 1989).

73. Ministry Paper No. 56, 3–4.

74. William R. Furtnick, "Jamaica Agricultural Sector Analysis" (prepared for the Jamaica U.S. Mission during March-April, 1986), 15.

75. Ibid.

76. *Economic and Social Survey of Jamaica, 1984* (Kingston: The Planning Institute of Jamaica, c1984), 7.8.

77. *Economic and Social Survey of Jamaica 1982* (Kingston: The Planning Institute of Jamaica, c 1982), 8.11.

78. "New Role for Banana Company," *The Daily Gleaner,* Jan. 13, 1985, 1. Also see "Assessment of the Effects of Structural Adjustment on the Agricultural Sector: Jamaica Technical Report" (Rome: FAO, April 1995).

79. *Economic and Social Survey of Jamaica 1982* (Kingston: The Planning Institute of Jamaica, c 1982), 8.11.

80. *Economic and Social Survey of Jamaica 1984* (Kingston: The Planning Institute of Jamaica, c 1984), 7.6.

81. The plan to deregulate the Coffee Industry Board was announced in June 1982. Subsequently other commodity boards were treated similarly.

82. Ivoral Davis, "Deregulation of the Coffee Industry-Coffee Industry Board sets Terms, Conditions," *The Daily Gleaner,* Saturday, 13 August 1983, 10.

83. Cargill (a regular *Gleaner* columnist) decried the policies of CIB that resulted in the blending of Blue Mountain coffee with other coffees of lower altitude. He lamented "What to my mind is worse is that the Coffee Industry Board has done that old colonial thing of making Jamaica a bulk seller, with no brand name to protect good will." Morris Cargill, "Blue Mountain Coffee Blues," *The Daily Gleaner,* Friday, 12 August, 1983, 12.

84. According to former director of Grace Kennedy, Mabel Tenn, Halse Hall started before AGRO 21. In fact, it was on the drawing board before the JLP assumed office in 1980, but cultivation commenced after two years of preparation and study of marketing conditions, etc. When AGRO 21 was established all such projects were subsumed within its expansive ambit. I conducted interviews with Ms. Tenn.

85. According to Ms. Tenn, the Company had been approached since 1977 to shift to production and, prior to cultivation in 1980, had carried out feasibility and marketing studies.

86. Grace, Kennedy & Company Limited, Halse Hall Project Experience, mss., n.d., 3.

87. Ibid.

88. Ibid. and interview with Mable Tenn.

89. Ibid.

90. Agrocon Ltd.(1986) "Case Study on the Halse Hall Winter Vegetable for Export Project," mss., 34–35. This study details the nature of problems experienced by the project and the benefits that accrued during its operations. My interview with Ms. Tenn revealed some of these problems: the unreliability and uncertainty of transportation, and the total lack of knowledge of company personnel of marketing operations and the export market in vegetables, despite advice got from consultants like Agridevelopment and marketing studies done by the World Trade Institute in New York.

91. "Government's Agricultural Policy Blasted" *The Gleaner* 11/86, 1 & 27.

92. Mr. Ramtallie was at the time the shadow Minister of Agriculture of the PNP.

93. Speculation was rife about the amount of money actually lost on the project. Mr. T. G. Minott, chairman of the All Island Cane Farmers' Association, felt that far more than $100 million had been lost. "They also accused the government of ignoring and neglecting small farmers in preference to high-technology projects such as winter vegetables" such as were produced on Spring Plain. See also Milton Robinson, "Some 'Human Failures' At Spring Plain," *The Daily Gleaner*, 1/11/86, 15 for a discussion of Spring Plain's failures.

94. The statement was drawn up by the bank's former director, Dhiru Tanna, and the then current chair, Meyer Matalon.

95. Dhiru Tanna (former Chairman) and Meyer Matalon (then current chair).

96. "Spring Plain: The Losses and the Prospects," *The Daily Gleaner*, 5 September, 1986. The directors argued that feasibility studies showed the parish to be a fairly dry one and the area of Spring Plain, though not ideal for vegetable production, had this advantage of being dry. There were severe floods most of which caused a major disaster in the parish of Clarendon. The Rio Minho river broke its banks flooding large expanses. The extent of the damage is measured by the fact that 23 people lost their lives during this short time. *The Daily Gleaner*, Sat. 7 June, 1986, 1. It was a joint statement made by Dhiru Tanna, former director, and Meyer Matalon, then chair of the National Investment Bank of Jamaica.

97. To counter rampant rumors about the closure of Spring Plain the directors announced that there was significant diversification in the wake of the demise of winter vegetables at that specific location. The production of winter vegetables had shifted to Bernard Lodge.

98. According to Seaga, high-technology banana farms were producing 15–20 tons an acre. Whereas, in 1980, growers resisted taking control of the industry, due to uncertainty, the current climate of stability and certainty had diminished such resistance, and the industry was now being run by the growers themselves. "P.M. No wrong-doing at Spring Plain" and "Seaga outlines gains and failings of farm policy," *The Daily Gleaner*, 25 September, 1986, 1, 13.

99. C. Roy Reynolds, "The Ruins of Agriculture," *The Daily Gleaner*, Saturday, 29 July 1989, 28.

100. Jamaican creole, in this context refers to the larger high-technology farm operators.

101. "A combination of high technology, sizeable land, capital: AGRO 21-A Commercial Venture, not Government Supported Farms," *The Daily Gleaner*, Saturday, 28 May, 1983, 10.

102. "Small Farmers Said at Odds with Farm Policy," *The Daily Gleaner*, Friday, 1 August, 1986, 23.

103. *Social and Economic Survey of Jamaica, 1982*, 8. 4.

104. See Table 1 in Appendix: Table 8.3 "Agricultural Credit Bank's Loan Allocation to Agricultural Projects in *Economic and Social Survey of Jamaica 1982*, 8.5.

105. I have discussed the nature of modernization schemes in earlier chapters.

106. Margaret Newman and Elsie Le Franc, "The Small-Farm Sub-Sector," in *Consequences of Structural Adjustment*, ed. E. Le Franc (1994), 132.

107. For a brief discussion of this practice see Mogens Buch-Hansen & Henrik Secher Marcusse, "Contract Farming and the Peasantry: Cases from Western Kenya." In *Review of African Political Economy*, no. 23 (January-April): 9–36.

108. In conversation with Mabel Tenn, director and coordinator of Grace's Halse Hall farm project. I will speak more directly to this project later.

109. These comments were made in the wake of the Spring Plain winter vegetable project collapse. *The Daily Gleaner*, 25 September, 1986, op. cit. 1 & 13.

110. "Spring Plain: The Losses and the Prospects," *The Daily Gleaner*, 5 September 1986, 8.

111. The Economic and Social Surveys also chronicled the declining recurrent and capital expenditure for agriculture. "In 1974/75, of the total national expenditures, Government's recurrent and capital expenditures on the agricultural sector were 4.5% and 14.8%. By 1990/91, these had fallen to 1.99% and 1.5% respectively." Adapted from a quotation in *Consequences of Structural Adjustment*, ed. E. Le Franc (1994), 125.

112. IFAD loaned US$6.7 million to the GOJ covering 47% of the project costs. Another 10% of the project, US$1.4 million, was financed by the Government of the Netherlands, US$3.9 million, or 27%, came from "government and agency contributions" and the rest, 16% or US$2.2 million, from farmer contributions. See "Jamaica Hillside Farmers Support Project Appraisal Report." Report no.0073. Jamaica March 1988, IFAD document, 40.

113. Hillside Agricultural Project: Report on the Survey of Phased out Sub-projects, June-September 1995 (Kingston: Data Bank and Evaluation Division, Ministry of Agriculture and Mining), 1.

114. The practice of soil conservation, watershed protection, and water access.

115. The project aimed to provide credit and assistance only to farmers who made their living primarily from farming.

116. Calculated from *The Farmers' Register 1982*.

117. Intercropping was encouraged, since it was recognized that farmers actually survived from crops like gungo peas and red peas during the time that it took for tree crops to mature.

118. Jamaica Hillside Farmers support project: Report No.0073-JA, March 1988, 33.

119. Ibid.

120. Ibid, 56.

121. The Jamaica Hillside Agricultural Project reviewed six phased-out subprojects viz., Rio Minho Cocoa Expansion, Manchester Rural Agricultural Development Association, Agro-Forestry, North West St. Catherine, Kellits/Crofts Hill,and North Clarendon Processing Company. A total of 420 farmers were interviewed, 163 male and 47 female, in a random stratified sample.

122. Hillside Agricultural Project, 32.

123. "Agriculture and the Environment: Jamaica Case Study" by USAID, mentioned in "Hillside Agricultural Project."

124. M. Newman & E. Le Franc, "The Small farm Sub-Sector" (1994), 127.

125. See for example, Luis Llambi, "Emergence of Capitalized Family Farms in Latin America," *Society for Comparative Study of Society and History* 31 (1988): 745–774.

126. *The Daily Gleaner,* Wednesday, 23 January, 1985, 11.

127. Morris Cargill "Why the Decline in Bananas?" *The Daily Gleaner,* Jan. 21, 1985, 1.

128. I discuss these issues more substantively in relation to the state and small farmer relationship in the final chapter.

129. "Assessment of the Effects of Structural Adjustment on the Agricultural Sector: Jamaica Technical Report," mss. (Rome: FAO, April, 1995). See chapter 7 for a discussion of "downsizing" in the public sector.

130. In retaliation to the PNP's public outrage at government's failed policy, Seaga countered by pointing to the failure of the sugar cooperatives. He stated that by 1980, the sugar cooperatives had lost J\$111 million, and that it had cost the government J\$355 million, to rehabilitate the industry. Furthermore, he argued that high-tech farms were far more productive than others. The banana industry, he posited, had almost been bankrupted under the PNP regime and it had cost the government J\$200 million to revive it. "Seaga Outlines Gains and Failings of Farm Policy," *The Daily Gleaner,* Thursday, 25 September 1986; also in same edition, "PM: No Wrong Doing at Spring Plain," 1.

131. "AGRO 21 to be Phased Out," *The Daily Gleaner,* Tuesday, 20 June, 1989, 11.

132. Kari Polanyi Levitt, *The Origins and Consequences of Jamaica's Debt Crisis 1970–1990* (UWI Mona: Consortium Graduate School of Social Sciences, 1991), 24.

133. Later, in defense of the AGRO 21 program, Seaga itemized the costliness of the PNP agrarian programs. See endnote 86.

134. As I have shown in chapter 4, much dissatisfaction among participants had set in during the execution of those projects. I focus more exclusively on this issue of protest in the final chapter.

135. Kari Polanyi Levitt (1991), 7.

136. For a discussion of how adjustment policies handcuffed the state's agenda, see Omar Davies, "Adjustment and Stabilization Policies in Jamaica, 1981–87," mss. (Department of Economics UWI, Mona, Kingston, Jamaica, 1988).

137. "Assessment of the Effects of Structural Adjustment on the Agricultural Sector, Jamaica Technical Report" (Rome: FAO, April 1995), 33.

138. See section entitled, "Export and the role of the smallholder" in chapter 6.

139. "Assessment of the Effects of Structural Adjustment on the Agricultural Sector." FAO report, 36.

140. Margaret Newman and Elsie Le Franc (1994), 130.

141. Gary Allen, "The Decline in Bananas," *The Daily Gleaner,* Saturday, 7 June, 1986, 8.

142. As part of the deregulation program, the Banana Board was divested of its commercial functions, and these were transferred to the new BECO. Other boards operating in the agricultural sector were also restructured.

143. From areas like Palmetto Grove, Middlesex, Albany, Belfield, Fontabelle, and Draxhall.

144. Gary Allen, "The Decline in Bananas," *The Daily Gleaner*, Saturday, 7 June, 1986, 8.

145. Ibid.

146. "Assessment of the Effects of Structural Adjustment on the Agricultural Sector." FAO report, 36, 37.

147. Ibid.

148. Ibid.

149. "Assessment of the Effects of Structural Adjustment on the Agricultural Sector." FAO report, 80.

150. These are general figures pertaining to large groups categorized, on the one hand, as "estates" which we know to be large-scale high-technology farms and "farmers," including medium and small holdings. While not very precise, they do offer a sense of the goings-on in the agricultural sector. See Margaret Newman and Elsie Le Franc (1994), 130.

151. Patricia Anderson and Michael Witter, "Crisis, Adjustment and Social Change A Case Study of Jamaica."In Elsie Le Franc ed. (1994): 1–55, 27.

152. Crouch and de Janvry discuss this in relation to the wider region of the Caribbean and Latin America in "The Class Basis of Agricultural Growth," *Food Policy*, 5,1 (February 1980): 3–13.

153. For a clarification see, for example, Philip McMichael, "Globalization: Myths and Realities," *Rural Sociology*, 61, 1 (Spring 1996): 25–55.

154. Newman and Le Franc, in somewhat of a rational choice perspective, determine that **winners** are "those small farmers who have managed to expand their enterprise, or livelihood/resource base. **Losers** are those whose livelihood/resource base has decreased" 175. In short, the welfare of small farmers is to be understood only within the context of household and personal decision-making. Thus, structural or historical factors do not receive equal weight or consideration. See Margaret Newman and Elsie Le Franc (1994), 180.

155. Moreover, microstudies of small farming communities, rich as they are in providing detail, because of their obvious methodological and empirical limitations, need to be relocated in the constitutive context of national and global developments.

CHAPTER 6

Inseparable Autonomies: Of State Spaces and People Spaces

> [T]he category peasant, whatever validity it may once have had, has been outdistanced by contemporary history. Within an anthropology and within peasant studies generally, 'the peasant' was constructed from residual images of preindustrial European and colonial rural society. Informed by romantic sensibilities and modern nationalist imaginations, these images are anachronisms, but nevertheless they remain robust anachronisms even at the end of the twentieth century. As such, they are appropriate targets for a house-cleaning that clears space for alternative theoretical views.[1]

Introduction

Up until the 1990s, Jamaica's agricultural sector consisted of highly developed relations of dependence and inequality. These relationships masked other prevalent processes which call into question the traditional conceptualization of that sector's dynamic, in terms of "peasant" and "plantation." Diverse farming "systems," households, and sectors are linked symbiotically through production and labor provisioning. In short, multiple processes are mobilized to "work for capital," to use Michel-Rolph Trouillot's construction in his analysis of the Dominican peasantry. Interestingly, as development policies have sought and succeeded in large measure in encompassing significant sections of the agricultural sector, creating complex state spaces, they have resulted in the informalization of relations of production and labor and general income-earning activities. These are people spaces. As land-based working people have been reconstituted through these modernization policies, the latter have also facilitated the manipulation of state institutional connections to constitute or remake alternative strategies of production and patterns of income earning. These alternative strategies reflect an exteriority typified for the most part by informalized relationships existing within and outside of the interior of these development created spaces and temporalities.

Since the start of the project of decolonization, agricultural modernization has involved the attempt to encompass rural space, channeling the energies of land-based working peoples into the primary state project of export agriculture and state-controlled domestic production. Forms of production, family, land ownership, even of respectability, not conforming to the specifics of a somewhat Eurocentric modernizing project, were considered backward and subject to modern techniques of incorporation and control. At least that was the plan—to root out forms of backwardness within the nation-state and to recreate new subjects capable of reaching for a future in the hierarchical racialized world economic order. Such was the hegemonic nationalist ideology. In agricultural terms, this meant a policy preference for monocrop export agriculture, and a particular technique for the spatialization of these crops.

These socioeconomic, cultural practices were sustained by ideas about building community and providing rural working people access to land, however inadequate. Thus the production of rural spaces was a function not only of rural policy, but of the notion that property ownership led to civic responsibility and support for the early developmentalist state, despite the inequalities. For its programs created, even as they attempted to remedy, long-standing economic disparities.[2] But a brief word about the narratives about "peasantries."

Although the expansion of European capitalism created the Caribbean, Caribbean peasantry is quite unlike its western European namesake.[3] Caribbean "peasants" reputedly originate through a slave labor process, not through a free proprietorship system, as in most western European societies.[4] During the post-emancipation period, peasants were "villagers" living on the outskirts of the plantations, and their decline was attributed to the restoration of plantation production and the restrictive role of government policies. They were reconstituted, "becoming peasants in some kind of resistant response to an externally imposed regimen," and their emergence was "simultaneously an act of Westernization and an act of resistance."[5]

Because the so-called peasantry emerged from the plantation labor process, we are also persuaded to track its emergent identity along this trajectory, which, to its credit, highlights the ex-slaves' agency in shaping their own present and future agendas. An unfortunate outcome of this trajectory is the sort of transhistoricizing and essentializing of the smallholder's emergence so pervasive in the work of plantation economy theorists,[6] even as other analysts highlight the in-

ternal differences that distinguish members of the postemancipation smallholder.[7] Often disregarded is the influence of the world economy, in which the
state, through its institutional appearances, shapes and reshapes the conditions
under which rural Caribbeans and their diverse cultural practices are constituted.
Rather than contemplate an unchanging "peasant," it is far more fruitful to consider the rural Caribbean as constituted discursively, materially, and historically
under conditions of a dynamic coloniality, and now, postcoloniality. This involves focusing on the ambivalencies and multivalencies inherent in rural
Caribbeans' economic and sociocultural practices as duly constituted transnational subjects, as Mintz implies in his assertion that "peasants" are influenced by
political, economic and social forces *far removed* from those "emanating from the
domestic urban centers of power holders" for reasons beyond productivity or tax-
ability.[8] To be sure, neither smallholder, capital nor colonial powers respected the
geographical edges constituting the colonial spaces of authority, and, in their
own way, they manipulated it by defying such dichotomized labor processes, spa-
tialities and conceptualizations.

Specific pronouncements on culture in the Caribbean evince a similar short-
sightedness. They isolate "peasant" practices, highlighting their African dimensions, and read these solely as expressions of resistance to dominant Eurocentric
ideologies or practices.[9] They speak of Redfieldian-like "peasant cultures" that resist and adapt, but fail to explore the mechanisms and dynamics of adaptation
inherent in new and reconstituted practices, as if adaptations were exclusively
about choices.[10] Implied is that "peasant cultures" are to be contrasted with
"nonpeasant cultures" almost like the Redfieldian folk-urban continuum, rendering Silverman's 1979 comment on the anthropological production of the
Redfieldian tradition of community studies, relevant still.[11]

The production of rural spaces cannot be accounted for in terms of these
binarisms, though one might argue that peasantlike and proletarian-like social
relationships may be perceived simply as historical tendencies in the complex
history of the world economy. The concept "peasant" is a residual category from
an industrial society, whose present form has no need of the category, as Kearney reminds. Deployed in the internationalized and globalized Caribbean region to depict land-based working people, such a concept succeeds in "reifying
or enclosing them in narrow(er) systemic boxes," to use Cook's remark in a different context.[12]

The employment of the concept "peasantry" in the Jamaican and other
Caribbean settings implies an amnesia that the consolidation, even in some instances, appearance of land-based working people was rooted in a political project, an artifact of an enduring, abiding colonial and postcolonial/postnationalist
perspective that ownership of property commands civic responsibility. This is by
no means a capitulation to a view that diminishes land-based working peoples'

agency; it recomposes it within a discussion of the wider terrain of class, strata and state re-formation and maneuvering in the region. It is to move beyond the glorification and reification of "the peasantry" and to implicate the world economy in the making of the local, to link as it were, modernity's diverse representations, and as Bhabha in a different context urged, to think in terms of ambivalence, which in this sense, is to complicate the relationship between land-based working peoples and development and to foreground the specific modernities of such constituents.[13]

As I have argued earlier, in the early developmentalist state land-based working peoples, perceived as smallholders, represented a key constituency. The stratum needed to be stabilized and reconstituted through various modernization policies and technologies, assuring them a foothold in the agricultural sector, though advancement into the ranks of larger, more economically viable strata was not guaranteed. Constrained by historical circumstance, the close association between freedom and land ownership, inherent in free people's socioeconomic and cultural practices, the developmentalist state, like its colonial progenitor, made possible the coexistence of formal and informal relationships among, between, and within enterprises. Each producer in the agricultural sector was allowed the space to incorporate formal and informal methods of production, based on his or her resources. This approach reinforced certain meanings of development among all enterprises, especially among smallholders considered central to the success of agricultural policy, making it possible for them to stake and frame their discourses and practices of citizenship, or the acquisition in the context of the inadequacies of development, and not outside of it. In this instance, the existence of an "outside," an "exteriority," refers to alternative ways of seeing and practicing development within the context, and toward the goals of these policies. It can be claimed that an exterior represents a discourse that combines elements of hegemonic discourses and recycles them according to notions of marginality. But what constitutes an exterior in the context of societies created in and outside of modernity's other image? What I mean to ask is that, when the modernizing project fails in any of its objectives, or it comes up against common sense ideas about ways of practicing agriculture, do land-based people counter its claims or methods? When they are deliberately left out, they may engage in counterdiscourses, which aim to rationalize or rectify their inclusion.

As I have stated in chapter 1, the argument guiding this text is not about the forceful superimposition of agrarian structures over rural space, but rather the structural outcomes of a certain vision of development that I believe was, if not widely shared, not widely opposed, especially by those who seemed to have benefitted less. At the same time, I do not intend to argue that these are the only structures through which, to use Trouillot's phrase, smallholders "work for capital," but they allow a certain amount of a "beneath-the-radar," perhaps exterior existence, allowed by the state, which is incapable of controlling them, permitting large numbers of smallholders to work for themselves, and to perceive their existence in that light. What I am suggesting is that the representation of rural space, or a great part of it, should at least be read along a two-pronged axis, that is on the one hand, as the means through which state institutions enter rural spaces and shape them accordingly, and on the other, as the way in which smallholders more often than not out of the need to survive, engage in informal practices and with others like themselves or with others in different enterprises, and with state institutions themselves.[14] These informal practices may constitute traditions of practices adhering to a different modern period, that get carried over given their practicality into a new era of development.

In short, the institutional legitimation and control of smallholders necessitate the engagement of certain "rules" of informality that engender the particular mix of labor processes and occupations between enterprises and also within them as well. Take the Brown family of a small community in the parish of St. Anne's. According to Nora, she worked her family land (noncommodified) for 14 years planting cabbages and other vegetables. Her family employed hired help, other similarly placed smallholders, for certain tasks, e.g., weeding and crop harvesting. When prices for these crops drastically declined, following a glut on the market, there was no money to pay workers, and there developed an informal exchange of labor.[15] Smallholders were forced to seek work in the tourist industry to maintain the farm. Discrimination within the hotel industry, resulting in a preference for younger workers, forced Nora and her sister to leave for Kingston, where they found work as domestic workers. In another instance, people like Nora who stay in the rural areas participate in government projects in order to maintain small plots. In this way, owners were able to engage in a variety of farming and nonfarming projects, even as they appeared statistically as smallholders or smallfarmers.

The development narrative ought therefore to include informality as a witting and unwitting mechanism—an expression, if you will—of stateness; that is to say, the type of relationship which the state officials wittingly and unwittingly facilitated in the relationships with working peoples. Development policy established and reinforced an array of linked enterprises that accommodated informality even as institutional actors (from extension workers to policy implementers) sought to impose agricultural policy formalities in rural areas. Moreover, the absence of a sustained agricultural production whether as wage work or as smallholder farming caused a number of working people to combine several types of occupations. Formal and informal social relations are therefore quite fluid tendencies embedded in the relations of people in the nonstate arena and policy makers and implementers. Therefore, the success of such formal techniques of production geared for a deeply regulated world market relies on the individual operator harnessing noncapitalist, informal familial networks. These cultural configurations are sheltered and altered under the developmentalist state's strategy of development. This is capitalist development's paradox—"mātis to the rescue, as James Scott would say: "the nonconforming practice is an indispensable condition for the formal order."[16] The nonconforming practice is made to facilitate the formal order, undermining its nonconformity and transforming its objectives.

Though the enterprises discussed below represent highly unequal structures of production and structures of control, the assemblage that they create, loosely referred to as the agricultural sector, ought to be considered as a somewhat intended space that allowed land-based working people and others to maneuver through and with the state bureaucracy. Farmers established agendas outside of those formally represented or given by the state. Given the enduring conditions of smallholder existence, one may argue that translated, development meant not so much the creation of mechanisms facilitating economic social mobility, but carried the idea of betterment of self and household even if one stayed put, inculcating a devotion to state-policy and state-bureaucratic perspectives on what had to be done, by whom and to whom.

The purpose of this chapter is to show the interconnection of structures through which these formal and informal negotiations take place among agricultural enterprises and the state, and which, for the most part, reveal the fuzzy labor processes that define agrarian social relations. The chapter also demonstrates the fluidity of agrarian social relations. The discourses of development in Jamaica, while they linked development and citizenship, smallholder welfare and the fortunes and future of the nation, choreographed socioeconomic structures that limited the realization of those ideals. In other words, development policy that incorporated this population, labeling it as backward, was also that which sustained that condition, undermining the idea that development could fulfill its promises of emancipatory deliverance.

In reconceptualizing Caribbean smallholders' experiences in the context of state-led development, I argued earlier that the incorporation of Jamaica and the Caribbean into the developing world economy led early to the erosion of precapitalist production forms. By the same token, in the seventeenth century, regional forms of production were linked to colonial-driven emergent capitalist production. With the capitalist world economy well formed by the mid-nineteenth century, the emergence of a diverse smallholder sector was not isolated from this process.[17] Quite applicable here is Dale Tomich's idea of rearticulating the terms of the discourse on the nature of capitalist development, entertained by world systems and mode of production theorists, in terms of market versus modes of production: "(t)hus in the world economy, commodity production and exchange unite multiple forms of labor and diverse groups of producers at the same time as they establish specific conditions of material and social interdependence among them."[18] This is precisely the issue here. The regeneration of smallholder production was a result of the way in which the state was continuously incorporated into the global market and the historical specificity given the political triangulation of development, sovereignty and citizenship, noted earlier. More important, locally, a mix of social relationships, embodied in land, labor, and technology, combined to create agricultural forms/enterprises with their distinct temporalities, enabling capital accumulation linked to the world economy, through the production of various cash crops, and wage work deployed by members of rural households. And so it is that state spaces have become symbiotically intertwined with people spaces.

In the Caribbean, the kinds of transformation occasioned by development policies have not involved a transition from precapitalist to capitalist forms of production, as in the universalized partial histories of Western Europe. Even so, a number of analysts point to the customary tradition of wage labor supplementing "peasant" households in Europe. Though the focus was on proletarianization, many of these writings suggest that peasant and proletarian were not fixed, but flexible historical tendencies. Bottomore and Roseberry, for example, noted that wage labor was vital for such households. "Work off the farm . . . could also be seen as an essential means for survival of the family as a 'peasant' family."[19] As discussed in chapter 1, Caribbean transformation evinced a polyvalent capitalist development. Thus the question that guides this chapter's analysis turns on the conditions under which commodity production, subsistence production, wage labor, tenantry and others are/were produced and on the structures with which working peoples mark their relationships to development, and the institutions which chart its various projects. A secondary but important concern is my desire to demonstrate the fluidity of social relationships marked by the differential occupational flows that define rural households in Jamaica and elsewhere throughout the Caribbean region—a phenomenon noted also for Latin America.

While some rigidity in the social relations of production persists, working people operating as smallholders have become increasingly dynamic producers and doers, even as their social location in the agrarian sector, and society in general, remains relatively marginal, but it is hardly a marginality of old precapitalist traditions, say of indigenous people, but very modern ones created and sustained by state institutions.[20] It would be useful, therefore, to see the units of production and consumption identified here, as representing overlapping social strata which tap into several different labor processes but which go beyond them.

To elucidate some of the main aspects of the Jamaican agricultural sector, I sketch a set of sociotypes, each representing a hierarchical division of labor in the agricultural sector and illuminating the comparative sociolocations of Jamaican working people. The fluidity and permeability of these locations is assumed. As

Mintz and Wolf advised in their 1957 paper distinguishing between types and systems:

> [S]cientific procedure in cross-cultural comparison cannot do with-
> out some such typological constructs [. . .] The use of such models
> in cross-cultural enquiry can be profitable, however, only if they are
> not endowed with a life of their own but are used simply as heuristic
> devices. A type is not a "thing" found in nature, but a mental con-
> struct. Just as the concept of a social system involves a series of inter-
> related statements about recurrences of observed behavior, so the
> concept of a type of social system represents a series of interrelated
> statements about the recurrent features of a number of social systems.
> Such features are never identical from system to system, but may be
> said to bear resemblances within certain specifiable limits.[21]

Though not derived from a cross-cultural study, these sociotypes are loose agrarian forms and relationships that more or less channel and determine the flow of social relations in the agricultural sector, spilling over into other sectors as well. Data imprecisions as well as changing categorizations constrain tracing continuous/discontinuous developments in the agrarian sector and also limit conclusions as to what has changed precisely and how, and what has remained. To compensate for this problem and to facilitate comparisons over time, I have in several cases re-aligned many census categories. In spite of these problems, the available data still offer a working impression of the Jamaican agricultural sector, along which we can plot the connections between commodity production and the global market, understanding ways in which state- and nonstate-derived modernities have been framed and structured. They are but development's creations.

I have differentiated types according to the scale of operations (acreage and intensity of production), the dominant method of labor, the level of technology, tenure status, and other economic activity additional to agriculture, as well as the ways whereby these characteristics are articulated.

Estates or Large Farms

Estates, sometimes referred to as plantations, were and still are considered the most modern and resourceful agricultural enterprises within the schema of development. The initial decline of estates was occasioned by significant losses of agricultural land between 1942/43 and 1954, estimated at 474,540 acres.[22] Consequently, the concentration of acreage held by these enterprises increased. In 1942/43 there were some 540 plantations, compared to 295 in 1978. In 1942/43, they occupied approximately 1,067,497 acres, while in 1978, they occupied only 585,616 acres. In 1942/43 the average size of a plantation was 1,976 acres; in 1961/62 this increased to 2,569 acres in 1961/62, though it fell again in 1978 to 1,985 acres. Despite such numbers, large estates continued to occupy a disproportionate share of agricultural land. Even in 1978, though estates constituted less than 1%, they controlled 44% of total acreage under cultivation.[23]

Estates operated under various types of ownerships, partnerships, companies, or individuals. Although wage labor predominated, estates' owners/operators sometimes provided marginal land to members of their work force as a substitute for wages. Estates also sometimes provided lands "free."[24] One recommendation of the 1944/45 Commission of Enquiry[25] was a minimum wage for smallholders, assuming that "the average worker would derive a part of his food supply and a small portion of his cash income from the cultivation of an allotment of at least one-third of an acre in area and for this reason, we consider that the estates for regular workers should make this area available, that is, those working for at least five days per week for 75% of the working year."[26] In that same year the Commission found that 16% of the field labor force rented land from estate owners or their operators, whose average allotment size was 5.4 squares, of which dependents of the estate labor force cultivated 3.4 squares.[27] Utilizing a variety of labor processes, estates created various social relationships aimed at producing commodities for the export market, and generally securing labor.

Large plantations/estates have benefitted tremendously from the emphasis on export agriculture. Although in 1968/69 most owners/operators (64% to 81%) were engaged in full-time farming,[28] as employers of labor, they were able to diversify operations in order to be linked to the commercial, manufacturing and industrial sectors.[29] As shown earlier, the economic power of planters and the biases of both the colonial and postcolonial states valorized monoagriculture in Caribbean economies, which engaged state support in the areas of marketing and research.

Small Estates

The little documentation available on farms of 100 to 500 acres makes clear their decline in accordance with the general trend in the agricultural sector. In 1942/43, though their share of total holdings remained at 1%, their acreage decreased. Between 1942/43 and 1978, these farms lost approximately 23,421 acres, and the average farm size decreased from 213 acres to 200.[30]

Like large plantations/estates, small farms concentrated for their agricultural earnings on the production of export crops such as bananas, coconuts, and to a lesser extent, pimento. Nevertheless, small farming households tended not to rely exclusively on their farms for most of their income. Households farming full-time were increasingly rare. In 1954, when the total number of holdings was approximated at 881, 56% of the operators farmed full-time. By 1968 this rose to 63%, while those participating in nonagricultural employment increased from 30% to 33%. By 1978 the percentage of those who farmed full-time had fallen to 56%, while those engaged in part-time agriculture, other agricultural and nonagricultural economic activity increased to 36%.[31] Some farming households might have exited production altogether.

Small enterprises have superseded plantations in their level of mechanization, using tractors, ploughs, trucks, trailers, and fertilizers. The ratio of mechanical, motorized, and hand-operated agricultural implements and machines to acreage bears this out, particularly the comparable figures for 1961 and 1968.[32]

Due to the emphasis on export production, these smaller estates received aid/credit from the state, as well as from regional and international bodies. Like the plantations, they employed significant amounts of wage labor, linked to other forms of labor such as piece work. Increased mechanization suggests less reliance on labor-intensive farming.[33]

Upper Medium-sized Family Farms

Farms between 25 and 100 acres are the quintessential family farms. These farms may be considered large, undercapitalized family enterprises. Although family members combined with wage labor drawn from outside the household employ labor-intensive methods of production, their use of modern farming equipment has improved considerably.

The average size of farms in this group ranges from roughly 40 to 45 acres. According to the 1942/43 census, there were 4,045 farms in this category, forming 6% of all agricultural holdings; in 1954 the number increased to 5,603, but those farms' share of total holdings declined to 2%. This reduction highlights the marked increase in the number of agricultural holdings that year, from 116,173 to 198,883.[34]

Between 1954 and 1978, family farms' number and share of total holdings continued to fall. In 1968, they numbered roughly 3,004, 2% of holdings nationally. In 1978, this slid to 2,400 holdings, less than 1% of all holdings.[35] The share of total agricultural acreage fell from 9.79% in 1961/62 to 8% in 1978.[36] Nevertheless landholdings within this group remained relatively stable, even as the group's national presence has diminished.

The number of households involved in nonagricultural and/or alternative agricultural employment has decreased over time. Although in 1968/69 it was estimated that 80% of households were full-time farmers, decreasing by 1978/79 to 67%, those partaking in part-time farming increased significantly from about 3% to more than 11% in that span of time, and the percentage of those engaged in nonagricultural and other agricultural employment dropped. Participation in other agricultural employment was estimated at 16% for 1968/69, 2% in 1978.[37] Anything short of complete withdrawal from agriculture seems to be a less significant phenomenon in this stratum.

Lower-medium-sized Farms

Lower-medium-sized farms are those between 6 and 25 acres. These households I refer to as the upper level of the smallholder stratum. They comprise a mix of poor smallholders and less dependent small farmers. During the 1970s, many farms at the lower end of the scale were operated by state tenant farmers.

Crop production is typically mixed, export crops interpolated with domestic-market food crops, mainly ground provisions. The labor force consists of wage, family and task workers, who utilize both mechanical and manually operated implements.

Farms in this category declined from 11 acres in 1942/43 to about 8 1/2 in 1978. Estimated at 34% of all holdings in 1942/43, their proportional share plummeted to 8% by 1978, with a drastic decline in overall acreage, from 19% in 1954 to 14% in 1978, though the actual reduction from 1961 to 1978 was only about 4%.[38] Most of the recorded decline coincided with the period of urban industrialization between 1950 and early 1960.

More households have continued to pursue full-time agriculture than on any other stratum. While, in 1968/69, 86% of farming households with holdings of 5 to 25 acres were involved full-time on their own farms, by 1978/79 this share had decreased to 73%.[39] These figures might be inflated, considering the numbers of state tenant farmers who stayed on farms even when they did not work them. Smallholders so placed would have been reluctant to provide information on the sources of their livelihood, as state farms were established to encourage full-time farming, and farmers otherwise engaged might have been penalized by state officials.

There was a sharp increase in the number of ploughs on these farms, from about 92 in 1968/69, to 520 in 1978, despite the fact that the total acreage occupied by such farms had fallen from 340,757 to 253,09 during that period. This phenomenon can be attributed to the state farms and cooperatives established in the early 1970s. Farm equipment and machinery were made accessible to state tenants, i.e., land lease and project farmers.

Cooperatives and State Farms

As state instruments aimed at transforming the social relations of production in the sugar industry, cooperatives and state farms were superimposed upon this network of agrarian social relationships. In the case of the cooperatives, former sugar workers were expected to assume roles as part-owners of the sugar industry. For a brief period, incomes among workers/owners improved, but social relations within the industry remained relatively stable, as civil servants exercised greater control over the farms' production. Although the emphasis placed on food production made local food more culturally acceptable and available, it accomplished little of the planned integration of the domestic and export sectors. The export sector continued in its role as king.

Cooperatives and state farm workers and members built no new sets of relations with other classes or strata within the agricultural sector, but did develop new relations with the state. Moreover, the state sector was caught in the very system it sought to undermine. Like any other agricultural enterprise on the island, state farms hired labor, often at the expense of the more vulnerable smallholders.

A Beleaguered Multi-Sector

Decline characterizes most change in the agricultural sector and units fragment and farmers retreat from farming. The sort of change associated with rising levels of productivity and profitability, as with large units swallowing up less advantageously placed units, has not prevailed. Development of the sector relies on external factors, related to changes in government policy, itself linked to international phenomena, but also the decisions taken within households say, regarding urban or external migration. Though the rural social structure is not static, change occurs within a restricted choreography, manifested within structurally stable units, related to the contraction, expansion and fragmentation of holdings.

Contraction and Expansion of Holdings

Tables 6.1 and 6.2 below highlight three significant developments in agriculture between 1942 and 1978. The first is the reduction of total agricultural holdings, as depicted in table 6.1.

Between 1940 and 1978, over half a million acres were lost from the agricultural sector. Between 1954 and 1978/79, owners of less than 5 acres of land

Table 6.1.   Distribution of Farms by Size-Group for Selected Years

	<5–<6	6<25	25<100	100<500	500+	TOTAL
1942(+)	87,897	22,813	4,045	878	540	116,173
	57%	34%	6%	1%	1%	100%
1954	139,043	53,024	5,603	881	332	198,883
	70%	27%	3%	b	b	100%
1958	141,224	53,300	4,012	639	314	199,489
	71%	26%	2%	b	b	100%
1961	112,600	41,000	3,800	800	300	158,500
	71%	26%	2%	1%	b	100%
1968	144,604	36,881	3,004	699	295	185,483
	78%	20%	2%	b	b	100%
1978	150,633	29,839	2,400	821	295	183,988
	82%	16%	1%	1%	b	100%

Source: Adapted from censuses and surveys of the respective years, 1942/43–1978.
a. May not total 100% owing to rounding.
b. less than .5%

lost approximately 41,429 acres, 17% of their total acreage. Holdings in the lower medium category (between 6 and 25 acres) decreased between 1954/55 and 1978 by almost 50%, a total of 249,833 acres. The acreage of larger medium farms in the 25–100-acre range also experienced an acreage loss of roughly one-half (123,204). Farms of more than 100 acres lost some 180,781 acres, or about one-fifth of their land. Except farms larger than 500 acres, most major agricultural losses occurred between 1954 and 1968. These losses coincided with bauxite companies' earlier (1940s) purchases of large properties for mining, the expansion of the tourist industry, rapid urbanization and the spread of housing properties.

The actual number of farms that smallholders owned or operated grew, especially after 1961, although the acreage they commanded, decreased, causing the average size of their to fall from 1.79 in 1954, to 1.59 in 1968 and in 1978, to roughly 0.13.

The farms of lower and medium scale decreased in number, though their average size remained the same. The large- and medium-sized farms, i.e. those in the 25- to 100-acre range, experienced a double decrease in terms of numbers and acreage. Little wonder that the average farm size, of roughly 42 acres, remained unchanged.

On the other hand, large holdings of more than 100 acres actually increased their share of acreage. Farms larger than 500 acres, and of an average size of over 2,000 acres, constituted less than 1% of the holdings, but occupied 44% of agricultural acreage, compared to smallholdings, which had only 16% of the acreage.

Table 6.2.   Distribution of Farm Acreage by Size of Holdings for Selected Years

	<6	6<25	25<100	100<500	500+	TOTAL
1942/43	157,336	254,376	170,209	187,223	1,067,497	1,836,641
	9%	14%	9%	10%	58%	100%
1954	249,074	502,924	232,178	214,131	716,068	1,914,375
	13%	26%	12%	11%	38%	100%
1958	N.A.	N.A.	N.A.	N.A.	N.A.	N.A.
1961/62	198,000	389,441	167,607	185,596	770,786	1,711,430
	12%	23%	9%	11%	45%	100%
1968	229,216	340,757	127,208	148,048	643,959	1,489,188
	15%	23%	9%	10%	43%	100%
1978	207,645	253,091	108,974	163,802	585,616	1,319,128
	16%	19%	8%	12%	44%	100%

Source: Adapted from censuses and surveys for the respective years.
a. May not total 100% owing to rounding.

In 1954–1961 data observed a drop in the number of smallholders, resulting in a reduction in land fragmentation. Roughly 26,443 holdings from this group seem to have disappeared from the sector.[40] Statisticians hastily regarded the situation as "the rationalization of farms in terms of the average size of the economic unit" though they attributed its causes to general migration to urban centers and foreign countries from rural areas. Certainly migration was a key phenomenon that obtained at this time, but such a situation which they describe persisted only a relatively short period. In 1968, with the contraction of employment overseas, in Kingston and the surrounding environs, as well as the high rate of population growth, fragmentation among smallholdings once again became the norm.

The smallholding sector has continued its parlous existence. Historically, the sector has been portrayed as overcrowded and fragmented. In part because of this, smallholders have sought to diversify their economic activity in the agricultural sector and outside of it. I will take up this issue later. Even still, smallholders collectively produced as much or sometimes more for the export market, than larger owner-operators.

In spite of their disadvantageous socioeconomic position, smallholders have been integral to export production, hence involved in the spread and expansion of capital accumulation (locally and globally). Within the context of the island's global position, they are no more marginalized than their larger counterparts. Nevertheless, as Michel-Rolph Trouillot emphasizes in his study of the Dominican peasantry, smallholders work for capital without accruing many/any of its benefits.[41] Trouillot's account of the vulnerability that such an engagement engenders leads him to conclude that Dominica banana smallholders can never be winners in such a system, but very few are winners judging from the statistical representation of life in the agricultural sector. Nevertheless, the more vulnerable experience dislocates even more.

Export Production, and Living by Multiple Means

Production for the export market is not a new phenomenon among smallholders. In the period following emancipation, smallholders relied almost exclusively upon the production of ground provisions. As late as 1890, ground provisions accounted for three-quarters of the total agricultural output. Even then, smallholders' participation in export crop production was growing steadily.[42] With the introduction of bananas, smallholders and agricultural laborers, often coincident roles, began producing for export. The percentage of locally marketed ground provisions declined, and export crops increased. As shown in chapter 2, the production of ground provisions decreased from 74% of total agricultural production in 1890 to 69% in 1930. Export production increased from 23% in 1890 to 27% by 1930, an expansion due exclusively to the consolidation of banana production on the island.[43]

With the entry of smallholders into sugar production, at the turn of the century, cultivation for export became commonplace and in no way curtailed production of local foods, such as tree and root crops.[44] Small cultivators interpolated the export crops with these food crops, ensuring subsistence and additional sources of household cash. Smallholders' foray into export agriculture was not without problems. When the international market offered satisfactory prices, certain planters sometimes threw their tenant smallholders off the land in order to expand plantation production. Furthermore, general economic difficulties directly affecting small plot operations in 1930 resulted in a contraction of smallholders' agricultural output. In that year their share of agricultural output decreased to about two-thirds, from the 1850–1890 figure of more than three-fourths.[45] As smallholders sought to become more independent from estate monocrop production, they became more dependent on the world market.

Through a combination of personal and state initiative, smallholders have been drawn into the export market, vital components of development.[46] In 1968/69, out of a total of more than 229,000 acres of land, about 48,089 smallholders produced export crops on 92,251 acres. Another 59,583 smallholders cultivated food and tree crops as their main crop on roughly 95,838 acres of land.[47] During the 1970s, the deepening of state involvement in agricultural production led to an emphasis on food production on state-established food farms, with the result that, at least for the early part of 1978/79, production of food crops increased. Yet smallholders continued to produce for export market mediated by local entrepreneurs. Operating properties of less than 5 acres each, 30% of smallholders, 143,002 properties, occupying a little more than 200,000 acres of land, claimed that most of their income came from export production (on roughly 75,542 acres). Another 74,622 smallholders who were cultivating 101,967 acres credited the domestic market with the supply of most of their income. More than 12,000 smallholders earned income from mixed crop production on 20,513 acres of land.[48] Even in the maroon community of Accompong, relatively isolated at the edge of Cockpit country, smallholders cultivated according to state/marketing initiatives.[49] Spence observed that among this community,

> Coffee, sugar cane, pimento and ginger have become increasingly important and now feature significantly in the *village economy* (my emphasis). Although these crops rank behind traditional subsistence crops in their frequency of occurrence as main market crops, they surpass traditional crops in terms of market value. This is not only because these crops fetch higher market prices, but also because of the existence of a more guaranteed market, causing fairly stable market prices for these crops.[50]

These crops were incorporated not into a *village economy*, as Spence asserts, but into a world economy mediated by state and *village* initiatives. Such incorporation caused cultivators to become "increasingly tied to commodity agencies for marketing, for example, through external price determination, the physical transport of their produce and the introduction of a technical package of agrochemical inputs."[51]

However "primitive" the agricultural practices of smallholders may appear, they have often been lauded as innovative, environmentally sound and sustainable.[52] These spaces constitute the alternative spaces of working people's production. As in the past, smallholders continue to combine domestic production with export production and to practice mixed cultivation, an older modern tradition emanating from the postemancipation era, placing emphasis on food crops alongside export or cash crops. By intercropping, smallholders are able to cultivate food forests, defined as "an imitation of tropical nature, a many-storied cultural vegetation, producing at all levels, from tubers underground through an understory of pigeon peas and coffee, a second story of cacao and bananas, to a canopy of fruit trees and palms."[53]

Farmers themselves sum up their rationale for intercropping by stating that

> Plants can't take too much sun; yams need something to run around;
> corn and nuts don't harm each other; peanuts and potatoes don't

agree; corn and tomato don't disturb one another; corn is maturing high and tomato low; coconut branches cover ground and protect during any weather; put plants together and keep the soil cool; soil gets tired of same crop all the time.[54]

In his description of a banana-dominant food forest, Innis observes that

The Jamaican banana garden with its shady, moisture-rich renewing microclimate is probably as close as any type of tropical cultivation to a permanent, soil-renewing type of agriculture. Chocho (christophene) and pumpkin are vines which can climb on the bananas or trees, especially at the edges of the banana patch. Arrowroot grows under the shade of bananas in the same ecologic niche as taro. Corn, sweet potatoes, and yams are minor crops which grow with bananas slightly more often in the limestone than in the conglomerate areas. Sugar occurs with bananas more often in the conglomerate area, perhaps because there are fewer there. The Jamaican propensity to try out various crops in small amounts either because the farmer likes a certain crop, because he doesn't need much of it, or because a volunteer plant seems healthy and is left alone is indicated by completing the list of crops which grow with bananas.[55]

Through intercropping, smallholders helped to systematize various techniques of sustainable production. By relying on several crops rather than one, they reduce the risks at harvest time, as well as lower capital outlays.

By growing a variety of products the peasant can assure himself and his family a basic food supply all the year round and by selling any surplus, increase his standard of living by purchasing those consumer goods and production materials which he is unable to produce himself. But this policy also has technical advantages to recommend it: the judicious combination of crops can ensure a healthy soil and by using sheltering plants which, themselves, yield economic crops e.g., the ackee—the more tender growths such as cocoa and coffee can be protected.[56]

The soundness of such practice has been underscored scientifically, for example, in allelochemics, a field that focuses on the chemical interaction of various plant species, highlighting the durability of certain combinations.[57] One analyst concludes that

Traditional agriculture is an approximate ecologic balance with the environment . . . (and) interacts with the environment in two ways . . . it makes better use of the environmental resources of rain, sun and soil than does modern monoculture . . . it is less destructive of the environment because it does not use poisonous chemicals or excessive doses of mineral fertilizers.[58]

Hardly the primitives as they are often made out to be,

small-scale farmers are practical ecologists with an overall record of success. Within the limits of their technology, and in accordance with their dietary preferences, they have exhibited sound expertise in their crop selection and management to come to grips with the significant local environmental characteristics.[59]

Thus, the smallholders' agricultural techniques cannot easily be written off as inefficient or primitive and unscientific. Food forest yields are 30 to 70% higher than crops produced in pure stand or in monocultural agriculture.[60] As early as the 1930s, a researcher in Trinidad found that aggregate yields were higher on two acres planted in mixed crops than on areas planted in pure stand.[61] Nevertheless, mixed-crop cultivation practices rely on the use of very basic technology. Smallholders usually occupy limited-acreage farms in "awkward spaces" that necessitate the use primarily of machetes, hoes and spades.[62] Smallholders face the further disadvantage of insufficient access to suitable labor-saving agricultural tools. Without proper tools, land can be cultivated only with great difficulty. Accordingly, land ownership may mean little economically, though it confers higher community status.

Table 6.3.   Distribution of Machinery and Equipment Types by Farm Size, 1961–62

Type Of Machinery	Farm Size					
	<5	5<25	25<100	100<500	500+	Totals
Carts and Drays	136	210	223	95	250	914
Trucks, Vans Pick Ups Station Wagons	–	165	275	169	594	1203
Trailers	–	60	52	238	2078	2428
TRACTORS						
Wheeled Tractors	–	124	97	163	638	1022
Crawlers	–	64	32	48	392	536
Rotor Hoes & Motor Scythes	–	–	53	62	270	385
Total	136	623	732	776	4222	6488

Source: Adapted from *Agricultural Survey, 1961–62.* Kingston: Department of Statistics.

From 1961 to 1978, there was an increase in the availability, accessibility, and/or ownership of heavy equipment on smallholdings. This might merely have resulted from the pervasive role of the state in agricultural production, especially during the 1970s, rather than any significant transformation of the labor process. Because the 1978/79 census did not allow for several state farms owning one tractor, it was hampered by multicounting.[63]

In the sample survey of 1961/62, carts and drays were the only farm implements regularly used by smallholders.[64] Table 6.3 depicts the ownership and use pattern among the various holdings. All holdings above 5 acres, especially those of more than 25 acres, had access to or owned the sort of motorized agricultural equipment common to larger holdings. A similar pattern occurs for farm tools. Smallholders had access to only a few basic implements. On the other hand, both the medium and the large owners had greater use of more modern technology.

Table 6.4 shows that smallholders had no access to any of the 681 tractor-drawn ploughs extant islandwide. Similarly, smallholders had none of the 1,203 trucks, station wagons and vans reported in 1961/62. Neither did they own ploughs, or similar machinery, whether animal- or tractor-drawn.[65] By 1978/79,

Table 6.4.   Distribution of Farm Implements by Farm Size, 1968–69
No. of Implements on Farms in Size Range

	Size groups					
Type of Implement	0<5	5<25	25<100	100<500	500+	Totals
Ploughs Tractor Drawn	–	92	77	125	387	681
Ploughs Animal Drawn	–	30	44	29	57	160
Other Implements Tractor Drawn	–	–	61	139	665	865
Spray Pumps Mechanical	145	–	48	24	69	286
Spray Pumps Hand Oper.	125	625	585	273	578	2186
Millers, Shellers Feed Grinders, etc.	–	30	48	57	52	187
Water Pumps Hand	–	120	178	65	123	486
Water Pumps Motor	–	–	184	128	477	789
Total	270	897	1225	840	2408	5640

Source: *Census of Agriculture 1968–69 Jamaica* (Kingston: Department of Statistics, 1973).

Table 6.5.   Distribution of Farms with Machinery and Equipment Available by Size Group of Farm Ownership, 1978–79

No. of Farms in Size Range

Machinery/ Equipment	<5	5–<25	25–<100	100–<500	500+	Total
Ploughs Tractor Drawn	565	520	323	165	612	2185
Other Ploughs	219	105	36	69	44	473
Tractors	370	430	170	139	103	1212
Trailers	78	78	41	62	57	316
Trucks, Vans, Station Wagons	342	364	112	110	106	1034
Animal Drawn Vehicles	32	19	8	3	5	67
Mechanical Spray Pumps	346	230	49	51	71	747
Hand Operated Pumps	473	251	70	74	27	895
Mechanical Reapers	9	20	25	23	17	94
Mechanical Loaders	37	55	21	12	12	137
Other Machinery and Equipment	118	67	26	63	53	327
Total*	2589	2141	781	771	612	7487

Source: *Census of Agriculture 1978/79* (Kingston: Department of Statistics, Preliminary Draft Report, n.d., circa 1982).
*It is inconceivable that this is the actual distribution of agricultural holdings nationally; presumably it refers to the actual number of farms in the various size groups that had particular machinery or implements.
Note: In table 6.5, "a farm is counted for each type of machinery and equipment owned."[66]

use of these types of machinery increased substantially among smallholders, reflecting the involvement of the state in the creation, management and peopling of parts of the agricultural sector. During the mid-1970s, when state presence pervaded Jamaican society at least at a bureaucratic level, smallholders on state properties had greater access to modern agricultural equipment.[67]

Despite the increase between 1961/62 and 1978/79 in the availability of modern farm equipment, as before, the larger the farm, the greater its access to modern tools and machinery.

Increases in ownership and/or availability of technology often impact the cultivation practices of working people in a contradictory manner. Any modernization of the labor process that may have occurred on smallholdings, has clearly not translated into significant changes quantitatively or qualitatively in the relations of production, which ensconced smallholders. The upcoming section on occupational multiplicity evinces an increase in the number of smallholders for whom agriculture was a subsidiary activity. Due to the economic con-

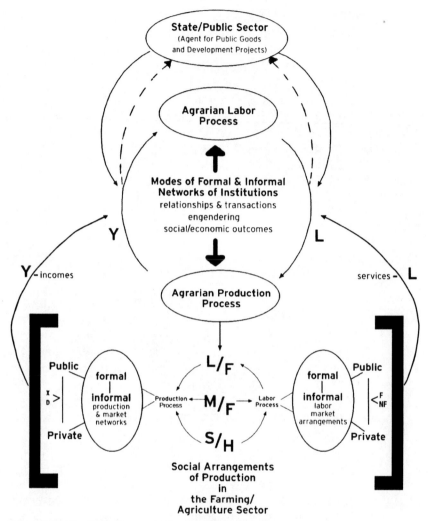

Figure 6.1.   Social Economy of the Agricultural Sector

straints of the small plot, such farmers augmented their income in alternative sectors and/or occupations, shifting judiciously between and among multiple social and economic identities. This was the case even on government-managed land settlements. It is a problem common to all holdings, regardless of size, a condition of agricultural production on the island. According to their economic vulnerability, farmers seek to enact multiple strategies to make farming work, and formality and informality become increasingly entwined. Intrinsic to farming is the engagement in other occupations. These arrangements are captured in figure 6.1 above.

Figure 6.1 portrays the flow of interconnections that constitute the social economy of the agrarian sector. The state is a critical "determiner" of social, economic and political economic relationships in the agricultural sector, and is itself shaped by the system it seeks to control or regulate. Its operations are funneled and embedded in structuring and integrating the labor and production processes through the informal and formal spheres. It is these networks of formal/informal relationships which, in large part, define the complex system of political, social, and economic relationships in the sector. Production, marketing networks and labor processes in the private and public sector, on the farm (F) and nonfarm (NF), are threaded through large firms (L/F), medium firms (M/F) and smallholder households (S/H) which also contribute to the sustenance of the informal and formal processes involved in production for the export (X) and domestic (D) markets.

Probing Multiple Social Relationships

However unsuited to or disarticulated (to use De Janvry's concept, without his epistemological baggage of linear capitalist development) the agricultural sector may seem, agriculture consists of articulated units of production, serving each other in myriad ways. I am certainly not advancing a structural-functionalist argument addressing various units' need for each other, as others have done.[68] Central to the book's argument is the attractiveness of development to smallholders, how their and the state's agendas became more or less intertwined, though they have registered discontent and pursued their own paths of development from time to time. I am concerned with how various agrarian strata, described earlier, are linked to each other, the wider society, and ultimately connected to the larger project of development, whether formally or informally.

While state policy operated under the assumption that the agricultural sector, and units within it, were relatively distinct and bounded, though many officials knew better, members of various agricultural strata considered such boundaries porous. Consider the rural-urban, rural-rural, and rural-overseas migration, all of which provided outlets for smallholders and others from the limits and dictates of state policy. Also, these units participated in formal commodified relations, deploying informal relations. Agricultural networks intertwine formally and informally in ways that undermine or advance development initiatives, dispelling notions of passivity among smallholders or members of other strata, and eliminating superfluous discussions about capitalist versus noncapitalist forms of production.

The number of smallholders involved in occupations other than agriculture has always been high. At the turn of the twentieth century, smallholders straddled many sectors of the Jamaican economy, extending well beyond them. In a survey of smallholders, 20% reported being migrants. Moreover, of the 69% who were farmers, 45% reported that they worked at other occupations while working on their farms.[69] Roughly half the men worked at several different occupations concurrently: carpenters, butchers, shopkeepers, property headmen, and estate laborers. In 1942/43 48% reported intense nonagricultural activity, while 52% were involved exclusively in agriculture. Given some census undercounting, the significance of this phenomenon was understated.[70]

By 1954/55, less than 38% (53,170) of those responding to surveys declared farming as their exclusive occupation. 16% (22,300) were involved in other economic activity, while 45% (62,573) regarded agriculture as a subsidiary activity.[71] This was also so for 1961/62. Although smallholders reported that most of their income came from agricultural activity, 53% (59,493) said that they generated that income from "own-account" or self-provisioned activity, meaning that they created their own economic opportunities, presumably in agricultural areas, though not specifically farming.[72] Of the 45% of smallholders whose income came from sources other than their own holding(s), 29% (32,689) said that most of their earnings came from specifically "nonagricultural" activity, compared with the 16% whose income was agriculturally derived, though it is unclear how this group was not counted under the category of "own-account."[73] Perhaps they sometimes sold their labor power to employers on larger farms or elsewhere, and therefore were counted only as wage workers. While smallholders do but would prefer not to work for other similarly placed smallholders, as it is socially infra dig to do so, they labor there for wages or other compensations and on larger farms, committing themselves and members of their households to other economic activities.

In a recent study of a small farming community, one analyst argued that there was no strict correlation between the incidence of occupational multiplicity (defined from an income perspective) and access to land; that is to say, occupational multiplicity did not lead to the necessary neglect of agriculture.[74] Other factors impinging on agriculture included the operators' skill, the opportunities for income diversification, and the operators' attitude toward farming.[75] There are, however, other data which suggest that the more access the farmer has to multiple occupations, the less land s/he cultivates. The smallness of landholdings, the low returns from agriculture, the pull from potential sources of livelihood, all combine to broaden the economic options of smallholders. The reverse holds true as well. Rural working people unable to compete or find jobs elsewhere turn or (re)turn to agriculture. People already gainfully employed in other areas might reinvest surplus income in agriculture. Yet, the notion that occupational multiplicity best describes the operation of smallholders allows for only a partial interpretation of their experiences. While the construct describes the multiple sourcing of income, it does not sufficiently capture the shifting and competing identities that its incidence entails. These data not only point to multiple sources of income, but to the diversity of social relationships which ensconce land-based rural people as they manipulate, negotiate and engage global processes of production locally.

Dependence on nonagricultural economic activities is not peculiar to smallholders. Many operators and owners of larger farms have also relied on nonfarm sources of income. In 1961/62 roughly 81% of those cultivating more than 500 acres of land earned most of their income from nondefined, "own-account" nonagricultural sources. The reasons for the participation of these two sectors differ. The agricultural survey of 1968/69 noted that "for very small farmers, agriculture may be mainly a subsidiary activity simply because households cannot make a living from agriculture alone on such small acreage."[6] The smallholders queried in this survey included bakers, truck drivers, artisans, shopkeepers, and laborers employed as wage labor on other farms or in government works, etc. On the other hand, the larger farmers may employ managers, overseers, etc., while engaged as employers or operating at managerial levels in other economic sectors. This of course is true also of the contemporary situation.

Smallholders migrated overseas throughout the twentieth century. Their destinations have included Cuba, Central America, and the United States. Since the 1920s, more recent migrations have been to the U.S., Canada, and, particularly in the 1950s, the United Kingdom.

In figure 6.1, typifying agricultural and labor processes networking, the work and contributions of women have been overlooked, partly because the agricultural extension model has typically perceived women "as being [solely] responsible for ensuring well-being in the socio-domestic domain."[77] The systematic collection of data on rural Jamaican women commenced only with the 1996 census, though women's work has been central to formal and informal agricultural production. It is true that farm operators tend to be overwhelmingly male, but agricultural households typically have equal numbers of men and women. Consider the figures provided by the 1996 census. Of the 186,115 holdings from which data were collected, there were 437,528 males and 401,131 females, and no significant age distinction between them. Twice as many men work on their holdings as women, though more than double the number of women work off the farms in nonagricultural employment. This may relate to the fact that generally more rural women than men were educated.[78] Educated people tend to seek off-farm employment, having a wider set of options.

Women who work on farms perform tasks associated with both family caretaking and farm duties. The testimonials of two Jamaican female smallholders describe the conditions of large numbers of Jamaican farmers, particularly single, female-headed households. According to one:

I wake up at 5.00 A.M., look after breakfast and send the children to school. Sometimes I go to the farm to do work or go with the pick-up to buy and sell farm produce. I go to the supermarket and return home. Sometimes I look after dinner or a female relative will cook. We share washing and ironing the clothes, and sometimes I do a lit-tle sewing in the night. I go to sleep at 12 midnight. I sell vegetables that I produce, and I also buy and sell tomato, lettuce, carrot, cab-bage, pumpkin and Irish potato to the hotel industry.[79]

The other chronicle states:

I wake up at 5:00 A.M. and help my daughter to prepare for school. Then I tidy the house; go to the field; cook lunch; wash; and cook dinner. On Tuesday I collect and process cassava. On Wednesday, I bake bammy and on Thursday deliver it to supermarkets. On Satur-day I go to market and on Sunday I go to church. At 1:00 A.M. I go to bed. I sell peanut and vegetables to higglers at the farm-gate, and bammy to supermarkets.[80]

The statistical invisibility of women belies their presence in agriculture, another link in the formal and informal production of agricultural commodities. Women who farm have access mainly to family land, that is, land held in perpetuity by families, access to which is available with some deviation to every member of the family. In a recent survey of 150 female farmers in five municipalities, it was found that 32% of women farmed family land, 20% rented land, 18% leased land and 19% farmed on privately owned land.[81]

Women and men utilize family land as a means to survive and to accom-modate the system, rather than solely as a means of opposition and resistance. Family land may be in some cases a noncommodified tenure practice, utilized to engage in commodified production and facilitated by informal labor processes. Except for the crop and the volume of production, the objectives of these farm-ers correspond to those farmers who produce, on private commodified land, crops for sale on the market.

Neither institutional nor systemic frameworks as censuses or surveys, cap-ture the provisionality of these informal practices.[82] In Jamaica and other Caribbean islands, evidence suggests that, while family land supposes land held in perpetuity by family members of legal or common-law union, often com-modified land markets have replaced family land.[83] Carnegie notes that:

Given the provision that family land be passed on in undivided units and the stricture against its alienation by heirs, it has surprised me, in my work in Sturge Town so far, to find there a lively market in real estate: small plots are bought and sold much as they might be in any large city. A few of these involve the buying or selling of somewhat larger tracts of farmland . . . but the vast majority involve minuscule plots within the village itself. Many of the purchases coincide with periods when outside earnings have been more readily available. Young men from the village who went to work in Cuba in the 1920s and earlier . . . all came back with extra amounts of cash which allowed them to buy houses and small plots of land of their own on which to raise their new families. Some of these sale transactions were between close kin or affines: brother and brother, father's brother and nephew, mother's brother and sister's daughter's husband, for instance, but most seem not to have been between close relatives.[84]

Highlighting the fragmentation between family land and tourism development in Negril in Jamaica, McKay posits that "peasants" became economically minded in the face of external forces and concludes that "if family land evolved as a means of existing independently of a dominant colonial system, that of plantation agriculture, then the use of family land can be seen as a means of competing with or maintaining an interest in a new export-orientated foreign dominated industry."[85] Of course other studies show continuity in family ownership patterns, a set of relatively stable practices associated with kinship arrangements.[86] Foremost among these, is the work of Jean Besson on the Martha Brae community in Trelawny, Jamaica. Besson's central argument revolves around treating family land as a resistant response to land scarcity and plantation monopoly.[87]

Family land plays a somewhat elusive or multivalent role among kin. Its uses are varied, serving to produce both subsistence food and commodified crops. Such land, however, is not entirely outside of the chain of commodified production insofar as family members draw upon its resources for their social reproduction, instead of depending on wage labor.[88] Women smallholders exercise a greater degree of control over family land tenure, both within and outside of production, than on properties held under different forms of tenure. It may be argued that more women operate informally than men, proportional to their numbers in farming. Family land notwithstanding, the desire for freehold property is pervasive throughout the island.

"Independence" and Land Ownership

The correlation between personal and financial independence and land ownership first drawn in the early antislavery and later anticolonial struggles is no doubt responsible for the perceived desirability for individual land ownership. No doubt the much-touted Facilities for Titles Act of 1955 simplified the smallholders' efforts

Table 6.6. Distribution of Farms by Basis of Occupancy and Size, 1954–55 and 1961–62[89]

Year 1954/1955	Owned*	Rent	Free	Owned Rent	Owned free	Rent Free	Owned Rented/	Other	TOTAL
0<5	75318	15481	8644	21489	8799	6341	2689	–	138761
5–25	31826	596	1180	5021	2673	458	1573	–	53327
25–100	459	200	33	393	492	18	26	–	5572
100–<500	894	2	3	28	20	–	10	–	957
500+	313	9	2	13	12	–	–	–	350
Total	112,941	16108	9862	26944	11996	6817	4298	–	198967

*Owned includes Squatted.

1961	Owned	Squat.—Rented	Free Rented	Owned	Owned Free	Rented Free	Rented Owned Free	Other	Total
0<5	84716	904	2860	11920	2837	808	424	130	113239
5–<25	31799	76	433	5841	1469	145	395	66	40769
25–<100	3216	–	31	363	105	2	18	8	3803
100–<500	689	–	7	50	9	1	1	–	779
500+	322	–	1	18	1	–	1	–	351
Total	44502	980	3332	18192	4421	956	839	204	158941

Sources: Sample Survey of Agriculture 1954–1955. Kingston: Department of Statistics; Survey of Agriculture. 1961–1962 (Kingston: Department of Statistics, 1966).

to register for individually owned land titles.[90] As a result, the landlord/tenant relationship has diminished significantly, giving way to freehold property. It has not entirely disappeared, though tenants are not treated as a separate stratum, since many themselves own small amounts of land and combine this with wage work on other agricultural properties or outside of the agricultural sector. Census data for 1942/43 show that roughly 20% of small farm operators were either part tenants and part-owners or pure tenants. By the 1950s the situation had changed. Tables 6.6 and 6.7 provide a glimpse of the changes that transpired between 1954 and 1961 and 1961 and 1968.

The categories in tables 6.6 and 6.7 are open to different interpretations. For example, in the 1968 data the categories of "owned" and "squatted" holdings were treated indistinctly, thus obscuring crucial developments concerning land access, as the two types of tenure often emanate from quite different processes. Those who owned land may also have squatted, and vice versa.[91] Data limitations aside, there is every reason to believe that freehold tenure has evolved as the norm in the agricultural sector.[92] Data for 1954/55 and 1961/62 indicate a decline of 7.25% in agricultural properties partly owned, and partly rented. For 1968, the categories reveal that individual operators owned the bulk of the properties. Rented land secured from larger farms or idle state or private lands prevailed among smallholders. Approximately 47,755 acres were "Rented-In" in 1968/69, the equivalent of the property of roughly 238,776 smallholders, if we assume 2 acres as the average property size. For 1968/69, it was reported that, of the 58,849 acres occupied under "Rented-In," farms in the smallholder category used nearly 50% (26,142 acres). This suggests a distinct shortage of owned land by members of this stratum. It also shows that rented land does not necessarily imply the classic landlord/tenant relationship. Smallholders also rent. Clearly more research needs to be done to assess what other kinds of relationships could emerge in a situation where land is "Rented" under unconventional arrangements.

Table 6.7.   Farm Acreage by Basis of Occupancy and Size of Farm, 1968[93]

Size	Owned	Rented-In	Rent Free	Other	Total Occupied Out	(Less) Rented Occupied	Net Acreage
<5	156243	47755	26142	2557	232697	3481	229216
5–<25	28343	41894	20013	2534	347872	7115	340757
25–<100	112494	12755	6582	1328	133159	5951	127208
100–<500	143534	12446	2760	100	158940	10892	148048
500+	650161	21592	3352	22	675127	31168	643959
Total	1,345,863	136,442	58,849	6,541	1,547,795	58,607	1,489,188

Source: *Census of Agriculture 1968–1969. Jamaica Final Report. Vol. 1. Part A* (Kingston: Dept. of Statistics, 1973).

In 1978/79, data were classified differently: for example, "single holder" referred to an individual owner.[94] For the smallholder, as for others, this is the most commonly held form of land tenure. Although ownership by itself is no guarantee of a stable adequate livelihood, it can allow for the "independence," however limited, that wage earners lack. Land ownership also confers upon the owner a higher societal status. Even still, the few exceptions to these rules challenge the commonly held view that land not under freehold is not cultivated seriously, due to the tenure's insecurity.

Following the dissolution of the land lease schemes of the 1970s, residents in Sawyers, a community located in the parish of Trelawny, continued to occupy lease land, a reflection of the low incidence of land ownership. Members of that community leased land from private landlords. In Meikle's study, there was little relationship between leasehold land and the cultivation of root crops, so that in Sawyers, regardless of tenure, smallholders planted cash crops and responded to state and market conditions as freehold cultivators.[95] Also, there was no discernible difference in labor arrangements among farms under land lease tenure.

Conclusions

Reading livelihoods through tabulations necessarily overlooks some vital realities. The people of Jamaica continue to eke out their livelihood via a myriad of methods, which cancel the possibility of capturing their inventiveness statistically. Not captured here are the stories which represent the will of smallholders and their families to exploit and negotiate the opportunities presented (probably) inadvertently by development. Consider Moyston's story, and the countless others, mostly unrecorded. Writing about three "peasant" women whom he knew, Moyston writes:

> The three peasant women are Miss Winnie, Miss Evelyn and Miss Jean. The setting was primarily in lower Stony Gut near the Morant Plantation and a good distance from Serge Island Sugar factory. As peasant farmers, those women would gather the goods for Coronation Market during the week. Thursday used to be a busy packing day and by midday Friday they began to move the goods to the crossroads at Mr. Segree's, in York. They would be picked up by Mr. Nicholas' truck later in the afternoon. They would arrive at Coronation Market very early Saturday morning, amide the "jam" of handcart men hustling as they take the "one-day" market specialists to their stalls. The male peasant farmers—some of them—work on nearby estates while having their domestic agricultural holdings. Others plant sugarcane on their plots alongside other crops. They sell

their cane to the sugar factory. There was a dynamic connection between the plantation sugar/estate and the peasantry. During crop season all the members of the family unit would help to cut, load and "pilot" the donkey or mule through the meandering tracks to the "truck stop." The cane was loaded in V-shaped branches. Two V-shaped branches were placed on either side of the mule or donkey as receptacles for the cane. The three women did not work on the plantation. They, along with the rest of the family unit, maintained the productivity of the holding for the "betterment of the family." These women were one day market-specialists. They had to sell all or most of their goods in one day—that was Saturday. Sometimes they would complain, "Market was bad." During the week, they organised their goods. For example, if Miss Winnie needed 75 lb of plantains for the next market day and her holding could produce only 50 lb, then she would mount her mule to other farmers to "bargain" for the other 25 lb. . . . When Miss Winnie's "husband" went to America on farm work, she kept the "fires burning." Her husband worked on the plantation in his earlier years until he acquired lands by leasing and buying. During crop season the entire family would help to reap the cane. It was sold to Serve Island sugar factory. I used to hear the talk of receiving bonuses a few times for the years. This relationship with the factory provided a needed boost to the family. Miss Winnie worked in times of weeding and planting. She had greater responsibility in the planting of the domestic crops. The children were primarily responsible for tending the livestock. The combination of the marked and plantation/sugar factory relationship created a relatively secured earning for the family unit.[96]

Moyston's story speaks for itself of the practices of land-based working people to negotiate the terrain prepared by development and the state.

The persistent developmental social reconfiguration of the smallholder takes place against a background of disaccumulation within the agricultural sector. This disaccumulation is manifest in the decline of the number and acreage of agricultural holdings, the stagnation in technological investment and the increasing numbers of persons engaged in other "own-account" economic activity. Consider that three-quarters of the poor are located in rural areas. In 1991, 57% of the rural population lived below the poverty line.[97] Rural poverty outstrips urban poverty. Among the reasons for this disparity, are larger households, a predominance of elderly householders, and restricted access to modern amenities, like running water, toilets and health care.[98] Moreover given the incidence of larger households among the poor, it is children who bear the brunt of poverty, constituting 49% of the poor in 1998.[99] These findings reflect the situation facing households where the main earner works in agriculture.

Add to this a brand of development which attempts to bureaucratize production structures and create cultures driven by commodification, and an environment results in which processes of informalization inseparable from the formal both proliferate and decline. Each enables the other's survival, comprehended and created by a development policy that apprehends members' imbricated identities.

Despite diminishing resources and returns, land-based working peoples from a variety of occupational vantage points contribute to agriculture in the production of both export crops and food crops bound for the domestic market, as well as in the sale of their labor power in other agricultural and/or nonagricultural areas, thereby participating in the burgeoning self-provisioning (informal) sector. The image of class formations in the course of state or private capitalist accumulation, of an increasing polarization of the population (of a locale) into relationally formed historical classes, *klassen an sich*, namely, bourgeoisie and proletariat, jointly formed by class struggle, does not hold here. However useful in projecting tendencies inherent in capitalist development of productive forces, such an image is, like most such "laws," only a tendency, as Marx maintains.

Such processes exist within Jamaica's agricultural sector. On the one hand, there is an increasingly bounded and self-conscious elite and an increasingly well-defined and self-conscious working poor—a "sufferer" in local parlance. But there are far more significant processes at work, which shape the growth of social formations, other than "classic" proletarian tendencies—through land dispossession, and other means of production. It may be possible to discern a stratum that operates within, beneath, above and parallel to these others, of which I speak. There may be a stratum of commercial farmers, or better-off smallholders, developing as potentially independent producers. Its members may be households who are neither so deprived of the means of production nor of the means of subsistence, that they are proletarian, in the sense of being more or less fully dependent on wages gained from employment by private capital or the state. Neither do such households possess sufficient means of production in agriculture to gain a livelihood by producing commodities for the domestic or export market, whether they choose to or not. Generally, their farming resources are either just enough for subsistence production, or augmented with the help of wage labor, hardly adequate to meet local standards of well-being. Smallholders operate small plots, allowing themselves more time to do as they please, and, given the arduousness of agricultural work, age often prevents them from doing too much. Ownership of small plots in Jamaica also allows the complication of a single form of production, thereby weaving a complex set of social relations in the agricultural sector, or in those places that link urban and rural activities. One small farm household may consist of squatters, subsistence producers, landlords (in a loose sense), and export producers. In another smallholding household, all of these activities may be consolidated in one person, usually the male, but sometimes, the female, head of household.[100] Households of this diverse stratum support themselves in several different ways. Members may engage in own-account or subsistence-production (from food crops primarily for households to garment-making and house-building), fishing, production of export crops or artisanal goods, or various forms of wage work.

Brodber's self-portraits of Jamaican men, though restricted to elderly men, portray the multiplex strategies that Jamaican men adopted to survive in Jamaica at the turn of the twentieth century. Many embodied these overlapping social identities as they tried their hands at farming, shopkeeping, trades and wage labor.[101] Man-boy was one of those who left rural Clarendon at age 18 for Cuba where he worked as a wage laborer, establishing himself as a fairly independent person, and returned to rural Jamaica with the resources to buy land to further his economic independence. Also featured among these portraits is a fisherman who owned land, was forced into wage labor to support his family and later became a postman.[102]

As the state has attempted to legitimize itself as the sole arbiter of conduct of the nation's working peoples, reconstituting them as small farmers, small-holders, etc., through the advance and accommodation of development, such policy has engendered much contradiction. It has reconstituted smallholders at a point in Caribbean history where purported independence depends largely on state largesse, now in short supply as chapters 6 and 7 show, and the manipulation and maneuvering through and around development projects. Development keeps smallholders in specific locations, curtailing their access to its alleged benefits, for some time, at the same time that its implementation allows for escape from the clutches of its demands. Incorporated by capital, smallholders are critical producers of commodities bound for international and domestic markets. Neither the laissez-faire developmentalist state of the early nationalist period, nor the active populist one of the 1970s, succeeded in dramatically altering this pattern. Indeed, it might be better to see development projects implemented from the 1940s as having rendered a pattern normative, though political rhetoric apprehends different processes. But rural space has undergone a significant make-over, and smallholders cannot ignore the government institutions. In fact state institutions provide them with certain spaces through which they could carve out people spaces, though this is achieved within the parameters set by the state. What results is akin to interdependencies of autonomous spaces.

The post-1990s present a different picture. The chronic indebtedness of the Jamaican state, punctuated by the institutionalization of Structural Adjustment Policies, the institution of a neoliberal economic globalization, portrays a paradoxical picture, reminiscent of the past documented in the preceding pages, albeit prefiguring new dilemmas, posed by the relatively new renunciation of the commercial viability of smallholder farming, as discussed in chapter 5.

Notes

1. Michael Kearney, *Reconceptualizing the Peasantry* (Colorado: Westview, 1996), 1.

2. Michaeline A. Crichlow and Fragano Ledgister, "Nationalists and Development: The Price of Citizenship in Jamaica," *Plantation Society of the Americas* VI, nos. 2–3 (1999): 191–222

3. Sidney Mintz, *Caribbean Transformations* (Baltimore: The Johns Hopkins University Press, 1974), 155.

4. Ibid.

5. Ibid.

6. George Beckford, *Persistent Poverty* (Oxford: Oxford University Press, 1971); George Beckford and Michael Witter, *Small Garden Bitter Weed* (London: Zed Press, 1982); Kari Levitt and Michael Witter, *The Critical Tradition of Caribbean Political Economy* (Kingston: Ian Randle Publishers, 1996)

7. Douglas Hall, "The Flight from the Estates Reconsidered: The British West Indies 1838–1842," *Journal of Caribbean History* nos. 10 & 11 (1978): 16–24 and Veront Satchell, *From Plots to Plantations* (Kingston: Institute of Social and Economic Research, 1990).

8. Sidney Mintz, "A note on the definition of Peasantries," *Journal of Peasant Studies* 1, 1 (1973): 91–105.

9. For a useful critique of this folkoric tendency, see Roland Littlewood, "History, Memory and Appropriation: Some Problems in the analysis of Origins," in *Rastafari and other African Caribbean World Views*, ed. Barry Chevannes (Syracuse: Syracuse University Press, 1995), 233–252.

10. Jean Besson and Barry Chevannes, "The Continuity-Creativity Debate: The case of Revival," in *New West Indian Guide*, 70 nos. 3 & 4 (1996): 209–228. Importantly the authors argue that continuity and change are integral to Revivalism and Rasta. Peasant culture is undergoing change they argue "from a culture of resistance to the still-persisting plantation system towards and even greater role in forging modern Jamaican identity," 217. The authors do not discuss in what ways cultural interpretations and performances undergo change. Furthermore, considering my general argument, the concept of "peasant" and "peasant culture" remains highly problematic.

11. Sydel Silverman, "The Peasant Concept in Anthropology," *Journal of Peasant Studies* no. 7 (October 1979): 49–69.

12. Scott Cook, "Book Reviews: Reconceptualizing the Peasantry," *Journal of the Royal Anthropological Institute*, nos. 3, 4 (December 1997): 789–790.

13. Homi K. Bhabha, "Signs taken for wonders: Questions of Ambivalence and Authority under a Tree Outside Delhi, May 1817," in Henry Louis Gates Jr. ed. *Race writing and Differences* (Chicago and London: The University of Chicago Press, 1986): 163–179. Bhabha's constructs, ambivalence, hybridization are deployed originally in the

context of the relationship between colonials and the colonizers. But it is a useful adaptation here.

14. I have written about the way this occurs in Trinidad and Tobago. See Michaeline A. Crichlow, "Reconfiguring the "informal economy" Divide: State, Capitalism, and Struggle in Trinidad and Tobago," *Latin American Perspectives* 99, 25, no. 2 (March 1998): 62–83.

15. Interview with Ms. Brown College Green, Kingston, 6 September 2003.

16. James Scott, *Seeing Like a State: How Certain Schemes to Improve the Human Conditions Have Failed* (New Haven: Yale University Press, 1998), 352.

17. See for example Immanuel Wallerstein, *The Capitalist World Economy* (Cambridge: Cambridge University Press, 1979).

18. Dale Tomich, "World of Capital/Worlds of Labor," in *Reworking Class: Cultures and Institutions of Economic Stratification and Agency,* ed. John Hall (Ithaca: Cornell University Press,1997), 287–311.

19. Juan Guisti-Cordero, "Labor, Ecology and History in a Caribbean Sugar Plantation Region: Pinones (Loiza), Puerto Rico 1770-1950 PT. 1 & 2" (PhD. diss. State University of Binghamton, New York, 1994), 46.

20. For a discussion, of this see chapter 1.

21. Eric R. Wolf and Sidney W. Mintz, "Haciendas and Plantations in Middle America and the Antilles," *Social and Economic Studies,* 6, 1 (March 1957): 380–412, 408–409.

22. See Tables on Numbers of Holdings and Their Acreage in Agricultural Censuses for 1942/43, 1968/69, 1978/79 and Agricultural Surveys for 1954/55; 1961/62.

23. Ibid.

24. That is, no immediate payment of rent.

25. The commission of enquiry was held to enquire into the conditions of workers in the sugar industry.

26. Report of the Sugar Industry Commission, Jamaica 1944/45.

27. It is not clear what "squares" mean in this context. In 1944 it was recorded that 56 out of every 100 field workers in the sugar industry were in possession of a cultivable plot. Five out of every 10 field workers possessed 1 acre of land; 28 out of every 100 possessed more than 3/4 of an acre, but less than one acre; 4 out of every 100 possessed more than ½ acre. See *Report on an Economic Survey Among Field Workers in the Sugar Industry, November 1944* (Kingston: Ministry of Labor, 1944).

28. This is a census interpretation. See Agricultural Censuses of 1968/69–1978/79. See Tables depicting "Farmer's Number of Years in Farming by Size Group of Farms 1968/69 All Farms," "Farmer's Purpose of Farming by Size Group of Farms 1968/69," Farmer's Principal Means of Livelihood by Size Group of Farms All Farms 1968/69." "Farmer's Major Source of Income by Size Group of Farms 1968/69."

29. I discuss this in chapter 2. Also Gisela Eisner mentions the fact that a number of new elites from the manufacturing, commercial and industrial sectors bought large holdings, becoming planters or owner/operators of large holdings. See chapter 2 in G. Eisner, *Jamaica 1830–1930* (1961).

30. See Tables on Acreage in Agricultural Censuses of 1942/43, 1978/79 and Agricultural Survey of 1961/62.

31. Ibid. also see tables cited in endnote 9 above.

32. See for 1968/69, tables showing the: Number of Farm Equipment and Implements by size group of farms, also Citizenship and Types of Operators by size group of

farms 1968/69. While the categories used over time defy comparison given their incon-
sistencies, each table in itself addresses the question of which particular farming size
group owned which equipment.

33. Ibid.

34. Calculations derived from respective Tables on Numbers of Holdings, and
Acreage in Census and Surveys of 1942/43.

35. Apart from the discrepancy in the 1942/43 census that made the 1954 situation
look out of proportion.

36. Ibid.

37. Sources for 1968/69: Tables indicating Farmers' principal means of livelihood
by size group of Farms all farms 1968/69; also Farmers' Major source of Income by
size group of Farms 1968/69. See set of Tables: Number and Acreage of Farms by Major Income Earning Agricultural Activity by Size Group of Farm by Legal Status of
Holder; Acreage of Farms by Major Income Earning Agricultural Activity by size
group of Farm by Holder's years in farming; Acreage of Farms by major income earning activity by size group of farm by use and source of technical advice; Acreage of
farms by major income earning agricultural activity by size group of farm by use and
source of credit. As will be observed, the particular method of culling data employed
here entailed the counting each farm separately for each variable. This is one of the
principal sources of double-counting which contributes to the unreliability of the
data.

38. Derived from Tables on Number of Holdings and their share of acreage of Agricultural censuses and surveys for 1961/62 and 1978/79.

39. For 1968/69, see Tables depicting "Farmers' Principal Means of Livelihood by Size
Group of Farms"; also "Farmers' Major Source of income by Size Group of Farms." For
1978/79, I looked at the table entitled "Number and Acreage of Farms by Major Income
Earning Agricultural Activity by Size Group of Farms."

40. This is only a rough estimate.

41. Michel-Rolph Trouillot's formulation in *Peasants and Capital: Dominica in the
World Economy* (Baltimore: The Johns Hopkins University Press, 1988).

42. G. Eisner (1961), 233–234.

43. Ibid.

44. For a substantial treatment of this phenomenon see George Cumper, "Labor Demand and Supply in the Jamaican Sugar Industry 1930–1950," *Social and Economic
Studies* 2, 4 (1953): 37–86.

45. Gisela Eisner (1961), 233–234.

46. One study noted the pressure placed on small cultivators to use chemical fertilizers and to apply for credit to get them. See Balfour Spence, "The impact of modernization on Traditional farming communities. Case study of the Accompong Maroon Village" (M. Phil. Mona: Department of Geography, 1985).

47. See relevant Tables for 1968/69 in Agricultural Census on "Utilization of Land in
Farms by Size Group of Farms."

48. See relevant Tables for 1968/69 in Agricultural Census on "Utilization of Land in
Farms by Size Group of Farms.

49. Maroons were escaped slaves who established communities on the outskirts of
plantations. Accompong, a community of runaway slaves, signed a treaty with the British

in 1739 that allowed their legal existence. Such villages were highly autonomous. The treaty accorded them 1.500 acres and later in the 1950s they got access to a larger acreage, 7,000, from the colonial regime. See Barbara Klamon-Kopytoff, *The Maroons of Jamaica: A Historical Study of Incomplete Politics 1955–1960* (Ph.D. diss. Michigan: University of Michigan, 1973).

50. The reference to village economy is odd given the data and Spence's argument showing the incorporation of the Maroon economy into the world economy. See Balfour A. B. Spence, "The impact of modernization on traditional farming communities: a case study of Accompong Maroon Village" (M. Phil. Department of Geography, University of the West Indies, Mona, Kingston, 1986), 131.

51. David Barker and Balfour Spence, "Afro-Caribbean Agriculture: A Jamaican Maroon Community in Transition" *The Geographical Journal* 154, no. 2 (1988): 198–208, 205.

52. Charles Kingsley, *At Last, a Christmas in the West Indies.* London, 1872); C. Y. Shephard, "Peasant Agriculture in the Leeward and Windward Islands" *Tropical Agriculture,* no. XXIV (April/June 1947): 61–71, 4–6.

53. C. O. Sauer, "Economic Prospects of the Caribbean," in *The Caribbean-Its Economy* (Gainesville: University of Florida Press, 1954), quoted in "The Caribbean Peasant Food Forests, Ecological Artistry or Random Chaos," in *Small Farming and Peasant Resources in the Caribbean.* ed. John S. Brierley and Hymie Rubenstein (Manitoba: Manitoba Geographical Studies 10, The University of Manitoba, 1988), 1–29, 6.

54. Quoted in Theo Hills and Stanley Iton, "A Reassessment of the 'traditional' in Caribbean Small-Scale Agriculture," *Caribbean Geography* 1, no. 1 (1983): 24–35, 27.

55. Theo Hills (1988), 12–13.

56. G. Eisner (1961), 225.

57. Ibid.

58. Innis (1981), quoted in Hills and Iton (1983), 31.

59. Hills and Iton (1983), 32.

60. A number of studies such as Boucher (1985), "Intercropping Research: An Ideological Analysis." Discussion Paper no. 23. Centre for Developing Area Studies, McGill University; A. H. Kassam (1973), "In search for Greater Yields with Mixed Cropping-A report on Agronomic Work," mimeo., Institute for Agricultural Research, Ahmadu Bello University Samaru, all quoted in Theo L. Hills (1985).

61. R. C. Wood, "Rotation in the Tropics," *Journal of Imperial College of Tropical Agriculture* XII (1934), 44–46, quoted in Theo L. Hills (1985).

62. G. C. Wilken, "Microclimate Management by Traditional Farmers," *Geographical Review,* V no. 62 (1978): 544–560.

63. One tractor used on a land settlement scheme comprising a few hundred smallholders appeared as several tractors, if each cultivator responded affirmatively. Also, because of the way information was presented, household data may be ambiguously interpreted as pertaining to several different households.

64. These are rudimentary two-wheel, sideless wagons.

65. See relevant tables depicting usage of Agricultural Implements and Machinery as cited in earlier endnote 37.

66. See introductory section of the Agricultural Census of 1978/79, which explains the incidence of multiple-counting, referred to as "double-counting" in the census tables.

67. I say in theory, because, during my visit on Nyerere Farm in 1978, where I stayed at the home of one smallholder family, several farmers whom I met complained about tractors not being available when they needed them.

68. For example, De Janvry's (1981) explanations about the survival of the Latin American peasantry deploys a structural-functionalist position, premised on the needs of capital for reserve labor and cheap food production.

69. Erna Brodber (1983), 121–122.

70. This has been undercounted by roughly 50,000.

71. See specific tables cited in footnote 37; also, "Numbers Of Subsidiary Farms classified by main activity of operator, and by size groups, 1956," "Number of Farms Classified as (I) Exclusive, (ii) Main, (iii) Subsidiary Interest of Operators, by Size Groups." For 1943, I looked at the following tables: "Number of Farm Operators and Number Working off Own Farms by Size of Farm," "Occupations of Farm Operators by Size of Farm." For 1961/62, "Farms Classified by Main Source of Cash Income and Size Group."

72. Even if we assume that what is meant here is income from plots, then this confirms the notion that there is an instability about agrarian strata which makes it difficult to categorize them.

73. This represented an increase of 7% from 1954.

74. This concept was first coined by Comitas. See Lambros Comitas, "Occupational Multiplicity in Rural Jamaica," in *Work and Family Life: West Indian Perspectives*, ed. Lambros Comitas and D. Lowenthal (Garden City: Anchor Books, 1973), 157–73.

75. See Margaret Newman and E. Le Franc, "The Small-Farm Sub Sector Is There Life After Structural Adjustment?" in *Consequences of Structural Adjustment A Review of the Jamaican Experience*, ed. Elsie Le Franc (UWI Mona: Canoe Press, 1994), 118–210.

76. See introductory section to Agricultural Census of 1968/69.

77. Brenda Kleysen, *Women Small Farmers in the Caribbean* (Costa Rica: IICA/IDB, 1996), 54.

78. Ibid.

79. Jamaican woman farmer, 34 years old, 6 children, 12 members in household. Kleysen (1996), 91.

80. Jamaican woman farmer, 53 years old, 4 children, 6 members in household. Kleysen, Ibid.

81. Ibid.

82. See Jean Besson, and Charles V. Carnegie (1987). See the debate on family land in *Afro-Caribbean Villages in Historical Perspective*, ed. Charles Carnegie (Kingston: African-Caribbean Institute of Jamaica, 1987).

83. Charles Carnegie, "Is Family Land an Institution?" in *Afro-Caribbean Villages in Historical Perspective*, ed. Charles V. Carnegie (Kingston: African-Caribbean Institute of Jamaica, 1987): 83–99, 88–89.

84. Leslie McKay, "Tourism and Changing Attitudes to Land in Negril, Jamaica," in *Land and Development in the Caribbean*, ed. Jean Besson and Janet Momsen (Warwick University Caribbean Studies: London: MacMillan, 1987), 132–52.

85. As I stated before in a previous article, "McKay's work would have been more insightful, had she captured the decision-making process involved in the sale of family land, given the large number of heirs associated with it. Nevertheless, both Mckay and Carnegie highlight the importance of approaching the family land question without any priori assumptions about its stagnation, neglect, and sacrosanctity or the separateness of its existence." See Michaeline Crichlow, "Family Land Tenure in the Anglophone Caribbean," *New West Indian Guide* 68, nos. 1 & 2 (1981): 77–99.

86. Jean Besson and others (see my work).

87. Jean Besson, "A paradox in Caribbean attitudes to land," in Besson and Momsen (1987), 13–45; Idem, *Martha Brae's Two Histories: European Expansion and Caribbean Culture-Building in Jamaica* (Chapel Hill: University of North Carolina, 2002).

88. I do not wish to pursue a functionalist argument here, which poses the issue of the "survival" of these forms of tenure as a function of the needs of capital. Rather, I would like to point out, in the tradition of Bernstein, that these "producers are not fully expropriated nor dependent for their reproduction on the sale of labor-power through the wage-form." See Henry Bernstein, "Concepts for the Analysis of Contemporary Peasantries," in *The Political Economy of Rural Development: Peasants, International Capital and the State*, ed. Rosemary E. Galli (Albany: SUNY Press, 1981), 3–24.

89. The headings in the following tables are defined as follows:

Owned: Land completely owned by holder or operator by way of title.

Rent Free: Occupied land, for which holder lacks title of ownership, and has no type of contract with the legal owner for its specific use.

Owned Rent: Where part of the holding is owned and part is rented.

Rent: Farms that are completely rented for a sum of money from owner/holder.

Free: Where the operator is using the land, but has no title to ownership, and is free to use the land for his or her own purposes with no obligation to the owner. This includes squatters.

Owned Free: Holdings that are both owned and partly squatted upon.

Owned Rented Free: These holdings consist of three mixed forms of tenure, partly owned, rented and portions for which neither rent is paid, nor any title of ownership is possessed, but is occupied with or without the owner's permission.

90. See discussion in chapter 3.

91. This might also be a class in transition. Unfortunately, the data's limitation impinge on a discussion of this possibility.

92. The numbers (farms, acreage) listed under "Rented in" cover land rented for money, represented by sharecroppers (rent payment in kind from produce of the farm). "Rent free" may also include squatting, insofar as operators may occupy it with or without the permission of the owner. This may also include land that is "rented out"; the term includes all land rented out to others, operated by others free of rent or in exchange for services. The category "Other" covers squatting and sharecropping of various types, erroneously construing classification, so that farms classified as different may be the same, or those classified as the same may be very different.

93. In 1968, the categories describing land tenure in the agricultural sector, included the following definitions:

Owned: Land for which the holder has legal title, consequently the right to determine its use as well as the right of exchange or transfer. This would include property that the operator has occupied uninterruptedly for thirty years without any payment of rent.

Rented-In: Where the holder rents the land for a fixed sum of money or any legal payment-in-kind. This includes land held under arrangements where the crop is shared with the landlord or any type of mutually agreed upon agricultural arrangement.

Rent Free: Where land for which occupier has no legal title or contract with the owner, but is occupied rent free, with or without owner's permission but without owner's interference.

Rented Out: This includes all the land that is rented out to others, operated by others free of rent or in exchange for services.

Other: Includes outright squatting on public or private land; also land for which occupier must work free for the landlord for a specified period, for one reason or other; where the holder is granted land for some service in return or must take care of the property.

94. These were as follows: single holder, partnership, cooperative and government. It seems that they organized such categorization with the sole intention of depicting certain developments such as the government ownership of land. But it was not done to provide comparative data, by which they could comparatively assess the state of the agricultural sector historically. Thus, comparisons with any earlier period are difficult.

95. Meikle interviewed 163 farmers in Cascade, Hanover, located on the Western side of Jamaica, and Sawyers in Trelawny on the northern side of the island. See Paulette Meikle, "The Changing Patterns of Root Production and Marketing in Jamaica." (Department of Geography, M. Phil., University of the West Indies, Mona, 1993).

96. Louis E. A. Moyston, "A Summer's Tale," *The Daily Observer*, 1 June 2001. I am grateful for Louis' permission to reproduce this large portion of his column.

97. See table 5.1, "Incidence of Poverty by Region," in *Report on the Jamaica Survey of Living Conditions, 2000* (Kingston: Planning Institute of Jamaica, 2000).

98. Patricia Anderson, "Poverty in Jamaica: Social Target or Social Crisis," *Souls: A Critical Journal of Black Politics, Culture and Society* 3, no. 4 (Fall 2001): 39–55, 43.

99. Ibid.

100. In conversation with someone from Wait-a-Bit, Trelawny, she described her parents as squatters, who employed labor casually, and who also rented out lands to other similar socially positioned smallholders.

101. Erna Brodber, "Portrait of the Jamaican Male," unpub. (UWI Mona: Institute of Social and Economic Research, c 1980). See George Beckford's introduction, a commentary on these unedited portraits. Idem, *Standing Tall: Affirmations of the Jamaican Male: 24 Self-Portraits* (Mona, Jamaica: Sir Arthur Lewis Institute of Social and Economic Studies, 2003).

102. Ibid.

Re-making the State and Citizen: The Specter of Formal Exclusions[1]

> If the widespread consensus of the 1950s and 1960s was
> that the future belonged to a capitalism without losers, se-
> curely managed by national government acting in concert,
> then the late 1980s and 1990s have been dominated by a
> consensus based on the opposite set of assumptions:
> namely that global markets are basically uncontrollable and
> that the only way to avoid becoming a loser—whether as a
> nation, or organization, or an individual—is to be as com-
> petitive as possible.[2]

This chapter serves both as a conclusion and an epilogue. It links the issues raised throughout the text, the role of the state, the fluidity of social relationships, and development, as well as highlighting the new developments underway on this is-land, that spell the rupturing of that triangulated relationship between citizen-ship, development and nation building. In this scenario, decolonization's core constituents, smallholders, stand to lose out bitterly unless they organize as for-mal economic interest groups, within the neoliberal economic order. Also, throughout the text, the formation of the state is seen as a continuous process, shaping the conduct of those whom its elites govern, and redefining the conduct of its institutions of governance. This sets up new conditions for the re-production of strata who "fit" (so deemed pivotal to) particular moments of this re-formation. It also sets up the possibilities for citizens to rearrange their rela-tionship to state elites creating "new states of imagination."[3] Consider David Nugent's portrayal of how the people of the Chachapoyas region of Peru imag-ined the state as they encountered elites' exercise of power. He deftly shows that the contemporary view of nation-state modernity as alien and polluting to tra-ditional local community is a modern response to the contemporary exercise of power, and does not at all resemble that imaginary which obtained during the 1930s when local people felt that they had reaped benefits from their support of the state. Since 1980 the people of Chachapoyas region feel betrayed and therefore re-imagine a different and distant relation to the nation-state.[4] In the case of Jamaica and the rest of the region this changing relationship to the state, and of the state's relationship to the populace has been evident as I will discuss later.

As we have seen through chapters 3, 4, and 5, smallholders have always stood squarely within development's embrace, whose projects have become their sites of struggle, negotiation and hope. Though the emergence of that stratum was part of the struggle against colonialism, partly rooted in radical protest, land-based working people as a whole became recycled within the development policies of a newly constituted national elite. This alliance formalized but informalized as well that relationship. Colonialism's projects were designed to generally marginalize these informal arrangements, prevent their emergence, or failing that, control their labor if not their labor processes or the forms that they assumed. The postnational, postcolonial regimes in Jamaica have reconstituted these arrangements, setting forth new rationalities for their existence as well as that of state institutions.

As we have seen, especially in chapter 1, critics of the development industry's operation argue against any analyses focusing solely on development projects' failures.[5] They emphasize the importance of understanding development's product beyond the intentions or objectives of developers and the relationship between knowledge and power that underlies development projects.[6] This text analyzes the state's relationship to land-based working Jamaicans and eschews the typical discussion of failure, instead highlighting a dynamic relationship between state and land-based workers (or society), a relationship in which as in many postcolonial places, development's sell connects the promise of modernization of economies and/or enterprises with the idea of citizenship in the early national period and, later, in a postnationalist phase rejuvenates citizenship and state/society relations within the body politic by popular cultural appeals and by the promise "betta mus' come." As shown in chapters 3 and 4, such refurbishment carried with it a sense of culture suitable for an independent and postnationalist state. National elites possessed certain ideas about the kind of citizen Jamaica needed. They articulated a set of values that citizens should possess, and so set about creating community, preparing Jamaicans for the task of nationhood, the mantle of a politically independent status. Like most projects of nationhood, it involved not only top-down initiatives, but also broad transactions in an anti-colonial front, and silenced, as Michel-Rolph Trouillot would put it, alternative perspectives, a common trait of nationalism and citizenship.[7] As many have noted, citizenship is instrumentally exclusive. All members of the nation are never included, which makes nationalism a high-maintenance project. Although the process of citizenship in Jamaica was largely an inclusionary project, in so far as, unlike Latin American countries, whose nationalisms excluded indigenous peoples, its rhetoric excluded no one, still critical segments felt excluded on the basis of class, race and/or culture. Rastafarians for example and their sympathizers felt that the nation was especially hostile to their cultural values. Even today, Rastafarians remain excluded from membership in the nation's armed forces, on the spurious grounds of their hairstyle, their beliefs, and, no doubt, their partaking of ganja, which is still criminalized on the island. Literal translations of Rastafarians' antiestablishment/anti-Babylon stance breed suspicion that they are antipolice.[8]

The outbreak of social unrest at the end of the 1960s, though simmering for some time, was an outcome of such silencing and exclusion. Not every perspective, and thus not everyone could be automatically presumed to be part of this "imagined community." Certainly the incorporation of popular cultural expressions into the PNP's political mobilization efforts of the 1970s was an attempt to break some of those silences. To some extent, it succeeded, within the architecture of the secular modernization project. As Scott put it, the Left and the liberals shared similar rationalities in the ways in which they imagined postcolonial Jamaica.[9] According to Escobar, though rhetoric and vocabularies differed, as well as targeted populations,

> Even those who opposed the prevailing capitalist strategies were obliged to couch their critique in terms of the need for development, through concepts such as "another development," "participatory development," "socialist development," and the like. In short, one could criticize a given approach and propose modifications or improvements accordingly, but the fact of development itself, and the need for it, could not be doubted. Development had achieved the status of a certainty in the social imaginary.[10]

As chapter 4 argues, postnationalist political elites of the 1970s and their supporters openly addressed the power dynamics of resource ownership in Jamaica, and they sought to rectify such inequalities through the state with appropriate appeals to the nation. They attempted to suture the nation's socioeconomic cuts. As shown, these projects seemed to blur the line between state and society and at the same time, widen it procedurally, because decision making remained within the domain of the civil service. Thus, state-led development was yet another means through which ideas about development were tied to people's well-being, though they were themselves marginalized from its procedures and outcomes.

Discourses about power and resource inequality in Jamaica—a staple of the political rhetoric of the 1970s—have shifted away from political parties, barely recorded among state elites, though they remain embedded variously in popular consciousness. Such discourses do not figure prominently in the PNP's contemporary political agenda, the party which, during the 1970s, made such discussion nationally respectable, even if the Jamaican people, enslaved and free, had raised these issues and demonstrated their discontent repeatedly.[11] Since the 1980s, a different discourse has sought hegemony. The discourse is reconstituted development discourse stripped of its sociological baggage operating as an "anti-politics machine." Insofar as development's "instrument effects" tend to constitute an "anti-politics machine," the conditions of development's target populations are depoliticized and the power dynamics in which social relationships are bundled become distorted development projects; when reworked into the histories of territories that constituted "plantation economies" with their colonial heritages, this involves an attempt to reconstruct or reinvent histories sensitive to notions of citizenship and nationhood.[12] Such reworking invariably results in the interweaving of political concerns that usually link the agendas of the state to working people's emancipatory histories. Up until the mid-1980s, the island's political independence was hinged to people's independence, concepts of self and well-being and later in the postnationalist phase, to organic forms of social order, which incorporated popular alternatives. Thus, understanding development's workings requires close scrutiny of the relationship between the state and citizens.

As has been shown throughout the text, the relationship between state and land-based working people is pivotal to understanding how development remains an active framework that allows people to imagine and regard their present and future lives in particular ways framed by the production structures in which they are enmeshed. However, to avoid imagining Caribbeans as inescapably trapped into disciplinary habits and positions from which there is no exit, one must remember that the rules defining the operations of production enterprises are also used, by land-based working peoples, to regain lost ground, to capture new territory, or to reinvest with alternative meanings than those generated by projects or state institutions. These spatial locations facilitate land-based working peoples' struggle for more inclusionary participatory techniques, making it possible for them to make contact with state institutions, and to make their demands on political elites, and oftentimes outside of those structures. I do not necessarily believe that using the vocabularies or participating in development projects necessarily negates certain liberatory potential. Nevertheless, a good part of development's discourse was believed and acted upon by the people, whom it eventually marginalized as partisans to state policies. As I have noted throughout the text, the complexity of this relationship underscores the inadequacy of such oppositional frames as state/society, peasant/state, and even residual plantation/peasant, in understanding the ways in which socially (re)constructed modern subjects, "the people," have maneuvered within these discourses and their material outcomes in order to alter the more blatant forms of exclusion and marginalization. These interstitial developmental instrumentalities remain insufficiently theorized in development perspectives. I have started the process here, by building on the recent work of poststructuralists.

In the Anglophone Caribbean region, since the mid-1980s, preoccupation with social development issues has diminished, and the ideological baggage accompanying efforts by states to modernize their economies, not least their agricultural sectors, has been sorely tested. The ability of states to supervise their domestic economies has increasingly been challenged by the neoliberal economic global order, as well as by citizens' doubts about state institutions' capacity to verify their emancipatory claims, scarce though they now are. Nevertheless, as seen in chapter 6, the fundamental structures of agricultural production remain embedded in people's imagination. These structures have become critical ingredients of land-based people's sociocultural and economic habituses (to use Bourdieu's term), to be called forth in their articulation of their condition and needs and as mechanisms through which land-based working people could grapple with the demands of the postnationalist, postcolonial state, whose institutions for the most part now function to facilitate neoliberal economic policies and to deal with the social disorder created in its wake. Perhaps this relationship that land-based working people have with the state constitutes techniques of hybridity, which characterize the postcolonial condition of which Akhil Gupta elegantly speaks, and which also inform the new methodologies to which postdevelopment theorists and postcolonialists allude.[13] These hybrid strategies extend not only to land-based groups of working peoples, but to the state as well.

In his influential book depicting how development discourse has (re)configured the Third World, and targeted certain populations, Escobar points to the emergence of new discourses within Third World countries which offer fresh alternatives to development. In some cases he refers to these as postdevelopment discourses. By this he means that these groups no longer deploy images, ideas, or the essentialized categories of a positivistic development discourse in relation to class, gender, ethnicity, culture, economic need, or their own condition. Escobar posits that the idea of modernization strategies constituting attempts to replace tradition with the modern, a pivotal tenet of development discourse, no longer holds, as working peoples engage multiple hybrid strategies to institute different kinds of modernity. In his words:

> Neither on the way to the lamentable eradication of all traditions nor triumphantly marching toward progress and modernity, Latin America is seen as characterized by complex processes of cultural hybridization encompassing manifold and multiple modernities and

traditions. This hybridization, reflected in urban and peasant cultures composed of sociocultural mixtures that are difficult to discern, determines the modern specificity of Latin America.[14]

The hypothesis that emerges is no longer that of modernity-generating processes of modernization, whose aim is to replace the traditional with the modern. Neither are working peoples any longer concerned with force-fitting schemes and with projects that are irrelevant to their reality. What has emerged instead is a hybrid modernity characterized by continuous attempts at renovation by multiple groups, which take charge of the multitemporal heterogeneity peculiar to each sector and country.[15] In short, instead of people attempting to see like the state, they are interested in agendas which aid them in seeing through the state. Hybridity is worth ethnographic investigation. It is not confined to the people, but is also symptomatic of the state, given the state's institutional diversity and the cross-purposes it comprehends and its link to the political arena, where votes count. Because political elites rely on votes, much maneuvering is possible, as elites attempt to balance the demands of diverse constituencies. Hybridity applies to many different conditions, states of being and acting: it is merely a heuristic device, that enables scrutiny of the myriad ways by which people and states engage development across time-spaces.

Escobar recognizes that the essentialized targets of development à la modernization are flexible in their reinterpretation of tradition and modernity and capture elements of either sociocultural practice, cutting across gender, ethnicity and class, making it difficult to conceptualize social relationships in terms of dominated and the oppressors. Forms of cultural hybridization "result in negotiated realities in contexts shaped by traditions, capitalism, and modernity."[16] Escobar at times posits a nihilistic perspective, whereby the production of any aspect of the development discourse leads to the reproduction of its disempowering effects.[17] Though he himself engages its vocabularies in deconstructing its powerful discourses, there is a sense in which only those capable of escape from development's grasp, like cultural hybrids, or those within new social movements, may lead us and themselves out of the disabling confines of distorted identities and the exclusionary socioeconomic practices perpetuated by such discourses.[18]

Land-based people exercise options coincident to their agenda and to development's expectations at several levels. They believe in different forms of progress that take them from early modern to late modern forms of production and consumption, involving differential relations to state institutions. Occupying different positions spatially and ideologically, they maintain practices that recall a range of functions of the developmental state, and its stated goals and discourses, from "backward" or traditional to the modern, and from the more modern, to the global, the new horizon of success. Development's various reincarnations are periodically marked. The old and the new interpretations of what people need coexist within the nexus of relationships that characterize state and agricultural clientele relationships. In other words, land-based working peoples who inhabit these locations call forth or produce positions that recall earlier development states.

These strategies are embedded within differential modern temporalities. In the Anglophone Caribbean, attitudes toward government's development policy emerge from within contradictory paradigms, which reflect the developmentalist state policy on the one hand, and, on the other, the present phase of state reformation, where institutions are transitioning, have transitioned, or even acquiesced to neoliberalism's demands. Transitions bring institutional lag times. Change is never instituted evenly. Institutional changes are staggered, depending on the priorities of the state, and on state-society relations, now new global actors. This situation allows political elites inhabiting these disjunctive spaces to pursue agendas at times contradictory. These responses are part of the overlay of the hybrid practices of most politicians in the region who rely on patron-client politics, unwilling to relinquish old-style approaches to politics and development, given the reality of getting votes, dependent on the interplay of competing discourses on development strategies and citizenship. These are not necessarily residual conditions, however. Ong's concept of "graduated sovereignty" might be adapted here to capture a process of uneven state surveillance. In her analysis of the Malaysian state in the period of globalization, she argues that in so far as it favors indigenous Malays, they have been accorded preferential treatment above all other ethnic groups since the 1970s, allowing them to take advantage of transnationality.[19] Considering that citizenship always excludes, even in more or less racially homogeneous sociocultural contexts, one can argue that graduated sovereignty is not a new, post-1970s phenomenon; new is its metamorphosis in the context of the current neoliberal economic agenda. We may ask what new interests or groups might be favored to implement or facilitate the state's repositioning and recomposition of its institutions to engender accumulation in the new era and with what consequences for the reshaping of citizenship and the conditions for its renewal.

Given the new priorities of the Jamaican state, how have land-based working people responded to development? Their responses have been framed within an understanding of development projects' inadequacies. That is to say, though working peoples accept much of development's claims and promises, they have tested and challenged its exclusionary practices, seeking to enhance their inclusiveness. In short, while working peoples seldom oppose projects' implementation per se, they subject them to discursive and material scrutiny that may lead to important revisions either at the level of operation or of the mechanisms of participation. Beyond Scott's "hidden transcripts" of discontent and resistance,[20] land based working peoples may flout the rules, leading to outcomes that incorporate forms of organic change. This double take on development is associated with the ways in which people relate to competing discourses of development though, since the 1980s, the neoliberal globalization project approach has dominated.

Land-based working people often rely on earlier articulations within older forms of agricultural enterprise, by appealing to state institutions and personnel to assist them at a time when such assistance in the dominant local development discourses is considered to be irrelevant to the "needs of globalization." In 2001, with the head extension officer, Marcia Forrester, I visited several small farms to get a closer look at their condition and needs. Marcia was surprised to find that Project Land Lease farmers (discussed in chapter 4) were still active in St. Catherine and clamoring for state assistance, as if nothing had changed. According to Farley, a farmer I spoke with, there were over a hundred farmers operating lease projects. Farley worked the property himself, and had captured an extra piece of land, whose tenure he hoped to regularize soon. Farley's wife was ill. He claimed her illness had "bruk" (bankrupted) him. He was a worker on a large property, but after the manager disrespected him, he quit the job, and turned to farming. He subleased the land from the original lessee, who was now in the U.S. On the land, he grew calalloo, which he sold on the export market. Exporters would pick up the crop at his farm gate. When export prices fell, he sold his crop to higglers, who in turn sold it on the island's local markets. Apart from calalloo, he was planning to cultivate cassava. He admitted to have visited demonstration plots during training provided by extension officers. Farley believed that the market was good for cassava, since there was a processing plant nearby to which he could sell the cassava. The processing plant manufactured bammies (round, flat cassava bread), some for export, some for domestic markets.

On another farm, the farmer and his help were digging holes for okra seeds. It was a newly leased area. This farmer, Joey, was in partnership with another, and, in addition to okra, they had a crop of sorrel underway. Joey complained that a virus was wreaking havoc among the potato crop of one farmer. We searched for this farmer, but instead encountered a female farmer, Lorraine. Dressed in knee-length socks and boots, she came to greet us, and appeared quite enthusiastic about meeting Marcia, the supervisor for that parish. The farmer whose potato crop had been devastated by the virus was out, but Lorraine said that she and the farmer worked closely on their farms, helping out each other on their adjoining plots of land. Lorraine and seven other farmers had worked on the potato crop. She was subleasing the land and complained that she had not made enough profit to warrant continuing. Her gungo peas (pigeon peas) crop had not done well. It had been attacked by bugs. Her second planting had benefited from knowledge she secured from that experience. She now knew when to spray to save the crop. She had "got a little something from her second crop." She had been able to save a bit. She had "got a little something" from her sorrel crop as well, but she complained that she had not been advised in any way by the extension officer. She did not even know his name. Marcia advised her how to get more out of her sorrel crop. We bent low under a barbed-wire gate to get to see the damaged potatoes. The potatoes she dug up were all big but dry, with sure signs of rot.

Marcia said that Lorraine should talk to her crops, treat them like human beings, and that they would respond well. Lorraine said they were coming along fine, and when "one big rain" came "them gone, (because) water settle pun de roots, and that is the end of them." She complained about the complete loss of crops after rains because the soil on the farms was clay. The other farmer too had complained about losing pumpkins and other cash crops because of a "big rain." Lorraine was advancing her agenda, seeking help from the Ministry.

Marcia made notes in her diary and promised to send Lorraine some sorrel seeds from the Kingston office. She advised Lorraine to "Get a backhoe to put in some deep drains." She reasoned, "you might save some of the crops instead of losing all of them." She also told Lorraine to "pray to the Lord," to which Lorraine replied "me speak to him everyday."

People like Lorraine and other similarly situated land-based working peoples strategize across a set of options, which further state involvement in their lives, but also allow them to enact their own agendas. They constantly challenge development's explicit failures, by querying and clamoring for state support. Also, sometimes posing as ineffective, even helpless, though their situation hardly warrants that description, they appeal to government institutions to fulfill their obligations, and Ministry personnel oblige.

Maximizing Possibilities on Government Farms

The struggles within the farm enterprises of the 1970s are crucial because they enable us to see the ways in which ideological appeals to self and nation are deployed in development projects, as shown in chapter 4. Attempts by the political elite to incorporate and legitimize key popular institutions reinforce state/society links, enabling working people to engage in new forms of agricultural production. Such policy bespeaks notions of citizenship, based less on the Western free-floating individual than on a collective spirit, and inorganic communities, jump-started by people's participation in state-led development projects. Under the rubric of democratic socialism, operating as Escobar would say, within the architecture of development, a new citizen would emerge, who would institutionalize socialist cooperation in the agricultural sector. Though these agricultural enterprises were inorganic structures, political elites felt that they, rather than the myriad of freeholding plots, or the large-scale estates, could better harness the people's will and productivity. New farm enterprises offered working people the opportunity to become settlers, farmers, participants, as well as an opportunity to wean themselves away from a relationship based on the capital/labor antagonism, inherent in wage labor relations.

State intervention in production and the organization of households and communities greatly influenced the emergence of a contradictory mode of struggle by smallholders. Although the struggle assumed a more systematic form in the 1970s,[21] state involvement proved an inadequate basis for workers in the reform and nonreform agricultural sector to radicalize their traditional forms of struggle. Indeed, the reorganization of production, discussed in chapter 4, created the basis for new initiatives to be undertaken, shaping the ensuing forms of conflict. Cooperative and land settlement schemes, such as Project Land Lease and State tenant farms, highlight this argument. Since issues of conflict on these properties were mentioned in chapter 4, I will summarize only those aspects which throw light on the influence of political unionism, which was a means of inclusion, open to all, but not to many, linked to the dominant political parties, and consequently, indirectly to the state. As seen in chapter 3, both the PNP and the JLP utilized trade unions as a mechanism of national inclusion. Unionism in Jamaica is historicized only in a political context.

In the sugar cooperatives workers expressed confidence in the traditional strike action they had used repeatedly before co-ops were established. Even as members of the co-ops, owners of property, they had not relinquished their union membership. Supported by their unions, co-op members at the Frome and Bernard Lodge sugar factories staged two strikes in 1976 to support their demands for the payment of severance pay, thus setting back the start of the 1976 crop by at least one month.[22] As one analyst put it:

> As economic pressures have sharpened within the coop farms, the SWCC has weakened while renewed interest in trade union membership and representation has grown. . . . As the movement's leadership shifts from agitational opposition roles to assuming authority positions popular support has waned and increasingly cooperators see the trade unions as a machinery for bargaining and pressuring the new democratic elite in the estate system.[23]

They struck again to back their demand for an aftercrop bonus of 12 1/2% of their gross crop earnings during the crop year of 1982/83.[24]

Though the space created by the state, and the formation of broad-based committees, were inadequate to participation, this space and these committees were nonetheless something novel and different and lent themselves for some time to working people's resolution of conflict outside the traditional mechanisms of conflict resolution. In the early stages, political elites permitted SWCC to mobilize sugar workers, inadvertently committing themselves to the blossoming of nontraditional politics. However, as the leadership assumed positions of authority in the cooperatives, the SWCC's agitational programs weakened, and the cooperators became even more reliant on the unions "as a machinery for bargaining and pressuring the new democratic elite in the estate system."[25] Co-op members were simultaneously supportive of both old and new forms of conflict resolution. Party/political unionism was refreshed, reinvigorated, ready to carry on where it had left off.

On Project Land Lease, where most of the participants were small cultivators, the problems that arose tended to be determined and contained by structural aspects of the scheme. Unlike the cooperatives' workers who were previously unionized wage workers, Project Land Lease participants were inner-city dwellers, who worked individual plots of land to supplement their income as wage labor under various employers. Moreover, the structure of the scheme reflected customary work practices of the individual small cultivators. Surveyed by central management, each participant managed his/her own small plot of land, individually seeking to enhance his/her own income. Neither Project Land Lease nor Project Food Farms had the benefit of a mobilizing nongovernmental agency like the SWCC. Protest action within the schemes was limited to outright withdrawals from the scheme and to rule circumvention. Dissatisfaction also percolated through official outlets; the major complaint centered around cash shortages.

Cash facilitated expenditures related to land preparation and the hiring of labor. Although discouraged, the hiring of labor was necessary, because the government's policy of distributing small economically unviable parcels of land to "encourage

Table 7.1.   Complaints over Project Land Lease

Complaints	Percentage Of Farmers With Complaints
Shortage Of Cash	35%
Water Supply And Internal Roads	12%
Inadequacy Of Land	11%
Low AMC Prices	10%
Absence Of Buildings On Farm	7%
Burdensome Terms Of Credit Repayment	8%
Administrative Delays And Failure	11%

Source: C. Stone, "A Sociological Survey of Tenant Farmers on Project Land Lease." mss. (Mona: Dept. of Govt. UWI, 1976), 18.

peasant involvement in agriculture" placed the responsibility of earning additional income onto the tenant cultivator. As mentioned earlier, 85% of the plots were less than 3 acres in size; over 60% were less than 2 acres.[26] Additionally, the large number of children within farm households created a shortage of adult labor. Moreover, many older adults were unable to handle demanding agricultural chores, resorting to employing younger laborers.[27]

Government's unrealistic appraisal of the agricultural sector forced land-based working people to redefine priorities according to their needs. Hiring labor, thereby flouting the reform's requirements, was one consequence. Another challenge surfaced in marketing arrangements. As discussed in chapter 4, worker/participants sold their produce to private individuals, like higglers, rather than to the state-owned Agricultural Marketing Corporation (AMC).

These demands reflected the extent to which the positioning of rural working people shaped their grievances and their operations within development's configurations. Such strategies may have limited their chances of improving their life chances, though as "conscripts of modernity," to use David Scott's construct,[28] working peoples do not lack the wherewithal to transform their relationship to certain forms of modernity, expressed in development projects.

This abbreviated account of land-based people's negotiations and maneuverings in the agricultural sector ignores migration as a strategy through which people escape from and may later return to the agricultural sector, reinvigorated. In her extensive interview of men in rural Jamaica, all born at the turn of the last century, Brodber discovered that many men had left home as boys in order to fend for their families. They either went to Kingston or left the island to work in Cuba, Panama, the U.S. or Great Britain. Not all these men were land-based, but the conditions under which they lived made for similar strategies of living and surviving. They were referred to as "manboys," because they were really child laborers responsible in part or sometimes wholly, for the welfare of their families. Beckford summarizes their strategies thus:

> Internal migration began for these 'manboys' at an early age. We find these cases of movements from the arid St. Elizabeth area and the sugar-dominated Clarendon plain across the island to St. Mary parish where the rainfall, climatic and land environment is more favourable and where economic opportunities had opened up in banana production through the efforts of the peasantry there. This latter internal movement such as represented by Migrant Farmer was characteristic of many youth men moving from a rural environment to urban environments like Kingston, Spanish Town and other towns, to acquire new skills—artisan skills for the most part; whereas Migrant Farmer and Landless Farmer remained within the agricultural sector.[29]

Many migrants would return to Jamaica's agricultural sector and engage the state from a position of financial strength and newly learned bargaining strategies. Migration is another strategy which rearranges this state/society relationship but from within the architecture of development, locally and internationally.

The above discussion of land-based people's strategies suggests that in Jamaica development is multitemporal, in which different modernities, even apparently contradictory ones, are linked. A new language is generated in the process, ably spoken by members of the state's administrative class. It is manifest in farmers' conversations, marked by their concerns about prices going "up" and prices going "down," and the global influences, by which the country finds itself tossed around on the ocean of these determinations (to use Hardy's metaphor).[30] There is the sense among land-based working people that things could be better if policy was better tuned to the local situation and to the needs of working people, including the "sufferers." The irony is that while smallholders, working people and others focus on what is needed locally in order to project outward, the language and policies of institutions like the World Bank, the IMF and now the Jamaican state and political officials articulate a vision that seeks to unseat some of these perspectives, while reinforcing others.[31] The latest documentary about the island, *Life and Debt*, poignantly portrayed this.

Life and Debt

The informative, superbly edited documentary *Life and Debt* captured the contradictory scenarios elicited by the neoliberal economic order in Jamaica, a modern/postmodern space. The narrator, Jamaica Kincaid, was able to transpose her Antiguan experience to Jamaica, describing the luxuries tourists were treated to, all the while oblivious to the developmental decay which punctuated the lives of Jamaican working peoples. Jamaica's efforts to sell itself as a premier tourist destination have further exacerbated its Janus-faced development policy. Many who saw the film lamented the dire straits that Jamaican farmers and other entrepreneurs found themselves in, given the unfairness of neoliberal policy toward small islands like Jamaica, a consequence of which was the rampant importation of less expensive goods undermining local production.

The documentary further revealed that Jamaicans had accepted the idea of neoliberal development, the critical sell of market accessibility, and believed that if they followed the rules, they would eventually get a fair break. As the film outlined, this was the appearance of a different reality. Female factory workers in the Export Processing Zones (EPZs) of Kingston, banana and vegetable farmers, milk producers and meat processors, were all agreed that "nutting nuh gwan like dat" (things did not happen like that). Foreign imports flooded the Jamaican market at cheaper prices than locally produced goods; the concessions awarded EPZ companies allowed them to treat workers with little respect. Such firms became even more "footloose" and pulled out of the country, leaving in their wake, angry unpaid workers. In the film the only people benefitting from such a situation were merchants who now had access to cheaper products. They were depicted loading up their trucks for islandwide distribution, satisfied that the floodgates had been flung open to allow the importation of various consumer goods. Tourists and Jamaica shared the same imported diet to the extent that the latter could afford it.

Development Discourse: Twinning the Old with the New

This filmic depiction of Jamaica's development dilemma hardly alters conversations in the agricultural sector about its commercialization. I now highlight the overlapping development discourses, extant in Jamaica's social space generally and specifically those related to agriculture, contextualizing the machinations of land-based working people.

Officials in the Ministry of Agriculture speak about the "need to focus on productive farmers," mainly medium-and large-scale producers. Officials hope these farmers lead the restructuring of the agricultural sector. The neoliberal developmental thrust fits the concerns about the need to realize economies of scale, in order to compete in international markets. Officials speak expectantly of the shift away from "subsistence" farming though they readily agree that even this group of farmers are involved in the export trade. The consensus in this circle seems to be that larger farmers have better potential and that the monies spent on smallholders over the years have not produced value. One gets a sense of policy makers going for broke as they begin to focus on larger producers.

These corporatist concerns have been reshaping the agricultural sector, since the structural adjustments of the mid-1980s, continuing into the 2000s. What began as enforced guidelines to restructure the Jamaican economy became the mantra of the Jamaican state—that a market-led economic model was far more efficient than a state/developmentalist model in reducing levels of impoverishment leading to economic recovery and competitiveness. Note the technicist nonpolitical or "antipolitics" orientation of the diagnosis, which erases the political dimensions of development and simplifies or ignores the basis of the actual division of labor in agriculture. The resolution represents the standard neoliberal economic fare: divestment of government properties, the elimination of import restrictions and food subsidies, the adoption of market-related credit terms in place of agricultural subsidies, all key coordinates of the new agricultural policy, aimed at making the sector competitive.[32]

In the light of WTO requirements that necessitate the dismantling of protectionist provisions to allow for free trade to release agriculture's competitiveness globally, the sector has to prove its social and/or private profitability. As summarily outlined in an official document:

> Internal competitiveness implies the ability of a productive sector to continuously attract labour and capital because it is able to provide adequate rates of return to those resources when compared to other sectors. . . . International competitiveness implies the ability to sell on domestic markets alongside imported goods and in overseas markets alongside goods from other countries.[33]

Workshops conducted on the island aimed to acquaint agricultural and private sector officials with the mechanisms for measuring commodity competitiveness. In October 2000, one official from the USA held a two-week training seminar entitled "Measuring the Competitiveness of Agricultural Commodities in Jamaica." There, workshop representatives from Jamaica and other Caribbean islands learned how to measure and evaluate eighteen commodities' competitiveness. These training sessions created the environment for Jamaicans and Caribbeans to survey their own practices and to internalize the rules for their continued participation in the global marketplace. Thus is globalization facilitated willingly from below.

The IDB-supported Agriculture Support Services Program (ASSP), the pivotal incipient agricultural project, worth $US31.5 million, is directed by an MBA whose previous job was in Jamaica's corporate arena. The director speaks of a new corporatist approach to agriculture that will favor medium- and large-scale producers, commercial farmers whom he believes are those most capable of responding to the new WTO's demands and placing the agricultural sector on a competitive footing. The project seeks "to enhance the competitiveness of Jamaican agriculture in domestic and global markets, making a substantial contribution to the goal of increasing the incomes of agricultural producers."[34]

The project has three components. The first seeks to enhance extension, research marketing and strategic information to producers and exporters, by way of establishing five Agribusiness Development Units (ADUs) which would "link agricultural services providers with producers, establish a fund to partially finance services supplied by selected providers, organize and train farmers, and improve facilities and train technical personnel";[35] the second component seeks to ensure that food systems meet domestic and international safety systems, by way of training and hiring personnel, and updating associated laboratories; and the third identifies and develops new, nontraditional areas of production, financing such activities with up to $US300,000.

The ASSP promulgates some of the assumptions of the "new" agricultural projects begun in the 1980s, during the era of structural adjustment. Adjustments persist even if the country is no longer tied to IMF arrangements. Perhaps such edicts are unnecessary since the country now censors itself, but I will return to this point later. Although the ASSP is only vaguely similar to AGRO 21 of the 1980s, discussed in chapter 5, the philosophy of free trade and market liberalization link the two. ASSP, like AGRO 21, equates growth and development of the agricultural sector with commercial farms; it does not seek to create such farms; it identifies them and works with them, the engines of agricultural growth and efficiency. In other words, ASSP takes as given the existence of commercial farms and seeks to enhance their export production and to reward innovation with large loans and services. Moreover, Ministry officials argue that AGRO 21 failed in part because it brought farms with no history of success into agricultural production, and add that, "There are Jamaican farms that are relics of plantations, but we can't overlook them now."[36]

To facilitate this transformation farmers are expected to organize themselves into interest groups, groups with the resources to tap into ASSP services. These groups will provide their own collateral to take advantage of loans and the ASSP services. The manager recounts how in the past, farmers were asked to grow particular crops, then markets were found for them. Now however, markets had to be identified in advance of production, and the ASSP would act as the middle "man," putting farmers into contact with overseas buyers and consolidating contracts accordingly. Emphasis would be placed on viable farmers, those already operating at a certain level of production and organization, capable of providing the necessary collateral in exchange for services.

The fundamental shift from governmental and societal concerns now reshaping agricultural policy is reflected in the Social Development Commission's (SDC) approach to community development. The five-year development plan for 1990–1995 states that, in the light of the disparity between the numbers of community centers and their functionality, within the framework of economic growth nationally, resuscitation of these centers would involve increasing community members' participation in economic activities. Accordingly, "the government (through the community-based Enterprises Project within the informal sector) will provide credit and support services to approximately 10,000 new and previously existing community enterprises over a five year period."[37] In this way, rural or urban enterprises with up to ten persons employed, with assets of up to J$120,000 (US$27,270), become central to the regeneration of communities.[38] A reorganized central government agency, the SDC would "permit a more responsive role that will enable communities to be integrated into the development process."[39] To facilitate this new role, the SDC would have to increase its technical capacity and become active in creating community organizations as well as train and educate community leaders on the issues of community and national development. No longer considered to be a service provider, the SDC would assume a catalytic role, "empowering community groups to assume responsibility over local needs."[40] In one researcher's words:

> The Report of the Committee of Advisors on Government Structure extends the description of the problem to include that of the implementation of the dogma of private sector-led development, and thus the concomitant location of greater responsibility at local and community levels.[41]

This new arrangement makes it possible for the private sector to become directly involved in community development. Through various inducements, the Jamaican government makes it possible for the private sector to adopt various projects or tasks within the rural and urban areas as part of its civic responsibility. Cunningham remarks that:

> In Jamaica the barrage of recantations such as "together with the private sector" is evident of the type of new consensus/agreement within which "success" as it relates to community development will be measured as well by the total dollar-value contributions the private sector can make to projects. In other words, the "consensus" will be as much a success as the contributions. The community development illusion will be more widely shared. The public will buy it because it makes for order and nationalism of which the save-the-dollar initiative is a prime example staving off community "problems."[42]

This is one way in which social services become privatized. The state weans itself away from services that it once provided gradually. Marketization and privatization become embedded into new spaces.

Advertisements in Air Jamaica's in-flight magazine hail the dawn of a new era, endorsing and contributing to the domination of the official discourse on development and social order.

In this 2000 advertisement in *Sky Writings*, an in-flight Jamaican magazine, the oldest leading investment firm on the island, which specializes in money-market investments, corporate banking services, and foreign-exchange trading, features a mulatto or a Jamaican white or light skin mixed-race child between seven and ten years old with a hairstyle of braids or cornrows looking out at the reader with a somewhat wry smile. The caption reads, "I WANT JAMAICA *to become a first-world country by the time I grow up.*"[43] The first part of the advertisement is rendered in bold large

print, the rest, in small print, as if there were a sober realization about the second, a whispered wish, that Jamaica might fail to become a first world country in, say, two decades. In the right-hand corner of the advertisement, a yellow flame is superimposed over a black circle, encircled by the company's name, inviting all kinds of mischievous interpretations. According to a company spokesperson, the flame is the significant symbol, and the black circle nothing more than a graphic against which the flame is highlighted signifying that the company is lighting the way forward in the field of financial investment.[44] In very tiny print at the bottom of the layout, the investment firm's logo reads: *"For People Busy Making Money."* The symbol's colors are the same colors of the Jamaican flag, linking the nation with the message of the advertisement. The firm has other advertisements that underscore the importance of investing for the future, one of which mentions the commonly cited saying that "money does not grow on trees."

Another advertisement in that same issue of *Sky Writings* hails speedy Internet services under the banner of *"Go the distance."* There, track and field runners caught in a photographic whirr compete to win the race. The advertisement states, "In Jamaica, the quicker you put the right INTERNET SERVICE PROVIDER in place, the quicker you will be able to go the distance. . . . Every second counts." This advertisement likewise links the popular national concern of track and field with the orientation of business, suggesting one speedy way to bring the nation into the sea of globalization.

Discourses of hope in the context of evident economic and social decline are sometimes cloaked in a critique of agricultural policy. Such critique invariably ends with the mantra that Jamaica can compete in a globalized world, that globalization can redound to the benefit of all hard-working Jamaicans. An ethnography of economic decline might do well to focus also on the ways in which people remain wedded to beliefs about upswings or their ability to transform themselves in the face of decline.[45] Such an ethnography would need to investigate the crosscurrents of hope and despair intrinsic to the lifestyle and practices of those who inhabit vulnerable locations, even those who objectively seem on an everlasting downhill slide. Consider for example, the recent statement regarding agriculture by the President of the Montego Bay Chamber of Commerce and Industry, Kerr-Jarrett. Kerr-Jarrett links the rise in urban crime and general social decay to the decline of rural agriculture, which he blames directly on the Ministry of Agriculture. He states:

> The escalation in crime, urban decay and overcrowding in the inner city and in standing squatter settlements, stems directly from the failure of rural agriculture, resulting in rural to urban drift with the tourism centres becoming a recipient for the majority of displaced farmers and their families.[46]

Kerr-Jarrett appeals to the Ministry to "research new avenues and diversify, as those among us who have realized that banana and sugar are dying industries and have had to review our direction." He concludes hopefully, stating that Jamaica possessed "tremendous potential to revive its economy in the agriculture industry and to reposition it as one of the primary vehicles for foreign exchange."[47]

The shaping of such an agenda and the facilitation of such policy have so far occasioned little public discussion of the Jamaican intelligentsia, who played a critical role in articulating positions within the framework of dependency theory and the plantation economy thesis in the late 1960s and who, as shown in chapter 4, in 1970 played a supportive role to the PNP's democratic initiative.[48]

The Conduct of Nation-State: Jamaica's Promises to the IMF to be "World Class"

The irony of the discourses of hope is that they occur at the same time that the Jamaican government is adhering to IMF surveillance, of its own accord, justified on the basis of 1) an outbreak of violence in Kingston, 2) the aftermath of 9/11, which led to the decline of tourist arrivals and 3) major infrastructural damage and population dislocation as a result of widespread flooding that occurred during November 2001.[49] Though this appeal to the IMF is technically an informal one, not the same type of relationship that the government entered into from 1984 to 1990, Jamaica has become a prisoner in the panopticon.[50] It polices itself by the IMF standards initiated two years ago in a letter of agreement, in which the IMF requested "informal monitoring of (Jamaica's) economic and financial program for 2000 to 2002 by the IMF staff." The government argued that the Staff Monitoring Program (SMP) would "serve as a vehicle for maintaining a close dialogue with the Fund to convey a signal (to official creditors, donors, and financial markets) of Jamaica's commitment to a credible and consistent policy package."[51] Interestingly, the SMP came in the wake of the refusal of the Jamaica government to borrow from the IMF. Considered a "prolonged user of IMF resources," because of nine standby and four extended arrangements which the country has had with the IMF since the 1960s, in 1996 the Jamaican government stopped borrowing from the Fund. Contrary to the IMF's advice, it adopted a "home-grown" financial policy, which the IMF would later grudgingly admit worked, because of the rigor with which the Jamaica government had stuck to its policies. Without firm political commitment, it admits, such a "home-grown" alternative would not have worked. The IMF's contrition is worth citation:

> With the benefit of hindsight, the IMF should not have been so dogmatic in insisting upon its preferred strategy, which also involved substantial risks. However, the IMF was prepared to modify its position, once it was clear that the authorities had a strong commitment to an alternative strategy and were prepared to back it up with action, especially on fiscal policy. Indeed, records of recent Board discussions suggest considerably sympathy for the authorities' position, especially on the exchange rate/monetary policy framework.[52]

In her incisive critique of the pivotal tendencies of globalization, Kari Levitt argues that

> National boundaries which separate external from domestic markets have become porous and blurred. *Trade and Development, Market and State and Equity* have been the leading issues of development economics since its beginning. . . . At the national level governments are under pressure from productive enterprise, labour and civil society to respond to the real needs of the population—however reluctantly or incompletely. At the global level capital is insulated from popular protest and the constraints of democratic accountability. The responsibility of nation states for realising *Development with Equity* has been subordinated to the globalisation agenda of *Trade and Growth*. Doctrine now prevailing at the World Bank is that 'growth is good for the poor' (David Dollar 2000) and global freedom of capital is good for growth. Debt dependence has provided the international financial in-

News Brief: Jamaica Revises Targets Under the Staff-Monitored Program

The Jamaican authorities have revised the macroeconomic targets under their Staff-Monitored Program (SMP) for 2001–2002 to take account of recent economic shocks. Over the past months, the Jamaican authorities and the staff of the IMF have been pursuing a close dialogue on policies designed to consolidate macroeconomic stability and regain the momentum for higher growth. All quantitative targets under the SMP for end-September 2001 were met, with the economy growing at an annual rate of 3 percent—its highest level for seven years—partly reflecting a rebound in agricultural output and a recovery in mining. However, a decline in tourism after the tragic September 11 attacks in the United States, and the floods caused by hurricane Michelle, which damaged around one fifth of Jamaica's crop acreage, have adversely affected the economy. Tourism revenues are expected to decline by 12 percent in the fiscal year through March 2002, the current account deficit to widen to about 8 percent from 5.3 percent, and unemployment to rise. The authorities now expect GDP growth to decline to 1 percent from the 3 percent initially projected under the SMP.

The government is facing a deterioration in the fiscal situation, owing partly to extra spending on security, tourism promotion and flood relief, as well as lower revenues on account of a decline in economic activity. The government aims to contain the widening of the fiscal deficit to a new target of 4.1 percent of GDP from an original target of 2.8 percent. The authorities have pledged to keep social safety net expenditures unchanged.

Jamaica is committed to maintaining the progress achieved so far under the program and to continuing their fiscal adjustment efforts to reduce the heavy public sector debt burden. IMF staff will continue to monitor the implementation of the SMP.

IMF EXTERNAL RELATIONS DEPARTMENT

stitutions with the leverage to tell developing countries—in microeconomic detail—how to restructure their economies.[53]

As the discussion below demonstrates, Levitt's comments above describe the Jamaican dilemma. But note that Levitt is not arguing that the state has somehow been eclipsed. More to the point is its relocation, which as, Saskia Sassen would argue, involves repositioning the state to an intersection between global and national interests, not resulting in its entire absorption by global entities, nor its unraveling. Sassen's point is that global economy needs states so as to reproduce constantly the conditions of its existence.[54]

Jamaica has to provide the IMF proof that it is assiduously servicing its public sector debt, which, at the end of March 2002 stood at J$494 billion or 133.1% of GDP. Of this most was the domestic debt, estimated at J$300.2 billion or

80.7% of GDP, while the stock of public and publicly guaranteed external debt was J\$194.7 billion (US\$4089.2 million) or 52.4% of GDP (also) for March 2002. As well, the government promises to "resist pressures to increase trade restrictions, in order to identify areas for further liberalization with the belief that excessive protection would work against Jamaica's long-term interest." It will also use IMF standards to collect statistical data. Moreover, the government has promised to measure the informal sector to "develop a robust estimation of the informal and hidden economy."[55] It has also promised the IMF that it would continue with its program of public sector modernization. Such a reform would allow it to make areas like education and health more cost-effective, or more prone to privatization. Its modest social safety net programs will be reformed as well. Duplicative excesses have been cited as a common problem, which needs to be addressed, and the privatization of public sector properties will continue apace. For the most part the SMP is concentrated on fiscal and monetary reforms related to the servicing of the country's enormous debt. Incidently, all of these plans resemble the programmatic items in the Washington Consensus, emphasizing privatization, fiscal policy, reformation of taxation, removal of protectionist trade barriers, deregulation of markets, etc.[56]

In the budget address of March 2002, the Minister of Finance and Planning, Omar Davies, remarked that the late Prime Minister Michael Manley and the present Prime Minister, P. J. Patterson, "recognized that there was no future in appealing to the rich developing countries for mercy. Each government had to learn that there is no space on the global map for countries seeking special dispensation on the grounds that they are poor struggling third world countries. Put simply, in every area you are either 'world class' or you are 'no class.'"[57] This is the mantra of the neoliberal global order, localized, the "anti-politics machine" stripping away considerations of global inequalities, denouncing the importance of local politics and dismissing the inequitable distribution of the world's resources. The budget, the Minister noted, was not an old-fashioned "Electoral Budget," which promised the people "goodies," but one which laid out facts. Its target audience was: 1) the people, particularly voters, affected by public expenditure, 2) the domestic business sector, which commits resources for the expansion of the economy, 3) the domestic financial sector, 4) leaders of international financial institutions, multilateral and bilateral, 5) foreign investors, and 6)

> the international private capital market, "rating agencies, pension fund managers, banks, insurance companies, investment houses, all of which now assess Jamaica's credit worthiness each week as they have committed billions of US dollars of their clients' funds to this country. The members of this latter group carry out analysis—not in terms of local politics, not in terms of populist utterances but in terms of whether what an Administration says is what it does, and

furthermore, what it intends to do is feasible and credible. This is a
new dimension to the context of Budget presentation and it is one,
which not everyone recognizes.[58]

The relationship of the state to such interests masks a preferential treatment of
the interests of one segment of society over another, a certain kind of "embedded autonomy," to stretch Evans' concept. In analyzing larger states, like North
Korea, Brazil and India, Evans argues that deployment of government's development policies facilitates and is based on an embeddedness within the society that
it governs and simultaneously a certain amount of independence from any one
interest.[59] Such a "balance" enables a state to pursue policies that may benefit
several groups, without being captured by any single interest group. Yet, in the
case of Jamaica, a very small state, such embeddedness is partial, for it involves
global constituencies, and the state's "autonomy" is limited, though correcting
historical socioeconomic inequalities may generate preferences for particular interests. Don Robotham's argument that the post-1990s Jamaican state sought
unsuccessfully to facilitate the emergence of a black financial sector, suggesting
that states may pursue "home grown" policies, but a point which Robotham does
not discuss is how such policies may effectively "coincide" with global agendas.[60]
Nevertheless, it is important to recognize that governments rely on local votes to
exercise continuity, locally and nationally, and that their selection of groups is
structured by the local class and racial dynamics. Though for the Jamaican state,
and any small peripheral state within the world economy, sovereignty, defined as
the ability to act fairly autonomously within the interstate system, is severely
compromised, such states still have the power to reconfigure local institutions
and shape and channel the influences of globalization. More likely, however, in
places like Jamaica, states cognizant of local interest groups have the power to engage in "graduated sovereignty," to use Ong's concept. In this way, sections of the
population enable universalisms to appear particular and local, strengthening the
role of state elites engaged in facilitating globalization in this reciprocal fashion.[61]

In his budget address, Minister Davies noted that a new generation of highly
trained professional, young Jamaicans had now internalized world standards and
experienced "no difficulty operating in a more tightly regulated, yet more competitive financial sector."[62] This generation is poised to receive state support, as
they produce and reproduce the instrumentalities of the neoliberal order. In
short, the transformation of the Jamaica economy to fit the neoliberal world order is well underway locally. The process is believed to be ineluctable. Even if a
new government had emerged in the aftermath of the last general elections, it is
certain that it would pursue similar paths of economic management.

Though the budget does not mention agricultural sector development per
se, the ASSP, discussed earlier in this chapter, operates within globalization's regulatory frames, and the project's objective is to advance Jamaica along the route

to "world-class status" by articulating the concerns of organized interest groups. ASSP personnel will assist such groups in securing contracts, by locating demands outside the country. Groups will produce for such contractors. Whereas the "anti-politics" effects of development discourse once operated at the country level, now they operate globally. Deploying IMF and World Bank standards, the government polices itself for the purposes of transforming its formal and informal institutions. It is in the country's interest to do so. After all, the state is also under strict global surveillance. It is accountable to at least six concerns, some of which are more important than others. The nation-state gains credibility only if the government placates its six watchdogs, though their interests diverge.

However modern the Caribbean has been, it has now entered a new era. Sassen and others have noted that globalization is a new phenomenon reshaping states and places. Hardly a declining state, the Jamaican state is now vying to reposition itself within the world economy. It does so partly through facilitating the spread of "state effects" to traditionally nonstate arenas. As shown in chapter 5, AGRO 21 was the start of the neoliberal project and, as such, represented an attempt by the state to alter its relationship with land-based working people, in preference of newly created and established farming entrepreneurs. Those efforts were significantly affected by past relationships agricultural institutions maintained with the sector. The marginalizing of the Ministry of Agriculture meant that many of these relationships endured, albeit in a hostile environment. During the 1980s, attempts at shedding a particular kind of state-society identity were hampered by deafening public proclamations about the failures of the project's objectives, and also the short-shrifting of land-based working people. The media likewise chronicled the projects' failures, as chapter 5 describes. What now seems certain is that the postnationalist state under the political hegemony of the PNP has benefitted from this early, incomplete state-society disentanglement and is now finishing the job—institutionalizing the process.[63] Its identity shedding project proceeds, seeking to rationalize its procedures amidst the rumblings of the "sufferers," Jamaica's Children of Sisyphus.[64]

Development is now being reattached to a new identity in which working people face the market with few social safety nets and a renewed relationship to the state. As stated in the budget speech, working people constitute but one constituency. They compete with several others inside and outside of Jamaica, though these lines are increasingly blurred. A postnationalist state operating in a new economic environment, facilitated locally, Jamaica functions to summon the nation to perform in the interest of global concerns for the pursuit of the nation's self-interest in the accumulation process. National interests become equivalent to global interests and to state interests, even as they maintain their discursive/ideological, spatial and institutional boundaries.[65] Land-based working people are being exhorted to produce under these conditions. When they do, most face a life of debt, vividly portrayed in the eponymous video cited earlier.

National interests have not only recently, since the 1980s, become unhinged from the state, contrary to what postcolonialist theorists contend, though the possibilities exist for far more disjuncturing now.[66] There have always been tensions between members of national communities and states which govern them, leading to connections and disruptions. As the text shows, development, at least that which has taken place up until the 1980s has facilitated a papering over of these tensions, even as the state has, through macro and micro techniques of management, become a more pervasive influence in the lives of land-based workers and citizenry in general, through the various technologies of government operating through agricultural policy. This relationship will not expire, as others have hastily concluded. Surveillance is increasing. So is escape.

In this redefinition of political and social space, national interests are being reconstructed to suit the new position of the Jamaican state. It is a work in progress. The institutions at the helm of this neoliberal globalization project have facilitated redefinition, making it possible for state elites to enter into new kinds of discourses that rationalize reorientation. The global and the local become intertwined. The budget speech articulates these new relationships quite clearly, and the ASSP echoes and seeks to reorient agricultural actors to this new economic and political environment, for political and economic elites alike believe that globalization is "irreversible." The choice is to be "World Class" or "No Class," a phrase that conjures up the specter of progress or being left behind. Who wants to be left behind?

In this climate, the cry of the Children of Sisyphus to the guardians of the developmental state, to "save we and give we wuk" as conveyed in Patterson's novel, seems rather like the good old days.[67] Their struggles for inclusion, and the remaking of the postnationalist Jamaican state, are not likely to be concluded.

Notes

1. I wrote this chapter after several discussions that I had with Dr. Patricia M. Northover, Research Fellow at the Sir Arthur Lewis Institute for Social and Economic Research, Mona in Jamaica, on postcolonialism and development. An economic philosopher, Pat joined me in informal study sessions on the poststructuralist development literature at her "yard" in Kingston, during the summer of 2002. It was she who alerted me to the fact that Escobar's text on development was also a critique of positivist methodology. I am deeply indebted to her for our conversations about the notion of *hybridity*.

2. Paul du Gay, "Representing Globalization: Notes on the Discursive Orderings of Economic Life," in *Without Guarantees: In Honour of Stuart Hall*, ed. Paul Gilroy et al., (London and New York: Verso Press, 2000): 113–123.

3. I refer to the discussion in chapter 1 in which I reference *States of Imagination: Ethnographic Explorations of the Postcolonial State*.

4. David Nugent, "Before History and Prior to Politics: Time, Space and Territory in the Modern Peruvian Nation-State," in *States of Imagination: Ethnographic Explorations of the PostColonial State*, ed. Thomas Blom Hansen and Finn Stepputat (Durham: Duke University Press, 2001).

5. Arturo Escobar, *Encountering Development* (Princeton: Princeton University Press, 1995); James Ferguson, *The Anti-Politics of Machine: "Development," Depoliticization, and Bureaucratic Power in Lesotho* (California: University of California Press, 1994); Timothy Mitchell, "The Object of Development: America's Egypt," in Jonathan Crush, *Power of Development* (New York: Routledge, 1995).

6. Michel Foucault, *Power/Knowledge: Selected Interviews and Other Writings, 1972–1977*, ed. C. Gordon (New York: Pantheon Books, 1980).

7. Michel-Rolph Trouillot, *Silencing the Past: Power and the Production of History* (Boston: Beacon Press, 1995).

8. Despite Jamaica's efforts to recruit 1000 new members in 18 months, they will disbar any Rasta membership. See Phyllis Thomas, "No Room in the Force for Rasta," http://www.go-kingston.com/whatsnew/200203. In this sense Rastafarians are perceived as not quite equal to other Jamaican citizens.

9. David Scott was addressing Don Robotham's critique of the pluralist paradigm advanced by M. G. Smith. See David Scott, "The Permanence of Pluralism," in *Without Guarantees: In Honour of Stuart Hall*, ed. Paul Gilroy et al., (2000), 282–301, 293–294.

10. Arturo Escobar (1995), 5.

11. I refer here to the many rebellions and strikes that compose working people's responses to the sociocultural excesses of colonial and postindependence states. See, for example, Swithin Wilmot, "Politics and Labour Conflicts in Jamaica 1838–1865," in *The Critical Tradition of Caribbean Political Economy: The Legacy of George Beckford* ed. Kari Levitt and Michael Witter (Kingston Jamaica: Ian Randle Publishers, 1996), 101–117; Ken. Post, *Arise Ye Starvelings* (The Hague: Martinus Nijhoff, 1978); "Report with Appendices of the Commission Appointed to Enquire Into The Disturbances Which Occurred in Jamaica Between the 23rd May and 8 June 1938" (Kingston: Govt. Printery, 1938); *Reports of Department/Ministry of Labour 1943–1964* (Kingston: Govt. Printery, n.d.); NPA, *Economic and Social Surveys* (1965–1970) (Kingston: National Planning Agency); Department of Statistics, *Statistical Abstract* (Kingston: Department of Statistics, Jamaica, 1971–1974), 27. The Commission of Enquiry on the Sugar Industry of Jamaica 1959–1960 held that violence was "inspired in part at least, by speeches which must be considered provocative when regard is had to the uneducated and excitable workers in poor circumstances to whom they were addressed. The Unions also submitted that management also used provocative language and sought to discourage workers from paying their union dues." From this account therefore, it would seem that such acts of violence as perpetrated during the 1959 strike were the direct spin-offs of the conflict between capital and labour.

12. James Ferguson, *The Anti-Politics of Machine: "Development," Depoliticization, and Bureaucratic Power in Lesotho* (Minnesota: University of Minnesota Press, 1994).

13. Akhil Gupta, *Postcolonial Developments: Agriculture in the Making of Modern India* (Durham: Duke University Press, 1998).

14. Calderón 1988, 11, quoted in Escobar (1995).

15. Arturo Escobar (1995), 218.

16. Arturo Escobar (1995), 220.

17. I thank Patricia Northover for her astute observations about hybridity, and on the Escobar text generally; also, for our elaborate discussion of positivism, and the particularities of the poststructuralist method.

18. See also Arturo Escobar, "Imagining a Post-Development Era? Critical Thought, Development and Social Movements," *Social Text* 10, 2 (1992): 20–56.

19. Aiwa Ong, *Flexible Citizenship: The Cultural Logics of Transnationality* (Durham & London: Duke University Press, 1999), especially chapter 8.

20. *Workers Time*, 3 August 1976.

21. See chapter 4, for a fuller discussion of these issues.

22. See *Workers Time*, 3 August 1976.

23. Carl Stone, "An appraisal of the Cooperative process in the Jamaican Sugar Industry," mss., Mona: University of the West Indies, 25.

24. *The Daily Gleaner*, 4/22/82. See also *Daily Gleaner* reports on the findings of the Drummond Commission appointed to look into the operations of the cooperatives, 9/29/82.

25. C. Stone, "An Appraisal of the Cooperative Process in the Jamaican Sugar Industry. Also see discussion under section headed "Project Land Lease" in chapter 4.

26. Ibid.

27. Ibid.

28. I first came across that phrase in David Scott's lecture at the University of Iowa, in Spring 2000. During that lecture, one member of the audience expressed discomfort with the construct, because he felt it ignored agency. To the best of my recollection, Scott replied that this was not what he intended. Having read *Refashioning the Futures: Criticism after Postcoloniality* my sense is that Scott was referring to the ways in which people's conduct was shaped by modernity, and the cognitive/political space that they occupied, or were made to occupy did itself generate or make available alternative imaginaries to the present. I like the phrase because it captures the sense in which people's conduct and experiences are social constructs within particular historical moments, something akin to Marx's idea that we do not make history as we choose, but within the context of the cognitive/political/cultural place in which we find ourselves, but it goes beyond that by pointing to the shifts in the way in which institutional expressions of modernities reform the relationships between knowledge and power. The way I use this phrase, is to identify the sociological and political structures which structured the presents of land-based working people, and their responses to them—their responses to particular forms of state ideology, and development projects. Dilip Parameshwar Gaonkar's article, "On Alternative Modernities," has been very useful in helping me to think through questions of modernity. Idem., *Public Culture* 11, no. 1 (1999): 1–18.

29. George Beckford's introduction to Erna Brodber's manuscript, *Profile of the Jamaican Male*, unpub. mss. circa 1980s. Beckford's mention of Migrant Farmer, Landless

Farmer refers to a couple of Brodber's interviewees. All the men that Brodber interviewed were born between 1893 and the 1920s. I do not believe the situation has changed in any real sense since then. Chapter 6 shows that the sector loosely comprising "smallholders," constituting the bulk of land-based working people, has contracted significantly in terms of numbers and acreage held. An abridged version of that manuscript has been published: *Standing Tall: Affirmations of the Jamaican Male-24 Self Portraits* (Mona: Sir Arthur Lewis Institute of Social and Economic Research, 2003).

30. Thomas Hardy, in reference to his rendering of the character Giles Winterborn's struggle against the forces of class privilege. *The Woodlanders* (Clarendon Press: New York: Oxford University Press, 1981).

31. The IMF and the World Bank are not the same. They have different cultures. See, for example, "The Odd Couple of Global Finance: The Spat between the IMF and the World Bank Reflects Very Different Cultures, says Ed Crooks," *Financial Times* Weekend, July 6, 2002.

32. "Development of the Agricultural Sector over the last 10 years," 2.

33. Ibid.

34. Project Document: Agricultural Support Services, 1.

35. Ibid.

36. Personal interview with top officials in the Ministry of Agriculture in June 2000.

37. See Bentley Cunningham, "Community Development in Jamaica the Administration of an Illusion," in *Grass-roots Development and the State of the Nation Symposium in Honour of Carl Stone*, mss. (UWI, Mona, Jamaica, November 16–17, no pagination, 1992).

38. *Five Year Development Plan 1990–1995*, 127.

39. Ibid.

40. Five Year Development Plan quoted in Cunningham (1992).

41. Bentley Cunningham (1992).

42. Ibid.

43. *Air Jamaica: SkyWritings*, Air Jamaica's Inflight Magazine, Issue #128, June 2000, 29.

44. Three years ago (2001) I garnered this information from a telephone conversation with the manager of marketing services at the financial firm, Bunting, Dehring and Golding.

45. See, for example, James Ferguson, *Expectations of Modernity: Myths and Meanings of Urban Life on the Zambian Copperbelt* (California: University of California Press, 1999).

46. "Ministry Blamed for Decline in Agriculture," *The Daily Gleaner*, Wednesday, July 17, 2002, B9.

47. Ibid.

48. A debate about the contemporary role of the University of the West Indies raised important issues about the academic's role in the current neoliberal project; the Finance Minister, Dr. Davies', speech was given at the opening ceremony of a SALISES conference, Wednesday, April 3, 2002. Davies was critical of the use of scarce financial resources to tertiary institutions as opposed to primary ones. In the process he cast doubts about the UWI's relevance. See Dr. Stephen Vasciannie's piece, "The Cost of 'Free Education' versus Scarce Resources," *Sunday Gleaner*, May 26, 2002; "UWI, Mona-a Myopic Sanctum," Elombie Mottley, *The Sunday Gleaner*, July 2, 2002, G4; "UWI responds to Mottley,"

Sunday Gleaner, July 14, 2002, B6; "UWI Responds to Mottley," *Sunday Gleaner*, July 14, 2002, B6.

49. For a good synopsis of the effects of the flooding see "May Floods Damage Economy: Inflation could move into double digits; 2%-4% growth no longer likely," *Insight* June 1st–15th, Vol. XVIII, 5, (2002), 6.

50. Michel Foucault, *Discipline and Punish* (New York: Vintage Books, 1991)

51. See http://www.imf.org/external/np/loi/2000/jam/01/index/htm, Jamaica letter of Intent, July 19, 2000.

52. IMF report: "Lessons from Jamaica: Implications for ownership and "seal of approval" issues. The letter states that this excerpt dealt specifically with "ownership and the "seal of approval" issues and was not a summary of "all aspects of IMF's relation with Jamaica." #1416568 v1-Jamaica Excerpt, June 26th, 2002. In a recent issue of *Carib News* columnist Basil Wilson calls attention to the conundrum over the economic data on Jamaica. See "The Poverty of Economics in Jamaica," 30 July 2002, 17.

53. Kari Polanyi Levitt, "The Right to Development," *The Fifth Sir Arthur Lewis Memorial Lecture* (Castries, St. Lucia, November 8, 2000), 28–29.

54. Saskia Sassen, *Cities in a World Economy* (Thousand Oaks, CA: Pine Forge Press, 2000); also idem, *The Global City: New York, London, Tokyo*. Second edition. (Princeton, NJ: Princeton University Press, 2001).

55. Ibid.

56. Washington Consensus was the term coined at a Washington D.C. conference in 1990 sponsored by the Institute for International Economics, at which were present members of the Latin American intelligentsia. The consensus was on issues related to trade liberalization, fiscal policy, privatization, reduction of debts, etc.

57. Opening Budget Presentation 2002/2003, Minister of Finance and Planning, Dr. the Hon. Omar Davies, MP, Wednesday, May 1, 2002, circa 3.

58. Ibid., circa 5.

59. Peter Evans, *Embedded Autonomy: States and Industrial Transformation* (Princeton, NJ: Princeton University Press, 1995).

60. Don Robotham, "Blackening the Jamaican Nation: The Travails of a Black Bourgeoisie in A Globalized World," *Identities: Global Studies in Culture and Power* 7, no. 1 (March 2000): 1–37.

61. I am adapting the phrase of Roland Robertson that "Globalization is the two-fold process of the particularization of the universal and the universalization of the particular." Roland Robertson, *Globalization: Social Theory and Global Culture*, quoted in Paul Streeten, *Globalisation: Threat or Opportunity*. (Copenhagen: Copenhagen Business School Press, 2001), 177–178.

62. Budget Address, March 2002, mss. (Kingston: Ministry of Finance, Jamaica., c 2002).

63. Such state projects are never completed, since every action incurs a reaction.

64. I adopt the phrase as used in Orlando Patterson's *The Children of Sisyphus*. (Essex: Longman Group, 1964).

65. In this respect, Timothy Mitchell's rethinking of state theorization is particularly helpful. See "Society, Economy, and the State Effect" in *State/Culture: State Formation*

after the Cultural Turn, ed. George Steinmetz (Ithaca: Cornell University Press, 1999): 76–97.

66. Akhil Gupta (1998).

67. Orlando Patterson, *The Children of Sisyphus* (Essex: Longman Group, 1964). Patterson's fiction captures the raw clientistic relationship between Premier and supporters and the expectations and promises that bound these constituents during the early phase of nationalism. The scene is a of a motley group of Jamaicans descended upon the Ministry of Labor, seeking jobs, soon after their party has been swept into office (85–87).

Bibliography

Abrams, Philip. "Notes on the Difficulty of Studying the State." *Journal of Historical Sociology* 1, no. 1 (March 1998): 58–89.

Air Jamaica: SkyWritings. Issue #128, June 2000.

Alavi, Hama. *Capitalism and Colonial Production*. London: Croom Helm, 1982.

Anderson, Patricia, and Michael Witter. "Crisis, Adjustment and Social Change A Case Study of Jamaica." Pp.1–55 in *Consequences of Structural Adjustment A Review of the Jamaican Experience*, edited by Elsie Le Franc. UWI Mona: Canoe Press, 1994.

Arrighi, Giovanni. "Globalization and the Rise of East Asia: Lessons from the Past, Prospects for the Future." *International Sociology* 13, no. 1 (March 1998): 59–77.

Augier, Roy. "Before and After 1865." *New World Quarterly* 2, no. 1 (1965): 21– 40.

Bairoch, Paul. *The Economic Development of the Third World since 1900*. California: University of California Press, 1975.

Banaji, Jarius. "Modes of Production in a Materialist Conception of History." *Capital and Class* 3 (Autumn 1977): 1–44.

Barker, David. "The Changing Caribbean: New Directions for Jamaican Agriculture." *Caribbean Geography* 2, no. 1 (1985): 56–66.

———. "Recent Developments in Agricultural Planning in Jamaica: The AGRO 21 Programme." Conference Paper, Caribbean Studies Association, Caracas, Venezuela, May 1985.

Barker, David, and Balfour Spence. "Afro-Caribbean Agriculture: A Jamaican Maroon Community in Transition." *The Geographical Journal* 154, no. 2 (1988): 198–208.

Barkin, D. "The End to Food Self-Sufficiency in Mexico." *Latin American Perspectives,* 14, no. 3 (Summer 1987): 271–297.

Beachey, R. W. *The British West Indies Sugar Industry in the late Nineteenth Century*. Greenwood: Greenwood Press, 1957.

Beckford, George. *Caribbean Economy: Dependence and Backwardness*. Mona: Institute of Social and Economic Research, 1975.

———. *Persistent Poverty: Underdevelopment in Plantation Economies of the Third World*. Oxford: Oxford University Press, 1971.

Beckford, George, and Michael Witter. *Small Garden . . . Bitter Weed, The Political Economy of Struggle and Change in Jamaica*. Morant Bay: Maroon Publishing House, 1980.

Beckford, George, Norman Girvan, Louis Lindsay, and Michael Witter. *Pathways to Progress: The People's Plan for Socialist Transformation, 1977–1978*. Morant Bay: Maroon Publishing House, 1985.

Bernstein, Henry. "Concepts for the Analysis of Contemporary Peasants." Pp. 3–24 in *The Political Economy of Rural Development. Peasants International Capital and the State. Case Studies in Colombia, Mexico, Tanzania and Bangladesh*. New York: State University of New York Press, 1981.

———. "Notes on Capital and Peasantry." *Review of African Political Economy* 10 (December 1977): 60–73.

Bernstein, Henry, and Pitt. "Plantations and Modes of Exploitation." *Journal of Peasant Studies* 1, no. 4 (July 1974): 514–526.

Besson, Jean. "A Paradox in Caribbean Attitudes to Land." Pp. 13–45 in *Land and Development in the Caribbean*, edited by Jean Besson and Janet Momsen. London: MacMillan, 1987.

Besson, Jean, and Barry Chevannes. "The Continuity-Creativity Debate: The Case of Revival." *New West Indian Guide* 70, nos. 3 & 4 (1996): 209–228.

Besson, Jean, and Janet Momsen, eds. *Land and Development in the Caribbean*. Warwick: Warwick University Centre for Caribbean Studies. London: MacMillan, 1987.

Best, Lloyd. "The Mechanism of Plantation Type Economies: Outlines of a Model of Pure Plantation Economy." *Social and Economic Studies* 17, no. 3 (June 1968): 283–326.

Bhabha, Homi K. "Signs Taken for Wonders: Questions of Ambivalence and Authority under a Tree outside Delhi, May 1817." Pp. 163–179 in *Race Writing and Differences*, edited by Henry Louis Gates, Jr. (Chicago and London: The University of Chicago Press, 1986).

Blake, Judith. *Family Structure in Jamaica: The Social Context of Reproduction*. New York: The Free Press of Glencoe, 1961.

Bogues, Anthony. "Nationalism and Jamaican Political Thought." Pp. 363–385 in *Jamaica in Slavery and Freedom*, edited by Verene Shepherd and Glen Richards. Kingston: Ian Randle Press, 2002.

Boone, Catherine. "States and Ruling Classes in Post-Colonial Africa: The Enduring Contradictions of Power." Pp. 108–140 in *State Power and Social Forces*, edited by Joel Migdal et al. Cambridge: Cambridge University Press, 1994.

Bourdieu, Pierre. *The Logic of Practice*. Cambridge: Polity Press, 1990.

Bradley, C. P. "Welfare Colonialism in the British West Indies. A Study of Development and Welfare Policy, 1938–1954." Ph.D. dissertation, 1955.

Brierley, John S., and Hymie Rubenstein, eds. *Small Farming and Peasant Resources in the Caribbean*. Manitoba: Manitoba Geographical Studies 10, The University of Manitoba, 1988.

Brodber, Erna. "Profile of the Jamaican Male." mss. Mona: University of the West Indies, c1980s).

———. "The Second Generation of Freemen in Jamaica 1907–1944." Ph.D. dissertation. Mona: University of the West Indies, Department of Sociology, 1983.

———. *Standing Tall: Affirmations of the Jamaican Male: 24 Self Portraits*. Mona: Sir Arthur Lewis Institute of Social and Economic Research, 2003.

Brown, Major Orde St. J. *Labour Conditions in the West Indies*. London: HMSO, 1939.

Bryan, Patrick. *The Jamaican People 1880–1902*. London: Macmillan, 1991.

Buch-Hansen, Mogens, and Henrik Secher Marcusse. "Contract Farming and the Peasantry: Cases from Western Kenya." *Review of African Political Economy* no. 23 (January–April, 1982): 9–36.

Cardoso, F. H., and Enzo Faletto. *Dependency and Development in Latin America*. Berkeley: University of California, 1979.

Carnegie, Charles. "Is Family Land an Institution?" Pp. 83–99 in *Afro-Caribbean Villages in Historical Perspective*, edited by Charles V. Carnegie. Kingston: African-Caribbean Institute of Jamaica, 1987.

Clarke, Edith. *My Mother Who Fathered Me: A Study of the Family in Three Selected Communities in Jamaica*. London: G. Allen and Unwin, 1961.

Comitas, Lambros. "Occupational Multiplicity in Rural Jamaica." Pp. 157–73 in *Work and Family Life: West Indian Perspectives*, edited by Lambros Comitas and D. Lowenthal. Garden City: Anchor Books, 1973.

Cook, Scott. "Book Reviews: Reconceptualizing the Peasantry." *Journal of the Royal Anthropological Institute* 3, no. 4 (December 1997): 789–790.

Corrigan, Philip, and Derek Sayer. *The Great Arch: English State Formation as Cultural Revolution*. Oxford: Basil Blackwell, 1988.

Cowell, Noel. "The Impact of the Bauxite Mining on Peasant and Community Relations in Jamaica." *Social and Economic Studies* 36, no. 1 (March 1987): 171–216.

Crichlow, Michaeline. "Family Land Tenure in the Anglophone Caribbean." *New West Indian Guide* 68, nos. 1 & 2 (1994): 77–99.

———. "Globalization and the Postcreole Condition: Notes on Fleeing the Plantation." mss. University of Iowa, 2004.

———. "La Politique Agricole, l'Etat et le Developppment Rural a Sainte-Lucie." Pp. 39–64 in *Enjeux Fonciers dans la Caraïbe, en Amerique Centrale et a la Reunion*, edited by Christian Deverre. Paris: Inra et Karthala, 1987.

———. "The Limits of Maneuver: Caribbean States, Small Farmers and the Capitalist World Economy 1940–1995." *Comparative Studies of South Asia, Africa and the Middle East*, xvii, no. 1 (1997): 81–98.

———. "Recentering Resistance in the Context of Globality: Afro-Caribbean People under Colonial Rule." *Contours: A Journal of the African Diaspora* 1, no. 3 (Spring 2004): 54–81.

———. "Reconfiguring the Informal Economy Divide: State, Capitalism and Struggle in Trinidad and Tobago." *Latin American Perspectives* 99, 25, no. 2 (March 1998): 62–83.

Crichlow, Michaeline, and Fragano Ledgister. "Nationalists and Development: The Price of Citizenship in Colonial Jamaica." *Plantation Society of the Americas* vi, no. 2 & 3, (Fall 1999): 191–222.

Crichlow, Michaeline, and Trevor Spence. "The Case for Land Reform in the Third World: Government of Jamaica." mss. Department of Sociology, UWI, Mona, 1978.

Cross, Malcolm, and M. Arnauld, eds. *Peasants, Plantations and Rural Communities in the Caribbean*. Surrey: Department of Sociology, University of Surrey, 1979.

Crouch, Luis, and Alain de Janvry. "The Class Basis of Agricultural Growth." *Food Policy* 5, no. 1 (February 1980): 3–13.

Crush, Jonathan, ed. *Power of Development.* New York: Routledge, 1995.

Cumper, George. "Labor Demand and Supply in the Jamaican Sugar Industry 1930–1950." *Social and Economic Studies* 2, no. 4 (February 1953): 37–86.

Cunningham, Bentley. "Community Development in Jamaica the Administration of an Illusion." In *Grass-Roots Development and the State of the Nation Symposium in Honour of Carl Stone*, mss. UWI, Mona, Jamaica, November 16–17, no pagination, 1992.

Curtin, Philip. *Two Jamaicas: The Role of Ideas in a Tropical Colony, 1830–1865.* Harvard: Harvard University Press, 1955.

Davies, Omar. "Adjustment and Stabilization Policies in Jamaica, 1981–87." Mona: Department of Economics, UWI, 1988.

———. "An Analysis of the Management of the Jamaican Economy: 1972–1985." *Social and Economic Studies*, 35, no. 1 (March 1986): 73–109.

De Janvry, Alain. *The Agrarian Question and Reformism in Latin America.* Baltimore: The Johns Hopkins University Press, 1981.

Dominguez, Jorge. *Democracy in the Caribbean: Political, Economic, and Social Perspectives.* Baltimore: Johns Hopkins University Press, c1993.

Dos Santos, Theotonio. "The Structure of Dependence." Pp. 225–236 in *Readings in U.S. Imperialism*, edited by K. T. Fann and Donald C. Hodges. Boston: Porter Sargent, 1971.

du Gay, Paul. "Representing Globalization: Notes on the Discursive Orderings of Economic Life." Pp. 113–123 in *Without Guarantees: In Honour of Stuart Hall*, edited by Paul Gilroy et al. London: Verso, 2000.

Duncan, Neville. "The Political Process in a Jamaican Parish Council." *Social and Economic Studies* 19, no. 1 (March 1970): 89–113.

Edwards, David. "Agricultural Development in Jamaica 1943–1961." mss. Mona: University of the West Indies, 1968.

———. *An Economic Study of Small Farming in Jamaica.* Kingston: Institute of Social and Economic Research, 1961.

Edwards, Nadi. "States of Emergency: Reggae Representations of the Jamaican Nation-State." *Social and Economic Studies* 47, 1 (March 1998): 21–32.

Eisner, Gisela. *Jamaica 1830–1930: A Study in Economic Growth.* Manchester: Manchester University Press, 1961.

Escobar, Arturo. *Encountering Development: The Making and Unmaking of the Third World.* New Jersey: Princeton University Press, 1994.

———. "Imagining a Post-Development Era." Pp. 211–227 in *Power of Development*, edited by Jonathan Crush. New York and London: Routledge, 1995.

———. "Imagining a Post-Development Era? Critical Thought, Development and Social Movements." *Social Text* 10, no. 2 (1992): 20–56.

Evans, Peter. *Embedded Autonomy: States and Industrial Transformation.* Princeton, NJ: Princeton University Press, 1995.

Femia, Joseph. "Hegemony and Consciousness in the Thought of Antonio Gramsci." *Political Studies* xxiii, no. 1 (March 1975): 20–48.

Ferguson, James. *The Anti-Politics of Machine: "Development," Depoliticization, and Bureaucratic Power in Lesotho.* California: University of California Press, 1994.

———. *Expectations of Modernity. Myths and Meanings of Urban Life on the Zambian Copperbelt.* California: University of California Press, 1999.

Feuer, Carl. "Jamaica and the Sugar Workers Cooperatives: The Politics of Reform." Ph.D. dissertation. Ithaca: Cornell University, 1983.

———. *Jamaica and the Sugar Worker Cooperatives: The Politics of Reform.* Westview: Westview Press, 1984.

Floyd, Barry N. *Agricultural Innovation in Jamaica: The Yallahs Valley Land Authority.* Occasional publication No. 4. University of the West Indies Mona: Department of Geography, 1969.

Foner, Nancy. *Social Change and Social Mobility in a Jamacian Rural Community.* London: New Beacon Books, 1971.

———. *Status and Power in Rural Jamaica: A Study of Educational and Political Change.* New York: Teachers College Press, 1973.

Foucault, Michel. *Discipline and Punish.* New York: Vintage Books, 1991.

———. *Power/Knowledge: Selected Interviews and Other Writings, 1972–1977.* Edited by C. Gordon. New York: Pantheon Books, 1980.

Francis, Sybil. "The Evolution of Community Development in Jamaica (1937–1962)." *Caribbean Quarterly* 15, nos. 2 & 3 (June–September 1969): 40–58.

Frolander, M., and F. Lindfeld. "A New Earth: The Jamaican Sugar Workers' Cooperatives, 1975–1981." mimeo, n.d.

Frucht, Richard. "Caribbean Social Type: Neither Peasant Nor Proletarian." *Social and Economic Studies* 16, no. 3 (September 1967): 295–300.

Furtnick, William R. "Jamaica Agricultural Sector Analysis." (prepared for the Jamaica-U.S. Mission during March–April, 1986).

Gaines, Kevin. *Uplifting the Race: Black Leadership, Politics, and Culture in the Twentieth Century.* Chapel Hill: University of North Carolina Press, 1996.

Galli, Rosemary F., ed. *The Political Economy of Rural Development: Peasants, International Capital and the State.* Albany: SUNY Press, 1981.

Gaonkar, Dilip Parameshwar. "Alternative Modernities." *Public Culture* 11, no. 1 (1999): 1–18.

Gilroy, Paul. *The Black Atlantic: Modernity and Double Consciousness.* Cambridge: Harvard University Press, 1994.

Girvan, Norman, ed. *Working Together for Development D.T.M.* Kingston, Jamaica: Institute of Jamaica Publications, 1993.

Girvan, Norman, Richard Bernal, and Owen Jefferson, eds. *Readings in the Political Economy of the Caribbean.* Kingston: New World Group, 1971.

Girvan, Norman, Richard Bernal, and Wesley Hughes. *Foreign Capital and Economic Underdevelopment in Jamaica.* Kingston: Institute of Social and Economic Research, 1971.

———. "The IMF and The Third World: The Case of Jamaica, 1974–1980." *Development Dialogue reprint from 1980*, no. 2: 113–155.

Gocking, C. V. "Early Constitutional History of Jamaica: With Special Reference to the Period 1838–1866." *Caribbean Quarterly* 6, nos. 3 & 4 (1960): 113–133.

Goodman, David, and M. Redclift. *From Peasant to Proletarian Development: Development and Agrarian Transitions.* Oxford: Basil Blackwell, 1981.

Gramsci, Antonio. *Selections from the Prison Notebooks of Antonio Gramsci.* Edited and translated by Quintin Hoare and Geoffrey Nowell Smith. New York: International Publishers, 1971.

Gray, Obika. *Radicalism and Social Change in Jamaica, 1960–1972.* Tennessee: University of Tennessee Press, 1991.

———. "Rogue Culture or Avatar of Liberation: The Jamaican Lumpenproletariat." *Social and Economic Studies* 52, no. 1 (March 2003): 1–33.

Grosfoguel, Ramon. "Depeasantization and Agrarian Decline in the Caribbean." Pp. 233–253 in *Food Agrarian Orders in the World-Economy*. Westport, Connecticut, London: Praeger, 1995.

Grueso, Libia, Carlos Rosero, and Arturo Escobar. "The Process of Black Community Organizing in the Southern Pacific Coast Region of Colombia." Pp. 196–219 in *Cultures of Politics: Politics of Cultures*. Boulder, Colorado: Westview Press, 1998.

Guha, Ranjit, ed. *Selected Subaltern Studies*. New York: Oxford University Press, 1989.

Guisti-Cordero, Juan. "Labor, Ecology and History in a Caribbean Sugar Plantation Region: Pinones (Loiza), Puerto Rico 1770–1950." PT. 1 & 2. Ph.D. dissertation. Binghamton: State University of New York, 1994.

Gunder Frank, André. *Latin America: Underdevelopment or Revolution*. New York: Monthly Review, 1969.

———. *World Accumulation 1492–1789*. New York: Monthly Review, 1979.

Gupta, Akhil. *Postcolonial Developments: Agriculture in the Making of Modern India*. London, North Carolina: Duke University Press, 1998.

Hall, Douglas. "The Flight from the Estates Reconsidered: The British West Indies, 1838–1842." *Journal of Caribbean History*, no. 10 and 11 (May 1978): 16–24.

———. *Free Jamaica 1838-1865. An Economic History*. New Haven: Yale University Press, 1959.

Hall, Stuart. "The Local and the Global: Globalization and Ethnicity." Pp. 19–39 in *Culture, Globalization and the World System*, edited by Anthony D. King. Minneapolis: University of Minnesota Press, 1997.

Hanchard, Michael George. *Orpheus and Power: The Movimento Negro of Rio de Janeiro and Sao Paolo, Brazil, 1945–1988*. Princeton: Princeton University Press, 1997.

Hansen, Blom, and Thomas and Finn Stepputat, eds. *States of Imagination: Ethnographic Explorations of the Postcolonial State*. Durham: Duke University Press, 2001.

Hardy, Thomas. *The Woodlanders*. Oxford: Clarendon Press; New York: Oxford University Press, 1981.

Harris, John, ed. *Rural Development: Theories of Peasant Economy and Agrarian Change*. London: Hutchingson & Co., 1982.

Harrison, Mark. "Chayanov and the Economics of the Russian Peasantry." *Journal of Peasant Studies* 2, no. 4 (July 1975): 389–417.

———. "Chayanov and the Marxists." *Journal of Peasant Studies* 7, no. 1 (October 1979): 86–100.

———. "The Peasant Mode of Production in the Work of Chayanov." *Journal of Peasant Studies* 4, no. 4 (July 1977): 323–336.

Heuman, Gad. "The Struggle for the Settler Vote: Politics and the Franchise in Post-Emancipation Jamaica." Pp. 1–28 in *Peasants, Plantations and Rural Communities in the Caribbean*, edited by Malcolm Cross and Arnaud Marks. Leiden: Department of Sociology/Caribbean Studies, Royal Institute of Linguistics and Anthropology, 1979.

Hills, Theo, and Stanley Iton. "A Reassessment of the 'Traditional' in Caribbean Small-Scale Agriculture." *Caribbean Geography* 1, no. 1 (1983): 24–35.

Hintzen, Percy C. *The Costs of Regime Survival: Racial Mobilization, Elite Domination and Control of the State in Guyana and Trinidad*. Cambridge: Cambridge University Press, 1989.

Hobsbawm, Eric J. *The Age of Capital 1848–1875*. New York: Charles Scribner's Sons, 1975.

———. *Pre-Capitalist Economic Formations*. New York: International Publishers, 1965.

Holt, Thomas C. *The Problem of Freedom: Race, Labor, and Politics in Jamaica and Britain, 1832–1938*. Baltimore: The Johns Hopkins University Press, 1992.

Huber, Stephens Evelyn, and J. D. Stephens. "A Changing Development Models in Small Economies: The Case of Jamaica from the 1950s to the 1990s." *Studies in Comparative International Development* 27, no. 3 (Fall 1992): 57–92.

———. *Democratic Socialism in Jamaica: The Political Movement and Social Transformation in Dependent Capitalism*. Princeton: Princeton University Press, 1986.

———. "The Political Economy of Structural Adjustment: The Seaga Government of Jamaica." Paper delivered at the Caribbean Studies Association XIV annual conference Barbados, 23–26 May 1989.

Hymer, Stephen. "The Internationalization of Capital." *Journal of Economic Issues* 6, no. 1 (March 1972): 91–123.

Jayawardena, Chandra. *Conflict and Solidarity in a Guianese Plantation*. London: University of London, The Athlone Press, 1963.

Jefferson, Owen. *The Post-War Economic Development of Jamaica*. Kingston: Institute of Social and Economic Research, 1972.

Jessop, Bob. "Narrating the Future of the National Economy and the National State: Remarks on Remapping Regulation and Reinventing Governance." Pp. 378–405 in *State/Culture State-Formation after the Cultural Turn*, edited by George Steinmetz. Ithaca: Cornell University Press, 1999.

Johnson, Irving, Marie Strachan, and Joseph Johnson. "A Review of Land Settlement in Jamaica." Pp. 110–132 in *Proceedings of the 7th West Indian Agricultural Economics Conference, Grand Anse, Grenada*, April 9–15, St. Augustine: Trinidad, 1972.

Kasaba, Resat. "A Time and a Place for the Nonstate: Social Change in the Ottoman Empire during the 'Long Nineteenth Century.'" Pp. 207–230 in *State Power and Social Forces: Domination and Transformation in the Third World*, edited by Joel Migdal, Atul Kohli, and Vivienne Shue. Cambridge: Cambridge University Press, 1994.

Kearney, Michael. *Reconceptualizing the Peasantry*. Colorado: Westview, 1996.

Kingsley, Charles. *At Last: A Christmas in the West Indies*. London: McMillan and Co., 1872.

Klamon-Kopytoff, Barbara. "The Maroons of Jamaica: A Historical Study of Incomplete Politics 1955–1960." Ph.D. dissertation. Ann Arbor: University of Michigan, 1973.

Kleyson, Brenda. *Women Small Farmers in the Caribbean*. Costa Rica: IICA/IDB, 1996.

Kruijer J. G., and A. Nuis. "Farm Development Scheme 1955–1960. A Report on an Evaluation." First Plan. Kingston: Ministry of Agriculture, 1955.

Lacey, Thomas. *Violence and Politics in Jamaica 1960–1970*. Manchester: Manchester University Press, 1977.

Laclau, Ernesto. *Politics and Ideology in Marxist Theory*. London: Verso, 1977.

Ledgister, Fragano. *Class Alliances and the Liberal-Authoritarian State*. Trenton, New Jersey: Africa World Press, 1999.

——. "Political Activists as Political Theorists: Norman Manley, Eric Williams, Democracy, and Decolonisation in the British West Indies." mss., n.d.

Le Franc, Elsie. "Peasant and Community in Jamaica." Ph.D. dissertation. New Haven: Yale University, 1974.

——, ed. *Consequences of Structural Adjustment: A Review of the Jamaican Experience*. UWI Mona: Canoe Press, 1994.

Levitt, Kari, and Michael Witter. *The Critical Tradition of Caribbean Political Economy*. Kingston: Ian Randle Publishers, 1996.

Lewis, Arthur W. "An Economic Plan for Jamaica." *Agenda*, no. 3 (November 1944): 154–63.

——. *Growth and Fluctuations 1870–1913*. London: George Allen & Unwin, 1978.

——. "The Industrialisation of the British West Indies." *Caribbean Economic Review* 2 (May 1950): 1–61.

——. *Labour in the West Indies: The Birth of Workers' Movement*. London: New Beacon Books, 1977.

Littlewood, Roland. "History, Memory and Appropriation: Some Problems in the Analysis of Origins." Pp. 233–252 in *Rastafari and other African Caribbean World Views*, edited by Barry Chevannes. Syracuse: Syracuse University Press, 1995.

Llambi, Luis. "Emergence of Capitalized Family Farms in Latin America." *Society for Comparative Study of Society and History* 31, no. 4 (October 1988): 745–774.

Lowe, Lisa, and David Lloyd, eds. *The Politics of Culture in the Shadow of Capital*. Durham and London: Duke University Press, 1997.

Mandle, J. R. *The Plantation Economy: Population and Economic Change in Guyana 1888–1960*. Philadelphia: Temple University Press, 1973.

Manley, Michael. *Jamaica: Struggle in the Periphery*. London: Third World Media Limited/Writers and Readers Publishing Cooperative Society Limited, 1982.

——. *The Politics of Change: A Jamaican Testament* (rev. edition). Washington: Howard University Press, 1990.

——. *Up The Down Escalator: Development and the International Economy: a Jamaican Case Study*. London: Andre Deutsch, 1987.

Marshall, O. R. "West Indian Land Law: Conspectus and Reform." *Social and Economic Studies* 20, no. 1 (March 1971): 1–14.

Marshall, Trevor, ed. *A Bibliography of the Commonwealth Caribbean Peasantry 1838–1974. Series 3*. Cave Hill, Barbados: Institute of Social and Economic Research, 1975.

Marshall, Woodville. "Metayage in the Sugar Industry of the British Windward Islands 1838–1865." *Jamaican Historical Review* 1 (May 1965): 28–55.

Marx, Karl. *Grundrisse. Foundations of the Critique of Political Economy*. New York: Vintage Books, 1973.

——. *Capital. Volume One*. New York: Vintage Books, 1977.

Mazumdar, Dipak. "The Urban Informal Sector." *World Development* 4, no. 8 (August 1976): 655–679.

McKay, Leslie. "Tourism and Changing Attitudes to Land in Negril, Jamaica." Pp. 132–52 in *Land and Development in the Caribbean*, edited by Jean Besson and Janet Momsen. Warwick University Caribbean Studies: London: MacMillan, 1987.

McMichael, Philip. "Britain's Hegemony in the Nineteenth-Century World Economy." In *States versus Markets in the World System*, edited by Peter Evans and Dietrich Rueschemeyer and Evelyn Huber Stephens. California: Sage Press, 1985.

———. "Globalization: Myths and Realities." *Rural Sociology* 61, no. 1 (Spring 1996): 25–55.

———. "Incorporating Comparison within a World Historical Perspective: An Alternative Comparative Method." *American Sociological Review* 55, no. 3 (June 1990): 385–97.

McMichael, Philip, and David Myhre. "Global Regulations vs. the Nation State: Agro-Food Systems and the New Politics of Capital." *Capital and Class*, no. 43 (Spring 1991): 83–105.

Meikle, Paulette. "The Changing Patterns of Root Production and Marketing in Jamaica." Department of Geography, M. Phil. Mona: University of the West Indies, 1993.

Meillassoux, Claude. "From Reproduction to Production." *Economy and Society* 1, no. 1 (1972): 93–105.

Mintz, Sidney. *Caribbean Transformations*. Baltimore: The Johns Hopkins University Press, 1975.

———. *From Plantations to Peasantries in the Caribbean*. Washington D.C.: The Woodrow Wilson International Center for Scholars, 1984.

———. "A Note on the Definition of Peasantries." *Journal of Peasant Studies* 1, no. 1 (October 1973): 91–105.

———. "Slavery and the Rise of Peasantries." Pp. 213–242 in *Roots and Branches. Current Directions in Slave Studies*, edited by Michael Craton. New York: Pergamon Press, 1979.

Mission of the International Bank for Reconstruction and Development. *The Economic Development of Jamaica*. Baltimore: The Johns Hopkins University Press, 1952.

Mitchell, Timothy. "The Object of Development: America's Egypt." Pp. 129–156 in *Power of Development*, edited by Jonathan Crush. New York: Routledge, 1995.

Munroe, Trevor. *Jamaican Politics: A Marxist Perspective in Transition*. Colorado and Kingston: Lynne Rienner Publishers and Heinemann Publishers, 1990.

———. *The Politics of Constitutional Decolonization: 1944–1962*. Mona: Institute of Social and Economic Research, 1972.

Munroe, William A. *The Moral Economy of the State: Conservation, Community Development, and State Making in Zimbabwe*. Athens: Ohio University Center for International Studies, 1998.

Nelson, Keith, and Novella Z. Keith. *The Social Origins of Democratic Socialism in Jamaica*. Philadelphia: Temple University Press, 1992.

Nettleford, Rex. *Manley and the Politics of Jamaica: Towards an Analysis of Political Change in Jamaica, 1938–1968*. Kingston: Institute of Social and Economic Research, University of the West Indies, 1971.

Newman, Margaret, and E. Le Franc. "The Small-Farm Sub Sector: Is There Life After Structural Adjustment?" Pp. 118–210 in *Consequences of Structural Adjustment A Review of the Jamaican Experience*, edited by Elsie Le Franc. UWI Mona: Canoe Press, 1994.

Nugent, David. "Before History and prior to Politics: Time, Space and Territory in the Modern Peruvian Nation-State." Pp. 257–283 in *States of Imagination: Ethnographic Explorations of the Post-Colonial State*, edited by Thomas Blom Hansen and Finn Stepputat. Durham: Duke University, 2001.

O'Brien, Philip J. "A Critique of Latin American Theories of Dependency." Pp. 7–27 in *Beyond the Sociology of Development*, edited by Oxaal, Barnett, and Booth. London: Routledge and Kegan Paul, 1975.

Olivier, Sydney H. *Jamaica the Blessed Isle*. London: Faber and Faber, 1930.

Ong, Aiwa. *Flexible Citizenship: The Cultural Logics of Transnationality*. Durham and London: Duke University Press, 1999.

Parry, M. L. "Land Use in the Christiana Area." M. Sc. mss. Mona: University of the West Indies, 1968.

Patterson, Orlando. *The Children of Sisyphus*. Essex: Longman Group, 1989.

Perera, M. S. *Project Land Lease I-III*. Kingston: Ministry of Agriculture Report, 1982.

Phillips, James. "Fe We Land A Come: Choice and Change on a Jamaican Sugar Plantation." Ph.D. dissertation. University of Michigan, Department of Anthropology, 1976.

Pile, Steve. "Oppositions, Political Identity and Spaces of Resistance." Pp. 1–32 in *Geographies of Resistance*, edited by Steve Pile and Michael Keith. New York: Routledge, 1997.

Polanyi Levitt, Kari. *The Origins and Consequences of Jamaica's Debt Crisis, 1970–1990* UWI Mona: Consortium Graduate School of School Sciences, 1991.

———. "The Right to Development." *The Fifth Sir Arthur Lewis Memorial Lecture*. Castries, St. Lucia, November 8, 2000.

Portes, Alejandro. *The Informal Economy: Studies in Advanced and Less Developed Countries*. Baltimore and London: The Johns Hopkins University Press, 1989.

———. "The Informal Sector: Definition, Controversy and Relation to National Development, *Review* vii, no. 1 (Summer 1983): 151–174.

Portes, Alejandro, and L. Benton. "Industrial Development and Labor Absorption: A Reinterpretation." *Population and Development Review* 10, no. 4 (December 1984): 589–611

Post, Ken. *Arise Ye Starvelings: The Jamaican Labour Rebellion of 1938 and Its Aftermath*. The Hague: Martinus Nijhoff, 1978.

Premdas, Ralph. *Ethnic Conflict and Development: The Case of Guyana*. London: Avebury Press, 1995.

Price, Richard, ed. *Maroon Societies: Rebel Slave Communities in the Americas*. Garden City: Doubleday, 1973.

Quijano, Anibal, and I. Wallerstein. "Americanity as a Concept, or the Americas in the Modern World-System." *International Social Science Journal*, no. 44 (November 1992): 549–557.

Ragatz, Joseph L. *The Fall of the Planter Class in the British Caribbean 1763–1833: A Study in Social and Economic History*. New York and London: The Century Company, 1928.

Raynolds, Laura T., et al. "The "New" Internationalization of Agriculture: A Reformulation." *World Development* 21, no. 7 (July 1993): 1101–1121.

Redwood, Paul. *A Statistical Survey of Government Land Settlements in Jamaica B.W.I. 1929–1949*. Kingston: Government Printer, 1945.

Reid, Stanley. "An Introductory Approach to the Concentration of Power in the Jamaican Corporate Economy, and Notes on Its Origin." Pp. 15–44 in *Essays on Power and*

Change in Jamaica, edited by Dr. Carl Stone and Dr. Aggrey Brown. Kingston: Jamaica Publishing House, 1977.

Riviere, William W. "Labour Shortage After Emancipation." *Journal of Caribbean History* 4 (May 1972): 1–30.

Roberts, George W. *The Population of Jamaica*. New York: Kraus Reprint Co., 1979.

Roberts, George W., and Don O. Mills. "A Study of External Migration Affecting Jamaica, 1953–1955." Mona: Institute of Social and Economic Research, 1958.

Robertson, Roland. *Globalization: Social Theory and Global Culture*. London, Newbury Park: Sage, 1992.

Robotham, Don. "Blackening the Jamaican Nation: The Travails of a Black Bourgeoisie in a Global World." *Identities: Global Studies in Culture and Power* 7, no. 1 (March 2000): 1–37.

Rodney, Walter. *History of the Guyanese Working Peoples*. Baltimore: The Johns Hopkins University Press, 1981.

———. *How Europe Underdeveloped Africa*. London: Paul Bogle Press, 1970.

Ronsbo, Henrik. "State Formation and Property-Reflections on the Political Technologies of Space in Central America." *Journal of Historical Sociology* 10, no. 1 (March 1997): 56–73.

Russell, Roy. "The Impact of the Bauxite Alumina Multinational Corporations on Rural Economy and Society in Jamaica: A Survey of Farmers in Five Selected Bauxite Mining Areas." mss. Mona: Institute of Social and Economic Research, 1983.

Sachs, Wolfgang, ed. *The Development Dictionary: A Guide to Knowledge as Power*. London: Zed Books, 1992.

Said, Edward. *Culture and Imperialism*. New York: Alfred A. Knopf, 1993.

Salmon, Michael. "The Impact of Bauxite Alumina: Land Utilization within Jamaica's Bauxite Land Economy after the Emergence of the Bauxite Alumina Industry." mss. Mona: Institute of Social and Economic Research, 1983.

———. "Land Utilization within Jamaica's Bauxite Land Economy." *Social and Economic Studies* 36, no. 1 (March 1987): 57–92.

Sampson, Faye U. "Making Agriculture Jamaica's Business." mss. Kingston: AGRO 21, 1989.

Sassen, Saskia. *Cities in a World Economy*. Thousand Oaks, CA: Pine Forge Press, 2000.

———. *The Global City: New York, London, Tokyo*. Second edition. Princeton, NJ: Princeton University Press, 2001.

———. *Losing Control? Sovereignty in an Age of Globalization*. New York: Columbia University Press, 1996.

Satchell, Veront. *From Plots to Plantations*. Mona: Institute of Social and Economic Research, 1986.

———. "The Jamaican Peasantry 1866–1900: The Relationship between Economic Growth of the Peasant Sector and Government Policies." mss. Kingston: Dept. of History, University of the West Indies, 1982.

Sauer, C. O. "Economic Prospects of the Caribbean." Paper delivered at annual conference on the Caribbean, 3rd vol. (1953) in *The Caribbean: Its Economy*. Gainesville: University of Florida Press, 1954.

Scott, David. "The Dialectic of Defeat: An Interview with Rupert Lewis." *Small Axe* 10 (September 2001): 85–117.

———. "The Permanence of Pluralism." Pp. 282–301 in *Without Guarantees: In Honour of Stuart Hall*, edited by Paul Gilroy et al. London and New York: Verso Press, 2000.

———. *Refashioning Futures: Criticism after Postcoloniality.* Princeton: Princeton University Press, 1999.

Scott, James. *Domination and the Arts of Resistance: Hidden Transcripts.* New Haven and London: Yale University Press, 1990.

———. *Seeing Like a State: How Projects to Improve the Human Condition Failed.* New Haven and London: Yale University Press, 1998.

———. *Weapons of the Weak: Everyday Forms of Peasant Resistance.* New Haven: Yale University Press, 1985.

Senior, Olive. *The Message is Change: A Perspective on the 1972 General Elections.* Kingston: Kingston Publishers Limited, 1975.

Sewell, William. *The Ordeal of Free Labour in the West Indies.* London: Samson Low, 1861.

Shanin, Teodor. *Peasants and Peasant Societies.* New York: Penguin Books, 1971.

Sharpley, Jennifer. "Economic Management and the IMF in Jamaica: 1972–1980." *DERAP Working Papers A235*, 1981.

Shephard, C. Y. "Peasant Agriculture in the Leeward and Windward Islands. *Tropical Agriculture* xxiv, nos. 4 & 6 (April–June 1947): 61–71.

Shepherd, Verene, and Glen Richards, eds. *Jamaica in Slavery and Freedom.* Kingston: Ian Randle Press, 2002.

Silverman, Marilyn. "Dependency Mediation and Class Formation in Rural Guyana." *American Ethnologist* vi, no. 3 (August 1979): 460–490.

Silverman, Sydel. "The Peasant Concept in Anthropology." *Journal of Peasant Studies* 7, no. 1 (October 1979): 49–69.

Simey, Thomas S. *Welfare and Planning in the West Indies.* Oxford: Clarendon Press, 1946.

Smith, Elaine. "Ethnic Foods: Farmgate to Florida Market Cost/Return Models." Kingston: Strategic Planning Department, 1988.

Smith, Joan, Immanuel Wallerstein, and Hans Dieter Evans, eds. *Households and the World Economy.* Beverly Hills: Sage, 1984.

Smith, Michael G. *The Plural Society in the British West Indies.* Berkeley: University of California Press, 1965.

———. *A Report on Labour Supply in Rural Jamaica.* Kingston: Government Printer, 1956.

Spence, Balfour. "The impact of Modernization on Traditional Farming Communities: A Case Study of the Accompong Maroon Village." M. Phil. Mona: Department of Geography, University of the West Indies, Faculty of Natural Sciences, 1985.

Stavenhagen, Rodolfo. *Social Classes in Agrarian Societies.* New York: Anchor Books, 1975.

Steinmetz, George, ed. *State/Culture: State-Formation after the Cultural Turn.* Ithaca: Cornell University Press, 1999.

Stone, Carl. "An Appraisal of the Cooperative Process in the Jamaican Sugar Industry." mss. Mona: University of the West Indies, n.d.

, Kennedy & Company Limited, Halse/Hall Project Experience." mss., n.d.
de Agricultural Project: Report on the Survey of Phased-Out Sub-Projects, June-
ember 1995." Kingston: Data Bank and Evaluation Division, Ministry of Agri-
ure and Mining, 1995.
nent Potentials in Commercial Agriculture Vol.1: Winter Vegetables. Kingston: Strate-
Planning and Monitoring, Unit AGRO 21 Jamaica Conference Center, Landell
s Associates (Caribbean Ltd.), n.d.
a, Agricultural Policy Committee of Jamaica 1945. "Special Report on Land Set-
nent." Kingston: Government Printer, Duke Street, 1945.
ca Agricultural Sector Analysis." mss. Kingston: Government of Jamaica, 1986.
ca Hillside Farmers Support Project Appraisal Report. Report No.0073–JA 1988."
gston, Jamaica: IFAD, 1988.
er Plan: Agro 21 Making Agriculture Jamaica's Business."
try of Agriculture Report. An Evaluation of Project Land Lease and Project Food
ms, n.d.
stry Paper No. 56." Kingston: Ministry of Agriculture, n.d.
ional Plan for Jamaica 1957–1967. Kingston: Government Printer.
e of the Prime Minister. The Emergency Production Plan, 1977–1978. Kingston:
vernment of Jamaica, 1977.
rson, P. J. "Q. C." Deputy Prime Minister and Minister of Development, Planning
d Production, 1989.
ort of the Agricultural Policy Committee." Kingston: Government Printer, 1945.
ort of the President of the World Bank to the Executive Directors for an Agricul-
ral Sector Adjustment Loan for Jamaica." Jamaica: World Bank. Feb. 9, 1990, annex
46–53; subnumbering annex iv: 1–8.
ort of the President of the World Bank to the Executive Directors for an Agricul-
ral Structural Adjustment of the Jamaica Economy 1983."
rt on an Economic Survey among Field Workers in the Sugar Industry, November 1944.
ngston: Ministry of Labor, 1944.
rts of Department/Ministry of Labour, 1943–1964. Kingston: Govt. Printery, n.d.
ort with Appendices of the Commission Appointed to Enquire into The Distur-
ances Which Occurred in Jamaica between 23 May and 8 June 1938." mss. Kingston:
overnment Printery, 1938.
stical Abstract. Kingston: Jamaica Department of Statistics, 1974.
tus Report on AGRO-21: Corporation & Affiliated Companies." n.d.
uctural Adjustment of the Jamaican Economy (SAJE) 1982–1987."
st India Royal Commission: Report and Recommendations, 1938–1939." London:
IMSO, 1945.
ny, F. "Memorandum on Five Year Agricultural Sector Plan." Kingston: Ministry of
griculture, March, 1978.

———. "Democracy and Socialism in Jamaica: 1972–1979." Pp. 235–255 in The Newer
Caribbean: Decolonization, Democracy, and Development, edited by Paget Henry and
Carl Stone. Philadelphia: Institute for the Study of Human Issues, c1983.
———. "Political Aspects of Post-War Agricultural Policies in Jamaica." Social and Eco-
nomic Studies 23, no. 2 (June 1974): 145–175.
———. A Sociological Survey of Tenant Farmers on Project Land Lease. mss. Mona: Uni-
versity of the West Indies, 1976.
———. "Socio-Political Aspects of the Sugar Cooperatives." Pp. 146–170 in Essays on
Power and Change in Jamaica, edited by Carl Stone and Aggrey Brown. Kingston: Ja-
maica Publishing House, 1977.
Streeten, Paul. Globalisation: Threat or Opportunity. Copenhagen: Copenhagen Business
School Press, 2001.
Tabak, Faruk, and Michaeline Crichlow, eds. Informalization: Structure and Process. Bal-
timore: Johns Hopkins University, 2000.
Thomas, Clive. Dependence and Transformation: The Economics of the Transition to So-
cialism. New York: Monthly Review Press, 1974.
———. Plantations, Peasants and State: A Study of the Mode of Sugar Production in Guyana.
Mona: Institute of Social and Economic Research, 1984.
———. The Rise of the Authoritarian State in Peripheral Societies. New York: Monthly Re-
view Press, 1984.
Thomas, Deborah. "What We Are and What We Hope to Be." Small Axe, no. 12 (Sep-
tember 2002): 25–48.
Thomas, Nicholas. Colonialism's Culture: Anthropology, Travel and Government. Prince-
ton: Princeton University Press, 1994.
Thomas, Phyllis. "No Room in the Force for Rasta." http://www.gokingston.com/what-
snew/200203.
Tomich, Dale. "Colonial Slavery in the Transition from Feudalism to Capitalism." mss.
Binghamton: SUNY, 1981.
———. Slavery in the Circuit of Sugar: Martinique in the World Economy 1830–1848. Bal-
timore: The Johns Hopkins University Press, 1990.
———. "World of Capital/Worlds of Labor." Pp. 287–311 in Reworking Class: Cultures
and Institutions of Economic Stratification and Agency, edited by John Hall. Ithaca: Cor-
nell University Press, 1997.
Trouillot, Michel Rolph. "Culture on the Edges: Caribbean Creolization in Historical
Context." Pp. 189–210 in Historical Anthropology and Its Futures: From the Margins,
edited by Brian Keith Axel. Durham and London: Duke University Press, 2002.
———. "Labour and Emancipation in Dominica: Contribution to a Debate." Caribbean
Quarterly 30, nos. 3 & 4 (September–December 1984): 73–84.
———. Peasants and Capital: Dominica in the World Economy. Baltimore: The Johns
Hopkins University Press, 1988.
———. Silencing the Past: Power and the Production of History. Boston: Beacon Press, 1995.
Wallerstein, Immanuel. The Capitalist World Economy. Cambridge: Cambridge Univer-
sity Press, 1979.
———. The Modern World System: Capitalist Agriculture and the Origins of the European
World-Economy in the Sixteenth Century. New York and London: Academic Press, 1974.

———. *Unthinking Social Science: The Limits of Nineteenth-Century Paradigms.* Cambridge: Polity Press, 1991.

Watson, Hilbourne. "When the Liberalist Solution is Part of the Problem: Capitalist Globalization and Contradictions of the Liberal Democratic State." Paper delivered at the Conference on "Interrogating the Globalization Project." University of Iowa, Iowa City, November 1–4, 2001.

Watts, Michael. "The Crisis of Development. " Pp. 44–62 in *Power of Development*, edited by Jonathan Crush. New York and London: Routledge, 1995.

———. "'A New Deal in Emotions': Theory and Practice and the Crisis of Development." Pp. 44–62 in *Power of Development*, edited by Jonathan Crush. New York and London: Routledge, 1995.

Weiss, Linda. *The Myth of the Powerless State.* Ithaca: Cornell University Press, 1998.

The West Indies Year Book 1940/41.

The West Indies Year Book 1936/37.

Wicker, E. R. "Colonial Development and Welfare 1929–1957: The Evolution of a Policy." *Social and Economic Studies* 7, no. 3 (September 1958): 170–192.

Wilken, G. C. "Microclimate Management by Traditional Farmers." *Geographical Review* 62, no. 4 (October 1972): 544–560.

Williams, A. N. "Agricultural Reorganization and the Economic Development of the Working Class in Jamaica." Ph.D. dissertation. Cornell University, 1976.

Wilmot, Swithin. "Politics and Labour Conflicts in Jamaica 1838–1865." Pp. 101–117 in *The Critical Tradition of Caribbean Political Economy: The Legacy of George Beckford*, edited by Kari Levitt and Michael Witter. Kingston, Jamaica: Ian Randle Publishers, 1996.

Wolf, Eric. "Specific Aspects of Plantation Systems in the New World: Community Sub-Cultures and Social Class." Pp. 136–146 in *Plantation Systems of the New World*, edited by Vera Rubin. New York: Pan American Union, 1959.

Wolf, Eric R. and Sidney W. Mintz. "Haciendas and Plantations in Middle America and the Antilles." *Social and Economic Studies* 6, no. 1 (March 1957): 380–412.

Wood, R. C. "Rotation in the Tropics." *Journal of Imperial College of Tropical Agriculture* xii (1934): 44–46.

Newspapers and Newsletters

The Daily Gleaner, 17 July 2002.

Insight, vol. xviii, 5, June 2002.

The Sunday Gleaner, 14 July 2002.

The Sunday Gleaner, 2 July 2002.

The Sunday Gleaner, 26 May 2002.

The Daily Observer, 1 June 2001.

The Daily Gleaner, 29 July 1989.

The Daily Gleaner, 20 June 1989.

The Daily Gleaner, 25 September 1986.

The Daily Gleaner, 5 September 1986.

The Daily Gleaner, 1 August 1986.

The Daily Gleaner, 7 June 1986.

The Gleaner, November 1986.

The Gleaner, 5 September 1986.

The Daily Gleaner, 13 April 1985.

The Daily Gleaner, 23 January 1985.

The Daily Gleaner, 21 January 1985.

The Daily Gleaner, 13 January 1985.

The Daily Gleaner, 17 September 1983.

The Daily Gleaner, 1 September 1983.

The Daily Gleaner, 13 August 1983.

The Daily Gleaner, 12, August 1983.

The Daily Gleaner, 28 May 1983.

The Sunday Gleaner, 7 August 1983.

The Daily Gleaner, 29 September 1982.

The Daily Gleaner, 22 April 1982.

Workers Time, 3 August 1976.

The Blue Book of Jamaica 1874.

Reports and Government Docume

"Agricultural Policy Committee of Jamaica." Kingston: Governn

"AGRO 21: Making Agriculture Jamaica's Business." Kingst Agency, 1983.

Annual Report of the Nyerere Managing Committee. Kingston: Soc mission, 1976.

"Assessment of the Effects of Structural Adjustment on the Agri Technical Report." Rome: FAO, 1995.

"A Case Study on the Halse/Hall Winter Vegetable for Export P AGRO 21, 1986.

Economic and Social Survey of Jamaica, 1986. Kingston: National

Economic and Social Survey of Jamaica, 1984. Kingston: National

Economic and Social Survey of Jamaica, 1983. Kingston: National

Economic and Social Survey of Jamaica, 1982. Kingston: National

Economic and Social Surveys (1965–1970). Kingston: National Pl

"Ethnic Foods Cost of Production per Acre (Small Farmer)." Strat ment, AGRO 21, 1987.

The Farmers Register 1982. Kingston: Ministry of Agriculture, 198

Government of Jamaica. *The Economic Organisation of Small Scale I nana, Coconut, and Cocoa-Highgate Area: St. Mary, 1958–1959.* I Agriculture.

Government of Jamaica. *Land Reform in Jamaica with Emphasis* Kingston: Ministry of Agricultural and Lands, 1962.

Index

About the Author

Michaeline A. Crichlow is Associate Professor at the University of Iowa, with African American World Studies, and International Programs, and chairs The Caribbean, Diaspora and Atlantic Studies Program. She is coeditor of *Informalization: Structure and Process* (JHP 2000) and editor of a forthcoming special issue of the journal *Plantation Society of the Americas*, on the banana crisis in the Caribbean. She has published many articles on land and citizenship in anthologies and various journals, for example, *New West Indian Guide, Latin American Perspectives, Social and Economic Studies,* and *Contours: A Journal of the African Diaspora.*

———. "Democracy and Socialism in Jamaica: 1972–1979." Pp. 235–255 in *The Newer Caribbean: Decolonization, Democracy, and Development*, edited by Paget Henry and Carl Stone. Philadelphia: Institute for the Study of Human Issues, c1983.

———. "Political Aspects of Post-War Agricultural Policies in Jamaica." *Social and Economic Studies* 23, no. 2 (June 1974): 145–175.

———. *A Sociological Survey of Tenant Farmers on Project Land Lease*. mss. Mona: University of the West Indies, 1976.

———. "Socio-Political Aspects of the Sugar Cooperatives." Pp. 146–170 in *Essays on Power and Change in Jamaica*, edited by Carl Stone and Aggrey Brown. Kingston: Jamaica Publishing House, 1977.

Streeten, Paul. *Globalisation: Threat or Opportunity*. Copenhagen: Copenhagen Business School Press, 2001.

Tabak, Faruk, and Michaeline Crichlow, eds. *Informalization: Structure and Process*. Baltimore: Johns Hopkins University, 2000.

Thomas, Clive. *Dependence and Transformation: The Economics of the Transition to Socialism*. New York: Monthly Review Press, 1974.

———. *Plantations, Peasants and State: A Study of the Mode of Sugar Production in Guyana*. Mona: Institute of Social and Economic Research, 1984.

———. *The Rise of the Authoritarian State in Peripheral Societies*. New York: Monthly Review Press, 1984.

Thomas, Deborah. "What We Are and What We Hope to Be." *Small Axe*, no. 12 (September 2002): 25–48.

Thomas, Nicholas. *Colonialism's Culture: Anthropology, Travel and Government*. Princeton: Princeton University Press, 1994.

Thomas, Phyllis. "No Room in the Force for Rasta." http://www.gokingston.com/whatsnew/200203.

Tomich, Dale. "Colonial Slavery in the Transition from Feudalism to Capitalism." mss. Binghamton: SUNY, 1981.

———. *Slavery in the Circuit of Sugar: Martinique in the World Economy 1830–1848*. Baltimore: The Johns Hopkins University Press, 1990.

———. "World of Capital/Worlds of Labor." Pp. 287–311 in *Reworking Class: Cultures and Institutions of Economic Stratification and Agency*, edited by John Hall. Ithaca: Cornell University Press, 1997.

Trouillot, Michel Rolph. "Culture on the Edges: Caribbean Creolization in Historical Context." Pp. 189–210 in *Historical Anthropology and Its Futures: From the Margins*, edited by Brian Keith Axel. Durham and London: Duke University Press, 2002.

———. "Labour and Emancipation in Dominica: Contribution to a Debate." *Caribbean Quarterly* 30, nos. 3 & 4 (September–December 1984): 73–84.

———. *Peasants and Capital: Dominica in the World Economy*. Baltimore: The Johns Hopkins University Press, 1988.

———. *Silencing the Past: Power and the Production of History*. Boston: Beacon Press, 1995.

Wallerstein, Immanuel. *The Capitalist World Economy*. Cambridge: Cambridge University Press, 1979.

———. *The Modern World System: Capitalist Agriculture and the Origins of the European World-Economy in the Sixteenth Century*. New York and London: Academic Press, 1974.

———. *Unthinking Social Science: The Limits of Nineteenth-Century Paradigms.* Cambridge: Polity Press, 1991.

Watson, Hilbourne. "When the Liberalist Solution is Part of the Problem: Capitalist Globalization and Contradictions of the Liberal Democratic State." Paper delivered at the Conference on "Interrogating the Globalization Project." University of Iowa, Iowa City, November 1–4, 2001.

Watts, Michael. "The Crisis of Development. " Pp. 44–62 in *Power of Development,* edited by Jonathan Crush. New York and London: Routledge, 1995.

———. "'A New Deal in Emotions': Theory and Practice and the Crisis of Development." Pp. 44–62 in *Power of Development,* edited by Jonathan Crush. New York and London: Routledge, 1995.

Weiss, Linda. *The Myth of the Powerless State.* Ithaca: Cornell University Press, 1998.

The West Indies Year Book 1940/41.

The West Indies Year Book 1936/37.

Wicker, E. R. "Colonial Development and Welfare 1929–1957: The Evolution of a Policy." *Social and Economic Studies* 7, no. 3 (September 1958): 170–192.

Wilken, G. C. "Microclimate Management by Traditional Farmers." *Geographical Review* 62, no. 4 (October 1972): 544–560.

Williams, A. N. "Agricultural Reorganization and the Economic Development of the Working Class in Jamaica." Ph.D. dissertation. Cornell University, 1976.

Wilmot, Swithin. "Politics and Labour Conflicts in Jamaica 1838–1865." Pp. 101–117 in *The Critical Tradition of Caribbean Political Economy: The Legacy of George Beckford,* edited by Kari Levitt and Michael Witter. Kingston, Jamaica: Ian Randle Publishers, 1996.

Wolf, Eric. "Specific Aspects of Plantation Systems in the New World: Community Sub-Cultures and Social Class." Pp. 136–146 in *Plantation Systems of the New World,* edited by Vera Rubin. New York: Pan American Union, 1959.

Wolf, Eric R. and Sidney W. Mintz. "Haciendas and Plantations in Middle America and the Antilles." *Social and Economic Studies* 6, no. 1 (March 1957): 380–412.

Wood, R. C. "Rotation in the Tropics." *Journal of Imperial College of Tropical Agriculture* xii (1934): 44–46.

Newspapers and Newsletters

The Daily Gleaner, 17 July 2002.

Insight, vol. xviii, 5, June 2002.

The Sunday Gleaner, 14 July 2002.

The Sunday Gleaner, 2 July 2002.

The Sunday Gleaner, 26 May 2002.

The Daily Observer, 1 June 2001.

The Daily Gleaner, 29 July 1989.

The Daily Gleaner, 20 June 1989.

The Daily Gleaner, 25 September 1986.

The Daily Gleaner, 5 September 1986.

The Daily Gleaner, 1 August 1986.
The Daily Gleaner, 7 June 1986.
The Gleaner, November 1986.
The Gleaner, 5 September 1986.
The Daily Gleaner, 13 April 1985.
The Daily Gleaner, 23 January 1985.
The Daily Gleaner, 21 January 1985.
The Daily Gleaner, 13 January 1985.
The Daily Gleaner, 17 September 1983.
The Daily Gleaner, 1 September 1983.
The Daily Gleaner, 13 August 1983.
The Daily Gleaner, 12, August 1983.
The Daily Gleaner, 28 May 1983.
The Sunday Gleaner, 7 August 1983.
The Daily Gleaner, 29 September 1982.
The Daily Gleaner, 22 April 1982.
Workers Time, 3 August 1976.
The Blue Book of Jamaica 1874.

Reports and Government Documents

"Agricultural Policy Committee of Jamaica." Kingston: Government Printer, 1945.
"AGRO 21: Making Agriculture Jamaica's Business." Kingston: National Planning Agency, 1983.
Annual Report of the Nyerere Managing Committee. Kingston: Social Development Commission, 1976.
"Assessment of the Effects of Structural Adjustment on the Agricultural Sector: Jamaica Technical Report." Rome: FAO, 1995.
"A Case Study on the Halse/Hall Winter Vegetable for Export Project." mss. Kingston: AGRO 21, 1986.
Economic and Social Survey of Jamaica, 1986. Kingston: National Planning Agency.
Economic and Social Survey of Jamaica, 1984. Kingston: National Planning Agency.
Economic and Social Survey of Jamaica, 1983. Kingston: National Planning Agency.
Economic and Social Survey of Jamaica, 1982. Kingston: National Planning Agency.
Economic and Social Surveys (1965–1970). Kingston: National Planning Agency.
"Ethnic Foods Cost of Production per Acre (Small Farmer)." Strategic Planning Department, AGRO 21, 1987.
The Farmers Register 1982. Kingston: Ministry of Agriculture, 1985.
Government of Jamaica. *The Economic Organisation of Small Scale Farming, Based on Banana, Coconut, and Cocoa-Highgate Area: St. Mary, 1958–1959.* Kingston: Ministry of Agriculture.
Government of Jamaica. *Land Reform in Jamaica with Emphasis on Land Settlement.* Kingston: Ministry of Agricultural and Lands, 1962.

"Grace, Kennedy & Company Limited, Halse/Hall Project Experience." mss., n.d.

"Hillside Agricultural Project: Report on the Survey of Phased-Out Sub-Projects, June–September 1995." Kingston: Data Bank and Evaluation Division, Ministry of Agriculture and Mining, 1995.

Investment Potentials in Commercial Agriculture Vol. 1: Winter Vegetables. Kingston: Strategic Planning and Monitoring, Unit AGRO 21 Jamaica Conference Center, Landell Mills Associates (Caribbean Ltd.), n.d.

Jamaica, Agricultural Policy Committee of Jamaica 1945. "Special Report on Land Settlement." Kingston: Government Printer, Duke Street, 1945.

"Jamaica Agricultural Sector Analysis." mss. Kingston: Government of Jamaica, 1986.

"Jamaica Hillside Farmers Support Project Appraisal Report. Report No.0073–JA 1988." Kingston, Jamaica: IFAD, 1988.

"Master Plan: Agro 21 Making Agriculture Jamaica's Business."

Ministry of Agriculture Report. *An Evaluation of Project Land Lease and Project Food Farms,* n.d.

"Ministry Paper No. 56." Kingston: Ministry of Agriculture, n.d.

A National Plan for Jamaica 1957–1967. Kingston: Government Printer.

Office of the Prime Minister. *The Emergency Production Plan, 1977–1978.* Kingston: Government of Jamaica, 1977.

Patterson, P. J. "Q. C." Deputy Prime Minister and Minister of Development, Planning and Production, 1989.

"Report of the Agricultural Policy Committee." Kingston: Government Printer, 1945.

"Report of the President of the World Bank to the Executive Directors for an Agricultural Sector Adjustment Loan for Jamaica." Jamaica: World Bank. Feb. 9, 1990, annex iv: 46–53; subnumbering annex iv: 1–8.

"Report of the President of the World Bank to the Executive Directors for an Agricultural Structural Adjustment of the Jamaica Economy 1983."

Report on an Economic Survey among Field Workers in the Sugar Industry, November 1944. Kingston: Ministry of Labor, 1944.

Reports of Department/Ministry of Labour, 1943–1964. Kingston: Govt. Printery, n.d.

"Report with Appendices of the Commission Appointed to Enquire into The Disturbances Which Occurred in Jamaica between 23 May and 8 June 1938." mss. Kingston: Government Printery, 1938.

Statistical Abstract. Kingston: Jamaica Department of Statistics, 1974.

"Status Report on AGRO-21: Corporation & Affiliated Companies." n.d.

"Structural Adjustment of the Jamaican Economy (SAJE) 1982–1987."

"West India Royal Commission: Report and Recommendations, *1938–1939.*" London: HMSO, 1945.

Zenny, F. "Memorandum on Five Year Agricultural Sector Plan." Kingston: Ministry of Agriculture, March, 1978.